1994

D

S0-AYE-933

Language
and Literacy Learning
in Multicultural
Classrooms

Language
and Literacy Learning
in Multicultural
Classrooms

LESLIE W. CRAWFORD

St. Cloud State University

ALLYN AND BACON

Boston   London   Toronto   Sydney   Tokyo   Singapore

Production Administrator: *Annette Joseph*
Production Coordinator: *Susan Freese*
Editorial-Production Service: *Kailyard Associates*
Manufacturing Buyer: *Megan Cochran*
Cover Administrator: *Linda K. Dickinson*
Cover Designer: *Design Ad Cetera*

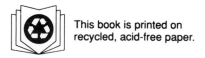

This book is printed on
recycled, acid-free paper.

Library of Congress Cataloging-in-Publication Data

Crawford, Leslie W.
    Language and literacy learning in multicultural classrooms /
Leslie W. Crawford.
        p.   cm.
    Includes bibliographical references (p.) and index.
    ISBN 0-205-13922-1
    1. Language arts–United States. 2. Reading–United States.
3. Intercultural education–United States. I. Title.
LB1576.C765 1993
428'.0071'2–dc20   92-28590
                                                        CIP

Printed in the United States of America
10 9 8 7 6 5 4 3 2   97 96 95 94 93

See page 458 for text credits.

To my parents, in appreciation for our home
environment that encouraged accepting and
valuing all people and creeds, and
especially to my mother for
developing my understanding and
concern for learners struggling to
become literate in a nonnative
language

Brief Contents

Contents

Preface

The student population in the United States is changing dramatically. Students from non–European American backgrounds will soon make up a substantial portion of the population of our schools (Kennedy, 1991). These students need to develop high-level language and literacy competencies to live and work as equals in a multicultural society. Language and literacy should be learned in a manner that supports and encourages diversity and respect for the rights of others, no matter what their race, creed, gender, or life-style. If culturally diverse students are to achieve high-level language and literacy competencies, educators may need to retool to be able to successfully meet their needs (Kennedy, 1991). Schools must change from a model of assimilation to one of diversity and equity.

This book is directed toward educators who are concerned that students from different ethnic, cultural, and language backgrounds learn effective use of language and literacy for access to education in a pluralistic society. Environmental, curricular, and instructional components and strategies that benefit all children are identified and are based on a premise of multicultural education: What is good for children from nondominant cultures is good for all children.

Students enter school with a wide range of experiences. Some may not speak a language other than English. Others come with nonstandard dialects. Immigrant school-age children may have had no formal schooling. Children of migrant workers may attend two or three different schools each year. The challenge for the educator is to provide an educational program in which students from all communities gain access to a body of knowledge, skills, and ways of thinking about language and literacy learning that will prepare them for the growing demands of society. These challenges require changing the traditional school—its program, curriculum, and instructional delivery system. A multicultural school and curriculum strives to remove all barriers to learning.

Although educators may support diversity, they are often complacent about restructuring school curricula and instructional systems to make them multicultural. However, programs must change. School experiences must be focused to raise attitudes and develop understandings of others. The future of our society depends on the attitudes, beliefs, and values that students develop as well as on strong language and literacy competencies that lead to cognitive abilities. Culturally diverse and European American students are not presently being prepared to deal with issues of racism and prejudice in U.S. society (Molnar, 1989), despite the changing nature of the population. Nor have first-language learning and cultural orientation been valued as important factors in developing literacy for culturally diverse students.

Language and Literacy Learning in Multicultural Classrooms places students at the heart of education in a redesigned multicultural school. When students are the focus for learning, the total program changes. All students are respected and trusted as competent learners who already know a great deal prior to any formal teaching (Reutzel & Hollingsworth, 1988). Students' cultural backgrounds are recognized in the design of classroom curricula and instructional delivery systems. Curricula are designed from a multicultural point of view. Children are invited to become active participants in the design and direction of educational experiences. Programs are developed that are relevant, functional, and meaningful. Students are encouraged to become social activists rather than mere recipients of knowledge and skills. Parents, primary caregivers, and community members are included as active participants in the design of the school and its programs. Parents are involved in planning and assessing their children's learning activities (Chrispeels, 1991).

This book is designed to assist teachers to develop student speaking, reading, and writing competencies through integrated multicultural themes and topics based on relevant children's literature. Most of the examples in the book focus on race, ethnicity, and culture. Social class and gender, although mentioned throughout the book, are not treated extensively; they are used in relation to race, ethnicity, and culture. Categories that deal with students with disabilities are also not included.

The framework of this book is based on four major requirements for teaching language and literacy in a multicultural school:

1. Educators must have knowledge of the foundations for learning, including an understanding of children's cultures, communities, and language and literacy development (both first- and second-language learning).
2. Educators need to understand the importance of the classroom environment, its relationship to culture and learning, and how to develop intellectually stimulating curriculum themes and topics

that embed multicultural literature and integrate speaking, reading, and writing.

3. Educators must facilitate language and literacy learning through learning strategies conducive to the learning of all students. Students must be assisted to develop critical communication, reading, and writing abilities.
4. Educators can facilitate learning by appropriately assessing and evaluating learning through a learner-centered model that involves students and parents or primary caregivers in decision making.

Children must be given the power to learn, to become literate, and to dream. Language and literacy programs must follow the paths students take as learners. Students must take control of their learning, respect their own backgrounds, and respect the backgrounds of others. When learners decide to become literate, they assume the responsiblity for learning and take the risks required to learn.

Although this book may challenge some of your previously held beliefs, I hope you will become passionate about the ideas as you consider and put them into practice. Both learning and teaching should be joyous situations.

ACKNOWLEDGMENTS

I wish to express my appreciation to the following individuals who made contributions during the development of this book: Susan M. Glazer, for her contributions during the last drafts; flo wiger, for consultation on multicultural concepts; Ethel Lowry and Bill Pogge, for reading and editing the first draft; Nancy Pearson and Sheila Gullickson, for reading and editing the second draft; Geoffrey Tabakin and Linda Scott, for reading sections of the book; Jo Tennison, for editing the third and fourth drafts; and Lisa Rarick, for typing and preparing the final draft.

I also which to thank the following reviewers for their comments, criticisms, and recommendations: Nancy A. Anderson, University of South Florida; Gloria Burke, Los Altos, California; Joan M. Donahue, John H. Wood Middle School, San Antonio, Texas; John J. Halcon, University of Northern Colorado; Barbara Kirk, Central Michigan University; John Madison, State University of New York at Plattsburgh; M. Lee Manning, Columbia College; Jackie Mathews, Orange County Public Schools; Donald R. Whitmore, Texas Woman's University; and Carmen Zuniga-Hill, California State University—Fullerton.

Language
and Literacy Learning
in Multicultural
Classrooms

PART ONE

Foundations for Language and Literacy in a Multicultural School

Students in U.S. schools have different educational needs, goals, and learning requirements from students of past decades. Since 1975 well over one million documented refugees, many of them children, have entered the United States from many areas of the world (NCBE Forum, 1989). Most of these immigrants have come from Asian and Latin American countries. Further, there is a dynamic growing non-Caucasian population in many regions of the country. The Hispanic population is growing faster than the African American population and represents a significant part of the metropolitan residents, which has policy implications for schools (Arias, 1986). *U.S. News & World Report* (October 22, 1990) reported that African American and Hispanic American students, who are disproportionately poor, are expected to make up 40 percent of public school enrollment by the year 2000 (Toch & Linnon, 1990).

Despite the changing population, U.S. society continues to be a stratified society that is based on race, gender, and disability. There has been little change in social policies since the 1960s. Although there has been some change in racial attitudes and some improvement in access to schools, African Americans, Native Americans, and Hispanic Americans are still distinctly educationally, economically, and politically disadvantaged.

European Americans continue to have the greatest access to available jobs because of their race. Unemployment of African Americans, for instance, is about double that of European Americans. This differential access to jobs as a result of race has a significant bearing on the level of housing and health services available to African American students (Sleeter & Grant, 1988) and implications for the quality of their education.

Mexican American and Native American students continue to be

1

victims of subtle racism (Grant, 1990). The evidence is found in school instructional language policies which are directed toward learning and using English exclusively and the continued representation of Native Americans in a romantic iconographic still-picture of tepees, toma-hawks, and feathered headdresses in textbooks. These result in serious learning limitations for students from these cultural groups.

Student background in the U.S. classroom is not interpreted neutrally, either. Wealth, power, and status are distributed unequally on the basis of race, gender, social class background, and disability. Conventional wisdom guides instructional practices based on the premise that students from less-advantaged homes are deficient in their preparation for school because their families have failed to give them the correct preparation for life (Knapp, Turnbull & Shield, 1990). They are deemed as having less potential and less intelligence and, consequently, are taught less of the high-status knowledge found in challenging studies. Teachers interpret the students' cultural and lin-guistic differences as indications of inability or lack of academic inter-est (U.S. Commission on Civil Rights, 1988). What they are taught and how they are evaluated is determined by the experience of the Euro-pean American population.

Multicultural schools recognize all students' potential for learn-ing. Multicultural schools are based on the premise that all students should receive an education that continuously affirms human diver-sity. Further, all students learn through the educational process how they can take charge of their own destinies. This process begins when the history and culture of the members of all racial groups are em-braced as part of the curricula and children learn how to eliminate race, class, and gender oppression. Teachers in multicultural settings hold expectations that challenge students trapped in the cycle of pov-erty and despair. Multicultural schools establish home and school relationships firmly built on trust and equity (Grant, 1990).

Multicultural schools recognize that although students may come from home backgrounds with few literacy experiences, they have other rich background experiences that are fertile references for learning. Multicultural schools accept the premise that acquiring literacy does not involve memorizing sentences, words, or syllables but rather creat-ing and re-creating through interaction with one's own context (Freire, 1973). The learner is *subject* rather than *recipient* of learning. The learner as subject discovers a creative and re-creative impulse and learns that one creates his or her own culture as well as responds to it.

The educator's role in the multicultural school can be likened to a dialogue with the learner in which he or she is offered the ways and means for self-learning and is empowered, as recommended by Freire

(1973). This dialogue must be linked and nourished by respect, love, humility, hope, faith, and trust. It provides the basis for a critical search for learning.

The foundation of the current American education program is based on the assimilation theory. This theory has resulted in the rejection of home communities and ways of responding by generations of learners from culturally diverse populations in order to gain educational access. In such a system, the acquisition of literacy can catapult a student out of family, community, class, or ethnic group. Students may not simply acquire a new way of using language or comprehending a text, but they may be under intense pressure to reject their cultural views of the world (Harman & Edelsky, 1989). "Family and friends may express resentment, jealousy, abandonment, or simply incomprehension at their loved one's movement away from them" (Harman & Edelsky, 1989, p. 399).

To overcome the cultural rejection pressure, educators in a multicultural school function as bridges for the students that take them as recipients of yesterday's culture and society to active participants and makers of tomorrow's society. These teachers know their students, believe in their power to make choices, and enable them to see mistakes as indications of learning development. They empower students for learning by accepting and supporting the students' culture while assisting them in understanding the expectations and procedures of the multicultural school. These educators recognize that students differ in their approaches to learning.

Educators in multicultural classrooms use student experiences as the basis for learning while exposing students to the new and unfamiliar. They focus on meaning and understanding (Knapp et al., 1990). Teachers who hold a multicultural framework for teaching understand and appreciate that students are interested in learning about their own cultural backgrounds and aspire to at least equal instructional time in their home language. Students in multicultural schools are not grouped on the basis of race, gender, social class, or achievement.

CHAPTER ONE

The Role of Culture, Family, and Society in Learning

- *What is the role of culture to learning?*
- *What are the characteristics of homes that facilitate learning and literacy?*
- *Are schools retaining culturally diverse students?*
- *What is a multicultural school?*

INTRODUCTION

The U.S. society is experiencing radical changes. Values, traditions, and beliefs once held as absolute have changed or been seriously challenged. There has been a significant change in population, through growth and immigration of peoples from nonEuropean cultures, races, and ethnic backgrounds. English has become the *lingua franca* of the world while the roles, values and traditions, and products of the predominantly European American English-speaking school have been under attack.

The traditional role of school in U.S. society has been to socialize and acculturate the young to the European American society. Considering the changing society and population of the United States, and the failure of schools to recognize the plurality of society, this role seems inappropriate. A significant change in the function, structure, curricula, and instructional practices of schools appears appropriate. Schools are the only remaining social institution that can assist students in analyzing their own lives to develop practical consciousness about the real injustices in society. They can prepare students to work toward social equality and cultural pluralism. They can provide a truthful and meaningful rendition of the whole of human experience (Hillard, 1992).

The changing nature of family life, society's changing cultural and ethnic makeup, and the development of rapid technological advancement have placed schools under tremendous pressure. Schools, however, still retain a Eurocentric focus in the curricula and teaching styles that are inconsistent with the needs of all students (Banks, 1988). This contributes to a continuing achievement gap between the haves and the have nots of society. As long as this continues, racial and ethnic conflicts and tension in the schools and society will continue.

The United States, founded on the Anglo-Saxon Protestant ethic, in the past glorified the nation as a melting pot of different peoples. However, in reality American schools melted diversity into conformity with their Eurocentric tradition. Schools stripped immigrant children of their Old World heritage, according to Meltzer (1976). Children were embarrassed by their native languages, and their history and traditions were not considered worthy of study. Those not conforming were often abused, expelled, or failed. Conforming groups were robbed of their cultural and language heritage. The cultures and values of the nondominant groups did not become part of the general culture and values of the United States.

Although educators today are more aware of the concepts of multicultural education, they find them difficult to implement for many reasons. Some school authorities see little need for multicultural curricula because their communities have few or no nonEuropean Americans. The dominant teacher force is European American. Many lack an understanding that their practices extol their own cultural backgrounds, which may be alien to some of their students. Many teachers do not have the strategies or comfort level for teaching culturally different or English second language (ESL) students. Further, there is confusion over multicultural education. Does it lead to diversity or polarization? Will it pluralize the curricula and ignore the necessary commonalities important for learning about a democratic country and pluralistic society?

One teacher's understanding about his mores, culture, and values began when he taught in the border area of Arizona and Mexico. He found his mores and values different and seemingly in conflict with those of his Mexican American students. He had to reassess his values. He had to learn how to facilitate his students' thinking about their actions and values without imposing his own. Although he changed, like many other educators with similar experiences, he found it difficult giving up values and mores that were a part of his nurturing. As a result, he was in conflict with the school organizational structure, the curricula, and the instructional materials and practices he was expected to use. Nevertheless, he had to change his classroom environment, the curricula, and the learning experiences if he were to make learning meaningful and relevant for his students.

The role of families, the value families place on school and literacy, and the nature of children's home literacy experiences have significant bearing on children's level of achievement in school. The role of society and the messages that children receive about the relevance, functionality, and meaningfulness of literacy in their culture are important factors that bear upon literacy.

CULTURE AND ITS RELATIONSHIP TO LEARNING AND LITERACY

An understanding of culture is fundamental for understanding children in modern classrooms. A child's culture has a significant influence on how well he or she will achieve. Banks (1980) reported that most social scientists regard culture as the way people use, interpret, and perceive values and symbols which distinguish one people from another. Because of culture, humans have differing values and perspectives of the world. They behave and act differently toward one another because of their values and world perspective.

According to Smith and Otero (1985) humans are captive of their culture. They act as they do because it seems logical to do so; their culture is their frame of reference. Nevertheless, Smith and Otero cautioned that there is also cultural diversity within cultural groups and that cultures are ever changing as well. What makes something cultural is that it is a world view shared by a group of people bound together through a common history, location, language, social class, and/or religion (Nieto, 1992).

Cultural differences in learning are particularly apparent in how children learn, interact, and communicate and in language-usage styles (Nieto, 1992). Similarities appear among racial social-class groups in how they receive and process information as well as in their language interactional styles that influence learning. In a study of three groups of culturally diverse families, Heath (1982) indicated that "learning style is learned in social groups in which the child is reared and in connection with other ways of behaving found in the culture" (p. 55).

Cultures give differing value and status to being able to read and write (Laquer, 1983). This greatly influences how literacy manifests itself in a culture. The use of literacy and the expectations of the society, as well as the impact that literacy has for the young in any particular culture, will vary (F. Smith, 1984). Cultures also value differently language dominance and ability to speak and function in more than one language.

Cultural differences in a society, however, should not mean that some cultures are deficient or culturally deprived. From the deficient viewpoint students from home backgrounds differing from those of the European American middle class would have a depressed ability to learn as a result of the substandard environments and language of their parents. Inability to speak English, from the culturally deprived point of view, is held as an educational determinant for the under-achievement of culturally diverse students.

Cultural differences in language and learning styles are not deficiencies but should be used to facilitate learning, according to Sleeter and Grant (1988). The discontinuity between a child's culture and the school culture is frustrating when he or she must function daily in the school's culture without having learned it. It is confusing to the child when normal cultural responses are misunderstood. The child in such a situation is required to make a cultural leap each day between home and school and back again (Sleeter & Grant, 1988). Teachers need to acknowledge the differences that all children bring to school, recognize that these differences may influence how they learn, and make provisions for their learning (Nieto, 1992). When home and school cultures are incompatible, students may fail to learn in school (Jordan, 1984).

Just how culture influences learning is not always clear, according to Nieto (1992). Spindler (1987) suggested that culturally diverse students may face failure because of the discontinuity between home and school culture rather than because of cognitive deficits or environment. Gardner (1989) shared an insightful observation explaining the differences between Chinese and U.S. parental cultural perception of teaching and learning that provides some insight. While in China Gardner's young son would carry the key of the hotel room and attempt to drop it in a receptacle in the hotel lobby. The child's lack of manual dexterity and his incomplete understanding of how to orient the key appropriately generally made him fail, but he enjoyed the sound the key made as well as the trials. The boy was allowed to experiment in problem solving and self-reliance, principle values of middle-class Americans.

Observing the boy's attempts, the Chinese hotel attendants would come over, observe the lad, smile, and gently but firmly guide the key into the slot. They felt that the child would become frustrated or angry by flailing around, and that he would be happier, learn how to accomplish the task sooner, and be able to proceed to higher levels of learning through their shaping of the task. Gardner surmised that the Chinese perceive that there are accepted means for achieving competence. Why bypass a long-established route?

Sleeter and Grant (1988) contrasted learning characteristics preferred for most middle-class classrooms with African American and Hispanic American children's learning modes. Characteristics that typify instructional approaches used in schools are, for example, task rather than person orientation, focus on parts rather than the whole, formal and nonpersonal attributes, decontextualized information, linear thinking patterns, nonemotional behavior, sedentary behavior, long attention spans, use of standard English, and ability to communicate without reference to context or nonverbal cues.

African American and Hispanic American children, according to the studies summarized by Sleeter and Grant (1988), tended to be more person oriented, to focus on the whole rather than the parts, to view the attributes of an object in relationship to the object's use rather than to a set of formal rules. They tended to be interested in content that has a human, social focus and to respond to teaching strategies that involve them with other people. African Americans were reported as having a strong interest in reading as a survival skill to counter hostility and learn social cues. Their homes fostered functional cognition skills.

Native American students, according to a study by Philips (1982), on the Warm Springs Reservation learned better in classrooms when the instruction more closely conformed to their learning styles. Their academic performance improved when students were not required to perform in public and when cooperation was emphasized over competition, as confirmed by Sandors (1987). In addition, she found Native American students value nonverbal communication group needs more than individual needs, an orientation to the present, sharing, privacy, and emotional relationships.

Children demonstrate strikingly different characteristics within cultures. Social class, family structure, psychological and emotional differences, home conditions, and order of birth can account for many differences (Nieto, 1992).

HOME CULTURES THAT FACILITATE LEARNING AND LITERACY DEVELOPMENT

Although there will be diversity in each culture, a range of home environments that encourage the development of literacy can be examined. Homes, not withstanding social class or culture, can be rich or sterile literate environments. Information about these environments can provide some insight into why children from various cultures may or may not succeed in the middle-class European American–focused school.

A small study conducted by Lynch (1989) examined affluent, poverty-level, and disabled children's families and homes for indications of literacy child-rearing practices. Although financial resources were an important factor, some single- and double-parent families, in what were determined lower income homes, were providing quality literacy experiences for children. The presence of two caregivers in the home did not ensure a fertile literate environment for children in either lower or higher income levels. Single-parent homes, sparse in furniture and lacking luxury items, were noted to have books for children's reading. These parents read to their children and provided literacy opportunities for them. An important factor appeared to be the value parents placed on literacy development.

Harste, Woodward & Burke (1984), in their study of children from all social-class levels, reported that when parents perceive themselves as middle class, despite the circumstances of their living conditions, they tended to provide literacy experiences more associated with the middle class. The quantity of literacy materials in the home did not appear as important as the nature of the materials and how accessible they were to both parents and children. (Books, pens, pencils, and paper are used when they are accessible.)

Taylor's (1982) study of family literacy of middle-class European Americans clearly demonstrated that reading and writing are cultural activities embedded in the daily lives of these families. Parents in the Taylor study always contextualized print into daily activities even when they made a conscious effort to make children aware of print. The transmission of literacy styles and values appeared to be viewed by these parents as a social filter through which the family lives were organized and accomplished. Children learned from parents the use of print as a medium for mastering their environment. In these homes children learned a multiplicity of socially significant literate activities as they engaged in different social activities. Reading and writing were cultural activities intrinsic to their daily lives. The meaningful, relevant, and functional experiences of the European American middle-class children, as identified in the Taylor study, provided them with a better foundation for the decontextualized literacy instruction of their schools.

The value and status the middle-class parents of the Taylor study placed on literacy would be rewarded in the school success of their children. Children in the Taylor study learned reading as a way of listening and writing as a way of talking. Reading and writing were a natural part of the daily experiences in the children's lives. The modeling and demonstrating of their caregivers provided them support and guidance as their literacy developed. Through these experiences they gained both status and identity because literacy was a medium for socioculturally shared experiences in their lives.

Although "many children have little opportunity to develop reading and writing as interpersonal language skills which complement and reinforce speaking and listening as interrelated forces of a communication system" (Taylor, 1982, p. 90), parents of various cultural groups in the United States provide the values and parental support necessary for school success of their children.

How do parents or primary caregivers overcome the limitations of socioeconomic level and education to help their children achieve? Goldberg (1990) painted a dramatic picture of how James P. Comer, a prominent African American professor of child psychiatry at Yale University Child Study Center and associate dean of the Yale School of Medicine, was school-acculturated as a result of the determination of his mother. A daughter of a sharecropper, Comer's mother was determined that her children get an education. Maggie Comer observed and learned from her work as a domestic how middle-class families functioned and applied the best to her children. She learned to use the telephone to intercede and intervene for her children. She and her husband, who was born in rural Alabama and barely completed the sixth grade, took the children to museums and places they considered educational.

Comer credits his family's values and the continued support of his parents for his success in college and being able to overcome the racism he encountered, particularly in college. Friends from his neighborhood were just as bright and able and yet were unsuccessful because their parents did not know how to mediate for them and to help teachers understand how afraid the kids were of the system and institutions.

Parents and extended family members of culturally diverse children may be concerned and anxious about the educational success of their children. One African American father brought his son to a university-run summer reading clinic. He was not a poor reader, but his father wanted to provide the maximum opportunities for him. The father overheard another parent, a mother, discussing the program on the phone when he was there doing some handiwork in her home, and he contacted the instructor. He later told the instructor how he used all the free resources of the community to assist his four children. For example, each child had a library card, was taken to the library early in his or her life, and had attended library programs for children in the community. The mother, who had limited reading ability, checked out read-along books for the children and played these on a discarded phonograph the father had restored. The children had attended Head Start programs and the mother went to all accompanying parental educational programs that were provided. In their home they made sure that each child did his or her homework, and when a child was having trouble in school, the father usually visited the school to get help.

In a home visit to an extended family of one of his students in the southwest United States, a teacher found a very small two-room house, sparsely furnished with only one bed, books, a framed art print, and records on loan from the local library. An older female child assisted younger children with homework during his visit and later read with one of the children. She cross-switched between the English of the book and her Spanish language in discussing and sharing the book. An apparently bright first grader played school outside the door, teaching her younger siblings and neighbor children the alphabet.

In the hills of West Virginia in a run-down, one-room, rural home with no apparent chairs and table, a teacher noticed books stored in makeshift shelves. The very poor grandmother told him she bought these books at rummage sales for a few cents or salvaged them from the garbage in a nearby town. Well worn, often dirty and torn, they were cherished and used by all the children in the family and shared with neighbor children. The grandmother appeared the focus and drive for the education of these children.

Kim (1983) reported studies of Korean parents that indicated they were concerned about and involved with their children's school experience. These parents held high expectations and standards for their children and supported them by taking an active interest in their school and by keeping track of their performance, which often resulted in tutoring them at home to aid in the schoolwork. Because parents felt that they were unable to gain success and acceptance in the United States, they intensified the importance of their children learning English and adapting to the majority culture as a means of ensuring success and acceptance for their children. At the same time they wanted their children to retain many of the Korean cultural traits, including the extensive use of the Korean language.

Chan and Tsang (1983) summarized several studies regarding the cultural characteristics of Chinese Americans. These studies, although providing a limited picture of the learning characteristics of Chinese Americans, indicated that Chinese American mothers appeared to give enthusiastic feedback to their children and were extremely specific in their instruction.

Literacy appears to be a powerful cultural component of many European American middle-class homes. Parents and primary caregivers of children from culturally diverse or ethnic backgrounds, however, may provide the access to literacy for their children, helping to prepare them for the European American school. However, the teaching and learning styles of these homes may not be compatible with the generally European American middle-class school and teachers.

Parental Perceptions and Values About Literacy

Literacy does not develop in a vacuum but in a cultural context as a result of the value placed on it by society. Literacy is dependent upon the culture for its role, function, and meaning to society. It is a complex cultural condition linked to expectations and circumstances (Cressy, 1983). How society uses literacy determines its value, who will need to be literate, and the degree of literacy needed. The values or cultural perceptions learned at home directly influence children's responses to school-like tasks. As children experience literacy events in their environments, they filter the learning through culturally conditioned expectations held consciously or subconsciously (Harris, 1982). Young children learn to take from the environment (Heath, 1982) according to their cultural perception of how and what they should learn.

Ogbu (1983) studied literacy and schooling in a subordinate African American culture of the United States. African American parents sought education to get jobs and believed economic opportunities were commensurate with education. The lives of these parents as observed by their children did not bear out these beliefs. The traditional African American social and economic position has not required the same level of education as expected by European American counterparts. *Focus 22* reported that African American castelike stratification influenced how children perceived their opportunities (Benderson, 1988).

Heath (1982) examined the early lives of three groups of children, which she labeled Maintown (middle-class children), Roadville (working-class European Americans), and Tracton (working-class African Americans from a recent rural background). Heath's work demonstrated that the cultural perception of parents about learning, schooling, and literacy has a significant effect on the school success of their children. Heath's study showed that children learned from their cultural settings ways of gleaning knowledge from books. When these ways modeled the school's, children were successful in school. The ways of knowing from books were interdependent with parents' perception that children either learned or were taught to talk.

Maintown children learned how to talk about books and how to interact with the text, as well as how to selectively attend to items in the text. Roadville children's bedtime or naptime stories were, in contrast to Maintown children, from alphabet, number, animal books, or Bible stories. These books were more discrete in nature, generally decontextualized, and illustrated with flat-line drawings. Roadville caregivers did not engage in questions and answers to establish meaning as did Maintown caregivers. Story events, if any, were not related to real life, as parents attempted to do for Maintown children; nor did Roadville parents fictionalize children's lives to relate to the reading as Maintown parents had. Instead there were formulaic questions and answers, morals to be learned, and a focus on the alphabet. As children grew they were forced to listen and required to be quiet.

Literacy was infrequently demonstrated for children by Roadville parents, indicating its lack of importance in their daily lives. Caregivers did not correct children's attempts at environmental reading (for example, "stop" for "yield"). They believed the children were too young to learn this. In school, Roadville children did well at first because of the school's emphasis on teaching children how to read. However, they were unable to answer affective, evaluative, or creative questions, and as instruction changed to reading to learn, they fell behind.

In contrast to both Maintown and Roadville children, Tracton children grew up in almost a nonbook environment. They experienced reading only occasionally in play with older children. They were accustomed to an oral story tradition with a much different story structure from European American storybooks. Oral stories had a truth value and human experience element. These were fictionalized through parallels with their own experiences. Tracton children were unfamiliar with labeling or responding to "what" questions. Parents ignored the children's developmental processes of talking until their children actually talked. Children observed some reading demonstrated from adults, but the model was much different from that practiced in school-type reading settings. Reading was more of a social event. Adults read in a group while the listeners related their own experiences, asked questions, expressed opinions, and, with group synthesization and oral discourse negotiation, constructed meaning.

Tracton children did not do well in school because the school organization called for knowing how to take meaning from books and labeling, not using the analogical skills the students had learned in their culture. Analogical skills, introduced in most American reading series as higher order thinking, were applied only when the child had learned to read. By the time these children were able to participate, they were frustrated by school.

Learning events are provided by parents or caregivers from their perceptions of the world and the values they have about the need and use of literacy. Traditional school curricula, environment, and strategies do not match the world perceptions and cultural learning styles of children from diverse cultures.

Parental Use and Demonstration of Literacy

Learners learn print by using and becoming involved in its use (Heath, 1982). In literate societies, literacy develops for complex and interrelated reasons. The degree caregivers use and demonstrate literacy for young learners influences their learning. Each culture may demonstrate the use of literacy in unique ways. The overall impact that literacy has on daily living, and the value that the culture places on it, make an impact on the learning of its young.

Literacy demonstrations are vicarious learning experiences for the young learner that specify how literacy is used in meaningful, relevant, and functional ways. These experiences serve to stimulate or initiate pretend reading and scribble or mock writing that may result in invented spelling. When children have literacy interactions with a literate demonstrator, these activities aid children in their development of actual reading and representational writing. Thus, when they observe how reading and writing work and are able to respond and interact to the experience with a demonstrator, literacy becomes focused. Fundamental to such development is the need for the learner to have a purpose and motive for learning (F. Smith, 1987). When the young learner has a reason and feels a real need to read and write, this is a stimulus to make it happen. Thus, the learner takes charge and decides to learn.

F. Smith (1984) reported that in literacy learning the learner apprentices to a literate demonstrator who uses reading and writing in meaningful and purposeful ways. The learner learns what being able to read and write does and means for the demonstrator. The learner finds out what the demonstrator is able to do because he or she is literate. Interaction with a literate demonstrator contributes significantly to reading and writing. The learner then begins using environmental aids and the interactive demonstrator to find solutions in the search for structure and form. Apprenticeship can happen in literate home environments for children and can occur with either caregivers or siblings.

A convincing ethnographic description of how literacy is learned by members of an ethnic culture through apprenticeship, modeling, and demonstration is given by Fishman (1987). Rural Amish children are acculturated to literacy through demonstrations showing the need, value, and uses of reading and writing for functional and recreational occasions. An Amish home is replete with print—bulletin boards, greeting cards, notices, clippings, magazines, newspapers, English and German Bibles, significant religious books of the culture, Amish directories, songbooks, hymnals in German, and children's books. Preschool writing and drawing adorn refrigerators along with schoolpapers of older children.

Amish children have their own personal copies of a songbook and young children follow the words from memory. The Bible is read regularly, both in English and German, and adults share their understanding with the children. Children also take turns reading the Bible aloud in the family. Older children will read a few words, allowing the younger to repeat. Children memorize Bible verses or hymn stanzas with nonreaders memorizing selections having less complex vocabulary. Parents share secular information as well by reading aloud information from books, papers, and children's books. Young children share their books by telling about them—what is seen or known.

Members of the Amish community are letter writers. Letters circulate from one person to the next, each adding a page and removing those he or she wrote. Children contribute to these, even before formal writing has been learned, by drawing and dictating. When letters are received, they are read aloud. A variety of other writing is carried on as well.

Amish children learn that literacy is a force that imparts power. They learn that to be Amish one must read and write. Reading and learning from the Bible and song and religious books, allows the children to affiliate with the community in primarily religious ways.

The works of Taylor (1982), Heath (1982), and Fishman (1987) illustrated that children learn literacy in homes where there is extensive literacy use and demonstration. Literacy was a fabric of life in these homes. Literacy in Taylor's middle-class families and Fishman's Amish family was deeply embedded in the social processes of family life and was not specific lists of activities added to the family's agenda. The Taylor parents paraphrased the text and talked about pictures as they "introduced each child to the act of reading stories" (Taylor, 1982, p. 68). They related real-life events to stories. Children were introduced to signs and symbols, like street and store signs, early in life in everyday social situations. Children were encouraged to experiment with letters, to ask what writing said, to copy from print in the environment, and to dictate ideas. Heath's study of the three groups of families showed that those children who succeeded in school had parents or caregivers who demonstrated ways to take meaning from books and how to talk about them that related to the school teaching model.

In the studies of nondominant culture homes reported above, when parents provided access to education, children were more likely to succeed. Home experiences often included literacy experiences, and parents interceded with the school on behalf of their children. One parent or caregiver seemed to be particularly influential in providing a sustained drive that promoted education and learning. These parents had the time or personal drive to be able to bridge the school culture and teaching practices on behalf of their children. If schools wish to provide access for children of diverse cultures, they can no longer continue to rely solely on parents to provide the bridges. Instead, schools must work with parents to change their environments and curricula. Teachers must understand their students and their students' cultures and become the bridges between home and school.

Clearly parents can play a significant role inculcating literacy for children. The significance of their role indicates the importance for developing culturally appropriate educational programs and implies the involvement of parents from various cultural communities who work with the school to change environment, curricula, and learning strategies.

Literacy: Access to Power for Multicultural Societies

All learners need to view literacy events as important aspects of life. Literacy provides power. Parents demonstrate its power when they model literacy in fulfilling their daily needs and activities. In the process of becoming literate the learner is changed. The literacy process develops different perceptions, increases understanding, develops language, and improves thinking. Literate people are not only perceived as being more productive but more easily trained. "Only the literate can buy, direct, or at any rate work with the range of technologies which are changing the wealth, organization and operation of societies" (Oxenham, 1980, p. 95). Thus literacy is a necessary component for all cultures, but for nondominant cultures it provides the access to education and improved occupational status—it provides power!

THE EDUCATION AND RETENTION OF CULTURALLY DIVERSE STUDENTS

Students of color or students from poverty-level homes appear to have lost motivation for schooling and have dropped out because of the hopelessness of their situation. Many find the school context alien to their cultural orientation. According to Ogbu (1983) African American youths' responses to school are directly influenced by values learned in the home and how they perceive their opportunities in society. The social and economic positions available for African Americans have not required much formal education; success for many of the underclass has been found through other less socially acceptable means. Poverty and a break down in societal norms appear problems that must be solved to keep culturally diverse youth in school.

European American perceptions have shaped the education of all of the culturally different communities in the United States. The African American and Native American communities have had a prolonged struggle with the European American community for equal education. An education that was culturally appropriate and well integrated schooling were goals African Americans sought. These goals are still not achieved in many areas of the nation. Ogbu (1983) states that the disillusionment of the African American youth has led to distrust of schools. Basic to solving the problem is changing society to raise economic expectations for youth that will result in their remaining in school and seeking a higher education.

School Retention of Culturally Diverse Students

Culturally diverse students have a higher dropout rate than European American students. Sandors (1987) provided figures from studies of other researchers that bear out this fact. She reported that approximately 29 percent of Native American students under the age of 21 in Wisconsin would not receive school diplomas. A study conducted by the National Indian Management also determined that 57 percent of Native American adults did not have high school diplomas.

Alarming figures for 1986 from the Center for Educational Statistics, U.S. Department of Education, indicated that 682,000 American teenagers dropped out at an average rate of 3,789 students per school day (estimate based on a 180-day school year). The dropout rate appeared higher in inner-city schools. Up to 50 percent of the students in some inner-city schools dropped out (Stern & Chandler, 1987). Gingras and Careaga (1989) reported that students from non-English-speaking homes had a dropout rate of 40 percent compared to a rate of 10 percent from English-only homes.

Waggoner (1987) reported that African American and Hispanic American youths were substantially behind European American youths and young adults in the extent to which they were graduating from high school. Despite improvement in the rate of dropouts, Hispanic Americans are nearly three times more likely than European Americans and twice as likely as African Americans ages 16 to 34 to have not completed secondary education. Only 51 percent of Hispanic Americans aged 25 and over completed high school compared to 78 percent of the non-Hispanics (Gingras & Careaga, 1989). This figure is even more significant when one considers that 95.5 percent of the increase in the population of ESL students are from homes where Spanish is the first language. Dropout rates for the 20- to 24-year-old youths indicated that one in seven European Americans, one in six African Americans, and one in three Hispanic Americans were not enrolled and had not graduated in October 1985. The figures improved for 16- to 19-year-old youths as of 1985. African American youths had virtually closed the gap and kept up with the European Americans while Hispanics were twice as likely as both groups to be dropouts.

Factors Governing School Dropout

Poverty and quality of education appear to be major factors for school dropout. According to Waggoner (1987) African American and Hispanic American schoolchildren were more likely to live in families below the poverty level than European American children. She reported figures from the 1980 census indicating that 36 percent of African American families and 27 percent of Hispanic American families reported incomes below the poverty level for their size and circumstances, while only 10 percent of European American families with children under 18 years of age reported below poverty level incomes. These findings are confirmed by Arias (1986). In summarizing studies regarding school attrition, she reported three factors associated with high school dropout: students are of (1) Hispanic ethnicity, (2) speak English as a second language, and (3) are of lower socioeconomic status. "Clearly, many families need the additional income which young people who drop out of school to work might provide, even though, just as clearly, the young people sacrifice opportunities and future earnings by not finishing high school" (Waggoner, 1987, p. 220).

On the brighter side, the *U.S. News & World Report,* December 25, 1989–January 1, 1990 cites that life for the poor inner-city African American has improved and the underclass has shrunk. Whitman and Friedman (1989/1990) reported that Christopher Jencks, a sociologist at Northwestern University's Center for Urban Affairs and Policy Research, estimated that about half of all working-age adults had regular jobs and only a third of all households received public assistance. However, Jencks emphasized that the proliferation of unwed mothers and jobless men has become more severe in the ghetto. In another study, Richard Freeman of National Bureau of Economic Research found the unemployment rate for African American male teenagers declined from a high 41 percent in 1980 to 7 percent in 1987 (Whitman & Friedman, 1989/1990). (Variances in these findings may be a result of different ghetto neighborhoods.) Recently, some employers have begun extraordinary minority recruiting programs to hire innercity workers.

This is movement in the right direction to assist African and Hispanic American populations who will be nearly half the labor force by the year 2000. Nevertheless, skill requirements, even for entry-level jobs, continue to rise rapidly meaning that low education level and poor work habits may cause ghetto residents to be passed by for suitable employment unless educational programs change.

Educational Testing Service in *Focus 22* (Benderson, 1988) reported a study that indicated that an underlying cause for school attrition for culturally diverse students was directly related to poor elementary and secondary education. According to the report if opportunities were equal, there would be no differences between the various racial groups. For example, differences for Hispanic American children are primarily a function of low socioeconomic status and education in a second language. By the age of nine the average reading and writing proficiency of Hispanic American children is considerably lower than that of European American children. Gingras and Careaga (1989) concluded that a clear reason for lower school performance in reading and mathematics for students from culturally diverse families was a lack of competence in English.

Such studies appear to blame the victim. Certainly, they ignore a deeper cause. Schools do not use the culture and language of their students in their programs. Schools and teachers clearly need to increase their expectations for achievement of culturally diverse students as well. Their present expectations place students in programs that focus on developing skills rather than on cognitive development. The problem is compounded further by social conditions in a society that limits opportunities and access to improved economic status for culturally diverse people.

Poverty must be considered a form of violence. It can do extensive damage to countless generations. Helplessness eliminates motivation and the drive for education. Poverty means poorer nutrition; poorer educational attainment follows. Marshall (1987) reported that studies show there is a correlation between nutritional improvement and achievement. Poverty also threatens the loss of literacy to future generations when literacy is no longer a viable, relevant, and functional need in life.

More single U.S. mothers are living at the poverty level than ever before. There is also an increase in births by teenage mothers. Generally, these mothers have poorer prenatal care, have poorer levels of nutrition, and, consequently, their children, born at risk, have a higher death rate. Since many of these mothers have not completed their secondary education, they are more apt to be unskilled workers with lower salaries. If, in addition, they are people of color, they have fewer job opportunities. Children from poverty-level homes have been found to have higher incidences of illness, absenteeism, and problems with concentration and may leave school early (Sutcliffe, 1987).

Examination of how well schools are doing in retaining students from culturally diverse populations indicates that a high dropout rate is precipitated by economic factors, lack of access to jobs, and failure of the schools to change programs and teaching to meet the cultural learning needs of students. Consequently, this provides a further reason why schools must change their curricula, environments, and teaching practices to develop social equality and promote cultural pluralism. This approach will go the furthest in improving society and will in turn further learning and growth.

THE RATIONALE AND FOUNDATION FOR
MULTICULTURAL EDUCATION

The society of the United States continues to withhold equal opportunity to all its citizens. People of ethnic backgrounds, for example, are often expected to display the same behavioral and linguistic styles of the European American middle class before they can be taken seriously. People of color are still distinctly subordinate economically and politically (Sleeter & Grant, 1988). They are more likely to be living in poverty than European American members of society because society also tolerates economic inequality for racial minorities regardless of education. African American college graduates earn nearly $7,000 less than their European American counterparts (Benderson, 1988). Clearly education may not even pay off for members of different racial groups. Being European American in the United States still holds greater economic and employment advantages.

Multicultural Problems of European American–
Focused Schools

Although there is not an official standard U.S. curriculum, most curricula are codified by standardized achievement tests and text materials, more alike than different. The content of text materials and standardized tests is the basis for what is taught. This material is then modified to fit the average skill level of a given class and, to a much lesser degree, student interest and experiential background (Sleeter & Grant, 1988). An examination of the curricula indicates content that has traditionally focused on the European American male with minor ethnic and female inclusions resulting from the social pressure of minority groups and feminists.

U.S. schools appear to have more commonalities than differences. There are teachers in the schools who are sensitive to culturally different students and attempt to provide more individualization involving learning centers and small-group instruction. However, there are more teachers who adhere to teacher-centered, large-group instruction focused on the tasks related to textbooks, duplicated materials, and workbooks which emphasize skills apart from context or real life (Goodlad, 1984; Cuban, 1984).

The teaching practices identified in the Goodlad (1984) and Cuban (1984) studies reflect a conception about learning that is irrelevant and inappropriate to students in a multicultural school. Instruction for all students must be student-centered and focused on learning about themes and topics that are relevant and meaningful. Duplicated materials and workbooks tend to focus on drills and skills removed from meaningful context. Learning results when students are involved in content having high interest and personal involvement.

Sleeter and Grant (1988) state that culturally diverse students will be at a serious disadvantage when teachers adhere to findings described by Godlad (1984) and Cuban (1984) because their learning styles will probably diverge from the predominant teaching style, and their skills may deviate from those of other students. They may then turn away from school because they do not identify with the school or their teachers and the content and instruction is uninteresting and alienating.

Implications of the Goodlad (1984) and Cuban (1984) studies, as determined by Sleeter and Grant (1988), have serious consequences for culturally diverse students in educational programs:

1. Students will be disadvantaged if their learning styles diverge from the predominant teaching style.
2. Students will present problems for the classroom teachers when their skills deviate from those of the majority.
3. Students may turn away from school because they do not identify with the schooling, their teachers, and the content, and instruction is uninteresting and alienating.

A culturally diverse student's different background experiences and learning styles may conflict with the school if, for example, he or she is more oriented toward cooperation, people centeredness, discussion, hands-on work, and whole to part, or if the student believes learning is private and does not display his or her best effort in taking a test. (Whole to part learning refers here not only to a style of learning but to a theory with a body of research which indicates that language and literacy are learned from whole to part rather than part to whole.) Schools traditionally stream students who fit these categories into nonacademic areas because they do not fit the school's curriculum and instruction.

Guidelines for Multicultural Education

There is growing pressure to make schools more inviting and supportive of culturally diverse students. In communities with large population diversity, there has been pressure to include additional languages in the curricula and to develop bilingual programs. More schools and educators have realized the importance of a strong English language program. Fewer have acknowledged the importance of a strong first language.

Students from nondominant cultural groups must be provided opportunities for success in society. They must also be empowered by learning decision-making and social-action skills and taught in strategies appropriate to their home cultures. On the other hand, schools must also teach students from the dominant cultural group how to respond positively and sensitively to diverse cultural, social, racial, and ethnic groups and to learn about the cultures of other ethnic subgroups in order to function appropriately within one or two other cultural contexts. This concept, when taken to the fullest, must be applied in all the curricula.

All students should learn about the beliefs, values, traditions, and contributions of all people in the society, whether it is in the arts, literature, social sciences, or physical science. This would mean including the scientific theories, music, and art of Native Americans for example, as well as European Americans. All curriculum areas should be taught multiculturally throughout the school (Sleeter & Grant, 1988).

Changing Schools to Facilitate a Multicultural Environment

Schools must strive to turn back the tide of hopelessness felt by children from diverse cultures. This can begin with educators knowing each child—the child's sociocultural history, the child's language and literacy development—and how all these characteristics might be incorporated for successful teaching and learning.

Multicultural curricula would be developed that included not only how the nation's people are different but also how they are alike, what they share as a nation, their ideals, values, and spirit (Ravitch, 1992). Curricula would be based on the assumption that ethnic diversity and educational equality are positive elements in society that will enrich the nation and increase the ways in which students learn to solve personal and public problems. Students learn equity and respect to overcome prejudice and discrimination (Banks, 1988). Students learn history, literature, and art in a manner that diminishes and combats prejudice (Ravitch, 1992).

Using Literature in Multicultural Education

Literature is an excellent resource for learning to understand how other people live and think. It provides the opportunity to talk about how people are alike as well as different. Good literature mirrors the culture and society it represents. Literature provides us the opportunity to explore cultural and ethnic differences. In schools with multicultural curricula, a focus on language, culture, and ethnic materials helps us teach democratic values for working together.

SUMMARY

Schools have not adapted, modified, or revised their curricula and instruction to account for the significant change in the makeup of the growing culturally diverse population. Culturally diverse children who succeed probably do so because of parental intervention and not because of significant changes in school programs.

Parents and primary caregivers of children from diverse cultural backgrounds are the key to the success of their children in school. Their view of the world, views about the status of literacy, the amount of interactive demonstration of literacy in their home, as well as the relevance, functionality, and meaningfulness of literacy modeled and demonstrated for the child can establish a learning course for the child in school.

The nature of the school's curriculum and instructional strategies must acknowledge and affirm all cultures within society. All students must be perceived as equal members of society and their diversity celebrated. Schools must not only celebrate the diversity of the population but the democratic values and history of the country.

IMPLICATIONS FOR INSTRUCTION

Schools and educators can respond to the need to restructure schools to become multicultural in the following ways:

1. Empower parents and primary caregivers to be equal partners in the education of their children. Involve parents in their children's education. Accommodate parental work hours by scheduling day and night school performances and conferences. Keep parents informed, keep interactions with parents informal and frequent. Listen to what parents have to share about their children. (See the report of a study by Lindle [1989].)

Establish parenting boards in a site-based management design that give parents equal voice in budgetary matters and program de-

150, 176

sign and development and to aid school personnel in selecting and suggesting culturally appropriate materials and practices. Have the boards meet regularly and work toward getting community involvement in the decision-making process of the school.

Designate parents who will provide assistance to teachers in learning what is culturally appropriate. Locate community speakers to bring awareness and understanding to nonspeakers of a language about the minority language, culture, beliefs, and traditions. Identify native speakers of a language who will assist and support bilingual children.

2. Develop parenting programs in conjunction with other agencies in society. Assist parents to create language-rich and literate home environments in keeping with their cultural traditions, beliefs, and values and learn how to help children develop skills and attitudes for success in the transformed school. Help parents learn how to select books appropriate to their value systems, read to children as an interactive demonstrator, facilitate children's early writing, make their homes into literate environments, and develop problem-solving skills. (See Lueder [1989] for a statewide effort begun in Tennessee as a good model for such a program.)

3. Assess and analyze the classroom environment and curricula and work toward making the classroom a literate environment. Embed language and literacy into the daily routines of the classroom. Demonstrate language and literacy as a natural part of what goes on in the classroom, a means for attaining goals. Immerse classrooms in print. Practice language and literacy in an open and informal classroom with a supportive psychological climate (Little Soldier, 1989).

4. Design and develop curricula that have cultural relevance for children. Hold high and realistic expectations for each child and provide equality in instructional practices for all children in a nonsexist manner. Develop curricula around multicultural themes and topics to provide for children's cultural backgrounds. Empower children to share in the control of their learning (Wells, 1987). Include adult language and literacy models and demonstrators from various communities. Use student native language in the instructional program to help students channel their conceptual backgrounds.

5. Design and develop curricula around interdisciplinary themes and topics (Gingras & Careaga, 1989). Use culturally relevant materials and learning experiences that enhance self-concept and pride in

identity. Provide a wide range of diverse learning experiences and instructional materials in each theme and topic that incorporates the contemporary and historic cultures of the students. Use material that presents different viewpoints, is gender fair, and inclusive. Design an instructional environment that reflects the culture through displays of pictures, books, and articles (Little Soldier, 1989).

6. Use a cooperative learning model to enhance sharing and communication. Help children from different backgrounds learn to work together and increase their interpersonal relationships, peer-group language, and problem-solving strategies (Sleeter & Grant, 1988; Johnson, Johnson & Holubec, 1986; Little Soldier, 1989).

7. Use a democratic problem-solving approach to teaching with limited use of large-group formal lessons. Help children with strategies that encourage participation in a variety of ways because asking and formulating questions can be a very culturally oriented activity (Little Soldier, 1989). (Vocabulary, phrasing of questions, and speed of speech may give bilingual children problems with questions, no matter how well the content is known.) Have children predict questions in cooperative groups that will be answered through reading. Listen to what children say, think, and what they want to know; praise them and support their efforts and progress. Assist student development by modeling standard language patterns and refraining from correcting pupils' oral language errors. Develop formal instruction only to fit children's specific needs (Little Soldier, 1989).

8. Work toward bilingual or multiple languages in the school. Encourage ESL speakers by using part-time aides, community and parent volunteers, recorded cassettes, or telephone tutorials (Troike, 1983) if logistics and funding for bilingual programs are not available. Provide literacy materials from each language represented in the student body. Have aides and parents translate appropriate materials into the communities' languages.

9. Revise the evaluation and assessment program of the school to reflect the content being learned. Refrain from grouping based on standardized tests. Make sure that students are not penalized in testing knowledge by lack of language skills or reading and writing. Use accurate assessment strategies that take into account individual differences in learning and the cognitive difficulty of learning academic language concepts (Sleeter & Grant, 1988) for students speaking English as a second language.

10. Work toward a better cultural balance in school staffing. Select a balanced staff of teachers, administrators, aides, and custodians in the school from the diverse populations represented in the community. (The ideal would be equal male and female membership.) Select school personnel who hold high expectations for all children and do not base their expectations on socioeconomic, language, race, or gender characteristics. Select people who model an ability to successfully interrelate with all people in the school community.

CHAPTER TWO

Language and Literacy Foundations for Multicultural Classrooms

- ■ *What is the nature of communication?*
- ■ *What factors govern first- and second-language and literacy acquisition?*
- ■ *How does culture affect language learning?*
- ■ *How successful are schools in developing literacy for culturally diverse students?*
- ■ *What factors should be considered in refocusing schools to become multicultural?*

INTRODUCTION

Attention must be given to language and literacy components of education that act as significant factors for student success in order to make U.S. schools more multicultural. The language children bring to school influences learning. A close link exists between language and multicultural education (Nieto, 1992). English second language (ESL) programs and many bilingual programs have had as their underlying purpose the assimilation of all non-English-speaking students by making them English speakers, but there now must be a forthright effort to develop bilingual programs and accept and recognize the language all children bring to school. Further, schools must develop programs that aid each child to fully develop competencies in both first and second language and literacy. When children have well-developed first-language (L1) skills, they acquire second-language (L2) skills with greater ease and success than children who are still learning a first language (Skutnabb-Kangas, 1981). Educators often lack understanding about L2 and literacy learning. The child coming to school speaking a first language is disabled only to the extent of the school's misunderstanding about L2 learning.

A young father, struggling to communicate in English, described how concerned he and his wife were about their children's literacy development. Should he and his wife stop speaking their native language to help their children improve their English? They were advised to retain their first language so that their children would be bilingual, and it was recommended that the children be taken to the public library for story hour on Saturdays. The father asked the librarian to help him select highly illustrative books for the children to enjoy at home. The parents were also advised to tell stories in their native language, because there were probably no children's books that used their language. The parents wrote the stories down in simple terms the children could illustrate. The parents also shared events with the children from a weekly paper and letters received in their own language. The father learned that his home language would help the children retain their native language. These parents could expand the type of language experiences parents normally provide by helping their children learn to read and write in their first language.

The young refugee parents knew that their children must learn to communicate well in both English language and literacy. They did not know how this would happen if their home was not conducive to the English language. They did not know that maintenance of the first language and the corresponding literacy development supports and facilitates L2 learning; then the learner is able to cognitively develop in two languages (Bennett, 1986). Such cognitive development is difficult outside a strong supporting L1 community without an effective school program.

THE NATURE OF COMMUNICATION

People must communicate to become fully functional human beings (K. S. Goodman, 1986). Communication is language, whether oral, written, or nonverbal. Communication occurs not merely as a message exchange from sender to receiver. It involves specially selected and shaped intents from a sender which are reconstructed by a receiver using prior knowledge and experiences. The environment or context in which the communication takes place is also important in the communication act. A communicative exchange, whether between speaker and listener or writer and reader, is easier when both participants in the language event share similar meaning as members of the same interpretive language community.

Recent thought on communication suggests that meaning is neither in the environment nor in the head of the receiver; rather it is a result of continued ongoing sign interpretation (Harste, Woodward & Burke, 1984). Language users of any community share similar meanings and understandings. For members of the same interpretive language community, learning occurs as a social event in the learning process. Since students in our schools come from diverse cultural communities, teachers need to understand the linguistic and cultural differences their students bring to the classroom. Although these differences can cause communication difficulties that impede learning if not anticipated, they can enrich the classroom learning environment for all children.

In the communicative process, whether oral or written, there are feedback loops from receiver to sender which constitute a change of role. Feedback shapes the message sent as part of the communicative process. Oral language, however, may not always stimulate feedback as we think of it. Listeners receive oral language heard on the radio or from television. The message is not designed to achieve oral response, only to transmit ideas or inform or entertain the listener or viewer. The intent is for the receiver to interact with the ideas being received, although the sender may never know what the interaction is.

Writers may not always get direct feedback from their writing either. Still, reading is a dialogue with the writer. A writer shapes his or her message for the reader. Readers have a long-distance transaction with the author about the interpreted message.

Learners from different language and cultural experiences bring different prior knowledge to the communicative event, whether listening and speaking or reading and writing. Their backgrounds affect how they comprehend the communiqué. Speech and written passages are interpreted differently as a result of prior information from each person's language and cultural background. For example, students from nondominant languages and cultures may need specific preparation for understanding common European American cultural events and activities—celebrating Halloween and Thanksgiving, and religious events, such as marriage ceremonies. Each culture has its own concepts about common everyday activities.

The opportunities for English-language communication and mutual growth and understanding of European American culture are significantly limited for culturally diverse students when they are grouped in schools according to race, class, and gender. When this grouping occurs, the students are taught in a manner that channels them into the roles currently occupied by members of their race, class, and gender. This practice has strong racist overtones. Hispanic Americans, for example, are the most segregated, interfering seriously with their English-language competence. The Hispanic American population is highly concentrated in urban areas, meaning that these stu- •lents attend schools in which Hispanic Americans predominate. The result is lack of native English–speaking peer models (Arias, 1986). Peer models from the target language are an essential factor for learning to speak and use a language as a native speaker.

Lack of English-language proficiency evolves for students at the secondary level into tracking and placement in classes with little academic challenge (Arias, 1986). Not only do these students fail to receive the program that European American students receive, but they fail to receive the opportunities to interact in natural communicative settings with native English–speaking students, which certainly interferes with their language development (Sleeter & Grant, 1988). Having another language besides English is not a hindrance to learning, according to Nieto (1992). She reports studies that indicate students proficient in their first language perform better on achievement tests.

LANGUAGE AND LITERACY CONCEPTS

Teachers in the multicultural school need a strong understanding about the nature of language and literacy. They need to fully understand the factors involved in acquiring language and becoming literate. Students enrolled in multicultural classrooms represent a wide range of cultures and home backgrounds. Teachers need to be able to provide an educational environment that will be conducive for students with a wide range of language and literacy competencies in the classroom. This is only possible when teachers comprehend all aspects of language and literacy acquisition, the role of culture in language and literacy acquisition, and when they can apply factors to their classroom environment, curricula, and instruction.

Factors Governing Language and Literacy Acquisition

Both Wells (1973) and Halliday (1973/1977) noted that children's language learning developed for functional reasons. *Functional* means that language is acquired in response to the learner's interaction with the environment as well as the need of the learner to gain control of his or her environment. Language functions emerge as young language learners have relevant and meaningful experiences. These experiences are necessary for the young child to consistently learn to discriminate sounds, words, and sentence patterns required by the various functions and to relate oral language to print. Such functional experiences occur in all languages and cultures. Oral language learning functions, derived from the works of Halliday (1973/1977) and Wells (1973), have application to literacy learning as well. Language and literacy emerge in the following ways:

1. Learners use language and literacy to direct and control. Language and literacy develop to satisfy needs or desires through requesting, suggesting, refusing, assenting, and giving orders or directions in all situations and language registers appropriate to the cultural community.

2. Learners use language and literacy to express and share feelings. Language and literacy develop to express and share personal ideas and feelings that are distinctive, reflective of family and culture in a multitude of situations and opportunities appropriate to the cultural community.

3. Learners use language and literacy to receive and transmit information. Language and literacy develop to acquire knowledge or explore the environment through naming, answering, questioning, denying, giving examples, reporting facts and conclusions, making summaries, forming generalizations, and advising in both formal and informal registers appropriate to the cultural community.

4. Learners use language and literacy to create and imagine. Language and literacy develop when learners use their imagination through prose, poetry, and dramatization to create and image the new and the different, to try out new roles and experience new situations through fantasy, to speculate as a scientist in wondering "what if" in registers appropriate to the settings and cultural community.

5. Learners use language and literacy for routines and formalities. Language and literacy develop as learners understand, respond, and use routines that are culturally and socially acceptable and appropriate in interacting sociocultural situations.

Two aspects of writing/reading make these communication processes different from listening/speaking. First, there is intent of writer/reader to communicate or receive communication that is more permanent, concrete, tangible, or can be used at some distance in time and space from the writer/reader or when the writer and reader are not able to be in an oral communicating mode. Second, the writer/reader desires to communicate or receive knowledge that can be gathered, recorded, kept, studied, analyzed, or used (McGee & Richgels, 1990). Consequently, the functional reasons for acquiring literacy might also include a learner's need for print permanency.

Conditions Conducive for Language and Literacy Acquisition

The conditions for language and literacy learning are clearly comparable. Both language and literacy emerge when the conditions are appropriate for the learner. Both emerge normally and naturally when interactive social situations are meaningful, relevant, and purposeful to the learner. Ideally, this occurs in the home language first.

Cambourne (1984) identified seven conditions that facilitated oral language emergence and acquisition for children:

1. Immersion in oral language
2. Modeling for the learner
3. Expecting to talk
4. Approximating speech
5. Opportunity to talk
6. Feedback for the content of talk
7. Responsibility for self-learning

Two additional conditions, identified by F. Smith (1984) and King

(1985), also are important conditions for language acquisition: self-control and creative construction. These conditions can be applied to literacy and are appropriate to all cultural communities.

Environmental Contexts

Language and literacy learning requires the learner to be immersed in an environment where language and literacy are used and practiced in meaningful, relevant, and functional situations. Both language and literacy learning require that each be modeled and demonstrated for the learner as important in relevant daily contextual situations. Learners must be in environments where they are expected to learn the language at a level that conforms with familial societal forms and registers and to develop the ability to read and write at a level that is appropriate to the expectations of their homes and families.

In language learning, a learner must receive positive oral responses to the content of the message, not the form. In other words, what is said is more important than how it is said. Generally, in L1 learning the parent responds to a child's meaning. In literacy learning, the learner must receive responses to the reading and writing that focus on the message, not the code. Learners in both language and literacy need the opportunity to use language and literacy in meaningful, relevant, and functional settings appropriate to their needs and interests. When this happens in the first language it more easily transfers to the second language.

Language learning requires that the learner receive oral feedback or response that can contribute to feelings of self-worth and interpretation of the social context of the oral communication. In literacy learning, the learner needs to receive meaningful responses from written messages. When the learner is able to receive written communication or make communicative meaning in print, the experience contributes to a feeling of self-worth and membership in the literate community and leads to further strategies for interpreting the written message's meaning.

Learner Requirements

The language learner must develop a take-control attitude for learning and have a feeling that he or she is responsible for learning. This, too, must occur in literacy learning if the learner is to learn to read and write. The take-control mode requires the oral language learner to takes risks to create new constructions, patterns, and word uses. In literacy learning the learner needs to take risks to interact and transact with the author in exploring meaning and messages.

L1 Acquisition Processes

The observation of young children using all languages clearly indicates that they are active experimenters with language. They acquire oral language through transactions with adults, other children, and siblings in functional and meaningful settings. They play with language as they learn, both by themselves and with others. Their environmental experiences provide meaning for the language they perceive. Children comprehend through actively listening and observing their world. Further, as they experiment in using the language they have heard, a set of rules for all the cueing systems internalizes. Gradually their language expands and refines until the speech they use reaches a societal norm. According to Harste et al. (1984) members of a particular language community discover the common patterns used around them. Language acquisition is basically a response to the environment (Halliday, 1973/1977).

The first language is acquired through interpretation and interaction as the learner attempts to make meaning from the social environment (Harste et al., 1984). Although imitation and modeling are involved, the child learns because of interaction. The knowledge and experiences children develop through learning their first language helps them develop cognitive schemas available for use in L2 acquisition.

Language Acculturates and Socializes

Very early in their lives young children appear to attempt to make their needs or desires known, or as Halliday (1973/1977) states, to better control their environment. The growing young child soon is actively comprehending and culturally responding to the language used in the environment through careful perception and cultural language interaction with caregivers. To be understood the child tries to conform to the sounds, structures, and cultural language behaviors experienced. The need to understand and be understood in communication is a very strong drive in the young child.

When children acquire their first language, they also learn a set of social rules for moving in the world. As children learn a language, they are also socialized into the culture and society of the parents and community. They learn when, why, and how to talk to people in their environment and what is or is not permissible in specific contexts. The primary caregiver's speech socializes the child to the culture of the family. The culture of the family has special language, customs, and ways of behaving and believing about events in society. Culture is introduced naturally without planning for it.

As children learn socially and culturally significant aspects of their lives, they develop in their abilities to express what Baker and Greenfield (1988) call the most informative element, the novel or different aspect. For example, a child may recall an important socio-cultural event and at the same time generate his or her own perception in the form of speech.

Language Organizes and Classifies

As children learn language and experience their environment, they learn culturally specific names for things in their environment. For example, some toys make sounds Americans ascribe to animals—cows say moo-moo, dogs say bow-wow. In some children's language dogs are bow-wows, cows are moo-moos, and so forth. Early vocabulary generally is heavily weighted toward dynamic objects which change as a result of the children's own actions (Baker & Greenfield, 1988). Thus, early vocabularies would rarely include names for common items that are stationary and noiseless.

Such learning establishes categories for children for classifying, retaining, and understanding their world. These classifications are refined through experiences by using specific words or testing hypotheses in communication. This testing and perception-checking continues as children develop.

Information and experiences are given order through the use of schemas—organized chunks of knowledge and experience often accompanied by feelings. Schemas develop as people transact with the world. They influence how one makes sense of the world, interacts or responds in the world. If schemas do not match what is heard or read, the learner may not be able to make sense of it (Weaver, 1988). If schemas are incompatible with incoming data, the learner may be confused and forced to revise the interpretation in such a way as to make the new information compatible. Schemas are the learner's concepts, beliefs, expectations, and processes used to make sense. They influence a person's recall and comprehension throughout his or her life.

Language Learning: Deduction and Generation Processes

Although the young language learner does demonstrate some imitation of adult speech, most language is deduced and generated. For example, children will deduce that -ed is the regular past tense form for verbs, but they overgeneralize its use. When a child uses the correct form it is probably only in imitation of an adult and will occur as an isolated incident. No amount of modeling or expansion can include that form until the child is ready through further development of the irregular verb form. According to Baker and Greenfield (1988) this overgeneralized use demonstrates how the child's language shows emphasis for the new aspect of the situation and could focus the listener's attention. It is not unusual for verbs with irregular forms (go, buy, see, and so on) to be overgeneralized. These verbs are regularized because of the internalized perceived patterns from the regular verbs.

Language: A Semantic Acquisition Process

Semantic (meaning) acquisition requires adding additional meaning to the known meaning or refining or delineating its use. For example, a child reasons that because there are hands, ears, and eyes, there should be foots. In this situation the child has semantically overextended. A four-year-old child was watching a PBS television program with her family and the station lost its signal. A message came on the screen saying "stand by." The child wanted to know what it said. When she was told, she immediately got up and stood by the television set. Clearly she demonstrated a narrow or limited understanding of the term stand by. However, her behavior in asking what the term said indicated she realized the functional aspect of literacy.

Factors That Facilitate L2 Acquisition

L1 learning plays an important role in L2 learning. It is a predictor of success in learning a second language (Hakuta & Gould, 1987). L2 learners have advantages in learning a second language they did not have in learning their first language. They now understand the meaning of language and how it works. They don't have to approximate the beginning stages of language learning and consequently use more sophisticated language. L2 children's linguistic abstraction skills mature earlier.

L2 learners demonstrate unique language usage patterns not found in L1 learners. Patterns of Southeast Asian learners are examples of usage not uncommon for adult L2 learners. Note that meaning is retained in each of the three utterances.

He nots eat.
She's dancings.
I have more rank first...

Cognitive Structure

Cognitive structure is an important factor influencing L2 learning. F. Smith (1975) described cognitive structure as the theory of the world in the head. He defined cognitive structure as the knowledge, opinion or belief, prejudice, taste, habit, hope, fear, love, hate, and expectation people have in their heads; how a person learns about the world; and how a person provides a useful summary of everything learned and a way to perceive and interpret new data, a source of useful hypotheses.

A child develops cognitive structure from the L1 environment through transactual experiences in the environment with adults and peers. As the schemas are developed and refined from experiences, a networking of interrelations develops among the schemas through active listening, participating, and experimenting with input from the environment. Learned societal and cultural rules govern and influence how the world is viewed. Cognitive structure, a personal theory of the world, imposes a formula for meaningfulness (F. Smith, 1975).

Ease in Learning the Second Language

It is often assumed that children learn a second language more easily than adults or teenagers. However, they probably learn the second language differently. Although they pick up what they hear and will remember it, older learners may use more socially acquired patterns for learning and may do more thinking about what they use. Children acquire conversational English relatively easily. Older learners, because of their more extensive L1 learning, may be able to infer more meaning from what they hear and observe. While teenagers and adults may have a strong motivation for learning, children may be willing to take more risks and be less afraid of making errors. Therefore, children may reach higher levels of competence than adults (Krashen & Terrell, 1983).

Environmental Influences in L2 Learning

Dulay, Burt, and Krashen (1982) emphasized the importance of the environment for success in learning a new language. They specifically pointed to broad overall environmental features—macroenvironmental—which influence learning. Further, they discussed factors characteristic of specific structures of the language the learner hears—microenvironmental—as perhaps having implications for success in L2 learning.

Macroenvironmental Factors. According to Dulay et al. (1982) a number of macroenvironmental factors affect L2 learning:

1. The naturalness of the language heard appears to enhance development of communication skills.
2. The learner's role in communication provides opportunities to

respond, not to respond, or respond in the first language during the initial stage and approximates natural learning. (Allowing children to have a silent period in learning a second language may be the most effective approach for the early phases of language instruction, according to Krashen and Terrell [1983].)

3. The degree to which extralinguistic factors are present aids the learner in grasping the meaning of the strange sounds of the new language from context, the here-and-now, the concrete. These factors include visual aids, motor activities, and nurturing language that explain what is happening in the target language as it occurs.

4. The availability of models from the second language, specifically peers over teachers or parents and same ethnic group members more than nonmembers is important. (The dialect of peer groups will be learned instead of the dialect of a high-quality teacher model.)

Microenvironmental Factors.   Dulay et al. (1982) stated that the following factors may have some effect on quality and rate of language acquisition:

1. The ease with which the structure is heard and seen does not always support the sequence of learning.

2. The quality of responses given to the learner's speech does not appear to make any significant difference—even in immersion types of programs. (Expansion, which is a systematic modeling of either the correct or a more complete version of the speech without identifying the problem, has not shown clear and positive results.)

3. The frequency with which the learner hears a structure may not affect acquisition order. (Learners learn certain structures that they do not hear or have never heard and some structures are heard in great frequency, like the articles *a* and *the,* and are delayed in learning.)

Importance of the First Language

Cummins (1986) has proposed a framework for empowering students from culturally diverse communities that strongly supports the importance of first language programs in schools. Students, according to Cummins (1986), are either empowered or disabled as a result of their interactions with educators in schools. Four interactions with educators are mediated on a continuum with one end promoting empowerment of students, the other contributing to disablement. These four institutional characteristics reflect the degree to which (1) language and culture of students from culturally diverse communities are incorporated into the school program; (2) the cultural community is encouraged to participate as an integral component of students' education; (3) instruction in the classrooms promote students' motivation to use their language actively and gain greater control over their own learning and meaning generation; and (4) the assessment program advocates for students from culturally diverse backgrounds rather than attributing psychological dysfunctions to explain academic difficulties residing within the students.

This conceptual framework of Cummins (1986) certainly supports the development of bilingual programs that maintain the first language while teaching the second language (Hakuta & Gould, 1987). Bilingual programs support *sheltered* learning of academic subjects, enabling students to develop academic language and literacy, areas of increased difficulty for L2 learners. Sheltered learning classrooms are most commonly found in middle, junior and senior high schools where the school curricula have been divided into subject areas. These classes are taught by second language specialists who provide learning experiences which support the second-language learner during a transition of instruction from first language to second language.

However, schools have not supported bilingual programs. Schools have been more concerned about getting students to quickly speak conversational English and then mainstream them into the regular program. This practice has serious consequences for L2 learners in academic subjects. These L2 learners may fail to learn concepts if not presented in their native language (Cummins, 1983).

L2 Learning Stages

Krashen and Terrell (1983) indicated that learning a second language meant first understanding what was being said—understanding the message one gets from listening. When students experience language in meaningful contexts they begin to comprehend the language. Krashen and Terrell stated that comprehension must precede production, just as the L1 learner understands language prior to using it. Production of a second language may gradually emerge in stages similar to those adapted from Krashen and Terrell (1983) and Urzua (1980).

Stage One: Nonverbal The learner responds to oral commands, directions, and questions through nonverbal communication.

Stage Two: Single Word   The learner responds with single words such as yes, no, okay, and so on. These are responses to questions, commands, greetings, politeness routines, and such.

Stage Three: Word Combinations   The learner responds in a variety of two- and three-word combinations, which may be the majority of the learner's speech but allows him or her to communicate needs, wishes, and information (telegraphic sentences). Examples of word combinations are *me no go, where book, don't go,* and so on. Intonation indicates when these combinations are used as statements or interrogatives.

Stage Four: Phrases   The learner responds using phrases that more closely resemble complete sentence elements: *I want to stay, Where you going?* Sentence formulas that have been learned from conversational speech are used for new word combinations.

Stage Five: Sentences   The learner responds using simple sentences and may use one or more in response to a question or to contribute in a discourse. New sentences will be invented. Overgeneralizations and overextension may result.

Stage Six: Complex Discourse   The learner's responses may include many questions about how the language works as speech expands from sentences to longer discourse.

Keep in mind that such stages may be transitory. Learners may show indications of more than one stage at any time, although acquisition is quite similar for children learning English from various language groups. The concept that groups of language structures are acquired at one time is held by researchers. L2 learners appear to learn to use word order at the same time they are able to use nouns in the nominative and accusative case (Dulay et al., 1982).

Relationship of L2 Learning to L1 Learning

L2 learning sequence is similar to L1 learning sequence in aspects of morphology and sentence structure. Specifically, both types of learners keep the grammatical frills to a minimum (*baby eat chocolate*), use only minimal cues to signal different sentence types, overgeneralize (*she writed me a letter*), and may use double tense markers (*I didn't went*). L2 learners also follow a hierarchical order similar to L1 learners.

Despite the developmental aspects of the L2 learners' language, their speech has a more sophisticated quality. Examples taken from adult and young adult learners demonstrate how L2 learners use progressive tense, add past tense, and use minimal cues to signal different sentence types in a continual process of refinement. Note in these examples that there never was a loss of meaning.

I did receive certificate.
I move from Thailand.
My family living in camp.
I did entry . . .
Now I think everything okay.

It is now generally believed that there is little interference from the first language to the second language. Dulay et al. (1982) indicated that children exposed to native language–speaking peers made very few errors reflecting the grammatical structure of their first language. There were more word order errors than morphological errors. What were once considered interference errors are really examples of falling back on the first language when the rule in the second language is unknown (Krashen & Terrell, 1983). For example, *It is the house of my mother.* The second language also has little influence on L2 learners' judgment of grammatical correctness in the second language.

Another thing we must remember about L2 learning is that no two languages have the same sound system and that learners, no matter what age, must discriminate the phonemes of the new language. Not all phonemes, even if discriminated, will be produced correctly at first. The first language may have more influence on L2 pronunciation than either morphology or word order.

Making mistakes is a natural part of learning, whether it is in language or literacy learning. In the beginning neither children nor adults produce their second language in a standard form (Rigg & Hudelson, 1986). Students should hear language and participate in real, meaningful experiences as they learn language. Some words used in English may have no reference to the new speakers' real world or schema. Southeast Asian learners may have no real-world concepts for words such as snow, furnace, violin, conductor, escalator, fire escape. However, teachers must not restrict their language because students might not know some aspect of the language. Instead, students must be given opportunities to grow from what they understand and to incorporate new information to expand their schemas.

L2 Learning Anxiety

Learners may worry about making errors. Some L2 children may not speak in class for months. Krashen and Terrell (1983) described these children as having a high affective filter. They should be allowed to remain silent or respond in their own language. Students who demonstrate understanding by responding in their own language are communicating their learning. Children who are silent may demonstrate understanding by actions.

Students must have good self-images to achieve in a second language. It is difficult to acquire a language when the anxiety level is high. Learners need to be open and receptive to learning. They must want to speak the language like native speakers. This is a further reason why L2 learners should not be segregated from peers who can be natural language models. Teachers of L2 students need to keep their communication comprehensible and the learning environment nonthreatening and supportive. Students will learn only when they become risk takers.

Difficulty of Academic Language for L2 Learners

Language proficiency has two dimensions: a less demanding level of speaking used for basic communicative speaking and a more demanding dimension of language required for academic purposes. The latter requires relatively complex, elaborate language (Cummins, 1981; Genesee, 1986) and is crucial for academic success in language and literacy because of cognitive-level requirements. Collier (1987) studied the length of time required for 1,548 advantaged-limited, English-proficient students to become proficient in English for academic purposes. She considered the age of the students on arrival, the number of years of schooling in English, and English proficiency upon arrival, among other variables.

Contrary to the commonly held belief that younger children do better, Collier (1987) found that students entering the ESL program at ages 8–11 were the fastest achievers, requiring two to five years to reach the fiftieth percentile on national norms. Students who entered the program at ages 5–7 were one to three years behind the performance level of their ESL peers who had entered at ages 8–11. Those who had entered at ages 12–15 experienced the greatest difficulties and were projected to require as many as six to eight years to reach grade-level norms in academic achievement. Research summarized by Hakuta and Gould (1987), however, supports teenagers as having less difficulty and taking less time than young children. These research reports should be interpreted as supporting the premise that the stronger a learner's first language, the better his or her opportunities for successfully developing a second language. Such research supports the development of bilingual programs and not hurrying the transition into English until students have established a strong L1 foundation.

Collier (1987) cautioned that the use of standardized tests was an inadequate measure of the cognitive academic learning proficiency of L2 students. The tests measure only a limited range of language proficiency. However, she pointed out that because these tests were used to move L2 students from one level to another, "these findings show that there is no shortcut to development of academic second language proficiency and to academic achievement in the second language. It is a process that takes a long, long time" (p. 638).

Many teachers and school administrators are unaware that academic language requires a more extensive learning period. ESL and bilingual teachers are often pressured to place ESL students in regular classrooms with little or no support services because the L2 learners appear to speak conversational English well. Although this may be the case, these L2 students may need years of supportive services to assist them with the academic conceptual development of content subjects available in bilingual programs. Teachers must be advocates and assist parents to insist that ESL students are provided adequate cognitive language content learning support.

Cultural Aspects Imbedded in L1 Learning

Cultural learning patterns are developed through social interaction in the language community. Each culture communicates with nonverbal as well as verbal communication. Each culture's social interaction patterns, both verbal and nonverbal behaviors, may vary from culture to culture. Nonverbal communication is part of the schema learned as the first language was learned in sociocultural development. Educators must be cognizant of the cultural interaction styles of children in the classroom.

Culture governs how individuals interact with one another and sets the guidelines for permissible behavior. For example, eye contact is permitted and acceptable with strangers in one culture but not in another. In some cultures it is extremely rude for young children to look at adults. Cultures also communicate at different distances. Some permit standing closer, others require greater distance. Closeness also varies with gender. Social controls regarding physical proximity are learned according to gender, social class, age, and work. Body messages cannot be separated from the culture (Levine & Ademan, 1982).

Schools as Cultural Institutions

U.S. schools are reflections of the European American middle-class culture. Children from other cultures entering these institutions may find their prior learning inappropriate both in behavior and speech. They may find that they do not learn in the school-approved manner.

Most American schools expect children to have certain culturally appropriate backgrounds for learning. These expectations are based on European American cultural values. When children come to school, and as they progress in school, they are expected to continue learning the cultural values and rules for appropriate behavior in the dominant society. For example, they are expected to have cultural understandings appropriate for interactions with peers and teachers in the classroom. If they are not from European American middle-class homes, they may find their verbal and nonverbal behaviors unacceptable to the teacher. They may be perceived as having inappropriate language for the classroom. They may also have difficulty in determining when and where to talk in classrooms. Even volume and pitch appropriate for classroom language differ from one culture to another and must be learned or unlearned if the cultural environment is changed. For example, in European American schools students do not call out across the room to the teacher, and they are expected to speak frequently in response to the teacher, generally with eye-to-eye contact.

Different appropriate social control from one culture to another becomes apparent in schools. What is effective for European American children may be inappropriate for children from other cultures. Children learn appropriate behavioral and interactional styles and roles from their cultural orientation. In some societies children may require an excessive amount of attention, prolonged eye contact, and threateningly close proximity for behavior management. In other cultures children would not even gaze at an adult because it is disrespectful. Many Native American children, for example, show respect by speaking softly and avoiding eye contact (Sandors, 1987). In most Native American nation schools competition that is used to motivate and control would not be a desirable cultural trait and certainly would not be used to encourage students to strive against one another.

Culture and Learning Styles

Cultural backgrounds also influence learning styles. Hakuta and Gould (1987) reported a study of oral English acquisition of Hispanic American and Chinese American children. Hispanic American children with poor initial English skills gained most through interaction with peers, while Chinese American children benefited most from interaction with the teacher. Wong Filmore (1986) found cultural variables influencing language and literacy learning of Hispanic American and Chinese American children. Chinese American children compensated for lack of clarity on the part of the instructor and became more attentive. They regarded the lack of real meaning for the content being taught as getting the real substance of school. Wong Filmore interpreted this as an indication that the Chinese American culture placed higher value on skill development than meaningful experiences and self-expression. Hispanic American children did well, on the other hand, in situations where they received clearly presented, well-organized instruction in meaningful content in which comprehension and student participation were emphasized.

Some students, because of their cultural orientation, may learn better from pictures, examples, demonstrations, or cooperative groups rather than from oral information or direct instruction (Hakuta & Gould, 1987). Students act the way they do because of learned cultural behavior. This clearly influences whether children learn best in collaborative and cooperative learning settings with peers or whether they learn better individually.

Culture and L2 Learning

In learning a new language, whether in a new country or the land of birth, perhaps the most difficult aspect is the sociolinguistic behavior. It is like taking on a new identity. Losing the first language may be a reluctant struggle akin to losing something of oneself. L2 learners may need to develop two sets of sociolinguistic behaviors, one for the European American school and one for the home and community. Consequently, a multicultural school may be the only solution for these learners.

School programs that provide for the development of the second language while maintaining and extending the first language provide an environment more conducive for children and teachers to understand the cultural features of language. The status of the nondominant language is upgraded and there is better social interaction between L2 students and their English-speaking peers in bilingual programs. Consequently, this improves the L2 learner's self-esteem (Hakuta & Gould, 1987; Cummins, 1986).

Relationship of Oral Language to Written Language

Oral language processes and written language processes have much in common. All language processes are part of a total communication process and involve conveying or receiving meaning through the use of oral or written symbols. Written language is not exactly talk written down. Although young children may incorporate elements of a story or written talk in their play, there are several differences that children must learn about written language that they did not acquire in learning how to talk. McGee and Richgels (1990) defined these differences as occurring in prosody, sustained language, text-bound language, and written language register. These four aspects develop as children gain a grasp of the relationship of oral language to print. Each aspect is illustrated from the writing of Drew, a first-grade boy in mid-October of the school year.

Prosody refers to how speakers use stress, intonation, and pause—features of oral language that communicate a significant amount of meaning. Young writers gradually learn that oral signals have to be communicated to the reader through written signals of underlining, italics, boldface, and other mechanics of writing for understanding.

> *She* sed a gen and a gen to the PePl in the velig that one day she wod banesh them a way in too the Forest Forevr.
>
> **She** *said again and again to the people in the village that one day she would banish them away into the forest forever.*

Sustained language refers to the monologic aspect of writing, which differs from the dialogic aspect of speech. Beginning writing generally resembles a single-sided conversation.

> boom boom baang the wor wint into the nigt biy moning thear wer PePil All ovr the Forest flor the spel waes brocin the velijars had acshle wan the wor and that is hew the store end
>
> *Boom boom bang the war went into the night. By morning there were people all over the forest floor. The spell was broken. The villagers had actually won the war and that is how the story ends.*

Text-bound language refers to the need to use information in writing that replaces the contextual aspect of oral language, the gestures, behaviors, and nonverbal responses (the looks, the raised eyebrows, the nods, and so on). Writing requires accurate, precise reference if understanding is to be achieved.

> she chokld as sh thot abowt wat a good Hoptoa he wod mac or broo
>
> *She chuckled as she thought about what a good hoptoad he would make or brew.*

Written language register refers to the need to include in the printed word the use of clarifying phrases, literary vocabulary, and literacy word order gained from listening to stories and books.

. . . bot nastenane thot it wod be nis too hav some sompane arown her lole casl and he wod be a nies srvnt too.

. . . *but Nasty Nancy thought it would be nice to have some company around her lonely castle and he would be a nice servant, too.*

Emergence of Reading and Writing

Many European American middle-class children entering schools have literacy experiences prior to coming to school. Print surrounds them in their homes, on television, in neighborhoods, and at shopping centers. They have had experiences of being read to and seeing and noting how writing is used in their daily lives. They may pretend to read and write like adults or older siblings and can create and generate text that sounds like reading. Perhaps they may be able to share a message from their own writings, to read and write their own names and even the names of others in the family. Some children even come to school considering themselves readers and writers.

Unfortunately, these experiences are not true for all children entering school. Some children enter school with little print experience in any language. Stories have not been read at bed- or naptime. These children may not have observed the functional uses of reading and writing; they may not have seen people in their environment finding pleasure and enjoyment in reading. While some of these children may have observed print in their neighborhood environment, they may not have had the type of interactions with the print that makes it meaningful or functional. Others may come from refugee families whose culture and society had little need for literacy. Some refugees, prior to arriving in the United States, spent years in a refugee camp where they were isolated from any normal daily literacy experiences common to their cultural community.

Literacy: A Natural Learning Process

The writings of a significant group of researchers have emphasized that literacy is a naturally developing process (Clay, 1982; Gollasch, 1982; Y. M. Goodman, 1980; Goodman & Goodman, 1977; Taylor, 1982; Sulzby, 1985; F. Smith, 1982a, 1984). These authorities proposed that literacy, begins to emerge long before formal lessons. Hall (1987), in synthesizing an extensive review of literature in the area of developmental literacy strongly argued in favor of the emergence of literacy. He supported his argument with four specific points:

1. Literacy development is a process within the learner.
2. Literacy processes appear over a period of time.
3. Literacy is acquired to make sense of the world.
4. Literacy requires specific conditions to emerge.

Emergence Theory Conflicts with School Programs

Hall's (1987) points about the emergence of literacy, however, conflict with instructional practice in many schools. These literacy programs present reading and writing as a visual learning task requiring focus on graphophonic relationships. Little, if any, attention is devoted to what F. Smith (1982a) referred to as the nonvisual aspect— what goes on behind the eyes. Instead, these programs present reading as translating symbols into oral language and writing as encoding letter sounds into words. These programs expect students to learn a set of prerequisite skills preselected, sequenced, and presented in a highly organized manner to be taught, practiced, and tested for mastery.

The emergence point of view holds that learners acquire the processes of reading and writing as they experience literacy, not as the result of learning literacy. This distinction is important in understanding literacy learning. The emergence point of view perceives literacy learning as a process, not the product of sets of skills.

Necessary Classroom Conditions for Literacy Emergence

Observations and analyses of children learning to read and write indicate that given the appropriate environmental context, writing and reading will begin to emerge. Reading and writing can emerge for students in a multicultural classroom when the following conditions are met:

1. Students engage in reading and writing experiences in a literate environment where literacy is modeled and demonstrated, literacy is embedded into the content across the curricula, meaningful print surrounds the learners, learners have stimulating and motivating access to books and tools for writing, and learning activities are based on rich content that stimulates learning.

2. Teachers assume learners are capable and competent, and they provide challenging and intellectually rigorous learning experiences.

3. Daily literate experiences are relevant, meaningful, and functional, and they integrate multiple language processes.

4. Teachers and students collaborate in developing experiences that are meaningful for learners, and they have ample opportunities to interact and respond in cooperative learning activities.

5. Students have interactive participation with teachers who are literacy demonstrators as well as literacy models.

6. Students take responsibility for their own learning through options, self-selections, goal-setting, and supportive assistance of others.

7. Students have opportunities to acquire literacy in sociocultural contexts in which they interpret reading and writing as an important function in real life for enjoying and learning.

8. Students are reinforced and facilitated as they take risks in developing ownership for appropriate graphophonic understandings.

9. Parents and community group members are collaborative in developing school programs and curricula.

Reading and Writing Learning Processes

Reading and writing processes have similarities as well as differences. Both are active, constructive, and interactive in nature. Readers construct meaning as they apply prior information about literacy, language, and teaching to reading text. They interact in a dialogue with the author relating their prior experiences in a transaction with his or hers. The more applicable their prior experiences and understanding are to the author's, the closer their interpretation is to his or her intent. This transaction does not imply that their reading must perfectly match what the author has written. Their understanding may go beyond the author's intent because of the differences in their experiences. Reading and writing are continuous processes of constructing, composing, interpreting, and integrating meaning, just as listening is a continuous process of constructing, interpreting, and integrating the oral symbols of the speaker or sender to construct and integrate meaning.

Writers sometimes know just exactly what they want to express as they compose meaning. Sometimes they know the ideas they wish to express but have problems finding the best way to state them. Sometimes they have insights into ideas only as they are constructed in writing. At other times their ideas change as they write. Writing heightens and refines thinking (C. B. Olson, 1984). Writers dialogue with the text as it emerges (Calkins, 1983). Writing aids them to realize what they know, it helps them formulate incomplete ideas and to have insight into ideas they are not conscious of before writing. As they write writers see what is written and decide if it is congruent with their mental plans (Peacock, 1986). Consequently, writing is as primary a process as speaking. Although related to oral language, it has its own form, structure, and process. In both oral and written language writers construct and reconstruct ideas or thoughts for expression.

The processes of reading occur simultaneously. In writing, although processes may seem more sequential, they are actually recursive. As readers or writers predict and prewrite, they use the language cueing system to formulate meaning, draft ideas, and edit predictions and ideas. As readers or writers move through the text drafting meaning or ideas, they may correct or confirm the ideas being constructed. This integrates, assimilates, and adds to the readers' or writers' prior information. Readers and writers both return to text either for rereading or rewriting. The intent of readers or writers directs rereading, study, underlining, notetaking, or editing and rewriting. The reading and writing process is diagramed in Figure 2.1.

Predicting and prewriting strategies change according to the purpose or text and the reader or writer's prior experiences. The reader predicts while the writer decides what questions to answer or ideas to

FIGURE 2.1   Language and Literacy Acquisition Functions

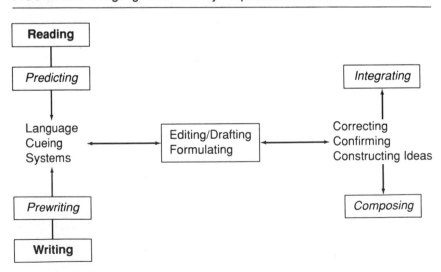

include in writing. This occurs through integrating the use of the reader or writer's language cueing systems: In semantic contexts prior information is used to predict or develop context based on the reader or writer's schemas and cognitive structure. In syntactic contexts grammatical and sentence patterns form the language schemas. In graphophonic contexts sound and symbol relationship is used to scan word elements or record information based on the relationship of the graphic system to the phonological system. These contexts provide the reader or writer with the ability to develop tentative meaning.

Confirming and correcting strategies occur as the reader or writer asks himself or herself, Does this sound like real language? Does this make sense? Depending on the responses the reader or writer may reread, rewrite, stop, study, or search for answers and ideas. Readers and writers strive to make sense.

Integrating and composing are meaning-getting and meaning-making strategies that result from the predictions or questions the reader is self-asking about the printed text and ideas the writer wants composed.

According to McNeil (1987) three types of schemas are used in reading:

1. Domain–knowledge of topics, concepts, and processes for reading a specific topic or type of material
2. General world knowledge–understanding situation-specific social relationships, causes, and activities
3. Knowledge of rhetorical structures–conventions for organizing and signaling the organization of texts

These are the same schemas required for writing, but writing also requires graphophonic schema. These three schemas applied to writing, however, are used differently, specifically as one writes with an audience in mind. In addition, these schemas may be used for assimilating, determining importance, inferring and elaborating, summarizing, and as a memory aid, whether reading or writing.

Literacy is an internal, intellectual state that cannot be learned without prior literacy experiences (Hall, 1987). If children are to become literate, they must learn what literacy is, and how it functions, and they must become actively involved in the process of learning. Literacy, like language, develops naturally and gradually; it develops when the learner takes ownership for learning.

Reading begins before the reader reads the page and continues throughout and after the reading. Writing begins before a word is written down and may be ongoing in the writer's mind after the pen or pencil is laid down. F. Smith (1982b) stated that "children should learn to write in the same manner that they learn to talk, without being aware that they are doing so, in the course of doing other things" (p. 211). According to Smith, reading should be a naturally developing process. Writing instruction should allow writing to be a naturally developing process as well.

Facilitating Literacy Learning in a Literate Environment

When a learner's life experiences are in a literate environment, an assumption develops that he or she needs and will learn to read and write. However, learners may enter school from backgrounds that do not value the need for print, or their families may not be able to provide a literate environment. These children need meaningful, functional, and relevant experiences with language and print in the school environment. Their literacy experiences in school must develop the value of literacy in relation to their sociocultural backgrounds. Learners must perceive that literacy is meaningful, functional, and enjoyable. This process most successfully occurs in a first language.

When children are L2 learners, teachers often mistakenly believe that literacy must await English-language development. On the contrary, reading and writing can be significant factors for oral language development, if the literacy experiences are real, meaningful, and functional and if language and literacy are integrated in the experiences. In school programs of this type, students will extend and develop language in conjunction with the development of written language. In these programs language learning is not hurried but facilitated by providing environments that support language and literacy learning.

The literacy backgrounds of many students from diverse cultural backgrounds may differ from that of the native English–speaking children from literate environments. An L2 student's strong conceptual background may be rooted in a rich oral heritage with little functional use or need for literacy, or it may derive from strong literacy experiences in the first language. Literacy experiences in the first language provide excellent background for learning. Readers of a first language learn how print works. If children read in the first language, they do not have to learn how to read all over again; learning to read happens only once. Reading skills transfer from the native language (Royer & Carlo, 1991). The best indicator of success for L1 students reading in a second language is reading ability in the first language.

A young Swedish lad of about six from a highly literate home of bilingual parents entered school with a well-developed first language and extensive literacy experiences in Swedish. These experiences had been particularly facilitated by an older sibling who, prior to coming to the United States, was learning to speak, read, and write English. By the end of the first quarter in school this youngster was speaking English to his peers and learning to read and write English. His language and literacy experiences in Swedish had prepared him for English. This child was an excellent example of the influence of environmental conditions on language and literacy learning. When these experiences are absent in a child's background, the school experiences must simulate those appropriate for a literate background of the student's home culture.

A Comparison of L1 and L2 Literacy Learning

The same principles for developing literacy in the first language follow for L2 learning (Hamayan & Pfleger, 1987; Freeman & Freeman, 1988). Further, if students are literate in one language, they will transfer that literacy from one language to another with ease and moderate assistance (Royer & Carlo, 1991). When students are not literate in the first language, literacy should be allowed to emerge naturally and gradually in a literate environment with a sensitive facilitating educator as the second language develops. This process is crucial for students who did not receive literacy instruction in their first language. They need time to learn to enjoy and value literacy through listening, experimenting, and risk taking. They need to experience language and literacy in meaningful, functional, and relevant situations before being confronted with skills that will be meaningless and will distort the nature of literacy.

Verhoeven (1987), in discussing sociolinguistic and psycholinguistic factors determined from numerous research studies, compared learning to read in a second language with learning to read in a first language. Verhoeven listed the following similarities regarding literacy learning:

1. Both the first language and the second language seem to follow a universal order of acquisition. Children appear to experience similar processes of discovery through interaction with their environment and in response to stimulation from it. The meaning of a written message is intuitively understood, guesses and hypotheses are formulated, the code is "cracked" through visual and aural comparisons, and words are reconstructed based on the synthesis of information.

2. Both L1 and L2 learners appear to employ similar learning strat-

egies. Reading follows a constructive process of assigning meaning in a selective and creative manner using integrative cueing systems.

3. Both the first language and the second language have similar miscue patterns as observed in oral reading (Verhoeven, 1987).

Verhoeven (1987) also cited differences in literacy learning. The L2 learner was less efficient in determining linguistic patterns and cues, had different prior information for reading text, and may have demonstrated some oral interference in reading from the first language. The latter, however, may not have always interfered with meaning. While mispronunciation generally caused little loss of meaning, lack of prior information or different world view may have resulted in a different interpretation than expected. Andersson and Barnitz (1984) cited a number of studies that clearly indicated that readers from different cultural groups achieved significantly different meanings from the same reading passages.

Second Language and Literacy Learning Principles

Teachers make assumptions about L2 literacy learning that influence their instructional practices. Often these assumptions appear to make common sense. However, they may limit the potential learning of L2 learners. Freeman and Freeman (1988) specified that the learning potential of students learning to read and write in the second language was limited when teachers failed to understand the following fundamental learning assumptions:

1. Learning is an active process. It does not occur because of a transfer of knowledge from teachers to students. What is explicitly taught is not always directly learned. Students need to interact with peers and teachers in their environment as they learn about the world. Children must be active contributors in the learning process, not passive recipients of the teacher's knowledge (Freeman & Freeman, 1988).

2. Oral language and literacy learning develop simultaneously. The delay in reading and writing for L2 children limits the use of crucial tools for academic success. L2 learners may already read environmental print; their literacy knowledge and expression may be better than their oral English performance. Integrated communication skills should be an integral part of language classrooms (Freeman & Freeman, 1988).

3. Learning should proceed from whole to part. Adherence to instructional programs that attempt to develop literacy as a mastery of parts of the whole is a faulty assumption. Although it may seem logical to break wholes into parts, learning then becomes a jigsaw puzzle for the learner. Language must be taught and learned as a medium of communication. Reading and writing must be developed as a whole for communicative competence (Freeman & Freeman, 1988).

4. Learning to read and write is not different in different languages. Learning one language is not different from learning another, nor is learning to read in one language different in another because the languages are different. Reading is a meaning-seeking process in every language. Learning to read in a language with greater letter/sound regularity does not make it easier. Children do not get confused learning to read two languages (Hakuta, 1986; Verhoeven, 1987). Research completed with children from many language backgrounds indicated that they were able to use the reading and writing processes and their prior knowledge of the real world to predict and hypothesize about print (Freeman & Freeman, 1988).

5. Learning in English may not facilitate assimilation. This assumption, based on a melting-pot mentality, requires people to conform to the majority language and culture. English-only instruction may not always improve students' learning. Cummins' (1981) work with bilingual learners clearly indicated that concepts, language functions, and forms taught in the first language are more accessible for transfer to the second language. When a child knows how to read in the first language, this proficiency more easily transfers to a second language. English-only instruction may not improve either language or content learning. Verhoeven (1987) stated that the acquisition of literacy in the second language when the first language is a nondominant language often has negative results. Bilingual programs have shown that simultaneous or successive reading instruction in two languages is feasible.

Erroneous assumptions about L1 and L2 learning and use touch the lives of children everywhere. A coordinator of a government-funded Native American education program identified a problem. A young Native American mother of a student in one of the schools had called the program to ask if it would damage or limit the learning potential of her child if she continued to speak her native language to her child at home. The child, about six years of age, was a fluent bilingual. The child's teacher told the mother that speaking the first language at home was confusing the child and limiting his literacy development. Nothing could be further from the truth. This young Native American's first language and culture were being totally ignored in his education. If it had not been, no doubt he would have been developing more successfully. When the first language is maintained the child may gain some measure of cognitive flexibility, according to research studies reviewed by Hakuta and Gould (1987). Bilingualism is a cognitive asset and may have positive effects on thinking flexibility. At the very least, according to Cummins (1986), subtle educational advantages may result from development of both languages.

The Literacy Success of Culturally Diverse and Low-Socioeconomic-Status Students

The Reading Report Card summarized results of four national reading assessments from 1971 to 1984 (Benderson, 1987). Although the gap between the performance of culturally diverse and low-socioeconomic, urban students and other students had narrowed over the period of the studies, the average reading proficiency of African American and Hispanic American 17-year-old students still was only slightly higher than European American 13-year-old students. Approximately 5 percent of the 17-year-olds had acquired advanced reading skills and strategies, while 16 percent failed to reach an intermediate level.

Concerning his research on achievement levels of Hispanic and non-Hispanic European American children, Luis Laosa, an Educational Testing Service researcher, stated that ethnic-group differences in achievement and development of school-relevant skills and abilities could be found in children as young as two and a half years of age. He reported that data suggested that these differences were primarily a function of low-socioeconomic status and language differences. Children who grew up speaking a different language in a country where English predominates probably have less cognitive stimulation than do English-speaking children (Benderson, 1988).

Applebee, Langer, and Mullis (1988) presented findings from the 1986 National Assessment of Reading Achievement of American Schoolchildren. The findings of Applebee et al. were taken from a nationally representative sample of students in grades 3, 7, and 11 attending public and private schools across the nation. Students from historically at-risk populations continued to perform poorly relative to the national population at each grade level.

These findings supported the need to incorporate the language and culture of students from culturally diverse populations into the school program. Culturally diverse populations are not failing; instead, society is failing because culturally diverse students have been disempowered in the schools as their elders have been in society. Schools must incorporate these students' languages and cultures before a significant change can be noted. Consequently, society, government, and educational institutions need to develop revised policies and attitudes toward nondominant languages and cultures in the United States.

Reading and writing, like oral language, are not learned just because students are taught skills. Literacy is a gradually developing process. The young learner's cognitive view of the world, developed in L1 acquisition, becomes the basis for the cognitive sociocultural blueprint or framework schema used for interacting and responding in language and literacy. L2 learners increase their cognitive framework through the acquisition of other language(s). L2 learners may bring different assumptions about the world to the printed page, so teachers must be aware that the L2 learners' transactions with the author may be different from native speakers of a language.

Refocusing Schools: Curricula and Language and Literacy Teaching

Curricula and instruction must be refocused toward multicultural goals. Schools in our high-tech world must teach and model democratic living to prepare students for active political participation as adults. This process requires a relatively high degree of reading and writing ability. Successful employment opportunities are more frequently related to advanced schooling opportunities, which require critical reading and writing competencies. Social issues of race, social class, disability, and gender continue to oppress and control the citizens of the United States. The very organization, curriculum, and instruction of schools can be contributing factors in oppression and discrimination. School curricula are often far removed from the lives of students, and the learning experiences are unrelated to their real-life experiences.

Schools must operate as a real democracy in which students collectively learn to make decisions. Students must learn to make decisions and to respect authority as they are empowered through real participation. They must become involved in solving problems that are part of their daily lives. They must examine all issues from their personal points of view (Grant & Sleeter, 1989). They must develop competencies to become social change agents (Sleeter & Grant, 1988). To achieve these worthwhile goals schools must do more than provide equal educational opportunities. The same treatment for all is inappropriate and inequitable. Instead, schools must provide educational opportunities that are appropriate for all students. Schools must address issues of social justice (Nieto, 1992). Social inequities must be challenged. Schools must promote social equality and cultural pluralism.

If a school's program were focused to facilitate the examination of social issues from the personal views of students (Nieto, 1992; Grant & Sleeter, 1989), the school's aspirations for literacy would change. Schools could no longer be satisfied with graduates having minimum reading and writing abilities as has been true in the United States since the great wave of immigration at the turn of the twentieth century. School educational goals would focus on developing literate citizens who need high-level skills in language and literacy for critical thinking about the issues facing the country. Schools would exist to serve all segments of society (Nieto, 1992).

Language and literacy are foundations for all learning and for learning how to learn. Language and literacy should develop thinking. Listening, speaking, reading, writing, and thinking must be woven into the total fabric of the school curricula. Language and literacy should affirm pride in student home cultures and languages (Nieto, 1992).

All students must experience the social, cognitive, and linguistic potentials the written language system holds for them (Harste et al., 1984). School is the primary introduction to literacy for some students. To assist students in becoming literate they must come to value literacy as well as value themselves. This begins with the school valuing and considering each child's language and culture in its educational program. Schools must value and consider all cultural backgrounds, not just the cultural background of the students from the dominant culture. Students are more apt to be successful learners when all students develop positive attitudes about all cultural groups, neither perceiving themselves as superior, inferior, nor alienated from their own roots (Cummins, 1986).

To fulfill their roles educators must understand their pupils and see their roles as adding a cultural affiliation to their students' lives (Cummins, 1986). Students' sociocultural backgrounds, value systems, and motivational forces can help to determine strategies and classroom environments involving both students and parents. Understanding L1 and L2 learning provides educators with points of reference for planning and facilitating learning appropriate for all students. Understanding the processes for becoming readers and writers aids in developing appropriate instructional environments and school curricula.

A teacher needs a point-of-view that guides his or her teaching of the communicative processes. The teacher must provide a framework for selecting content and learning experiences and organizing and managing these in a classroom that facilitates learning for all children. A teacher's point of view must be firmly rooted in the knowledge and understanding of language learning and students' sociocultural contexts; their curricula must be focused on social issues that develop critical thinking skills. Instruction must develop social action skills that empower students.

Students of all ages need control over their own communicative learning processes. Control requires being able to determine the pace of learning. Students need to interact with receptive, actively literate adults to develop language and literacy (Wells, 1981). Teachers should encourage students to interact with peers in the learning process. For students learning English as a second language it is crucial that they interact with native language-speaking peers. Cooperative group learning provides an opportunity for students to work collaboratively in problem solving and decision making; these opportunities increase pupil involvement in language practice and appeal to culturally conditioned learning styles of students from nondominant populations.

Schools must involve parents and primary caregivers in deciding the goals of education and the educational practices of each school. Most parents have high expectations for their children. Parents must be aided in how they can help their children improve their learning. For example, Cummins (1986) reported that children in Great Britain showed pronounced reading progress by reading daily to parents. In addition, children's interest in school learning increased.

SUMMARY

Communication skills are increasingly important aspects of life. They are essential for becoming educated; they empower learners. Schools need to develop high-level language and literacy communication skills for all students to address the changing needs of a pluralistic society.

The processes of literacy and language learning require learners to be immersed in meaningful, relevant, and functional situations. Learners must see processes of language and literacy modeled and demonstrated. The focus must be on the message, not the code. Learners of both processes require feedback. They must take control in the learning situation and take risks in learning. Literacy learning must occur in a literate environment.

A learner's first language is acquired through interacting with caregivers in language-rich experiences. Acquisition of the second language occurs under similar situations. Schemas and cognitive structure develop through L1 learning and influence L2 development. L2 learning requires a lengthy period for development, particularly if learners are to be able to use English for academic purposes.

Reading and writing processes involve interactions and transactions. Writing is a dialogue with the text. Reading is a transaction with the author. Both reading and writing should be naturally developing processes. A reader's interaction and transactions are influenced by linguistic and cultural factors. L1 literacy is an important factor for L2 literacy. There are similarities and differences in literacy learning in the first and second languages.

IMPLICATIONS FOR INSTRUCTION

Based on the constructs presented in this chapter, a number of implications can be drawn for developing curriculum and instruction in a multicultural classroom. These implications include the following:

1. Immerse students in print combined with rich and varied oral language experiences that are meaningful, relevant, and functional in a pluralistic society.

2. Relate literacy to the lives of the students. Student-written text will relate oral language to printed language through students' retelling of everyday events, recording of interests and knowledge, and using writing to address interests and solve problems.

3. Demonstrate and model speaking, reading, and writing through practices such as using teacher-prepared charts that provide input for language and literacy; reading books with predictable language and plot that have relevant meaning for students or that will extend understanding of other cultures and language use; using thinking-aloud problem solving from reading and writing; and using material and text sources written from a multicultural perspective.

4. Embed literacy into the fabric of classroom activities. When reading and writing are integrated across the curriculum, learning becomes meaningful, relevant, and functional. Use language and literacy in democratic processes that encourage student empowerment and develop their abilities for critical thinking.

5. Foster self-selected, high-quality reading and self-directed writing. When students select their reading, they are more likely to be motivated for reading. When students choose their own topics for writing or

reading, they are taking ownership for their learning. Provide books for reading that have appropriate ethnic and cultural role models and reflect social issues that are important for student learning.

6. Provide opportunities to practice language and literacy in simulated settings, such as stores, cafés, post offices, offices, newspaper and television studios, and so on, that correspond with topics or themes currently ongoing in the classroom and reflect the issues and experiences important in society. These should reflect the community in which the students are growing and living and provide means for solving problems that students face in real life.

7. Develop multicultural themes, projects, and units of study that provide learning in meaningful, relevant, and functional ways. In these situations real books are used for study and resource; children use reading and writing in a manner simulating the real world of work (i.e., newspapers, job applications, etc.) and they learn problem solving in a democratic tradition. An understanding and appreciation of diversity is developed.

8. Encourage and support the development of bilingual programs. When this is not possible develop a classroom environment that recognizes, affirms, and encourages the nondominant languages of the community. Invite community speakers into the classroom and use books, recordings and tapes of music, and stories both in the original language and translated into English.

9. Base instruction on an understanding and knowledge of the various diverse linguistic and cultural communities in society. Schools must develop positive relationships with community parents and involve them in curricular and instructional decisions regarding the education of their children.

10. Use instructional strategies that are in consonant with the learners' cultural backgrounds. These might include cooperative grouping, as well as strategies that provide more active student involvement in decision making and meaningful learning experiences.

PART TWO

Preparing to Teach in a Multicultural Classroom

Curricula and the classroom instructional environment must be based upon a foundation that is sensitive to and addresses the cultural complexities of U.S. society. Students must experience the classroom curricula through educational practices which will inculcate an understanding that one value system and perspective of the world is disadvantageous in today's society (Baker, 1983). Curricula and instructional practices must facilitate the growth of all students and contribute to the development of their self-concept if each student's academic potential is to be nurtured. The school's responsibility in society is to facilitate the development of individuals who are sensitive to and knowledgeable about the diverse cultures in society. Every person must have the option to support and maintain one or more cultures—the value systems, lifestyles, and sets of symbols (Baker, 1983). Further, as a citizen, each individual must develop a responsibility for contributing to and maintaining cultures that are common to all who live in a society.

What should be the focuses in developing multicultural classrooms? A classroom environment based on the principles of multicultural education includes the curriculum, the learning environment, and attention to the interaction among student, teachers, and the various communities of the school (Nieto, 1992). The curriculum integrates communities by focusing learning on themes and topics of interest of the communities; thus it is important to the development of the students.

How can teachers develop a multicultural classroom? Baker (1983) suggested that teachers will be able to develop a multicultural classroom when they acquire knowledge of culture—ethnic and racial, religious, and gender differences—supportive of multiculturalism; develop a philosophy that values multicultural education in personal, professional, and community dimensions; and become involved in implementing multicultural curricula through the use of appropriate instructional techniques, strategies, and materials.

Grant and Sleeter's (1986) ethnographic study of the quality of secondary schooling and teaching in providing equality of education found that teachers were not used to thinking in multicultural terms. Although they realized they were not supposed to discriminate on the basis of race, class, gender, or disability, and they tried to treat all students equally, they did little to broaden student understanding of racism, cultural pluralism, or sexism. They appeared to assume that working-class students could not be expected to achieve well in school. Grant and Sleeter noted that the content of the curriculum was watered down and taught in the secondary school through reading and writing, although student ability was low in those areas. Teachers blamed students for not learning rather than looking at their own teaching for part of the explanation. Students were taught to accept the European American culture and believe its interpretation of reality as well as accept working-class lives. (Working class is interpreted as meaning not aspiring to roles in society available through higher education.) Students were not supported to challenge racism in the school nor were they prepared to challenge it in society. Although the school had added courses and programs about people of color and included supplementary multicultural textual materials, there was no restructuring of the content of the curricula. Grant and Sleeter's findings concerning the secondary school probably would not be much different for most traditional elementary schools.

Burstein and Cabello (1989) reported modified success for a multicultural in-service program for teachers based on similar concepts suggested by Baker (1983). Teachers demonstrated change but reported struggling with their own belief systems about education and how things had been "traditionally done" as they attempted to implement strategies. These findings would support those of Grant and Sleeter (1986). Teachers need to have an instructional philosophy that applies cultural diversity to how they select or develop curricula, instruct, and interact with all students. They need to believe and trust in students' ability to learn.

CHAPTER THREE

Developing and Organizing Multicultural Curricula

- *What are guidelines for developing multicultural themes and topics?*
- *Why and how should multicultural themes and topics be selected?*
- *How can multicultural literature be selected for themes and topics?*
- *Why and how should multicultural literature be used in the class-room?*
- *How can a curriculum framework be constructed for curriculum development?*
- *How can an instructional web be developed and used?*

INTRODUCTION

Educators in multicultural schools should select, develop, and organize multicultural curricula to provide stimulating and enriching classroom environments where learners can be actively involved in meaningful learning experiences. The teacher's role is as guide, monitor, facilitator, model, and demonstrator for the learner. The teacher creates an environment for learning using multicultural themes and topics appropriate to the learners; he or she motivates the learners, monitors their development, and continues to provide relevant and appropriate learning materials that invite learners to participate and assist in planning literacy events and learning experiences.

Language and literacy instruction in the multicultural classroom should focus students on ideas and knowledge through relevant reasons for using language and literacy strategies. Literature can be a resource for learning language and literacy because the content of good literature is meaningful and relevant to learners. Literature suggests themes or topics that will assist learners in increasing their speaking, reading, and writing abilities. Student-relevant themes and topics encourage a desire to communicate and open windows to new and stimulating ideas, which in turn develop needs for increased language and literacy abilities. Reading and writing develop when students are stimulated by needs triggered by the functions for reading and writing. Functional reasons encourage the development of language and literacy experiences or events in themes and topics.

Multicultural curriculum development and learning is based on the premise that there is no hierarchy of subskills, no universal sequence for learning reading and writing skills. Students learn when they have relevant reasons and motivation. Language and literacy materials must be selected from multicultural literature that is meaningful and relevant to students. Some specific overarching learning principles, described by Freeman and Freeman (1988), appear fundamental to curriculum development. They are important to multicultural curriculum because children achieve when learning is an active process, oral language and literacy can develop simultaneously, and learning proceeds from whole to part. All students in a multicultural classroom will learn more effectively if they are empowered to be active learners instead of relying on teachers for the transmission of knowledge.

When students are active learners they interact with the learning environment, their peers, and teachers as they learn. Language and literacy can be learned as they are learning mathematics, social studies, or science. L2 students don't have to wait to learn to speak

English before learning to read and write. Integrated learning experiences in meaningful topics and themes contribute to the development of listening, speaking, reading, and writing. Each communication area assists the development of the other.

L2 students may have greater mastery of the written English language than the oral language. When literacy instruction is delayed, their development is hampered. Such delaying practices stem from a learning model in which language and literacy are learned from part to whole. Part-to-whole programs break language and literacy into smaller parts for identification, practice, and mastery. Research, however, supports a whole-to-part model that develops the internal structure of language, not the external patterns (Cummins, 1986; Freeman & Freeman, 1988).

The curriculum development process begins by determining themes and topics for learning. Because curriculum in most schools is skewed toward a European American perspective (Nieto, 1992; Hilliard, 1992), selection of appropriate children's multicultural literature and related material for teaching language and literacy is an important aspect in determining themes and topics. Next a curriculum framework is developed which focuses the learning of the study and provides specific instructional stages for incorporating suitable learning experiences for all students in the class. Appropriate instructional strategies include involving students in planning, designing instruction based on cultural backgrounds of students, and integrating language and literacy in the learning activities. Finally, the teacher assesses and evaluates learning.

GUIDELINES FOR DEVELOPING CURRICULUM THEMES AND TOPICS

Curriculum development can successfully be undertaken through a series of decision-making steps. These steps include the following:

1. Select a topic or theme arising from the interest and experiences of the students or related to the school's curriculum. Extend the topic by integrating content from appropriate curriculum areas. The most successful themes or topics are relevant to the learners and provide ample opportunities for integrating language and literacy. The topic must be free of cultural, racial, and gender biases and must provide students with a multicultural focus.
2. Locate material in a range of interests and levels from multiple content, textual (expository and narrative), and nontextual (me-

dia and realia) sources. Textual sources in a library can be located through using Carolyn and John Lima's *A to Zoo: Subject Access to Children's Picture Books,* third edition (Bowker, 1989). Sources such as Ginny Moore Kruse and Kathleen T. Horning's *Multicultural Children's and Young Adult Literature: A Selected Listing of Books Published Between 1980–1988* (Cooperative Children's Book Center, University of Wisconsin-Madison) and the 1990–1991 catalog entitled *The Olive Press: Multicultural Books and Teaching Resources* (5727 Dunmore, West Bloomfield, MI 48322) will be helpful in selecting multicultural materials. This source has a small, but helpful, selection of books for children in a few languages spoken in areas in the United States.

3. Develop a curriculum framework using the materials located. This helps to conceptualize the topic's scope, its theme and topic title, any subtopics or themes, and the learning intentions—the content, language, and literacy functions and identification of the multicultural focus.

4. Develop learning experiences in the following phases:

   a. The introductory phase develops orientation, focus, and purpose-setting activities with students. In this phase students are tuned in to what they know, their interests are determined, and teachers can adjust and modify any preplanning in reference to student interests and prior experiences. During this phase teachers develop new interests and motivation for learning.

   b. The theme- or topic phase develops the content intentions for this study using planned learning experiences that provide the following:

      (1) Appropriate language- and literacy-integrated learning experiences that contribute to the development of each of the major intentions given in the instructional framework

      (2) Student instructional groupings that encourage student opportunity for self-selecting interesting areas for the study, facilitate student achievement of specific learning goals, and develop appropriate social relationships and understandings

      (3) Classroom organization and management that establish centers for locating and using appropriate materials; create working space for the various groups and spaces so they can store and secure their work in progress; allow student access to the library and materials; include ample opportunities for working on projects and tasks individu-

ally and in small cooperative groups; include appropriate teacher-directed and student-directed learning activities; encourage frequent access to teacher assistance, feedback, and informal instruction; and integrate learning experiences from across the curriculum into the topic or theme

(4) Organization and management that include time for sharing ideas and experiences; allow students opportunities for discussing and interpreting learning and sharing experiences through a variety of activities such as interviewing, semantic mapping, and writing (descriptions, letters, dialogues, newspapers, poems, narrative stories, etc.); and encourage students to share ideas, learning experiences, and projects through displaying products by mounting, developing settings for display with labels and descriptions, and integrating art, drama, and music

c. The generalization phase assists learners to integrate the various learning experiences to increase their understandings — schemas. It includes opportunities for students to develop critical and higher level thinking ideas.

d. The culmination phase facilitates an awareness of fulfilling learning purposes and the realization of learning.

5. Assess the learning in the theme or topic in relation to the learning intentions of the study through observing and participating with students in planning, studying, and sharing activities; keeping a portfolio with anecdotal records; and conferencing with individuals and groups.

6. Develop a draft instructional web for the theme or topic to aid in graphically visualizing the activities and refining their functional relationships in developing the study. (Many teachers will use this for their teaching blueprint and record more detailed planning as they make their daily lesson plans.)

SELECTING A MULTICULTURAL THEME OR TOPIC FOR LANGUAGE AND LITERACY LEARNING

Planning for the instructional program begins with the selection of the theme or topic. The theme or topic might be selected from a school's curriculum or it can occur as a result of a spontaneous happening in the classroom, something a student does or something a student might bring to school. The theme or topic might be developed by teachers based on known interests of students.

How themes and topics are selected greatly depends on the teacher, the school, and the children. Some teachers may not feel comfortable allowing the children to self-select a theme or topic based on their own interest. In some schools students might be prohibited from selecting a theme or topic by a mandated curriculum. There are, however, many ways to involve students in making decisions even when it may appear there is little freedom in theme or topic selection.

Restructuring School Curriculum Topics

One teacher taught on the U.S. border with Mexico, where the curriculum was clearly the content that was in the supplied texts for each subject area. She realized, however, that she did have control over order, sequence, and focus of the topics. She arranged the various topics that she was required to teach in the most meaningful sequence possible, integrating all the topics that the school termed units of study into a curriculum with a meaningful, logical sequence. She then set about to refocus the topics so they would be more appropriate to the learners. When the teacher was finished, she had a listing of social studies, science, and health topics for study and had determined how the language arts activities or topics were going to be integrated in all the curriculum topics.

The teacher gave each topic or theme a tentative title and involved the students in planning by including their ideas about what they wanted to learn about the theme or topic. Thus, she gave the students control of the focus for the study. The elicited learning objectives were listed on a chart. As the year progressed objectives were written on the board with spaces left for answers. Later, students suggested having them typed with space left for recording answers. When all children had copies of the questions, they could record answers as they were determined or discovered.

The topics provided for a greater range of student interest. Through teacher/pupil planning the teacher also elicited how children would like to learn about the theme or topic and what activities they thought would be interesting. The children suggested learning activities they could carry out, topics and/or people they would learn about, resources and people they could use for the study. In subsequent planning with the students the teacher suggested choices of activities they could use in learning and sharing their findings. She located trade books and magazines from the local library for students to carry on investigative learning because there was no school library.

Themestorming

The object of themestorming is to broadly extend the possibilities of an idea or concept for a theme or topic in the initial planning stages (Baskwill, 1988). Teachers might carry on this process in grade-level teacher groups prior to involving students. This would develop a general framework for each theme or topic in a school or district. Themestorming appears to be an appropriate strategy for students when literature is the central focus. Baskwill (1988) provided the following guidelines for developing themes and topics:

1. Themes might be developed around single pieces of multicultural literature and extended and expanded to other books of the same genre; single authors or illustrators with biographic supporting materials; a single genre which includes many works by various authors; and themes found in books of narrative writing. Themes should contain both narrative and expository literature.

2. Themes and topics should provide rich opportunities for using and developing all the communication processes: speaking, reading, and writing.

3. A wide range of learning experiences should be used to develop themes. Literacy events appropriate to the theme and all learners should provide meaningful, relevant, and functional learning (planning, discussing, cooperative grouping, observing, journals, writing, books, reports, etc.).

Sparrow and Dawson (1987), from Sparrow Hill Primary School in northwestern England, recommended selecting themes or topics having opportunities for ample literacy-learning events. For example, they worked in teacher teams to plan and develop a television studio for children to present programs and newscasts. Children in this multicultural school learned and practiced speaking, reading, and writing in the context of this simulated television studio. Sparrow and Dawson pointed out that a theme or topic like "Jungles" fails because it is not applicable for developing literacy experiences.

4. Adequate time should be provided to develop each theme or topic. Children must become immersed in the theme or topic with sufficient time to explore a wide variety of literature relevant to it. Smaller themes and topics are drains on a teacher's energy, time, and resources.

5. The theme or topic should provide for several supporting subthemes or focus areas that provide for developing broader curricular aspects (Baskwill, 1988).

6. The theme or topic should include multicultural dimensions to account for the pluralistic nature of society (see Developing a Curriculum Framework below for criteria for multicultural dimensions). Although every theme or topic may not have a strong multicultural focus, each might have some specific multicultural dimension.

7. Types of themes should also be balanced throughout the year. Balance should be maintained between various genres of literature.

8. Themes and topics should reflect the interests and values of students and teachers. This does not mean, however, that the great themes, events, ideals, and values of cultures in literature should be neglected.

Basal Texts: A Source for Themes and Topics

Teachers often feel unable to develop themes and topics because they must use basal textbooks. Basal textbooks, however, should not be considered a hindrance to developing themes and topics. If the teacher uses the basal wisely, motivating and stimulating themes and topics can be developed for any age level.

One teacher used a combination language experience approach and individualized reading approach with children from a range of socioeconomic levels and racial backgrounds. The children asked the teacher if they could have books. The class was using a great range of materials in their language and literacy program, so the children were directed to go into the walk-in closet that contained all available basal texts and multiple-copy trade books in the school. They were advised to make their own selection.

Expecting them to select one of the multiple-copied paperback books, the teacher was surprised when they came out with a basal reader marked *Fifth Grade!* The students went through the books and decided which stories they wanted to read, and the teacher used these to plan themes and topics that would integrate speaking, reading, and writing. The teacher expanded the topics with other literature, both expository and narrative, on each topic or theme. Because most of the selections were especially written for the text, it was not often that he was able to find longer original versions or sources for the material that were more common in recent basal materials.

The basal story served as the introduction to the theme or topic. Each theme or topic was planned with the group following the reading and discussion of the basal story. Planning was conducted much like that done for a social studies or science topic. A story about a soap box derby lead to research of the topic which culminated in planning the building of a soap box racer. A selection on legends included listening to a record about legends from people of many cultures, reading many legends from around the world, comparing legends, and finally writing and illustrating modern-day legends. Because all the stories used as a basis for the topics were self-selected, the teacher found it easy to develop topics on issues and interests relating to the students' lives. The themes and topics led to reading paperback books on a topic when they could find enough multiple copies.

Trade books were suggested for reading in the library collection that were related to each topic or theme. The students read daily from these self-selected books, concluding with an entry in a journal about their reading. Individual reading was shared weekly in a variety of ways. Children chose daily activities to do. At first the activities seemed to be motivators for reading—as if the teacher had said "Do this and then you can do something fun." The teacher set a timer to aid students in increasing silent-reading time. (Many students neither have the time out of school nor the quiet environment necessary, he thought, to establish an initial recreational reading habit outside of school.) As the year passed, one of the students said to him, "You don't have to use the timer anymore. I don't mind reading. I kinda like it!" The teacher stopped timing and involved the students in determining activity selection on an individual basis. Readers had developed!

Schoolwide Themes and Topics

Teachers in a school or district who plan themes and topics together should not be concerned about each class carrying on the same activities. Activities will change appreciably when children are involved in brainstorming and planning in each class. In addition, when each teacher adds his or her own unique touch to developing a theme or topic by using different supplemental materials, selecting, focusing, and timing activities differently, as well as organizing students in different arrangements, each theme and topic develops a uniqueness. Yet, students will easily achieve the teacher/team determined common goals and objectives, and students will achieve their own self-determined purposes.

Accounting for Multicultural Backgrounds

Children from multicultural backgrounds may need help recognizing the familiar in a new setting. For example, one teacher found questioning her Hispanic students to elicit background information in introducing topics often unsuccessful. Had she stopped, she would have assumed that they had no prior information. However, two strategies proved successful in determining their background. The students were referred to a term, concept, or generalization in Spanish, and when that seemed inappropriate or insufficient (or the teacher did not know it), she used illustrations that clearly depicted the term, concept, or generalization. Clearly defined illustrations work well with children from many cultural groups. They often open a floodgate of information.

During themestorming a teacher might record recalled ideas, help students see relationships between terms, and then classify or categorize the concepts to form a web of concepts. This can aid them in organizing vocabulary or terms about a topic in their thinking. As students see their personal and collective ideas graphically displayed, they might also be led to develop personal goals and objectives for the study.

SELECTING CHILDREN'S BOOKS FOR MULTICULTURAL THEMES AND TOPICS

Literature is a requirement for increasing children's understanding and appreciation of cultural awareness. Through multicultural literature children learn to understand and to appreciate a literacy heritage that comes from diverse backgrounds (Norton, 1990). Well-selected children's literature can be a powerful medium for understanding others in the world (Diakiw, 1990). Through literature students can develop an awareness of various languages, dialects, and peoples from cultural backgrounds different from their own. Literature identifies significant values and beliefs for the student to share and discuss, as well as providing a model for their own language and writing. Norton (1990), pointing to the importance of well-selected literature for students, stated:

> *From the past they discover folktales, fables, myths, and legends that clarify the values and beliefs of the people. They discover the great stories on which whole cultures have been founded. From the present, they discover the threads that weave the past with the present and the themes and values that continue to be important to the people. (p. 28)*

Literature Contains Cultural Values

Children can learn from literature what a culture values and how it thinks. Good literary selections in the classroom not only open windows to the world, they provide insight into how other people live and think, and open windows to other worlds—past and future—and perhaps more importantly to the world of imagination. Good literature leads children to select their own reading and hopefully share it with others. Children gain social sensitivity to the needs of others and realize that people have similarities as well as differences. They gain aesthetic appreciation as they learn to respect the artistic contributions of people from other cultures. Further, the use of multicultural literature helps students learn geography and natural history, increases historical understandings and understanding of sociological change, and recognizes literary techniques used by authors with different cultural backgrounds (D. E. Norton, 1990). The stories that children read can transport them to distant lands and introduce them to cultures and traditions different from their own. Through literature the young learner is provided a bridge to understanding other cultures, values, traditions, and beliefs (Diakiw, 1990).

The values of a society are found in multicultural books. Patricia McKissack's *Flossie & the Fox* (Dial, 1986), a version of "Little Red Riding Hood," shows how good overcomes evil; Joyce Milton's *Marching to Freedom: The Story of Martin Luther King, Jr.* (Dell, 1987) provides insights into the life of a great person; Mildred Pitts Walter's *Justin and the Best Biscuits in the World* (Lothrop, 1986) and Joyce Hansen's *Which Way Freedom?* (Walker, 1986) provide relevant historical information for children today.

Literature Provides Language Models

Literature provides children with the opportunity to learn language models and usage because good literature reflects life in a culture—how people behave and talk. They should learn the power of language, how to use it to regulate their environment, express their ideas, and control their own learning and thought processes (Y. M. Goodman, 1989). Children's literature is an excellent means for developing language. This is supported in the research by a study conducted by Whitehurst et al. (1988) who found that parental reading and interacting with children through books increased language development of middle-class children. A study by Cummins (1986) indicated pronounced reading growth when children read daily to parents. Some teachers have observed that books read to second-language (L2) students increased their language, especially if the books were excellent pieces of literature rich in language that develops and expands language concepts.

Literature Provides Insight into the World

Children construct the world through stories. They "encounter and come to understand a wider range of feelings and relationships by vicariously entering the worlds of others, and in consequence they are likely to understand more of themselves" (*English for Ages 5 to 11,* 1988, p. 27). Children should be introduced to a wide range of literacy forms from many countries and peoples and to ideas and feelings of people from cultures different from their own. Through reading a wide range of literature children develop a resource of forms of expressions and modes of discourse that may be used in their own writing. Good literature provides enjoyment, understanding, and appreciation of others. It also provides children with a basic knowledge of literacy references for allusion and inference. This can be learned, for example, as a result of reading the fables of Aesop, East Indians, Ethiopians, and Native Americans. Fables are particularly excellent for learning about other cultures as well. Human behavior is taught by a culture through its fables. A study of fables provides opportunity for contrasting beliefs and behavior.

Literature Provides Understanding of Cultural Narratives

Van Dongen (1987) stated that the uses and forms of narratives are significantly different from culture to culture. The stories of a culture may be integral to the culture or merely serve as entertainment. To examine the role of narrative in a culture it must be analyzed from its uses in daily routines, traditions, and rituals. What does a culture teach about the value of narrative? Does a culture use narrative for entertainment? What can be learned about the culture from narrative literature? In Heath's (1982) study of children from three different cultural groups in the United States, she depicted the groups as Tracton (working-class African Americans of recent rural origin), Roadville (working-class European Americans of Appalachian origin), and Maintown (middle class, school-oriented). Narrative form and use differed across the cultural groups. Each used narrative differently.

Although Tracton and Roadville people told stories, their structure differed. The Tracton stories were highly creative, fictionalized accounts, while Roadville's were factual with little exaggeration. Maintown's children, on the other hand, had a strong literate tradition of story through oral reading experiences, story hours, and imaginative play (Van Dongen, 1987).

The narrative thought of a cultural community will shape the children's narrative competence. The Native American stories carry on cultural traditional teachings, instructions, and ritual tightly woven into their cultural fabric and belief system. Some children come to school who have been influenced by stories heard from storybooks, while others have developed narrative forms from stories that involve basic beliefs, traditions, and values of their culture. These cultural influences need to be noted, valued, and appreciated by the school because these influences can support literacy and literacy development.

The telling and retelling of personal and cultural stories needs to have a place in the school. Understanding cultural narrative thought modes of and uses in a community can help children build a bridge from home to classroom (Van Dongen, 1987). Books can provide linguistic insight into the variety of English spoken today. Routines, rituals, values, and beliefs are interwoven in the narrative. The works of John Steptoe, for example, are excellent linguistic and cultural sources of the African American dialect. Virginia Hamilton's African American folklore book, *The People Could Fly: American Black Folktales* (Knopf, 1985), uses colloquial language or dialect throughout the book while giving insight to the culture's concept of the "good life."

Poems as well are a part of the oral tradition of a people and are meant to be heard. Poems invite participation and stir feelings (Larrick, 1987). Poems show the moods, feelings, and experiences of children. Nikki Giovanni's *Spin a Soft Black Song* (Hill & Wang, 1985) provides poems of feeling and situations.

Literature also provides understandings about the socializing functions of a culture. For example, Lucille Clifton's *Everett Anderson's Goodbye* (Holt, 1983), Eve Buntings' *The Happy Funeral* (Harper, 1982), and Miska Miles' *Annie and the Old One* (Little, 1971) are sensitive books about how children and families deal with death. They provide excellent examples of the values of particular racial communities, their rituals and routines. Good multicultural literature not only expands a child's world, but it also expands his or her language and literacy abilities.

IMMERSE STUDENTS
IN MULTICULTURAL LITERATURE

Students must be immersed in good multicultural literature. Teachers need to respond to children's choices and introduce them to and encourage them to read unknown selections (Atwell, 1989). Students should be introduced to books that explore problems others have solved. Although there is a variety of good literature available for children, it is often difficult for teachers to quickly locate multicultural materials when they have limited time for planning. According to Bishop (1987) there also have been fewer books published about minority cultures since 1980. Norton (1990) cited two books in 1989—one African American and one Native American and nine books in 1990—seven African American and two Native American—as being multicultural books selected for the Best Books of the Year (Notable Children's Books, Booklist Committee). Good books about minorities may be out of print although still available in many libraries.

Sibley's Recommended Books for Multicultural Teaching Themes and Topics, provided in the Teacher Resource Kit, are not intended to be the only children's literature used in the classroom. Sibley has selected books available for children ages 5–12, across a range of cultural groups: African, African American, Asian, Atlantic and Pacific island cultures, Hispanic, Native American, and a sampling of European cultures. (The age listing follows the age divisions for *Children's Choices;* see October issues of *The Reading Teacher,* 1975–1992.)

The greatest amount of multicultural children's literature is available in realistic fiction (Bishop, 1987). The wealth of realistic fiction about a range of people and cultures provides children with opportunities for sampling the values and lives of people in a pluralistic society. In addition, realistic fiction provides children with models of respectable individuals in a particular society (Bishop, 1987).

Use Non-English Literature in the Classroom

It is also wise, although difficult, to locate books written in languages other than English. Non-English books are difficult to select unless one speaks the language or knows the book in its English translation. Choosing these books also poses another problem. Inability to read the language makes it difficult to ascertain if it is sexist and/or racist. A knowledgeable colleague or community member can assist in making these decisions. Nevertheless, children need books around them in other languages so that they can become aware of these languages and learn that people read and write in languages other than English.

Further, when the books are in children's native languages, their self-esteem is increased. An alternative or a supplement to non-English books is having parent speakers of other languages come into the classroom to tell or read stories in their primary language and in English to the children. Parents not wishing to tell or read stories might be persuaded to tape stories and books in their primary language as read-alongs.

Smidt (1985) suggested that books be made to fit the home languages of children in a classroom. This is done by selecting children's favorite trade books which can be easily translated and finding literate speakers of community languages, even dialects, who will translate them. Translations might be copied and adhered next to the English text or in place of the English version. These books can also be audiotaped in both languages for use in a listening center. The length of the book, of course, is an important consideration in doing this. Picture books seem to be the most suitable for accomplishing this task.

Some excellent examples of translated books by professional authors are available. Two favorites children enjoy are Sumiko Yagawa's *The Crane Wife,* translated by Katherine Paterson (Morrow, 1981), and Ai-Ling Louie's *Yeh-Shen: A Cinderella Story from China* (Philomel, 1982). The richness of the narration, illustration, and the values and beliefs that children can gain from these translated books warrant their use. In addition, it is especially important they be used, shared, and enjoyed when there are children in the classroom with a home-language match. When used they increase and support a child's pride in his or her family's heritage and often aid in developing greater understandings and appreciation of the values, beliefs, and traditions of the language community.

Another suggestion made by Smidt (1985) involved having parents write stories for children in languages represented in the classroom. Parents can share their beliefs, traditions, and values through topics about their childhood, schooling, and experiences. Parents should be encouraged to illustrate the stories, when possible. This project must be handled sensitively to ensure that grammar and spelling is appropriate to the language or dialect. Parents can also assist children in writing stories in their home language to be illustrated, bound, and perhaps photocopied. Smidt told of schools selling children's photocopied books to other schools. Photocopying of children's work, if it can be done inexpensively, can actually enhance the color and total product. Certainly, exchanging books written in languages other than English would provide greater opportunity for reading non-English books. A pen pal project might be the vehicle for such an exchange.

DEVELOPING A CURRICULUM FRAMEWORK

A curriculum framework is developed based on a curriculum topic or theme or on particular interests of students. A well-selected topic or theme serves as the overall concept or major concept around which the learning of a study is focused. Subtopics, major learning intents, language and literacy functions, and multicultural and instructional focuses are determined for the study. The curriculum framework provides the blueprint or structure for the study, a structure and focus for the learning experiences. The framework facilitates development of schemas.

In planning the study, the teacher should plan so that student ideas and learning options are included to involve students actively in their own learning. Students must have opportunities to select related or specific in-depth aspects to explore in a study. They should become involved in setting purposes for their learning to increase motivation and interest. Students can also select learning experiences.

Learning Intentions

Learning intentions guide the selection of the content of the study. When a teacher drafts the learning intentions, he or she identifies the content of the study and personalizes the study for his or her students. Ideally the intentions are founded on valid and significant content information. These are what a teacher intends at the onset for this group of students. They may not be, however, what is achieved in the final analysis as a result of elicited student interest and need.

What a student learns is related to his or her own particular needs, interests, motivations, and prior experiences. A teacher, determining these, orchestrates them in redesigning a text's theme or topic to make it more relevant to the students. When the theme or topic is determined by the students, the teacher focuses it for meaningful, coordinated learning experiences for the children. Student objectives and interests determine the learning intentions. When the theme or topic is teacher-selected, he or she will involve students in the study to develop reasons and purposes for learning to assist the student in relating the theme or topic to their life experiences. These become sources for new intentions and may necessitate refocusing or refining the teacher's intentions.

Curriculum development must be considered an ongoing process specific to a particular group of students. It is never completed; it is always being changed, adapted, and modified in relation to specific learners. Any curriculum guide or teacher manual should only be considered a resource. It should never be applied to teaching any particular child or group of children without modification or adaptation through teacher and student interaction. This is particularly true in working with children from diverse cultures. A piece of curriculum is a beginning point for learning, not the terminal point of what should be learned. The teacher must be able to adapt it to the students or it should be deleted from the course of study.

In the process of developing learning intentions, the teacher makes preliminary plans about the breadth, depth, and sequence of content and determines content that is current, relevant, and meaningful to the kind of world in which the students live or envision living in the future. Children from all cultures need to be challenged by stimulating topics and ideas. Children from diverse cultures do not need watered-down curricula—just creative teachers who value and respect their right to learn in their own way.

Language and Literacy Functions

Language and literacy functions are important considerations in developing any theme or topic. These functions (see Chapter Two) are reasons language and (it is assumed) literacy are learned. They support the multicultural focus for the theme or topic. Language and literacy functions are selected to focus the language and literacy learning of the study. Students' views of the study may also influence the selection of language and literacy functions in teacher/student planning. Consequently, language and literacy functions might be altered or changed following teacher/student planning.

Classroom learning experiences must place students in learning situations that integrate students of different cultures and genders and include children with and without disabilities. It is in these integrated experiences under the guidance of a skillful teacher that students have the opportunity to learn to understand and appreciate one another and work together. Students from L2 language backgrounds will have opportunities to observe language and literacy modeled by first-language (L1) students and interact in natural communicative settings. Students from the dominant culture will learn language and sociocultural behaviors of students from nondominant cultures.

The teacher should consider several questions when selecting language and literacy functions. What functions will provide meaningful learning experiences for multicultural themes and topics? How can the nature of the study provide functional reasons for needing and using language and literacy? How can the theme or topic provide reasons for using imagination and creative thinking? Language and literacy functions are selected for the study from the following:

1. *Language/literacy to direct and control*—suggesting, requesting, disagreeing, assenting, persuading, reaching consensus
2. *Language/literacy to express and share feelings*—praising, approving, rejecting, describing, listening, stating
3. *Language/literacy to acquire and transmit information*—stating, explaining, discussing, listening, defining
4. *Language/literacy to create and imagine*—speculating, fantasizing, exploring
5. *Language/literacy for sociocultural routines and formalities*—greeting, thanking, introducing, listening, order and sequence of talking, personal space for interacting

The Multicultural Focus

By including a multicultural focus in the curriculum framework, the teacher ensures that the study addresses pluralism and provides a focus for cultural diversity in the curriculum. Students may need assistance in realizing the rationale for a multicultural focus in a study. They might need consciousness-raising experiences to provide the necessary motivation for learning about and understanding multicultural dimensions. Unless feminist issues are initiated, they may not arise from the students. The multicultural focus determines what multicultural understandings are appropriate to be developed in the study. Sources for multicultural focuses should include, but not be confined to, the following learning dimensions (Tiedt & Tiedt, 1990/1979):

1. Aspects that aid students to respect and appreciate diversity
2. Aspects that aid students to identify and describe groups within the population
3. Aspects that aid students to make connections, noting similarities among people, their universal needs and behaviors
4. Aspects that will aid students to identify differences among people noting no two people are alike
5. Aspects that will aid students to discuss stereotypical thinking and how it leads to prejudice
6. Aspects that will aid students to critique or evaluate experiences
7. Aspects that will aid students to gain a better sense of self

A Model Curriculum Framework: Folktales

A group of teachers wanted to break away from basal readers used in their district for reading and language arts instruction. They expressed a desire to improve the quality of learning for their students by providing excellent multicultural literature for children to read, increasing children's use of self-selected reading, and integrating reading and language arts. The basal reader they had been using had versions of folktales. They decided this theme would be an excellent study because it was in keeping with the school curriculum, and ample multicultural literature could be secured in school libraries.

By using a topic or theme out of their basal reader, the teachers could still develop a curriculum based on real literature for their reading and language arts program while not venturing too far afield. They developed a curriculum framework for their study that could vary as it was implemented in each classroom through input from the students. The adapted initial curriculum framework that these teachers developed is shown in Figure 3.1.

DEVELOPING LEARNING EXPERIENCES

Learning experiences should be relevant to the statements listed by the teacher in his or her learning intentions. Multiple kinds of learning will contribute to understanding the theme or topic and hopefully to enjoying the learning. Learning experiences should actively involve the learner, and they should be conducive to whole-to-part learning. They should be consonant with each student's home culture. Learning is possible when the learner's prior information is activated and the learner is empowered to learn. Learning experiences can be sequenced or may occur simultaneously.

Introduction of a Theme or Topic

The introduction to the study should generally proceed through three stages. The orientation stage makes the student aware of and interested in the topic. The focus stage aids the learner to recall prior information and develop a mental organization of the known information. The purpose stage sets purposes or reasons for study.

The Orientation Stage

Study of a theme or topic should begin with stimulating and motivating experiences that introduce the students to the proposed

FIGURE 3.1   A Model Curriculum Framework

Topic/Theme: Folktales

Subtopics:

   Journey motif: Home-adventure-home themes

   Repetitive patterning

   Reflection of societal times and origin

   Stereotypic representations in folktales

   Theme similarity across cultures

Learning Intentions:

1. Folktales across varied cultures have a main character begin in a setting, go through conflict situations, and return to the original setting having been changed in some way.
2. Folktales are found in every culture. They were originally told; now many are written down.
3. Folktales have a repetitive nature, common plot structure, and stock characters in most cultures.
4. Folktales are a form of expression or commentary on an aspect of life retold generation after generation.
5. Folktales can be stereotypic and use stereotypic language in their writing and thinking.
6. Folktales reflect a society's perspective for acceptable behavior, attitudes, and values are related to age, gender, race, class, and disability.
7. The common themes found in folktales support a premise that all peoples in all regions and cultures in the world have great similarities.
8. Folktales are generally told or read for enjoyment.

Language/Literacy Functions:

   Sharing, creating, and imagining through telling and writing

   Identifying how folktales were used to direct and control behavior

Multicultural Focus:

   Folktales indicate that people have universal similarities, needs, and behaviors.

   Folktales have stereotypic representations of people and behavior.

---

study when the theme or topic comes from the school curriculum or has been selected by the teacher. What students know about the world is critical to what they will learn (Trabasso, 1981). Comprehension is dependent on the learner's available knowledge of the world (Schallert,

1982). To develop higher level understandings and make inferences, students need background knowledge, particularly when dealing with multicultural topics. They either need to recall various essential elements relating to the theme or topic or be provided concrete information for developing essential information. Students having misinformation will have difficulties with learning. Consequently, during the orientation stage the teacher should make every effort to relate existing knowledge to new concepts. When a topic arises out of the interest of the class, however, there may not be the time or need for formally introducing the study.

General Orientation Strategies. Planned curriculum themes and topics need to have a good start with learning activities that will capture the interest and imagination of the students. Five generic strategies have potential for linking readers with the content of study (Mathison, 1989):

1. Use analogy to make the new familiar or the familiar different for the learner in a manner that intrigues the learner through a connection with the learner's prior knowledge. This makes the learner feel more secure.

2. Relate personal anecdotes to the study to make the study more personal and capture the interest of the learners. Content or nonfiction texts generally do not provide personal anecdotal experiences. Help students to see the importance and relevancy of the content, and make content more personal by using biography or historical fiction. Literature is an opportunity to infuse multicultural content; for example, personal anecdotes from a historic person of color.

3. Disrupt the students' expectations to move them beyond their comfortable domains by creating surprise or confusion that will heighten interest.

4. Challenge readers to resolve paradox by presenting students with factual information that will contradict their present knowledge and beliefs and create interest for reaching equilibrium.

5. Present novel and conflicting information or situations to draw attention to what stands in contrast to past experience or life.

Create Interesting Bulletin Board Displays. Bulletin boards with a "clever hook" catch and create student interest, connecting their known with the unknown. Questions and statements with grouped articles, maps, illustrations, and realia to support a topic like "Was the New World really discovered?" are usually successful techniques to use in this stage. Interesting visuals are necessary for a good display. Children are fascinated with excellent pictures and realistic illustrations.

Use Audiovisual Resources. Audiovisual resources can be excellent sources for introducing a topic. Carefully selected films, filmstrips, and videos are particularly good for developing background experiences and language concepts, especially for L2 students who may not have appropriate language concepts or experiences. These resources create interest and raise questions for study. For example, periods of history can be introduced with recordings (condensed) of famous speeches, significant music important to the period, slides or newscasts of important events, and videotapes of places or events.

Use Community Resources. Community people are excellent resources for introducing a topic, particularly when they have significant experiences and/or resources such as slides and photographs and realia that could be shared with the students. They can present personal anecdotes, generally along with the history and geography of an area. A rabbi was a resource for part of a study entitled "Contributions of the Great Religions of the World." He was asked to be ready to talk to the students for about 45 minutes and show any realia, pictures, or slides. One group of students was studying Judaism and had read the Book of Ruth. The rabbi clearly demonstrated a love for people, as he shared his life experiences, and students developed an understanding of Judaism through many anecdotes. The students countered by sharing Jewish holiday songs and Israeli folk songs. They asked questions beyond those that had been generated for their study. Any misconceptions, misunderstandings, or bigotry toppled that afternoon. The rabbi showed no slides or pictures or any realia, and the students learned understanding and acceptance of another group's values and beliefs.

Use Dramatic Experiences. Drama can be a successful technique for introducing a study. It requires preplanning and often some creative thinking in locating or developing a suitable dramatic piece which will create and heighten interest in a topic. Radio drama, recordings the children have developed from a piece of literature and taped, dramatized historical fiction, and creative drama are all successful forms for introducing a study. A difficulty in developing these in a classroom is to keep the work relatively "fresh" for the other students in the class. Drama provides opportunities to integrate multicultural literature or topics from the onset of a topic.

The Focus Stage

The teacher should next select strategies which facilitate student development of a focus for the theme or topic. The focus stage develops direction and organization and narrows the content of the study. Well-planned discussion can assist students to recall prior experiences. Discussion and related learning experiences should develop familiarity with, interest in, and clarity about the purpose for studying the theme or topic. Two examples of focus-developing learning activities are (1) brainstorming and semantic maps and (2) prediction guides.

Brainstorming and Semantic Maps.   The teacher writes the main theme or topic title on the board and draws a circle around it. Students are asked to suggest what they know about it and the elicited terms are placed in clusters or categories. Children may revise, recluster, or recategorize the map as it develops. Slots may be left for unknown terms. (It is assumed that this will be modified or revised as the study progresses.) This activity results in better questions or purposes for learning about the topic (Heimlich & Pittelman, 1986). Students may need some assistance in categorizing terms (Nagy, 1988).

The students are asked to draw or locate illustrations that can be used on the maps with the terms. This is helpful for young students, students learning English as a second language, and students for whom the concept is completely unknown. L2 learners might be encouraged to share the term in their first language or to share information about the term and how they understand its use in their culture. Drawing is a process that seems to integrate the image of the L1 term with its L2 equivalent as well. Figure 3.2 is an example of a semantic map.

Prediction Guides.   The teacher develops a prediction guide for use prior to studying a theme or topic. A prediction guide contains statements about the theme or topic in true/false, matching, or cloze procedure formats. Prediction guides aid students to recall what they know and/or guess from information they have. Prediction guides let the students know what they should be learning.

Students from diverse cultural groups appear to do best in prediction activities when they are assigned to cooperative groups for completing the activities. This experience enriches all the students. The quality of the experience improves because of the interaction within the groups. When students share their conclusions and decisions, they should be encouraged to share from more than one point of view.

FIGURE 3.2 Semantic Group Brainstorming Map

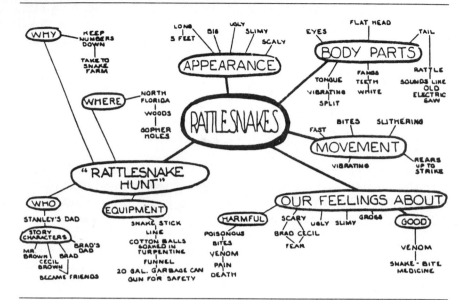

Source: J. E. Heimlick and S. P. Pittleman, *Semantic Mapping: Classroom Applications,*
International Reading Association, Newark, DE, 1986, p. 28. Reprinted with permission of
Joan E. Heimlich and the International Reading Association.

The Purpose Stage

In this stage the student develops purposes for study from known
information. Purposes for learning can be elicited from young children
and written on a chart. Older students might have their questions
recorded, typed, and duplicated, and they may be given copies on which
to jot notes or record answers as they study or read. This is particularly
appropriate when it is a topic that will take many weeks. As the
teacher records questions, involve children in editing for overlapping,
clarifying, and sequencing. This aids students to see related questions
or restate ideas for clarity. When this is frequently done, students will
soon be pointing out purposes that are alike or similar, those that could
be combined, as well as better ways to state a question. This particularly helps L2 students note how parts of sentences can be manipu-
lated and ideas restated to improve meaning. By the age of 10 and 11
students might write questions on the board as you elicit them from
the whole group.

Older elementary students may not have an easier time developing purposes for learning. Inability may reflect not having been involved in prior purpose-setting processes. They may need assistance in
learning how to state their objectives for learning.

An example is determining purposes for studying topics such as contributions of ancient societies. In studying Roman civilization, students were greeted when they came into the room with Latin writing everywhere. The teacher had assignments, a welcoming statement, all major titles on bulletin boards, and notices written in Latin. He pinned new Latin names on the students as they entered the classroom. Immediately, students started working in informal groups to determine what the words and sentences meant. What had been there before and what they anticipated would be there were excellent contextual clues. They examined and discussed the pictures, illustrations, and words that had word elements similar to English. It became a game to figure out the meaning.

This activity created curiosity and led students into thinking of questions in the study regarding the origins of the English language, in addition to wanting to know who these people were, when they existed, and what happened to them, their language, and civilization. Consequently, not only did the quality and quantity of purposes increase for this aspect of the topic, but the questions were applicable to future studies. The teacher was particularly pleased to have them curious about the relationship of Latin to English and other languages.

What was multicultural about the study of the contributions of ancient societies? Besides developing some respect and appreciation for people of the past, the study provided an opportunity to examine and compare pluralistic concepts as a basis for studying modern societies. Social studies curriculum often presents these societies to young people as models for their great accomplishments. Although true, these cultures, however, would not be acceptable models in a modern multicultural society. Students are generally able to study such societies without any bias. The students who studied Roman civilization determined that these ancient societies were classist in nature, even condoning slavery; sexist in that women held lower stations in life, had few or no rights, and were, in essence, owned by their fathers or husbands; and racist in believing one race or people superior to another. Most did not allow religious freedom. These points made for some lively discussions and often excellent comparisons with modern civilizations.

Development of the Theme or Topic

In this phase of the study the teacher designs learning strategies aimed at assisting students to achieve the learning intentions of the study. These strategies may take many forms, all directed toward achieving the intended content. Themes and topics should be studied from a cross-curricular dimension with language and literacy processes integrated for more thorough learning. Learning will be more effective if children's literature is used in the study of both themes and topics. Multicultural children's literature should be selected for topics across the curricula.

Development of Generalizations

Strategies selected for this phase of study aid the learner to develop understandings about the theme or topic. In this phase the teacher assists the learner in integrating the various ideas gained from the learning experiences to reach generalizations. This phase is often missing in the development of topics and themes because teachers do not assist students to reach higher level understandings about what they are learning.

Some former elementary students returned to chat with the teacher about what they were doing and how school was going. One of them said, "You're studying Africa this year?"—referring to the material the teacher was about to place in a display. She was immediately puzzled and responded, "Didn't we study it last year?" None of these young people could remember studying Africa, a study lasting about six weeks. The teacher began asking questions regarding activities they had done in the class in order to jar their memories. Most activities were remembered by one or more of them. However, there was no reference to why it had been done or how it had contributed to any specific understanding.

Where had the teacher gone wrong? Analyzing her teaching strategies, she reached an important conclusion. These learners had not been assisted in knowing what they had learned. Students had been left with a memory of many unconnected interesting activities which had been intended to be experiences to support the development of concepts and generalizations.

Teachers must assist students in learning how to develop important generalizations about what they are experiencing in each learning activity. Teachers might have to demonstrate how the ideas from learning activities merge into a generalization about a topic. Charting, graphing, and webbing are some ways that teachers can assist students in developing higher level thinking. These activities aid students to compare and contrast, as well as perceive, broader ideas about topics. Students need to learn how to learn these skills.

Culminating the Theme or Topic

In drawing a study to a conclusion, the teacher plans activities that facilitate and synthesize all the generalizations that have been developed in a study. These experiences should assist students to focus the ideas into a larger framework. Hopefully, they help students extend and develop schemas. Charts, time lines, webs, and hierarchical trees are extremely helpful in assisting students to place all the information into focus for understanding and learning.

In addition, students must see that they have determined answers for the purposes they developed earlier for studying the theme or topic. Older elementary students may want to record their newfound information in some manner. In organizing and managing topics, teachers should provide students with means for recording learning. Doing so is satisfying to the student and serves as a means for reviewing and summarizing learning experiences.

Folktale Learning Experiences

What follows is an example of the development of learning experiences for the folktales theme presented in Figure 3.1. The process includes introductory experiences, development of the topic or theme, developing generalizations, and culminating activities of the study. In addition, suggestions for using the theme or topic are included under the subtopic General Teaching Suggestions.

Introductory Experiences

Orientation. Since the origin of the folktale resides in the oral tradition, the study could begin with the teacher reading or telling a group of excellent folktales. A good starter is Ai-Ling Louie's Chinese Cinderella tale, which allows the teacher to assist students to compare it with Western versions of the tale, probably well known to most of the children. This beginning establishes a framework for enjoying and understanding folktales as literacy forms common to many cultures. Suggested folktales that will establish the multicultural nature of folktales include the following:

Ai-Ling Louie (reteller), *Yeh-Shen: A Cinderella Story from China* (Philomel, 1982)

John Steptoe, *The Story of Jumping Mouse* (Lothrop, 1984) (Native American)

Diane Wolkstein (reteller), *The Banza* (Dial, 1981) (Haitian)

Sumiko Yagawa (reteller), *The Crane Wife,* translated by Katherine Paterson (Morrow, 1981) (Japanese)

Focus. After each reading or telling, the children are asked what kind of story it was and if they know any other similar stories. These stories are then discussed. The teacher must determine if these are or are not folktales. Next, the students are encouraged to locate and bring in folktales to share that they know and enjoy. Children who wish to read or tell these to the class or to a group are given class time.

Purpose. The students are told they will be learning about folktales. They are then asked what they would like to learn about folktales. Students suggest activities that might be done in conjunction with the theme.

Development of the Topic or Theme

Small group reading or literature circle books (see Chapter Six) can be used for having children read folktales. Before reading each folktale students predict what it will be about. Selections will be easily found for these European common folktales for the study: *The Gingerbread Boy, Three Billy Goats Gruff, Rumplestiltskin, The Frog Prince, The Shoemaker and the Elves,* and *The Little Red Hen.* Folktales based on universal story plots across various cultures such as John Steptoe's *Mufaro's Beautiful Daughters: An African Tale* (Lothrop, 1987), or explore folktales across a number of cultures represented in the classroom. For example, Ashley Bryan's *Lion and the Ostrich Chicks,* and other African Folktales (Atheneum, 1986) or John Bierhorst's *Doctor Coyote: A Native American Aesop's Fables* (Macmillan, 1987).

These tales should be read by the students for enjoyment. It is probably best to have groups read two to three of the folktales. As these stories are read, children identify the story structure, characters, setting, theme, or plot through retelling. A story map is used for developing a sequence of events in each tale.

Activities

Different activities should be planned for each book. These can be shared with the total class or two or more groups may share an activity. Examples of activities include the following:

1. A modified panel discussion may be used for *Rumplestiltskin.* Have children prepare reasons for defending the little man, while others defend the Queen's actions.

2. For *The Gingerbread Boy* the Old Woman and Old Man might bring the Wolf/Fox to court for eating the Gingerbread Boy. Children will have to take parts and develop speeches for prosecuting or defending the Wolf/Fox. People in the tale should be called on to testify.

3. Puppet plays using hand or stick puppets can be created with folktales such as *The Frog Prince.* Other folktales, such as *Three Billy Goats Gruff,* are better for creative dramatics.

4. Have children choose favorite characters and dress and act out their parts on a special day. Each person must guess who each character is.

5. Large dioramas of various folktales can be made by the children. Have the folktale read in a Reader's Theatre style as the diorama is viewed (see Chapter Five).

Developing Generalizations

Comparing and Contrasting.   When the folktales are well known by the children, they must be assisted to compare and contrast the story structures. This is best done on a graph because it allows children to see the journey motif and repetitive patterns that are used. Similarities of folktales from the various countries and cultures may be discussed and behavior traits of characters in the journey motif folktales may be developed.

Stereotypic Nature.   This concept is begun by suggesting that children compare the folktales to find what these stories are telling them about how the best or perfect boys and girls or men and women should behave. Through discussion the students are led to note values being implied in the folktales. The elicited information is listed on a chart and the children and teacher discuss whether these ideas are appropriate for their lives and times. Other stereotypic aspects of the folktales—classism, sexism, racism—are discussed. In discussing racism, for example, students should note that many favorite or best-known folktales have characters who are European (Grant & Sleeter, 1989).

Writing Folktales.   Two writing activities are appropriate in this theme. In the first, students might write original folktales or rewrite familiar folktales using familiar structures and people from their own lives or well-known people in the country. This allows children to try storytelling in a particular setting, and it indicates how well the folktale story structure is understood by the students. These folktales could be illustrated and published if the students would like to share them. In the second activity the students might rewrite specific folktales with a nonstereotypic bias. This will probably be most successful if it is done in cooperative groups (see Chapter Four). Before and After plays could be presented by the class (Grant & Sleeter, 1989).

Culminating Activity

The delightful book *The Jolly Postman or Other People's Letters* by Janet and Allen Ahlberg (Heinemann, 1986) may be used to plan letter writing to characters in the folktales, as is demonstrated with fairy tales in the Ahlberg book. Questions can be asked about how other characters live or what actions they take. One idea that could be most effective would be to encourage students to question characters in folktales about their stereotypic actions. This activity provides an excellent opportunity to exchange letters with another class, perhaps an older group, who can answer in character. It will make the project more interesting when a letter is answered by an unknown writer who responds in character (see N. Pearson, 1989).

General Teaching Suggestions

The following suggestions will assist the teacher in planning, organizing, managing, and assessing the theme:

1. Select the most suitable versions of folktales for your group. Many folktales should be available in the classroom for student self-selected reading.

2. Assist children to find and read different versions or variants of the tales. Using a number of versions or variants will lead to excellent discussions and comparisons. If this does not happen, the teacher might read versions of *Stone Soup* for discussion (Marcia Brown, *Stone Soup,* Scribner, 1974, and Harve Zemach, *Nail Soup,* Follett, 1964).

3. Story maps are excellent to use in helping early readers develop a basic understanding of the plot. These are usually done by sequencing the events on a chart in a clockwise fashion. Making the map provides an excellent opportunity to discuss cause and effect. Story maps serve children as aids in retelling and dramatizing the tale.

4. An excellent source for locating folktale variants is Margaret Read MacDonald's *The Storytellers Sourcebook: A Subject, Title, and Motif Index to Folklore Collection for Children* (Neal-Schuman Publishers, 1982).

5. Establishing a portfolio for each student to use as a means of assessing progress and learning will be helpful. Students should be encouraged to keep their writing examples and include taped oral reading of folktales. Self-evaluation checklists concerning information about folktales might be included for the student to use. Students might also be encouraged to write down what they know about folktales at the beginning of the study and again at the end.

ASSESSING LEARNING

Throughout the learning experiences teachers need to make instructional decisions concerning how well students are learning in the theme or topic. Assessment of learning should occur daily to provide the teacher with accurate information for planning the next day. It is always wise throughout the study as well, to take time to consider each student's development. Daily assessment provides an opportunity for reteaching or redesigning a learning experience to fit student needs. Teachers need to allow time during daily activities for observing students and for interacting with a student or a group about learning. If anecdotal records are kept from observations and conferencing, data is available for noting daily progress and decision making. Children might have a portfolio especially designed for each theme or topic in which they collect samples of their writing and reading. The teacher might record conference notes and observations. This could include a checklist covering the learning intentions of the study. These become excellent sources for the teacher and students to determine growth and progress.

Ideas for assessment and evaluation using the folktale theme may be generated by asking the following questions:

1. Can specific examples be cited showing the degree to which the child actively participated in group discussions and sharing?
2. Did the student's participation, sharing, and/or conference indicate an understanding of the theme and an understanding of story structure?
3. Was the student able to create or re-create a folktale?
4. Did the folktale follow:
   ■ Folktale themes?
   ■ Story structure?
   ■ Journey motif or repetitive pattern?
5. What indications did the student give of enjoying hearing and/or reading folktales?
6. How did the student respond to the folktale writing experiences?
7. What indications did the student give that he or she understood that folktales are a common story form to people throughout the world?
8. Was the student able to identify any/some/all stereotypic features in folktales?
9. Was the student able to determine why the stereotypic features in folktales are not appropriate for today's multicultural, pluralistic society?

USING INSTRUCTIONAL WEBS
FOR CURRICULUM PLANNING

Instructional webbing is a useful tool in planning and organizing a study. It graphically presents the study and allows the teacher to develop better interrelationships among the learning experiences as well as determine if the study is meeting the teacher's learning intents. Instructional webbing might be used by teachers as their major planning vehicle.

Norton (1982) recommended that teachers use webbing to develop learning activities "that encourage elementary children to apply reading and language arts skills, search for information, work together in interest or research groups, share an enthusiasm for books, increase knowledge in social studies and science, and share their findings in creative ways" (p. 348). Norton finds that webbing allows teachers to provide differentiated instruction through trade books on several reading levels in a range of books, including aspects of fiction and nonfiction; provide heterogeneous grouping situations; and provide for integration of communication skills as students plan, discuss, and share their learning.

Steps in Developing a Web

Webs can be created for themes and topics as described above or used as an alternative curriculum development process. The webbing process adapted from Norton (1982) has some components similar to those used in developing themes and topics. The following steps will assist in developing instructional webs:

1. Identify a theme or topic for study. This may evolve from the content to be covered in the subject area and/or specific interests of students. Select potential language and literacy functions appropriate to the theme or topic.

2. Brainstorm ideas with the class that should be investigated around the central theme or topic. (This step substitutes for the introduction phase in the theme or topic procedure.) Next, have the group add specific topics for each of the ideas suggested around the central theme, or do some research for additional pertinent topics, subtopics, and details.

3. Assist the students to include multicultural dimensions to account for the pluralistic nature of society. (Use the learning focuses previously introduced.)

4. Select language and literacy materials for the study related to the web. Involve students for doing the research as is appropriate. (See the section on selecting a multicultural theme or topic for suggestions of materials.)

5. Relate the language and literacy materials to the ideas in the web. Help the children determine how the materials will be organized to study the topic. Have the children keep in mind that new ideas can and should be added to the web as the study develops.

6. Discuss learning activities and experiences that children think would be interesting and appropriate for the study. Have some learning experiences in mind to suggest that correspond with each topic in the web. Learning activities should relate to the aims of the study, integrate subject areas, and encourage children to develop language and literacy functions and processes as well as encourage the enjoyment of learning. Learning experiences should provide a balance of different learning opportunities for students in a large group setting, in small cooperative groups, or in collaborative arrangements that explore topics of interest independently.

Model Instructional Web

The instructional web is prepared prior to involving students, as a planning process. Although the model presented here (Figure 3.3) was developed to demonstrate instructional webbing, the focus book for the web was tried out with a group of students to ascertain its appropriateness and to sample some selected learning activities with students. This was followed by modifications and adaptations of the web from the learning success of the learning experiences.

The model web was envisioned to provide a range of interests and abilities typically attributed to elementary school-children. The theme "Living and Loving in Families" was developed for a group of L1 and L2 students who were readers and writers.

The theme was conceived with a multicultural focus of perceiving others positively – particularly focusing on gender stereotyping. Language and literacy functions that seemed appropriate for students studying this theme at this age were transmitting and informing and sharing feelings. The study was initiated by reading aloud Anthony Browne's delightful *Piggybook* (Knopf, 1986). This book illustrates what happens when families stereotype roles. The author illustrates this as males in the family gradually develop pig characteristics. The illustrations are particularly enjoyable as a pig motif develops throughout the house as the plot comes to a climax. This book provides

FIGURE 3.3   Instructional Web: Living and Loving in Families

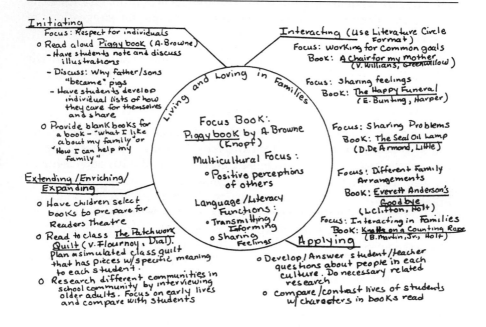

Initiating
Focus: Respect for individuals
o Read aloud Piggybook (A. Browne)
  - Have students note and discuss illustrations
  - Discuss: Why father/sons "became" pigs
  - Have students develop individual lists of how they care for themselves and share
o Provide blank books for a book - "what I like about my family" or "How I can help my family"

Extending/Enriching/Expanding
o Have children select books to prepare for Readers Theatre
o Read to class The Patchwork Quilt (V. Flournoy, Dial). Plan a simulated class quilt that has pieces w/specific meaning to each student.
o Research different communities in school community by interviewing older adults. Focus on early lives and compare with students

Living and Loving in Families

Focus Book:
Piggybook by A. Browne (Knopf)

Multicultural Focus:
o Positive perceptions of others

Language/Literacy Functions:
o Transmitting/Informing
o Sharing Feelings

Interacting (Use Literature Circle Format)
Focus: Working for common goals
Book: A Chair for my Mother (V. Williams, Greenwillow)
Focus: Sharing feelings
Book: The Happy Funeral (E. Bunting, Harper)
Focus: Sharing Problems
Book: The Seal Oil Lamp (D. De Armond, Little)
Focus: Different Family Arrangements
Book: Everett Anderson's Goodbye (L. Clifton, Holt)
Focus: Interacting in Families
Book: Knots on a Counting Rope (B. Martin, Jr., Holt)

Applying
o Develop/Answer student/teacher questions about people in each culture. Do necessary related research
o Compare/contrast lives of students w/ characters in books read

learning opportunities that enhance self-concepts, identify gender stereotyping, and can aid children to develop increased respect for one another in a family. The book also provides an opportunity to help students characterize people without considering gender stereotyping traits.

The study is designed to provide multiple reading and interacting experiences for the students through small discussion groups such as literature circles (see Chapter Six). The books selected for this theme for reading and interacting all deal with family life across various cultures found in society and were in print at the time of selection. They are listed under the subtopic used for developing the theme:

■ Working for common goals
  - Ian Wallace, *Chin Chang and the Dragon's Dance* (Atheneum, 1984)
  - Vera Williams, *A Chair for My Mother* (Greenwillow, 1982)
■ Sharing feelings
  - Eve Bunting, *The Happy Funeral* (Harper, 1982)
  - Valerie Flournoy, *The Patchwork Quilt* (Dial, 1985)

■ Sharing problems
  – Beverly Cleary, *Ramona Forever* (Morrow, 1984)
  – Lucille Clifton, *Everett Anderson's Goodbye* (Holt, 1983)
  – Dale de Armond, *The Seal Oil Lamp* (Little, 1988)
  – Madeena S. Nolan, *My Daddy Don't Work* (Carolrhoda, 1978)
■ Different family arrangements
  – Ruth A. Sonneborn, *Friday Night is Papa Night* (Viking, 1970)
  – Vera Williams, *A Chair for My Mother* (Greenwillow, 1982)
  – Lucille Clifton, *Everett Anderson's Goodbye* (Holt, 1983)
■ Interacting in families and in the community
  – Tricia Brown, *Hello Amigos* (Holt, 1985)
  – Ina R. Friedman, *How My Parents Learned to Eat* (Houghton, 1984)
  – Bill Martin, Jr., *Knots on a Counting Rope* (Holt, 1987)
  – Mildred Pitts Walter, *Have a Happy . . .* (Lothrop, 1988)

Although these books cover a range of cultures in society, the teacher might, in addition, locate other books that may be more appropriate to people in a particular area or region or be better suited to his or her students. The books in the study were selected considering the possible range of reading strengths identified for children ages eight and nine.

In deciding how to apply the selected books to the overall theme there appeared many choices for meaningful learning activities. Here again, the teacher must adapt and modify books and learning activities to fit the interests and backgrounds of the students. For example, children might research jobs to find occupations that are nontraditional for males and females. People holding these jobs could be interviewed and photographed for a class book project. Or family trees for important people or heroes who could represent a culture or group in a community, such as Martin Luther King, Jr., Malcolm X, or Rosa Parks could be developed. This might provide opportunities to write letters for information to descendants of people, if they are not presently alive. If this exercise is chosen, the teacher must be sure to select males and females from each culture to research for family trees.

Notice that this web presented a theme. Some teachers find webbing more appropriate to themes. Generally, the topics are more extensive in the cross-curricula content with extensive supporting material and learning experiences. Webs might be developed on the subtopics of these studies. The format followed in the web was taken from Goodman and Burke (1976). This format is very effective when the focus of the theme or topic is literacy development.

SUMMARY

Learning in multicultural classrooms will be enhanced if instruction stems from themes and topics that integrate learning across the curriculum and students are actively involved in the planning, learning, and assessment of instruction. Language and literacy should be integrated into each topic and theme and learning should proceed from whole to part. Attention to language and literacy functions will make learning more meaningful and relevant to the learner. When themes and topics have a definite multicultural focus, learners are more likely to consider their attitudes and actions towards others in society.

Multicultural literature should be an important element of each theme and topic in the multicultural school. Literature assists students to experience and relate to others different from themselves. Well written literature enables a reader to truly walk in another's footsteps and see through eyes of a person from another culture with another life experience. The wide range of literature available in most schools provides opportunities for students to satisfy their own interests about themes and topics.

Teachers developing instruction through themes and topics using literature sources can be liberated from the confines of textbook programs, even when a text may still be the approved learning vehicle of a district. Content topics or selections in the textbook can be utilized to develop themes and topics that will have more meaning and relevancy for students. Students will be empowered when they are involved in teacher-pupil planning, self-selection of learning experiences, active learning in cooperative and collaborative learning experiences or structured learning centers, and a part of the assessment of their learning.

IMPLICATIONS FOR INSTRUCTION

Implications for curriculum development for the multicultural classroom are as follows:

1. Select, develop, and organize curricular themes and topics that provide multicultural understandings.

2. Make children's literature the central focus for developing multicultural understandings. New ideas will be better understood by children using the story structure of literature. Choose selections that thematically link curriculum. Stories bridge children's understandings of other people, cultures, values, and lands to their own personal

experiences of the world. Literature can be an important facet in developing and extending schemas.

3. Integrate language and literacy across the curriculum. Language and literacy functions should serve as the medium for determining appropriate learning experiences.

4. Give children ownership for their learning by involving them in planning themes and topics, themestorming, and suggesting learning experiences. The format of the more formalized curriculum development theme or topic encourages children to increase understanding through learning experiences that aid in generalizing and assessing learning.

5. Use instructional webs to plan and visualize the content and learning activities of a theme or topic.

CHAPTER FOUR

Structuring the Multicultural Classroom Environment for Language and Literacy Learning

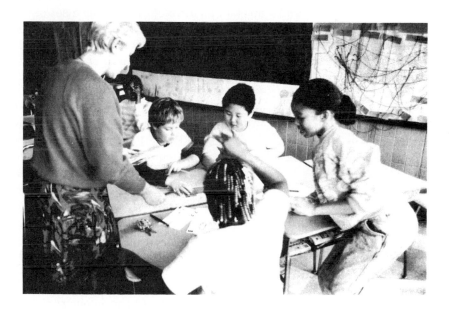

- *What are essential elements for a multicultural classroom environment?*
- *How can classrooms be made communicative environments?*
- *How can classrooms be made literate environments?*
- *How does cooperative learning contribute to a multicultural environment?*
- *Why should structured learning centers be part of a multicultural classroom?*

INTRODUCTION

Educators need to create classroom environments that are extensions, not rejections, of children's homes and communities (Sobol, 1990). This will contribute to children's self-esteem and signify respect for those who are culturally different. Teachers must have an understanding of the history and cultures of the major ethnic and cultural components of U.S. society as a basis for creating classroom environments. Classroom environments, through their organization and management, must respect and value students and their communities.

Thomas Sobol, Commissioner of Education of New York (1990), believes that students must explore the diverse roots of the peoples of the United States if the country is to become one society. He sees the American public school's mission as developing a shared set of values and common traditions to which all citizens can belong. For this reason students need an understanding of the values of a democratic society. This means that there is respect for the individual, rule of law, tolerance for differences, free elections, free speech, free trade unions, and freedom of religion.

These values are developed through daily experience in a classroom as well as through explicit instruction. A specific type of learning environment is required for achieving the values of a democratic society. The school must become a "caring community" imbued with democratic values (Shaps & Solomon, 1990). Traditional classrooms must be reconceived as communicative environments where children are organized to work cooperatively and collaboratively, empowered to be involved in learning and governing decisions, and where provisions are made for all young people to acquire the skills and knowledge they need to learn. The organizations, structures, and environments students are involved in must bridge home and school. When this is done, classrooms will also reflect the cultures of the community, and learning will encompass the diverse experiences of the learners.

Teachers can provide for diversity in a classroom environment that facilitates language and literacy learning. The classroom environment ultimately dictates and controls the type of curriculum and the nature of the learning experiences. The learning success of students in a multicultural school is contingent upon a classroom being a communicative, literate environment. The classroom must be structured to promote interaction. Cooperative grouping and structured learning centers are important for encouraging interaction, collaboration, and learning in a functional, meaningful, and culturally relevant manner.

ESSENTIAL CLASSROOM ENVIRONMENT ELEMENTS

Essential classroom elements are required to create a learning environment appropriate for all students. Classrooms can be made extensions of cultural communities and become language and literate environments.

Making Classrooms Extensions of Cultural Communities

Children leave one world and enter another every day when they move from their homes to their schools. When there are marked cultural differences from the learning patterns in the children's community and the learning styles in their school, children will not function as competently within the school setting as they would if their school, home, and community environments all contained similar elements. The classroom organization must adjust to reflect a community's spatial organizational needs and learning patterns and materials (Loughlin & Suina, 1983). The classroom organization must respect and reflect a community's belief systems about permissible materials and provisions for learning. This becomes more complex when the community is multifaceted and multicultural. Parents from the various communities can be involved as consultants for making the total school more accessible to students. Children can be observed in their communities by visiting their homes. Home visits give insights into cultural interactions and provide indications about how literacy is used and valued.

Loughlin and Suina (1983) suggested that teachers use the community for sources of teaching materials to reflect the community's environment and culture. These can be loaned from business or industry or by parents. Involving parents in provisioning the classroom avoids the use of materials that would be offensive to a community. For example, Loughlin and Suina described situations when animal skeletons were used that were unacceptable to the culture of the community or where water and food products were inappropriate because of the community's attitude about these essential raw materials.

Teachers build bridges between home and school when they select environmental provisions that reflect a community's environment and culture, whether it be plants and flowers or raw materials used for arts and crafts in the community. "By continuously reflecting the children's personal lives, rather than featuring their community now and then, the environment offers a constant message of acceptance and welcome to the children who come to work in it" (Loughlin & Suina, 1983, p. 21).

Environmental information sources, photographs, and natural materials selected from the community should be used in learning experiences.

Creating Classrooms that Sustain Learning

A classroom with a higher level of complexity in the learning environment tends to promote sustained involvement of children over a longer period of time as well as independence from teacher assistance and suggestions (Loughlin, 1978). The classroom environment sends a message to children, whether teachers realize it or not, and a poorly arranged environment usually causes strong negative responses, noise, ruined materials, behavior problems, and loss of learning. Well-organized classrooms reduce the time teachers spend in dispensing materials, presiding over routines, and managing behavior. When teachers have a good understanding of the relationships of the environment to behavior and learning, children's inquiry and learning are fostered.

Making Classrooms Communicative Environments

A classroom that is a communicative environment has continual, conscious use of the double learning potential in every facet of the daily life of the room, according to Enright and McCloskey (1985). Every aspect of learning is perceived as having language-learning potential, whether it be the directions and interactions during an art activity or the cleanup afterward. Teachers organize and use curricula to enhance language learning. Communication is the central goal and operating principle in the classroom. This requires making changes in how the classroom is organized and how learning events are organized and conducted. Enright and McCloskey (1985) specified that seven criteria should govern the organization of the classroom to make it a communicative environment. The criteria include the following:

1. Organize for collaboration. Classroom organization must facilitate collaboration between students and teachers and between students and other students. When children work together they are learning from and teaching one another. For many cultures this is an essential feature of society. Students should work together on tasks, discuss results, and adjust and adapt decisions rather than always being receivers of informational data from the teacher.

2. Organize for purpose. Classroom organization must focus on purposeful learning activities. Generally, these result in projects that have immediate application and goals for students—a play production, a classroom newspaper, or the enjoyment of shared student-written stories.

3. Organize for student interest. Classroom organization must account for student interest. Learning experiences must engage students fully in their own learning. Students are engaged when they are involved in planning and active in implementation. Children need to measure, for example, not engage in paper problems and drills in measurement. Doing this collaboratively meets communicative as well as mathematical goals.

4. Organize for previous experience. A multicultural classroom will have as a focus the application of diverse linguistic, social, and cultural experiences toward the understanding and appreciation of diversity. Classroom instruction would facilitate using students' previous experiences to learn new concepts. Teachers would adjust instructional communication patterns to accommodate and include communication patterns beyond those of the typical middle-class school.

5. Organize for holism. The classroom organization must provide for the integration of curricula and learning activities. Learning should be from whole to part, not segmented. Language and literacy are taught as integrated communicative competencies, not as separate subjects of reading, writing, and the language arts.

6. Organize for support. The teacher must provide support through the classroom organization for communication and all students' efforts for communication. Learners need opportunities for multifaceted language experiences. Although students might not always succeed, they should feel they can fail and yet learn without embarrassment. Opportunities for learning from failure should be more private and peer collaborative rather than public (in front of the total class). An excellent example of this is when a partner clarifies a pronunciation to aid a second-language (L2) learner's communication at the other end of a walkie-talkie (Enright & McCloskey, 1985).

7. Organize for variety. The classroom must be organized to provide for communication across a wide variety of diverse settings. The classroom must provide for diverse materials, purposes, activities, and ways for collaboration and interaction.

Making Classrooms Literate Environments

Teachers need to develop classrooms in which all children may live, grow, and develop to their fullest potential. This type of an environment must be a literate one. The classroom may be the only literate environment some children have experienced, or it may be the first literate environment for L2 children in English. In order to develop a literate environment, teachers should carefully examine their classroom environments and practices.

Is This a Literate Classroom that Reflects the Community?

Stroll through any community and its shopping areas to verify how literacy is used and whether more than English is used in communication. The classroom must reflect the way literacy is used in the real world. The use of literacy in the community must be embedded into the classroom curriculum. Real-life experiences should be closely simulated in the classroom to demonstrate use, value, and importance for all. When L2 students are in the classroom, this is even more paramount. Diffuse literacy materials throughout the classroom. Incorporate language materials from the students' native language whenever possible. Aspects to consider to determine if the classroom is literate and reflects the community include the following:

1. Are there comfortable multiple areas conducive for reading and writing that might seem to be extensions of student homes?
2. Are children's written works prominently displayed and available for other children to read in languages used by the students?
3. Does the room give a definite sense of child ownership or does it have a teacher-arranged look?
4. Are there places children can post notices or messages?
5. Are supplies, cupboards, shelves, boxes, cartons, cans for storage labeled? Are they labeled for children?
6. Are classroom displays in social studies, science, and mathematics posed with questions for study, research, or problem solving?
7. Are there child-originated written displays relating to current events or activities about the day or what is happening in the community?
8. Do books, magazines, and papers reflect the multicultural nature of the community?

Literate classrooms that reflect the community can provide and support opportunities to increase language and literacy learning.

Is the Teacher an Active Demonstrator of Literacy?

Students must see teachers use and value literacy. Teachers must demonstrate literacy for students. If all that children see or hear are written exercises on the board, notations on papers, or exercises read aloud, the teacher's behavior will have little meaning to the students. Real literacy must be demonstrated. Teachers can model real literacy use for children by reading when the children are reading silently, by writing when the children are writing stories or letters, and by sharing reading and writing when the children are sharing.

Teachers interact with students when they work out a tricky composition problem with a child, think aloud about a difficult passage that is causing problems in comprehension, or read aloud some complicated directions for a problem and actively solve it aloud with the children. When a teacher is literate in another language, he or she should model, demonstrate, and interact in reading and writing in that language as well. The following aspects may be considered to determine if a teacher is an active demonstrator of literacy:

1. Does the teacher read daily to and with children?
2. Does the teacher write daily for and with children?
3. Do the teacher and students confer about reading and writing?
4. Is the importance of reading and writing demonstrated in the teacher's life?
5. Does the teacher model or demonstrate reading for pleasure; writing notes, letters, stories, and poems; solving comprehension and composing problems?
6. Is the importance of reading and writing frequently demonstrated by the teacher?

Teachers must also include interactive demonstration with learners. This is particularly crucial for L2 learners because they will not have this experience in English. When teachers do not speak the first language(s) of the students, they should invite community members into the classroom to read and write with students in the community language(s). Encourage the visitors to participate in both English and their native language as ways to both model and demonstrate literacy.

Do Children Value Communication Competencies in the Classroom?

Children live in a rich social world of language. They are immersed in language daily and use it to express their own meanings. Through interactions with people they develop beliefs and expectations about language. They learn language to meet their needs and to communicate (Pinnell, 1985). Although children may be native speakers of a language, they may not develop adequate oral communication skills to function at a level commensurate with peers without appropriate motivational and learning experiences.

All students need to develop a repertoire of functional communication strategies and learn how to evaluate the effectiveness of their communication (Wood, 1982). This functional approach in considering language focuses on how people use language in their everyday lives to communicate, present themselves, find out about things, give information, negotiate, and interact. All students need to learn how language and literacy are used in functional settings in other communities in society. They will value communication functions if these are learned through meaningful, functional, and relevant situations. Aspects to consider include the following:

1. Do the learning experiences in the classroom provide for a variety of purposes for using language?
2. Do the learning experiences provide for language functions that allow students to develop strategies that direct and affect the behavior of others and to respond to the information and controlling functions of others?
3. Do the learning experiences provide for language functions that allow students to express feelings and to respond to the feelings of others?
4. Do the learning experiences provide for language functions that allow students to practice formal and informal societal forms for greeting, thanking, conversing, and so forth?
5. Do the learning experiences provide for language functions that allow the students to use language in creating, speculating, dramatizing, fantasizing, and storytelling?

Most communication experiences involve multiple communication functions at any one time. This information should be remembered when selecting experiences for inclusion in the curriculum. Multiple functional learning experiences will appear more real to the students.

Does the Classroom Environment Provide Meaningful, Relevant, and Functional Learning Activities?

The focus of study in the classroom must always be on themes or topics which are meaningful for the learner; these will have relevance for study and a functional connection to the real world. Learning experiences that are chosen or adapted to develop bridges between school and real-life literacy are appropriate as a medium for learning and communicating about learning. Consequently, the themes and topics of the learning experiences must reflect the multicultural nature of society. They should reflect the values and uses society places on language and literacy. The following aspects may be considered as the classroom environment is examined:

1. Do the themes and topics have meaning and relevance to the lives of the students?
2. Do the themes and topics reflect the multicultural nature of the society?
3. Are the learning experiences important to the lives of the students?
4. Would students understand from these learning experiences that language and literacy were important in their lives?
5. Are community members used as role models to create a need and use of language and literacy?

When meaningful, relevant, and functional learning activities are selected, children perceive that this learning is appropriate and important in their lives.

Are Language and Literacy Experiences Embedded into the Classroom Environment and Learning Experiences?

A classroom that demonstrates the uses of language and literacy in the real world will indicate how literacy is used in daily life. A class of young children may have a home center with a notepad by the telephone, recipe books by the stove, and papers and magazines for children to simulate adult roles; children will be able to use and practice the language and literacy they observe around them. Or the classroom may include a store, café, or beauty shop. Classrooms for older students may have a television studio, a travel agency, or perhaps students may even run a real school supply store. Aspects of language and literacy that are found in the particular setting should be provided in these learning centers. Teachers should demonstrate and model language and literacy uses in these centers and allow students to simulate real-life experiences through dramatic play.

Careful analysis of the topics, settings, and use of language and literacy functions is an essential prerequisite for developing centers that simulate real life community experiences. Parents, primary caregivers, or community members can share their work and expertise. Community members can serve as language and literacy role models as they explain and relate a center's activities to real life. Further, this might also be an opportunity for embedding nondominant language literacy materials, thus demonstrating that the language is valued, contributing to L2 learners' self-esteem.

The following aspects may be considered when examining the classroom environment to determine if language and literacy are embedded in the classroom:

1. Are there indications in the room of student activities using print materials from the real world or simulating the real world?
2. Do the various learning areas in the classroom require the functional use of language and literacy?
3. Are there changing dramatic play or structured learning centers that provide opportunities to use language and literacy in simulated real-world settings?
4. Do the dramatic play or structured learning centers provide cultural reference to the society of the community?
5. Are language and literacy experiences embedded across the curriculum?

A classroom portraying embedded literacy is a room where students are immersed in print. A classroom embedding language into the very fabric of the day is one where children are employing all the language functions necessary for communicating in society.

Are Quality Multicultural Materials That Have High Interest to Students and Facilitate Learning Used and Displayed in the Classroom?

Themes, topics, and projects necessitate the use of materials that are culturally appropriate to the setting. Literacy requires the use of trade books with high interest for students; plots and characters from diverse backgrounds that students will relate to and identify with; a range of content written from the specific point of view of the cultural community it represents; appropriate sociocultural, age, gender, and nonstereotypic role models; use of language that is genuine for characters and setting; and plots that have children interacting positively with authority figures from various cultural communities (Kendall, 1983).

The use of culturally appropriate "provisions and their arrangements in the classroom make it possible for children to work through the day with a great deal of independence and to make use of literacy throughout the day a natural part of their activities" (Loughlin & Martin, 1987, p. 19). The classroom that reflects the community is sensitive to community attitudes and traditions (Loughlin & Suina,

1983). For example, if pictures about ghosts and witches are offending to the community, they should not be included. The following aspects may be considered when examining the classroom (adapted from Ramsey [1987] and Loughlin and Suina [1983]):

1. Do books selected and displayed in the classroom indicate a range of ethnic, cultural, social, and economic perspectives?
2. Are selected books written to counteract negative stereotypical images, and do they present heroes of different color, gender, creed, and class?
3. Do the books used refrain from presenting characters from diverse cultures as having to adjust, cope, and avoid conflict with majority culture characters in order to succeed? Do the books refrain from placing members of these cultures in subservient roles? Are these people not portrayed as the source of problem in the plot?
4. Are family relations depicted in which men and women have equal voice and role and equal occupational opportunities in business, the professions, and industry at all levels of responsibility?
5. Are negative values not attributed to people of different color, creed, or language?
6. Are materials used in the classroom that will bridge the cultural differences between school and community?
7. Do materials used in the classroom reflect the community?
8. Are cultural materials displayed and/or used with the regard and respect accorded to them in the community?
9. Are the cultural materials displayed and used in the classroom authentic? If they are photographs, do they represent real individuals or representative figures, not stereotypical images?
10. Are culturally authentic materials used in the various learning centers, dramatic play centers, or structured learning centers? Do they keep to the cultural traditions of the people represented?

Multicultural materials must be selected and used in the classroom in every aspect of the curricula. These include books and learning materials as well as realia that are included in the dramatic play or structured learning centers.

ASSESSING CLASSROOM ENVIRONMENTS

Although classrooms will and should be different from each other, they should reflect the community, teacher and student interests, student backgrounds, and developmental stages. Taking a specific classroom model and duplicating it is usually not successful, even in a very monoethnic community. Facets of each classroom can be the same in principle by providing a language- and literacy-enriched environment that is an extension of the cultures of the school community.

Classrooms developed to provide language- and literacy-rich environments have multiple learning centers, reading and writing diffused throughout the room, decentralized supplies, work areas away from frequently used passage areas, child-labeled supply drawers and shelves, easily accessible materials clearly marked for getting and returning, bulletin boards for children to use, questions posed on pictures, displays, realia, and books displayed to show title and invite picking up to explore. In summary, language- and literacy-rich classrooms are immersed in print and are environments with opportunities for communication.

Classrooms developed as extensions of the cultures, homes, and languages of the school community include the home language as a significant feature of school instruction, provide themes and topics that are consonant with the community, have physical and organizational arrangements that are appropriate to the home cultures, and encourage student-to-student and student-to-teacher communications that are appropriate to dominant and nondominant cultures.

Classroom Environment Assessment Scale

The classroom environment assessment scale was developed through tryouts with undergraduate teacher education students and experienced teachers and administrators in graduate classes. The scale is based on the work of Hall (1987), Loughlin (1977, 1978), Loughlin and Martin (1976, 1987), and Loughlin and Suina (1982, 1983). The scale allows the teacher to easily assess his or her classroom for analyzing the quality of the multicultural classroom for language and literacy learning (see Figure 4.1).

To demonstrate how different teachers might apply these ideas for creating a language and literacy learning environment, two classrooms that incorporated these features were examined. Each community environment was different from the other and the two classrooms were of different grade levels.

Primary Classroom

The primary classroom was located in an inner-city school in a declining, heavy industrial city. Most of the children came from low socioeconomic–level homes. The school was surrounded on two sides by small attached homes, many opening directly onto sidewalks with

FIGURE 4-1 Classroom Environment Assessment Scale

Directions: Make observations about each category in the scale. Briefly note these. Rate each category on a scale of 0–5 (0 = not present, 1 = little, 2–3 = to some degree, and 4–5 = to great degree).

Categories	Observations	Rating
1. Physical arrangements conducive to learning/involvement		
2. Arrangements/practices conducive to student interaction		
3. Accommodations for cultural communities evident		
4. Learning areas include written self-directing activities		
5. Self-monitoring systems use reading/writing		
6. Areas for quiet reading/writing available and frequently used		
7. Writing instruments/materials available/accessible		
8. Displays/exhibits/materials include student writing		
9. Print accompanies nearby displays, objects, pictures, realia		
10. Space available for mounting/displaying student work/notices		
11. Student-written/dictated work displayed		
12. Labels/directions used through classroom		
13. Print materials from outside school included/used (English/non-English)		
14. Current events stimulate reading/writing		
15. Books displayed with covers visible (children's trade books)		

FIGURE 4-1 *(continued)*

Categories	Observations	Rating
16. Range/variety of trade books (fiction/ nonfiction) included		
17. Multicultural books and materials evident/used		
18. Reference materials available		

Comments and Recommendations:

Sources: From *The Emergence of Literacy* by N. Hall, 1987, pp. 82–84. Portsmouth, NH: Heinemann Educational Books; "Understanding the Learning Environment" by C. E. Loughlin, 1977, *The Elementary School Journal, 78*(2), pp. 125–131; "Arranging the Learning Environment" by C. E. Loughlin, 1978, *Insites into Open Education, 11*(2), pp. 2–6; "A Dynamic Teacher Role" by C. E. Loughlin and M. D. Martin, 1976, *Journal of Teaching and Learning, 2*(2), pp. 34–43; *Supporting Literacy: Developing Effective Learning Environments* by C. E. Loughlin and M. D. Martin, 1987, New York: Teachers College Press; "Reflecting the Child's Community in the Classroom Environment," by C. E. Loughlin and J. H. Suina, 1983, *Childhood Education,* (1), pp. 19–21; *The Learning Environment: An Instructional Strategy* by C. E. Loughlin and J. H. Suina, 1982, New York: Teachers College Press.

small private rear areas; on the third side were high-rise, public housing apartments. Some houses directly across from the school had been turned into small stores. For example, one was a quick-food place, popular in the neighborhood of single-parent or two-parent working families. This resource was used by the teacher in developing a classroom learning center, called the Café.

The school was located three blocks from a heavily trafficked business area. Between the school and this area were bars, some light industrial businesses, small stores (some boarded), and a community center covered with writing in at least two different languages. The school building was old and surrounded by a paved playground. The rooms on each floor opened off a central area that was used as a multifunctional room. The school was in good repair and appeared to be recently painted.

The school population was fairly stable, consisting predominantly of children of families from English-speaking homes. However, approximately 25 percent of the children in the school population represented culturally diverse communities; for nearly a third of these, English was a second language. There was no bilingual program and limited assistance in teaching English as a second language. Some of the first-language (L1) children and most of the L2 children in the classroom had been in Head Start programs (United States government compensatory programs established for the "culturally disadvantaged" children from the lowest socioeconomic levels in the 1960s focusing on early learning experiences).

Parents nights were held throughout the year. The important role of parents in preparing and supporting children for learning was discussed, curriculum and teaching were explained. Parents were consulted about teacher concerns and changes and additions to the program. Parents were encouraged to embed literacy in the home and continue language and literacy experiences in the first language.

The parent organization, headed by a dynamic African American single mother, provided the teachers with assistance and support and was gradually becoming more involved in the curricula and management of the school The organization was instrumental in encouraging and supporting all-school celebrations in relation to cultural and ethnic events. One important event was the Cinco de Mayo celebration. Every class took part and related content was integrated across the curricula. On the day of the celebration parents and many children came dressed in costumes, and a Mexican lunch was served to the children.

Community people were in the building daily, many participating as volunteer aids and assisting in classroom projects. Parents on night shifts, particularly fathers, came in the early morning to read and listen to young children read.

Ms. L. taught a class of children ages five and six, many of whom were in Chapter One (United States government funded pull-out program provided for students scoring below specific reading and mathematics achievement quantities). At the time of the year the assessment took place, the children were no longer receiving Chapter One instruction. Each item from the assessment scale in Table 4.1 was used to examine the classroom environment.

Current Events   Photographs of recent activities of a trip reported in the small community newspaper were on a cupboard in flip holders with news clippings to correspond. On a bulletin board was a teacher-elicited daily news report: major happenings of the day before, what the children had done in school, what was anticipated to happen, and the current weather.

Labels/Directions   All drawers in cabinets were labeled, some by students. Signs and directions identified a structured learning center called the Café. A menu was posted, directions were printed for using the café and wet center, students were invited to make books, make a design, and label it.

Student-Written/Dictated-Work   Student-made books were on display in a number of reading places. A bulletin board held notes and children's writings. Student-painted pictures with accompanying dictated sentences that retold a story the teacher had told ran along one wall.

Displays/Exhibits/Materials   Many child-made signs for the Café gave prices and directions. A teacher-made sign gave the cost of milk near the milk carton and described how to pay for the milk in different mathematical equations.

Self-Directing Learning Areas   Writing instruments and colored pens were near teacher-made blank books with a sign: "Write a book about your terrible, horrible, no good, very bad day" (Judith Viorst, *Alexander and the Terrible, Horrible, No Good, Very Bad Day* [Macmillan, 1972]).

Print Accompanies Displays   A display of items dealing with the food industry included realia such as a chef's hat, apron, jacket, cooking utensils, and pictures of food. Each item had a short phrase or one-line description accompanying it. Questions were asked about displays and space was left for student responses. ("Which do you like better for pets, cats or dogs?" "What is your favorite food?")

Mounting/Displaying Space   Student bulletin board space was available for placing notices, notes, and work in a number of places in the classroom. One spot was above a center where a phone, catalogue, and calculators were kept.

Writing Instruments   Paper, pens, pencils, and blank books were available at every working area in the classroom where they might be needed and used.

Reading/Writing Areas   One large carpeted reading area had pillows and accessible books at sitting level. At least two other smaller centers were in the classroom that held two to three children each. Writing areas were established in relation to the projects ongoing during the day. Smaller more permanent areas included the telephone/catalogue center and a spot where journals were kept that seated two to three people. The room had groups of tables identified for differing activities.

Reference Materials   Special dictionaries that accompany a structured language-experience program were available in the classroom. Picture books and topic books about restaurants and cafés, recipe books, catalogues to order restaurant utensils, and books about various types of foods were located in numerous locations.

Print Materials from Outside School   Besides the catalogues from the restaurant supply houses and the community newspaper, students had posted notices for various community activities coming up in the near future that they had brought from home and shared. A few notices were in languages other than English.

Book Displays   Books were stored so their covers were visible. Some were held on racks kept in place by narrow strips of wood running across the shelf. Books written by the children were included.

Range/Variety of Books   About 300 books were in the collection, fiction and nonfiction. These did not include any of the many sets of books that accompanied the big books in the classroom.

Multicultural Books   Numerous multicultural books were in the collection including a few books from the other community languages. Some books had been read aloud and translated for the English speaking children by a parent. An oversize book was developed from folktales, myths, and fables from one of the community's cultures by a mother. The book was illustrated by the children under her direction.

Accommodations for Cultural Communities   Displays that used two languages were evident in the classroom. The teacher read Ann Nolan Clark's *In the Land of Small Dragon* (Viking, 1979), a Cinderella variant, to introduce a study of folktales. Two children sat and named items in a catalogue, each in his or her own language. Books and items related to a forthcoming cultural event were on display. Posters of scenes and people from at least two community cultures were on the walls.

Student Interaction   Interaction was encouraged in small, cooperative learning groups, and personal interaction patterns were accepted. Learning activities located at the various tables appeared to facilitate this.

Self-Monitoring Systems   Students signed up for activities that would take place during the day (Which kind of cupcake would you like to make? Chocolate? Poppy seed?). Students signed in to indicate attendance and took care of signing up for milk, if they wanted it. Directions were provided to monitor use and activities in the various, changing centers. A tape recorder and read-along books were in the listening center. Children were able to use the tape recorder on their own.

Physical Arrangements The classroom was arranged in various learning areas to provide for child involvement. Children took part in making decisions about the use of the centers and activities. Tools, instruments, and materials were all convenient for use to develop independence.

Comments and Recommendations Very novel functional use of reading and writing was everywhere (Would you like to take a nature walk tomorrow?). Everything was at the children's eye level. Ms. L. modeled language and literacy through her interactions in the Café – she wrote a check and ordered from the menu. A parent volunteer helped children make cupcakes from a recipe printed on a large tagboard.

Intermediate Classroom

The intermediate classroom was located in a large school situated in a small midwestern city with light industry and commerce. The population of the school was drawn from single-family homes with well-maintained houses, yards, and gardens, and multiple-family buildings in what could be termed the low-rent district. Many of the homes were built after the school was erected. Apartment dwellers were located in a large section along a busy street across from a rail link. Some of the children were bused from other parts of town with comparable or newer, more expensive homes and from well-kept farms on rich irrigated land.

The original school building had two additions to meet the enrollment demands. The building had a large well-stocked library with an excellent librarian and staff person. The library was easily accessible to the classrooms and had comfortable chairs, couches, and study carrels as well as groups of tables, all attractively arranged. The shelves were dotted with displayed books, art prints, statues, and busts of famous people. In the library a bulletin board displayed book jackets about a special theme that encouraged children to read. In this library there was always some special display of books by author, illustrator, award, or season.

Over the years the school's population had changed from middle-class children from two-parent backgrounds to more children from lower socioeconomic levels, single-parent homes, homes where parents received economic aid. Included in the changing school population were also more English second language (ESL) students from migrant families and a few refugee Southeast Asians relocated in the community by various church and civic groups. Most of these children were Chapter One students.

The largest culturally diverse population in the school was from the migrant Hispanic community. Most of these children were in attendance only during the fall and spring of the school year, when their enrollment swelled the school population about 8–10 percent. Their parents, migrant workers, returned in the winter to Texas, which they considered home. However, more of this population was remaining throughout the year. They generally lived in the multiple-dwelling neighborhoods. Teachers believed these students' parents faced subtle discrimination problems in securing housing from landlords who may not have wished to rent to them because of their large extended families.

There was one ESL teacher in this building for approximately 75–80 ESL students in a pull-out program. Most of these children were in the early primary grades. One of the features of the program was a buddy system in which native language–speaking children became peer tutors of a non-English-speaking child. Tutors were taught how to teach words for real-world items in the school environment and help the new students get acquainted.

Mr. J's intermediate classroom was made up of children ages 10 and 11. His classroom was large and carpeted, students were seated at tables. Items from the assessment scale in Table 4.1 were used to examine his classroom environment.

Current Events Students were encouraged to read daily newspapers, and a special time was set aside for discussion. Items from the discussion often appeared in journals that students kept. News clippings of interest to students were placed on a bulletin board under appropriate permanent categories to encourage sharing and more discussion.

Labels/Directions Cabinets and drawers were labeled in student handwriting. Labels and directions were on items and activities in the science area.

Student-Written/-Dictated Work Student-made books were on display in a special area of the room. A bulletin board held reports written by children on a science topic. A display with a photograph and biographical sketch highlighted one student as Writer of the Week.

Displays/Exhibits/Materials Science-project displays included write-ups describing projects done by each cooperative group.

Self-Directing Learning Areas Students worked in literature circles and knew their tasks and routines. Directions explained to students what should be done at each learning area.

Print Accompanies Displays Besides the print accompanying science projects, there were detailed photographs of children, on a winter outing, on a bulletin board with questions about the prairie winter plant and animal life and human survival in the winter. (These were from the previous year's class and were used to introduce the upcoming study.)

Mounting/Displaying Space Student jokes, advertisements, and announcements were on a particular bulletin board. All displayed work, except the winter survival bulletin board, appeared to be student originated.

Writing Instruments Paper, pens, and pencils were provided by the students. Response journals and special illustration materials were readily accessible from shelves that were conveniently located in the room and labeled to assist students in getting and returning on their own.

Reading/Writing Areas Students read and wrote at tables or in the nearby library by checking out of the room. Only a small collection of books on topics under study was in the room. Some children read and wrote at tables on the outer edge of the classroom.

Reference Materials Dictionaries and encyclopedias were in the classroom as well as the special topic books.

Print Materials from Outside School Besides the papers that came daily, there were some student magazines in the classroom on loan from the library. (No non-English materials were noted.)

Book Displays Books available in the classroom were all standing in shelves or displayed on tables so their covers were readable.

Range/Variety of Books Both fiction and nonfiction books were available in the classroom, but it was obvious that the students were expected to use the library to locate reading and research materials.

Multicultural Books Mr. J. read Bette Bao Lord's *In the Year of the Boar and Jackie Robinson* (Harper, 1984) to the students daily, and the students were involved in literature circles with a focus on self-esteem. For example, Jean Craighead George's *Julie of the Wolves* (Harper, 1972) was read by one group.

Accommodations for Cultural Communities Labels and titles in the classroom used both English and Spanish. One of the books used for literature circles was Joseph Krumgold's *And Now Miguel* (Harper,

1953). Children in this group were discussing different Hispanic American communities with two students who were Mexican American. Cooperative grouping was used in topic studies. Mr. J. visited with each student in his or her home prior to the start of school. He made frequent calls and wrote to parents to keep them informed about their children. When necessary, Mr. J. sought help for communications from a Spanish-speaking, support staff person from the district central office. Semantic webs and illustrations were used to help develop topic terms. A web on winter survival was on a chart holder. Semantic webs aided children in developing greater conceptual understanding because of the profusion of terms elicited or developed around the major topic concept.

Student Interaction Interaction was encouraged in literature circles and cooperative groups. Students sat at tables that provided for interaction and collaboration. There were frequent discussions on spelling and reactions to passages a writer or reader was working on. There was a general low noise level in the room.

Self-Monitoring Systems Students understood the procedures for working in the major learning activities in both literature circles and cooperative groups. Directions were evident in learning centers. Students self-selected books, writing topics, and activities.

Physical Arrangements The children sat at tables located in a more central part of the classroom while other tables were available on the edges of the classroom for project work in groups. A total ring around the classroom could be walked to get at centers and provisions.

Comments and Recommendations The classroom appeared to run in a very democratic manner. Students worked in groups and made decisions by voting.

Reflections About the Model Classrooms

Both the primary and intermediate classrooms met Enright and McCloskey's (1985) requirements that communicative classrooms be flexible, functional, enticing, and student owned. The classroom environments were interactive and literate environments. These classrooms evolved to fit the changing needs of the learning activities. All materials were easily accessible to the learners and labels, questions, and directions all enticed the learner to learn. Print was used in the classroom contextually, thus encouraging reading and use for writing. Students communicated and interacted in all the various learning activities of the classroom.

Children participated in decision making regarding their learning activities in these classrooms. For example, the children chose making cupcakes over making chocolate chip cookies for their treat in Ms. L.'s room, while Mr. J.'s students made decisions about what they were learning, how much they would learn, and what activities they would do. Ms. L.'s classroom was small and crowded with many students, perhaps like the home of most of her students. Mr. J.'s classroom, although spacious, was divided into small areas that were inviting and comfortable for work, reading, and activities that accommodated the needs of the students. Two computers were used for instruction, writing, and games.

What makes these classrooms multicultural may not be obvious without seeing how children and adults interacted in the classroom learning environment. Ms. L. had carefully woven a multicultural focus into the curriculum. Her yearly focus was diversity. She focused on this topic whether studying animals or work people do in the community. For example, the subthemes for the Café structured learning center were gender-fair and equality.

Both teachers used community events and happenings for selecting themes and topics. Mr. J. opened the year with a study around a theme of people of the community. This allowed him to do some consciousness raising. He developed understandings and appreciations of the diversity of the community in this topic and stated that it had made for better student interaction. His topics and themes focused children on what they could do to change the society in which they lived. The themes of Mr. J.'s literature circles were easily identified as multicultural. The themes changed as the literature selections changed.

The organizational structures that these two teachers used contributed to the instructional success of their programs. Cooperative grouping was used by both teachers; structured learning centers were used by Ms. L. daily and by Mr. J. approximately once a week when the children put out the class newspaper. Cooperative grouping and structured learning centers are important components of the classroom environment.

STRUCTURING INTERACTION THROUGH COOPERATIVE GROUPING

Many teachers organize children for literacy instruction using ability grouping patterns. These traditional, small-group instructional organizations develop a type of classism by sorting children into better-to-worse categories and encourage a competitive atmosphere. When a classroom has a competitive atmosphere, students tend to develop an attitude that their achievement is dependent upon the failure of others. Johnson and Johnson (1987) described three types of common instructional delivery patterns in schools:

1. Cooperative grouping (We sink or swim together)
2. Individualization (We are each in this alone)
3. Competitive (I swim, you sink; I sink, you swim)

The latter two patterns contribute to attitudes that are destructive to desirable classroom environments. The first, cooperative grouping, contributes to healthy interactive attitudes.

Cooperative Grouping Increases Interaction

Cooperative learning offers the greatest opportunity for assisting students to work, learn, and live together; it is an excellent preparation for life. Cooperative learning can be equally effective for all children if used appropriately. Augustine, Gruber, and Hanson (1990) described dramatic improvement in learning over a year through the use of cooperative groups. Slavin (1991) reported that 61 percent of the 67 studies of achievement found cooperative learning significantly increased learning. Only in one study did the control group achieve higher.

Cooperative learning changes the atmosphere of the classroom. In classrooms where cooperative learning is the norm, students develop excellent relationships because they work together toward meeting common goals. Students will achieve more in cooperative interactive groups (Johnson, Johnson & Holubec, 1988). Although other types of learning patterns can be used in the classroom as well as cooperative learning, teachers may wish to use cooperative learning more than other types of learning delivery patterns. Cooperative learning gives students an opportunity to interact while practicing skills being developed (Slavin, 1991).

Using Cooperative Learning with L2 Learners

Cooperative learning is not a panacea or quick cure for the ills that plague instruction in heterogeneous classrooms. Although E. G. Cohen (1990) documented that cooperative learning can help teachers develop high-level academic and linguistic basic skills in English, she believes that teachers and students will be tuned out unless three key requirements are maintained for cooperative learning.

The first requirement is that materials must be developed and used differently from those used in the traditional classroom (the worksheet or textbook task or the right-answer variety). The latter materials require little interaction, and only students who know how to do the task in the first place benefit from them. Tasks must be designed that demand multiple abilities—spatial and visual, reasoning, role-playing, and abilities to be precise, accurate, and careful—not pencil-and-paper tasks. Tasks must provide opportunities for all students to read and write in the context of their performance, use one another as resources to prepare their own work, and take responsibility for what is happening to other members of the group. Materials should be sufficiently rich in context to provide language cues to the meaning of terms for non-English-speaking students.

The second requirement is that all students must participate in classroom activities or the quality of learning suffers. Consequently, rich, multiple-ability, motivating tasks must be prepared. Tasks must be designed that require many different intellectual and problem-solving abilities. Further, the teacher must explicitly state that no one will be good at everything and that everyone will be good at at least one task. Teachers must believe that intelligence is multidimensional and that the task requires a variety of abilities. This will encourage the most reluctant class isolates to interact.

The third requirement is that teachers must understand that cooperative learning is an instructional approach which necessitates a reconceptualization of the teacher's role. This new role requires increased management abilities and a greater need to work cooperatively with other teachers in developing and evaluating new tasks. Working together is an ideal way to present opportunities for developing collegial relationships among teachers.

Characteristics of Cooperative Learning

Johnson et al. (1986) stated that if learning is to be cooperative it must have the following five characteristics:

1. The learners must feel they need one another to accomplish their task(s).

2. The learners must have interaction and verbal exchanges through summarizing, giving and receiving explanations, and elaborating (relating to previous learning).

3. The learners must have each learned the material and have helped one another learn the material. This can be accomplished when

the teacher assesses individual accountability or randomly selects one member to give an answer for the entire group that is the group score or grade.

4. The learners must practice social skills such as encouraging others to participate, disagreeing without put-downs, taking turns participating, and using conflict management skills.

5. The learners must be given the opportunity and procedures to analyze how well their groups function and use social skills.

Teacher's Role in Structuring Cooperative Learning

The teacher's role in structuring cooperative learning situations includes seven strategies. These strategies were adapted from Johnson et al. (1988).

Strategy One

The teacher determines what the students are to learn and the collaborative skills necessary for achieving the learning. The content to be learned need not stem from the teacher, alone, but can be determined through teacher-pupil planning. Cooperative learning is equally good for new skills, discussion, and brainstorming (Edwards & Stout, 1990). Scott (1990) recommended that brainstorming done in small groups or pairs was more conducive for girls, males having low group status, and culturally diverse students.

Strategy Two

The teacher determines the group size most appropriate for achieving the goal, usually from two to four students. Larger groups require more time for the task and more skillful group members. Groups can be assigned in any number of ways, but placing class isolates with supportive students and mixing students of color, students with and without disabilities, and male and female members of the class probably is best for a multicultural and gender-fair mix. Diversity will increase the quality and quantity of student work (Scott, 1990).

Strategy Three

The children are prepared to work together and to get acquainted (if this is a new group). Students might be together for four to six weeks, depending on the study, or only for one task (Edwards & Stout, 1990).

Strategy Four

The assignment or task is structured so that the students know what they are going to do and how they are expected to reach the goal. The students must understand the concepts and procedures that will be used, what the final product is expected to be, and what each student will be expected to do. All students must know their individual responsibilities and work together (Slavin, 1990). Students can be involved in assigning responsibilities as well. Carefully designed assignments for groups will lead to positive interdependence, a breakdown of stereotypes, and acceptance of individual differences (Scott, 1990).

Assign roles to achieve interdependence. For example, a summarizer could be used to restate major conclusions or answers; a checker could be used, when it is necessary, to ensure that each group member can explain how to arrive at the answer or conclusion; a researcher-runner could be used when it is necessary to get materials and communicate with other groups and the teacher; a recorder could be used when the group is to write down group decisions; an observer could help develop group collaboration by keeping track of how well the group is doing (Johnson et al., 1988).

Jigsawing techniques that provide students with only pieces of the materials to be learned are one way to develop interdependence and individual accountability. These techniques require each student to be responsible for teaching the other group members his or her particular material. Jigsawing emphasizes the important skills of active listening and checking for understanding. Active learners focus on the speaker and ask for clarification to be able to summarize or give examples of what has just been presented.

Strategy Five

The effectiveness of the learning groups is monitored as they work; when the students need assistance the teacher intervenes by answering questions and assisting with group skills or assigned roles. Roles are rotated so that children have opportunities for different roles. Responsibility is encouraged and progress rewarded (Edwards & Stout, 1990). The teacher must look for signs of one student dominating and for lack of participation, as well as the interaction patterns being used. Small cooperative mixed-gender and multiethnic groups can contribute to girls, and culturally diverse and less-confident European American boys, becoming more assertive, if interaction is carefully structured and monitored (Scott, 1990).

Strategy Six

Closure for the lesson is provided by having students report, share, or summarize what they have learned. To support interdependence as well as individual accountability, a student is randomly chosen from each group to report. This technique ensures that students check and correct one another.

Strategy Seven

The quality and quantity of the students' learning is evaluated. The students are given feedback on how well they learned the assigned concepts or information and how well they collaborated. Students must know how well they are working. Students should also evaluate how well they think they did in their collaboration at the end of each working session, and they should have time to set goals for what they can do to improve the next time (Scott, 1990). The teacher should process with each group at least once a week, if the group is extending over a long period. Whole-class processing is also recommended each week. Processing enables the teacher to assess progress and aid students to determine progress and future goals and directions. It helps to keep the work moving along toward completion.

Cooperative Learning and Cultural Differences

Cooperative learning is reported by authors and researchers as appropriate for instruction because students from diverse cultures are more successful learners in classrooms using cooperative grouping. Slavin (1987) reported that positive effects have been found in creative writing, reading comprehension, problem solving, and language mechanics through cooperative group learning. "In general, achievement effects have been equivalent for high, average and low achievers, for boys and girls, and for students of various ethnic backgrounds" (Slavin, 1987, p. 10). In addition cooperative grouping provides opportunities for L2 students to practice English, language, and literacy in an environment that is nonthreatening. Positive effects from cooperative learning have also been found in race relations. If students are going to learn to work and live together cooperatively, they must do so in classrooms. Cooperative learning, according to Scott (1990), raises students' achievements and attitudes as they learn to respect one another's differences when working to solve cooperative problems more creatively.

To avoid opportunities for students to dominate, Scott (1990) recommended that groups be kept small, often using pairing and jigsaw activities that structure positive interdependent and individual accountability with equal status for all group members.

Cooperative learning fits the values, traditions, and beliefs of some non-Western societies. For example, Native American cultures have a conception of society as being collaborative in nature. They have a concern for the common good, a need to see that no one achieves at the expense of others—a sharing ethic. Teachers who have taught on Native American reservations tell of children who would delay finishing work, tasks, and activities so as not to be competitive. Children from other culturally diverse homes may also come to school expecting to work cooperatively and find the competitive nature of the schools alien and threatening to their nature.

DEVELOPING STRUCTURED LEARNING CENTERS

The structured learning center provides a vehicle for integrating language and literacy learning experiences in a simulated, community-related learning experience. The structured learning center provides opportunities for students to practice speaking, listening, reading, and writing in conjunction with social and functional real-life situations. This center may be content dependent, deriving its situation from a theme or topic of the curriculum, yet operating semiautonomously, such as the Café in the primary classroom discussed earlier. Structured learning centers may also be developed to operate as integral parts of the learning activities of the classroom. The teacher acts as a facilitator, stimulator, model, and demonstrator. An example of the latter would be Mr. J., the intermediate classroom teacher who acted as editor-in-chief when his classroom was set up as a newspaper office for putting out the class newspaper.

Research Supporting Structured Learning Centers

Hall, May, Moores, Sheaver, and Williams (1987a) reported a study of nursery-age children to determine if they made use of literacy-related objects in the structured learning centers. A situation was set up in which literacy was an embedded feature of a home center. In four days of unobtrusive videotaping, researchers observed 290 literacy-related events from fleeting bits of engagements in literacy to highly organized and sustained episodes of play in which literacy was a consistently embedded feature. For example, a young boy was told by one of the girls in family play to read the newspaper. He then spent five minutes manipulating and maneuvering the paper until he had it organized for reading, and he sat and gave it intense scrutiny. He appeared to explore the role of being a newspaper reader (Hall et al., 1987a, p. 8).

Children in the Hall et al. (1987a) study demonstrated not only knowledge of the purposes of print but also the social contexts in which these purposes were embedded. Children displayed a wide range of mark-making abilities and explored the use of written language to establish ownership, build relationships, recall, request, record, and imagine. Hall, Jones, and McCaldon (1987b) then extended the study by developing an office environment for another group of children. This group of young children used literacy terms and writing materials in ways that indicated that writing-type marks were intended.

These studies provided foundation for using language and literacy for older children as well. Students of all ages respond to learning that is meaningful, relevant, and functional. Structured learning centers provide a means for bringing community life into the classroom and integrating language and literacy that is meaningful, relevant, and functional.

Structured learning centers are powerful learning experiences for culturally diverse and L2 students. They provide practice for these students in a simulated setting before going out into the real world. The opportunity to practice language and literacy in simulated social and environmental situations may not otherwise be a part of their experiential backgrounds.

Primary Structured Learning Centers

Structured learning centers are probably more common at the primary level. Teachers using a structured learning center approach develop an environmental center that simulates real-world situations known to children. This environment allows the students to role-play using the language and literacy of the particular situation. Structured learning centers can embed literacy for younger children through cafés, stores, beauty shops, and offices that include use of all the simulated literacy appropriate to a particular situation. They allow the students to use and practice language and literacy through interaction with other students. In a post office, students would buy stamps and money orders, write letters, mail packages, fill in forms, receive papers, and deliver mail.

Intermediate Structured Learning Centers

Structured learning centers appear most successful for older students when the total classroom becomes the simulated situation for a period of time. For example, students studying the television industry would develop programs such as news broadcasts, plays, weather reports, special interest programs, and game shows to be presented. These learning experiences would require extensive research, discussion, planning, writing, and role-playing.

Other situations might include a full range of retail businesses found in a community. In the latter, stock could be sold, a board of directors elected, and materials developed, purchased, merchandised, and sold. These learning situations provide excellent ways to integrate mathematics for older children when they establish real situations for finding percentages for markups of stock or stock reduction sales. Students learn the power of advertising as well.

Another activity that works well for older students and provides extensive opportunities for use of language and literacy is to simulate one level of government—local, state, or national—with appropriate branches of government, such as judicial or legislative government. Government simulations lead to working in parties to develop political platforms. Laws can be written and passed necessitating speeches supporting and opposing platforms and legislative bills. After the children had developed their own laws in one sixth grade classroom, they were immediately faced with lawbreakers and the need to develop a judicial branch of government. This led to new bills before the legislature regarding punishments or fines and the need to have judges, lawyers, and juries. The study of both companies and government were excellent ways the teacher integrated a range of community members and resources into his classroom.

Guidelines for Developing a Structured Learning Center

A structured learning center can be a particularly significant aspect in structuring a classroom learning environment when the following conditions are met:

1. The center is conceived around situations that provide ample opportunities to use language and literacy in real-world settings.
2. The theme is one that provides for integrated language and literacy practice in simulated social and environmental settings.
3. The teacher models and demonstrates the use of skills required in the center.

4. The students clearly understand the use of the center. This includes the number of students allowed in the center, time and duration for use, and roles and responsibilities of users.

SUMMARY

There are many facets to consider in structuring a learning-centered environment for children in a multicultural school. Of the various criteria to use in designing the classroom environment, communicative and literacy criteria are essential for a multicultural classroom environment. The use of cooperative learning techniques and structured learning centers in a multicultural classroom are two strategies that provide opportunities to practice and use language and literacy in an interactive atmosphere, a requirement for multicultural learning.

IMPLICATIONS FOR INSTRUCTION

The following implications should serve as guides for developing a multicultural environment:

1. Develop classroom environments that reflect the communities and cultures of the students. The cultures and communities of students should be analyzed to provide for an environment that is conducive to learning.

2. Develop classroom environments that focus language and literacy learning on specific communicative criteria. Create an environment that encourages language and literacy learning in both dominant and nondominant languages in the community.

3. Develop classroom environments that are literate environments by immersing students in print to support literacy learning. These environments should value both L1 and L2 literacy by providing examples and opportunities for use and development of dominant and nondominant languages.

4. Employ cooperative grouping to facilitate students' learning to live, work, and study together in a multicultural society and to increase learning opportunities.

5. Include structured learning centers to provide students with meaningful, functional, and relevant learning environments for using language and literacy in the classroom.

PART THREE

A Multicultural Instructional Program in Language and Literacy

Language and literacy are acquired for achieving social, cognitive, and academic skills that will prepare students for successful adult lives in a free society. However, children labeled disadvantaged by society may bring to school speech patterns, cognitive predispositions, and behavior patterns different from those of middle-class European American children. These cultural manifestations often lead to lowered school expectations and misdiagnosis of student's abilities.

Educators need to realize that school is alien to culturally different children (Knapp, Turnbill & Shield, 1990). School environments, curricula, and instructional strategies may be deterrents for the success of culturally diverse and low-socioeconomic students. To achieve in school may mean that these children have to give up their allegiance to their own culture. Dana Brady's (1991) poem amply portrays the situation of a Native American child:

Being Native American
by Dana Brady, 6th Grade
Northern Cheyenne

Being Native American
is like being an eagle
   —soaring high above the earth.
Then there comes drinking
and it's like pollution
   —to the soaring eagle.
When you get an education
it's like being
   —abandoned from the flock.
or sometimes
   —you get helped out by the flock.

Conventional curricula and instruction for disadvantaged and second-language (L2) learners breaks up reading and writing into fixed sequences of discrete skills ordered from simple to complex. These skills are to be mastered in a linear progression. This instructional model, according to Knapp et al. (1990), underestimates student capabilities, postpones more interesting and challenging work, fails to provide a context for meaningful learning and functional use of skills, and tends to reinforce academic failure. Students in such a curriculum and instructional model must integrate the pieces without a means for coherence and intellectual challenge. They may fail to learn to think for themselves and may become dependent on the teacher for monitoring, motivating, and structuring all aspects of their work (Knapp et al., 1990).

To achieve the conventional, discrete, skills-centered curriculum with careful, teacher-centered, direct instruction, low-achieving students are grouped by ability for literacy instruction and supplemental services, such as Chapter One and English second language (ESL) instruction. This arrangement often permanently segregates students into groupings or tracts (Knapp et al., 1990; Nieto, 1992). The problem is exacerbated through misdiagnosis of students' academic abilities because ethnic or linguistic features are often interpreted as signs of low ability. Ability grouping leads to students being labeled and provided more limited curricula. They advance more slowly, are apt to develop lower self-esteem, and are more likely to drop out (Nieto, 1992).

Programs and instruction for multicultural classrooms should be designed based on student strengths and holistic teaching, not discrete and isolated skills and totally teacher-directed instruction. Guidelines the teacher should use for developing an instructional program in a multicultural classroom include the following:

1. Empower students by involving them in the selection of goals, themes, topics, instructional decisions, and evaluations. When students are involved, the learning becomes meaningful, relevant, and functional.

2. Develop instruction based on students' previous knowledge and personal experiences. This recognizes their cultural identities (Early, 1990).

3. Provide opportunities for students to observe and interact in meaningful language and literacy events (Knapp et al., 1990).

4. Integrate language and literacy in thematic and topic content that develops thinking skills and content knowledge simultaneously

(Early, 1990). The themes and topics should examine, clarify, and reflect on students' values, attitudes, beliefs, and feelings related to social and racial issues such as prejudice and discrimination. Highly developed thinking skills are essential for social criticism and social change (Banks, 1989b).

5. Accept first-language (L1) or dialect use, but encourage development of L2 standard forms for speaking and writing as well. Such learning empowers culturally diverse students to overcome social and political systems.

6. Develop instruction around multicultural literature. Literature provides models for developing competent writers and speakers and for understanding and appreciating diversity. It provides opportunities for students to examine attitudes, beliefs, and feelings about prejudice and discrimination (Banks, 1989b).

7. Involve parents and communities in the instructional program (Early, 1990).

CHAPTER FIVE

Facilitating Language and Literacy Emergence in Multicultural Classrooms

- *How can the classroom teacher facilitate second-language learning?*
- *How can the classroom teacher facilitate literacy emergence for students from dominant and nondominant cultures?*
- *What strategies can the classroom teacher use that are particularly successful for assisting second-language literacy learners?*
- *What strategies assist students to acquire the conventions of print?*
- *Why and how should the teacher become an interactive demonstrator of language and literacy?*

INTRODUCTION

Educators must rethink how students will best learn language and literacy. F. Smith (1987) pointed out that what children read and write, and who they read and write with are as important as any formal education. This can be said about oral language as well: What children listen to, what they talk about, and who they listen to and talk with are as important as any formal language instruction. Further, who listens to them and how the listeners respond or interact with them is essential in language learning. Each learner has his or her own time-table or schedule for learning language and literacy. Language and literacy can be facilitated and supported through modeling, demonstrating, and interacting in a communicative and literate environment; it can never be hurried. Sulzby (1988) reported that reading and writing emergence appeared to progress, then regress, or it may make a developmental leap; the same can also be noted about second-language emergence.

To facilitate the emergence of both language and literacy for children requires that the school environment be receptive and that teachers accept and value each student's cultural background. A cooperative relationship should be developed with parents and families, one that draws on their experiences with their children. The classroom should be a supportive environment where children feel free to explore and expand language and literacy learning in a meaningful instructional program that helps them learn about themselves, others, the community, and the world.

Teachers need to have confidence in children's self-learning abilities and to trust in their own professional instincts about what makes good learning for children. Teachers can learn from children to adapt, adjust, or modify learning experiences. Children should be given the opportunity to work through their problems with literacy rather than being rescued by well-intentioned teachers fearing they might become frustrated. A second language will be learned if teachers recognize the value of the home language and culture. Learning is not so much the struggle of learning but the struggle for understanding. Both language and literacy will emerge through functional, meaningful, and relevant communicative and literate interactions.

F. Smith (1987) stated that children learn literacy to become members of the Literacy Club; they are helped by family and society while learning how to learn in a meaningful environment. Children learn to read from authors of the books that are read to them and from those that they read. They read what they know—the story. They learn about the surface structure of the written language as a consequence of learning, not the cause for learning. They learn to write when writing is modeled and demonstrated in their environment and when their attempts are supported in a risk-free environment.

LEARNING A SECOND LANGUAGE IN A DOMINANT-CULTURE SCHOOL

If children entering school have neither the oral language of the school nor a cultural orientation for learning in their school, the experiences will be extremely stressful and everything will seem foreign. These children require a caring teacher and a supportive learning environment. Children have the right to be successful and their experiences should help them to succeed. Educators are needed in schools who receive job satisfaction from the success of their students (Cochrane, Cochrane, Scalena, & Buchanan, 1984).

Children learning a second language need to be immersed in oral language opportunities if they are to learn to read and write. Unfortunately, the language used in the classroom can be teacher dominated. Teachers should examine their classroom communication. Is teacher talk focused on explaining and evaluating student behavior, work, and progress? Such teacher behavior contributes toward students becoming highly dependent and discouraged with their roles in school. Culturally diverse children then learn through their failure that good school language is knowing behaviors such as when to talk or when not to talk; when and for what purpose to initiate talk; how long to talk; how to demonstrate knowledge; and how to anticipate the type of response that the teacher is expecting. These are all culturally dependent behaviors (Dillon & Searle, 1981). Children whose culture and language are different may find these expected school behaviors very foreign and speak less extensively and expressively than they do at home (Dillon & Searle, 1981).

When the school requires a new language code for students, success depends on their abilities to learn and use the school language code. The nature of the language the students are exposed to in the classroom, and the opportunities they have to practice language and literacy in a supportive environment, are crucial for developing language and literacy for second-language (L2) and nonstandard dialect students.

Teachers' Roles in Language Emergence

What can classroom teachers do to facilitate the emergence of standard English for culturally diverse children? The important things require neither money nor materials. Generally, what is required is a caring person with an instructional framework for planning, organizing, and implementing learning events for the emergence of language and literacy. This teaching framework should include, but not be limited to, the following activities:

1. Interact with students with language that is slower, more clearly pronounced and more fluent, shorter, and syntactically simple, yet formal, high pitched, redundant, and limited to the here and now. Use a high proportion of imperative and interrogative structures related to the students' behaviors (Enright, 1986).

2. Anticipate when unfamiliar concepts will cause confusion and follow the input of information with direct questioning or reformulating misunderstood information when there has been a communication breakdown (Genesee, 1986). Abstract concepts may cause difficulties as well as concepts foreign to students' background experiences.

3. Use students' cultural background experiences, values, and norms to increase the likelihood of learning (Early, 1990; Genesee, 1986; Tikunoff, 1985).

4. Integrate language and literacy learning in thematic content that will enable students to acquire spoken and written English in content (Tikunoff, 1985; Early, 1990). Figure 5.1 provides an example of an instructional web developed along a thematic focus. Books developing language concepts for word opposites are grouped to provide experiences and activities. The theme is designed for a classroom that includes both native English speakers and L2 learners.

5. Accommodate instruction to children's learning rates and English proficiency levels (Early, 1990).

6. Integrate language teaching into academic instruction to ensure academic performance. English medium instruction might begin with low cognitively demanding subjects that provide context-embedded support, such as physical education, art, or even mathematics, and then extend to more cognitively demanding areas (Genesee, 1986).

7. Select activities for learning that involve students in real language and do not fragment language learning (Early, 1990). The conventions of language use should first be implicitly experienced within their context. Emphasize learning from experience and demonstrations, not from completing skill sheets and rote exercises (T. R. Smith, 1990).

8. Provide experiences for students to experiment with language

FIGURE 5.1 Instructional Web: A Wonderful World of Opposites

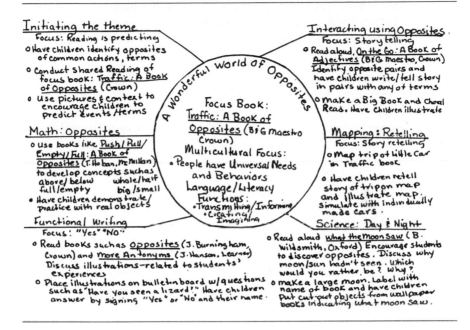

Initiating the theme
Focus: Reading is predicting
o Have children identify opposites
of common actions, terms
o Conduct shared Reading of
focus book: Traffic: A Book
of Opposites (Crown)
o Use pictures & context to
encourage children to
predict events/terms

Math: Opposites
o Use books like Push/Pull/
Empty/Full: A Book of
Opposites (T. Hoban, McMillan)
to develop concepts such as
above/below   whole/half
full/empty   big/small
o Have children demonstrate/
practice with real objects

Functional Writing
Focus: "Yes" "No"
o Read books such as Opposites (J. Burningham,
Crown) and More Antonyms (J. Hanson, Learner)
Discuss illustrations—related to students'
experiences
o Place illustrations on bulletin board w/questions
such as "Have you seen a lizard?" Have children
answer by signing "Yes" or "No" and their name.

A Wonderful World of Opposites

Focus Book:
Traffic: A Book of
Opposites (BIG maestro
Crown)
Multicultural Focus:
o People have Universal Needs
and Behaviors
Language/Literacy
Functions:
o Transmitting/Informing
o Creating/
Imagining

Interacting using Opposites.
Focus: Story telling
o Read aloud, On the Go: A Book of
Adjectives (BIG maestro, Crown)
Identify opposite pairs and
have children write/tell story
in pairs with any of terms
o make a Big Book and Choral
Read. Have children illustrate

Mapping & Retelling
Focus: Story retelling
o Map trip of little Car
in Traffic book
o Have children retell
story of trip on map
and illustrate map.
simulate with individually
made cars.

Science: Day & Night
o Read aloud What the Moon Saw (B.
Wildsmith, Oxford) Encourage students
to discover opposites. Discuss why
moon/sun hadn't seen. Which
would you rather be? Why?
o make a large moon. Label with
name of book and have children
put cut-out objects from wallpaper
books indicating what moon saw.

through made-up rhymes, riddles, songs, and so forth (Barrs, Ellis, Hester & Thomas, 1990).

9. Involve students learning English in collaborative activities with English-speaking peers using realia, equipment, and graphic materials.

10. Involve parents in the education of children at school as well as at home. Strive for a program that will make parents equal partners in the education of their children (Early, 1990; Quintero & Huerta-Macias, 1990).

11. Use a student's first language if you speak it to mediate effective instruction for English second language (ESL) students when you need to ensure clarity of instruction (Genesee, 1986; Tikunoff, 1985). If you do not speak the child's language, use a trained teacher, a bilingual aide, or parental assistance when needed.

12. Assist student understanding by using graphic, physical objects or realia that will develop interrelationships between language modes and meaning. Meaning will be negotiated through the provision of contextual support (Early, 1990; Genesee, 1986).

13. Allow students to use their native language at early stages (Genesee, 1986) and code-switch (alternate between languages) to enhance communication between students and the teacher or aide and to express thoughts and ideas in a natural and precise way (Quintero & Huerta-Macias, 1990).

14. Encourage student discourse by using culturally appropriate teaching strategies. For example, cooperatively group Hispanic American and Native American students. Encourage Chinese American children to proceed on their own, or assist them to acquire discourse rules through dramatic play and role-playing (Tikunoff, 1985).

If L2 children are to be well served in the schools, they should have continued language, literacy, and academic instruction in the first language. There is a high correlation between content-based instruction in the home language and command of English. Essential language, literacy, and thinking processes can be most efficiently learned in the first language and transferred automatically and unconsciously to the second language. The extent of relevant knowledge a learner has about a topic makes comprehension easier, whether the learner is listening or reading (T. R. Smith, 1990).

Classrooms That Facilitate Language Emergence

According to Norman (1990) there are three aspects for talking and listening that should be considered in the classroom:

1. The social aspect is concerned with how people interact as a means of getting along.
2. The communicative aspect refers to how people use talk to transfer meaning.
3. The cognitive aspect refers to how talk is used by people as a means of learning.

Generally, all three aspects should be included in most school activities. Although all need to be balanced in the curriculum, the focus in schools is toward oral language activities, communicative in nature.

These three aspects of oral language are essential for culturally diverse students to learning. These students' only opportunities to interact with majority language speakers may be in school. Further, because of possible differences in cultural orientations, they need to learn school listening and talking discourse for learning how to learn in school.

The classroom teacher can facilitate language emergence for L2 children and at the same time continue language development for other children in the classroom. The classroom should provide an environment that encourages interaction with experienced language users. Classrooms should be places where conversation, discussion, and sharing of knowledge take place. Conversations are opportunities for real talking between and among children and adults that are personal exchanges of ideas, information, or feeling (Eckard & Kearny, 1981). Children should feel that the way they talk is accepted and what they say is valued and important. Children should understand the valuable role of talk in the classroom (Barrs et al., 1990).

When speakers in conversations and discussions are from different cultural groups, misinterpretations may present significant barriers to successful communication. Speakers have to become aware of the verbal and nonverbal signals being exchanged if communication is not to be misinterpreted (Eckard & Kearny, 1981). This must be integrated into the social, communicative, and cognitive aspects of the oral language program for all children.

Classroom Arrangements That Encourage Communication

The classroom needs to be an environment that can be arranged to satisfy many learning contexts, whether children are working in pairs, small groups, or large groups. Most of the furniture in the classroom needs to be movable, adaptable, and multipurpose. Children need to feel free to move and use the furniture as they choose. Classrooms that encourage language emergence and continued development will have an organization and arrangement that provides areas for many learning activities.

Role-Playing Area.   Role-playing activities may be provided in structured learning centers that change in focus according to topics and themes of the classroom. These activities are developed by involving students in the selection, planning, and organization of the area.

Listening and Recording Centers.   Centers for listening and recording are developed with care given to sound absorption (Norman, 1990). Microphones, earphones, and tape recorders will be standard equipment in these centers. Listening tapes can consist of commercial, teacher-made, or parent-made tapes of songs, poetry, and stories. The children should be provided with their own tapes to record their stories, reports, and plans for stories and recording events (Norman, 1990).

Talk Corner. A setting is organized where children will be comfortable to go and talk. Such a spot in the classroom invites children to contribute ideas that would intrigue other classmates for talking. In this center the teacher can post pictures with questions, newspaper items, books, and a telephone with suggestions for characters to call (Norman, 1990). Children who are learning English as a second language are encouraged to use the corner for speaking their first language as well. A sign might be written in multiple languages: "More than one language spoken here!"

Computer Center. A computer center may be provided in the classroom where children might work together in small groups doing collaborative writing on word processors, work cooperatively on programs, or work with an older student or adult who acts as scribe for writing a book.

Whole-Class Sharing Area. An area for children to come together may be arranged where children may sit on a rug to share experiences, discuss, hear stories and books read, be prepared for group activities, and participate in shared reading, writing, and choral speaking. In this spot the teacher will generally adopt a more traditional role of talking (Norman, 1990). The teacher will direct and control the content, direction, and oral participation of students. The nature of the setting demands a more formal and controlled environment so that teacher and student speakers can be heard and responded to by the students.

Reasons Children Talk and Listen

When the curriculum of the classroom is organized with a focus on talk and listening, language will permeate classroom experiences. Children will talk about both school and out-of-school experiences and develop communication skills that allow them to obtain, present, and respond to information in a range of registers required for successful living. Norman (1990) stated that children will talk when they have a variety of purposes and contexts for talk. According to Norman (1990) the following conditions must be met:

1. Children must have someone to talk with and an audience for listening. This two-fold purpose focuses primarily on social and communicative language. Communication provides purpose for sharing information and stimulates need for developing clarity, audibility, self-rehearsal, self-criticism, and selection of appropriate style and register.

2. Children need to have something to say or discuss. The need to communicate is an important motive for speaking, but listening requires something interesting to hear (Norman, 1990). When children are active learners in a classroom they will be involved in sharing and reporting information they learn. When children are empowered to be responsible for their learning they are more likely to be interested in sharing, reporting, listening, and discussing. Topics and themes in a classroom can provide interest for hearing what other children have learned as they focused on some specific aspect of the study.

3. Children need something to learn and/or achieve. What children are to learn must be relevant to their prior experiences, needs, and interests. When children are involved in planning by selecting themes and topics, developing purposes, and deciding what to do, they develop ownership for their learning.

4. Children must have fun with language. Language activities should involve games that provide dimensions for language learning that are not always related to school. This is an opportunity to develop talking and listening that will assist the students with personal community relationships. Fun activities could include riddles and jokes, which can be collected from other cultures. However, riddles and jokes require a level of language sophistication for the L2 children and might require some graphic demonstrations for understanding.

Facilitating Communication Across the Curriculum

A classroom should provide speaking and listening activities in which narrative multicultural literature, poetry, song, role-playing, and drama are used. Children should have opportunities to interact in play situations, work with technology in solving problems and tasks, interact from observations and experiences with media, and use expository materials or academic content as sources and references for information.

When classrooms are organized around themes and topics, teachers can integrate learning across the curriculum and provide for speaking and listening through the use of literacy-related activities. Planning for talk and listening throughout the curriculum is crucial for all children. Norman (1990) suggested the following guidelines, which are appropriate for children in a multicultural classroom:

1. Determine what the children are to learn. (This is a process that children can be involved in through teacher-pupil planning.)

2. Draft the stages of the learning activities.
3. Decide where talk and listening will facilitate learning.
   a. How should the students be involved in planning?
   b. How might the learning tasks be done?
   c. Will students work collaboratively?
   d. What approximate time is needed?
   e. What resources and materials are needed?
   f. What will be the teacher's role?
4. Decide how the work will be monitored and, if groups are being used, how the groups will share with one another.
5. Determine how students might reflect on or learn from their work or project? For example:
   a. What was liked or disliked?
   b. How well did the group work? Did they listen to one another? Did they keep to the point? Was the group involved in the decision making? Did they achieve what they set out to do? If not, why not?
   c. Do they need to improve their talking to increase understanding of listeners? (This can result in taping language and sensitively handling weaknesses and strengths.)
6. Determine how children can record and evaluate their work.

Talking and listening will grow for all children when students are challenged to find words and expressions for explaining what they observe, feel, and mean. To this regard, every learning context in the classroom can be an opportunity for learning language.

STRATEGIES THAT ENCOURAGE LITERACY EMERGENCE

Preschoolers who can identify logos from merchandise commonly used, who recognize and write their own names and those of other family members, and who appear to "read" stories verbatim from their books, are not uncommon in a literate society. Schools might well emulate home environments where literacy emerges so naturally. C. B. Smith (1989b) suggested that "we surround young children with books and with storytelling rather than simply trying to teach them a specific sequence of letters, sounds and high frequency words" (p. 528). He recommended that the best thing for educators to do was to allow children to experiment and try to make literature and print as real as they could by trial and error. Informally having children identify and name letters as they experience writing helps them understand the spelling system and the conventions used in writing. According to Mason (1984) this practice seems preferable to traditional practice in beginning reading programs.

What learning activities will assist children to understand the functional use of print? What practices will give students pleasure and satisfaction from print? How can children learn the pleasure derived from using print for learning? Learning activities should establish concepts and attitudes about print that will facilitate children becoming readers and writers who use print for satisfying learning needs and who derive pleasure from reading and writing.

Activities Involving Environmental Print

Strickland and Morrow (1988) suggested that the classroom emulate functional life experiences of the children in the community. Some communities are so rich in print that there is print from more than one cultural or language group. Functional print is a part of modern life. Children should be involved in labeling functional objects. Daily routines, information and attendance charts, and calendars should be posted. Written explanations should be placed next to children's illustrations and theme or topic illustrations. Thermometers should be used for gathering weather information that is recorded daily. Children should post news or notes they wish to share on special bulletin boards or message boards.

When teachers focus instruction instead on letters, nonsense syllables, words, and print taken out of context, children will not see print used to guide, direct, suggest, entice, aid, announce, and inform, or be used for safety purposes in the world. The environment must be used to observe, predict, and determine print. Then literacy is demonstrated as being important.

Print Walks

The community environment can be a useful teaching tool for all children in a multicultural classroom. The community environment provides for multifaceted learning. All children have prior experiences to relate to the activity. The teacher and the children may explore the school, neighborhood, or nearby shopping centers. Walks into the area surrounding the school provide opportunities for children to use the environment to predict signs and symbols. A youngster of about five or six in Great Britain wrote to a teacher about the signs he had seen on a walk around his school's countrylike neighborhood. The teacher wrote back and asked the boy to draw pictures of the signs so he could see if they were similar to signs used in the United States. He filled a page with detailed signs and told the teacher that these would not be found in America! The boy's teacher, according to A. Robinson, Crawford and Hall (1990), incorporated this walk into a safety theme; the children increased their identification of traffic signs, learned to read vocabulary through predicting, and increased their understanding of the spelling system.

Excellent trade books are available that might either precede a walk in preparation for looking for and reading signs or be used to follow up an environmental trip. These books provide a rationale for learning to read and write. Some books appropriate for children to hear and discuss signs include (Roser & Wilson, 1986):

> Miriam Cohen, *When Will I Read?* (Greenwillow, 1977)
> Ron and Nancy Goor, *Signs* (Harper, 1983)
> Pat Hutchins, *The Tale of Thomas Mead* (Greenwillow, 1980)
> Betsy and Giulio Maestro, *Harriet Reads Signs and More Signs* (Crown, 1981)

At the beginning of the school year, a print walk around the school, combined with getting acquainted with the school and members of the staff, could involve taking Polaroid pictures of people and signs. A group shared writing experience (see explanation in this chapter), illustrated with the actual pictures of the people and sites, would follow. Short stories could be written about each person; who he or she is, what he or she does. An excellent reference for signs is Jann Huizenga's *Looking at American Signs: A Pictorial Introduction to American Language and Culture* (Lincolnwood, IL: Voluntad Publishers, 1985).

Shopping Area

A rich source for print in the environment is the community shopping area. It is also an excellent source for foods and items that are culturally related to children's home lives. Taking a trip (hopefully walking so that print along the way can be seen and predicted) to a shopping area is a learning experience beneficial to all children in a classroom. Whether the trip is to a supermarket, small grocery, or shopping area, students should be directed to locate all the print they can. Also, point out items that are culturally specific. These items should be identified in the languages of children in the classroom when possible.

A Planned Shopping Trip. Arrange with the management the best time to do some shopping. Plan to buy groceries for the children to use to make some item in the classroom. (At least do some simulated shopping if nothing else works out.) In preparation for the trip collect advertisements of food and prices out of the local paper, circulars, or leaflets; collect pictures of food from magazines and catalogues; and collect clean, labeled food packages and cartons. Read and discuss one of the books in the Teacher's Resource Kit about shopping and buying, such as Anne and Harlow Rockwell's *The Supermarket* (Macmillan, 1979).

Have the children identify and group the foods together into the typical categories that would be found in a supermarket or grocery. Plan shopping needs from a recipe with the children. This will be especially effective if the shopping items can be related to a theme or topic, perhaps with a cultural focus. Have students observe the teacher writing the list of items on a chart. Match items on the list with pictures and labels collected. Duplicate the list for all to carry and check off items as they shop. Look at newspaper ads or advertisement circulars and find brand names for the needed items that are on sale.

Have each child carry a pad to copy down any special words that he or she finds interesting along with the shopping list. (Tying half pencils to a small pad with a punched hole works well for young children.) This experience develops a vocabulary for the L2 children and develops speech-to-print relationships for the first language (L1) children.

Point out the print and ask "Why do you think this print is here? What might it say?" (If you have a Polaroid, snap photographs of print the children have found interesting and which have been excellent predicting experiences.) "How do you know that it says that? How is this sign or label used?" If the store uses bilingual signs, ask to have a bilingual worker assist you with reading the signs and follow by reading in English.

While shopping be sure to use signs in the aisles to determine where to find the items, and look on the shelves and decide on the item by brand, size, and price. (In some supermarkets there are computer screens that can be used to locate items by following simple directions shown on the screen. The items are all listed alphabetically. This can lead to an excellent literacy experience.) Have the children check off each item on their shopping list, matching oral or written name to item as they are located.

On your return to the classroom, make an overhead transparency of the computer printout of the items. Have children check off each item on their shopping list. Have L2 children identify the items in their language(s). When possible write these or, if you have a bilingual aide, ask the aide to write these for the children.

Use some of the following literacy-focused follow-up activities:

1. Follow a recipe printed out on chart paper to cook or bake food shopped for on the trip. If it is for a cultural event, have community members assist.

2. Prepare a large map of the neighborhood on butcher or mural paper by drawing out the streets and blocks and have the children trace their route to the shopping center and make the signs they noted at various places. (Polaroids are helpful here for remembering.)

3. Prepare a large piece of mural paper to allow children to plan a picture of the store. Encourage them to write labels and signs on their mural to make it more authentic or use the brand labels collected for a collage effect.

4. Make a collage that simulates the store window using collected labels. Remind children to try to use other languages found in the store. Arrange L2 children throughout the small groups to supply this information.

5. Make a store (structured learning center) in the classroom using real (but empty) cartons, packages, and so on. Discuss with the children how to use the center, the roles to be played in the store, when and how items will be bought and sold, and so forth. Include bilingual items. Include all the literacy experiences that would be required in a store.

6. Make collages of each alphabet letter with pictures from the circulars, newspaper advertisements, and food and clothing catalogues. Small or cooperative groups will take some days to get through the alphabet. (Some letters may have only a few items.) Display posters or collages and sing an alphabet song to help identify and place each poster in the correct order.

Activities Involving Book Talk

Stories are basic for developing reading and writing. Stories provide listeners and readers with a rich variety of language that can be used in talking and writing. Some children learn to read through being read stories. Children learn through this strategy when these become vicarious learning experiences and they have engaged in the demonstration. In the lap method the reader reads to the nonreader and points to the print as it is read. The reader involves the nonreader by asking questions and helping the listener to relate to the story. This is a valuable strategy for all children learning to read, whether in their first or second language.

Telling children stories encourages all children to want to read and write as well. Oral stories also serve as excellent examples of language for both L1 and L2 students. A good storyteller will adapt the story for the listeners and respond to questions and comments, which assists in clarifying meaning as the story progresses.

Some cultures, like the African American culture, have retained a strong oral tradition of storytelling. Virginia Hamilton's *The People Could Fly: American Black Folktales* (Knopf, 1985) is an excellent source for a range of stories in this culture. However, every culture has produced folklore that has been preserved by being told from generation to generation. Folktales from around the world reveal innumerable similarities in plot, style, and theme (Lunge-Larsen, 1981). Folktales are probably one of the easiest ways to initiate and integrate multicultural understandings into the classroom. They provide opportunities for comparison and appreciation of other cultures. They can enhance the self-esteem of children from other cultures. They are excellent opportunities for developing book talk.

Reading Aloud to Students

The language of good books should be seen as it is read. When big books are used, or when a small group gathers around a book and observes it being read, children not only see the language but also see the teacher act as a demonstrator. Elley (1981) pointed out that seeing the printed word may help the L2 learner sort out the tangles of where one word ends and another begins. Many studies (Wells, 1986; Thorndike, 1973; Butler, 1980) have shown that children read to at an early age are the best readers. D. Cohen (1968) found that teachers who read books aloud and did significant activities with them, produced readers whose comprehension and reading vocabulary were significantly ahead of students whose teachers did not.

McKenzie (1978) suggested that the child read back to the reader. For young children this is particularly appropriate with simple texts such as predictable books. McKenzie concluded that this procedure increased the oral language of ESL students. Language with unfamiliar meaning may require ESL learners and dialect speakers to hear the text again and again before they can easily take on the language of the text. Since children generally enjoy hearing a book over and over again, this process would gradually assist the learning reader "to accommodate to the visual constraints of the print, to repeated patterns, eventually recognizing a one-to-one correspondence between the word he says and the form he sees" (McKenzie, 1978, p. 50).

Selecting Books for Reading Aloud. Teachers need to carefully select books for reading aloud, especially when L2 and culturally diverse students are in the group. Well-selected books will be of interest to all children. Books that are read aloud should be selected based on the following qualities:

1. Content is of high interest to the students.
2. Content includes familiar situations, settings, and characters who represent the diverse cultures of society.
3. Unusual words and new structures are presented in good context and repeated frequently in the text.
4. Books are well illustrated, especially when humor and fantasy are involved.
5. Stories can be heard in one sitting, especially for a child who has a limited second language.
6. Major female book characters demonstrate strong nontraditional and traditional roles.

Procedure for Reading Aloud.   In reading aloud a book for a first time, show children the cover and discuss what comes to mind when they see the cover and title, which the teacher or a child reads. Page through the book, scanning the pictures and encouraging the children to predict what the story will be about. Read the story, pausing when appropriate to have children respond to their original predictions, share ideas, and further predict events. Give students an opportunity to discuss the story. Help students to relate to it, and compare characters, plot, and setting to other stories, similar or different. Assist students in recognizing multicultural themes in the book, the cultural behavior of a character, roles for women in society, and so forth.

Encouraging Retelling
Good books are shared with others. Talking about the story enhances story comprehension, sense of story structure, and language complexity of kindergarten children (Koskineri, Gambrell, Kapinus & Heathington, 1988). Retelling, or verbal rehearsal, requires the reader to reorganize the information for a personal rendition. This activity provides language practice and insight for the teacher regarding listening, comprehension, and language production. Retelling extends the enjoyment of a book.

Children will best learn how to retell if the story is read by the teacher who then retells it. Use of story structure may aid students in developing a sense of story when students have limited story experience. After the story has been retold, the children are asked to identify the important elements for telling the story (based on story grammar or structure). They identify the characters of the story, where the story took place, important things that happened, and how the story ended.

Then the children retell the story with the elicited information. This provides the opportunity to practice good language. Assistance in retelling may be provided if students need help. It is particularly important to provide support for L2 students to overcome any hurdle (see the discussion of scaffolding in this chapter). If the story you have selected is suitable, complete the experience by having the story dramatized. The story might be told as it is acted out. With classes having L2 students, this develops a correspondence between action and language. Puppets are another dramatic medium suitable for practicing retelling skills.

Books for the Emergent Reader and Writer

Four types of books suitable for emergent readers and writers support the integrating of speaking, reading, and writing in themes, topics, and student interests. The four types—language development, predictable, big, and literacy-focused—are discussed below.

Language Development Books. In the Teacher Resource Kit Carol Sibley suggested books that can be used in language development. (Sibley is a former school librarian and currently is Curriculum Librarian at Moorhead State University. She is a former teacher and has had experience working in international and urban schools.) These books support the premise that children can learn language through print, and they are particularly helpful in relating concepts to terms. Their illustrative nature pictorially demonstrates the language concept or meaning for young readers and developing L2 users. Further, for students learning English, these books help them see what they hear at the same time (Elley, 1981). The Sibley list is suggested in categories suitable for themes and topics. (Betsy and Giulio Maestro's *Traffic: A Book of Opposites,* Crown, 1981), the focus book in Figure 5.1, is an example of one of these books.)

Moustafa (1980) has an excellent collection of picture books suggested for non-English-speaking children as well. Her list indicates terms and concepts the books are helpful in developing. Most of the books will be found in a good school library, despite the list being dated.

Predictable Books. Highly useful and popular with emerging readers and writers are types of books called predictable. Predictable books have repeating refrains, sentence patterns, or context so rich in clues that the reader or listener can predict what comes next in print. Books with patterns based on rhyming words are popular and are often combined with repetitive refrains. Some books employ the use of enumeration, others are set to music. Teachers working with culturally different children find these books extremely helpful in developing both language and literacy. (They also present patterns that children can use in their own writing.)

Numerous research studies have found that kindergarten and first-grade children using the predictable patterned materials learned significantly more sight words than children using traditional basal materials (Bridge, 1986). Children used semantic and syntactic clues in addition to graphophoneme clues while reading predictable materials. Predictable materials enable the child to learn to read while reading. Heald-Taylor (1987a) reported that children can learn to read naturally through a language arts program based on stimulating literature read to them, without formal instruction. This was also confirmed by Elley (1981) for bilingual readers. Learners scored significantly higher on all tests of comprehension, word recognition, and oral sentence reading in learning to read with predictable material.

Predictable materials allow the emerging reader to interact with print, a process readers do as they read. The emerging reader is able to interact because he or she is confident of the content and uses cueing systems from reading. Relating the oral language to print is an important strategy in the development of a learner's reading ability. Sulzby (1985) determined that when children could build a story across a book's pages, their speech took on the characteristics of either the oral or written language of the book and they demonstrated book-reading behaviors.

Because young children enjoy books with repeated refrains, the repetitive phrases or sentences are easily and quickly learned as they are heard and read. Children usually spontaneously chime in as you read these. Heald-Taylor (1987a, 1989) suggested that predictable books be at the children's level of understanding and contain illustrations that support the text. Ideas adapted from Heald-Taylor (1987b, 1989) for using predictable books with emergent readers from diverse cultures as well as the majority culture include the following:

1. Introduce the book as was suggested in "Procedure for Reading Aloud."
2. Read the book so that the group can see the illustrations and text. Point to the print as it is read. (Demonstrate how to handle and care for the book as it is read.)
3. Stop in appropriate places as the book is read to encourage partic-

ipation. Continue children's prediction of what will happen. (Children from some cultures participate by reacting and responding as the story unfolds. Accept the behavior and encourage it.)
4. Follow the story with a few questions that seek to get students' reactions: What did you think about the story? What was best? Was there a problem in the story? How was it solved?
5. Begin the practice of evaluating books. (This can be expanded as children develop into independent readers.) Encourage the students to rate each book and discuss. Ratings can be recorded on a chart and graphed. (This contributes to functional reading and writing.)
6. Carry on one of the following activities after the book has been read and enjoyed:
   a. Tape the book and place in a listening center for students to listen to and follow along as they hear.
   b. Write repetitive refrains on a sentence strip. As you are re-reading the book, have the children pass the strip along and whoever is holding it stand as the refrain is repeated and hold for all to see it.
   c. Suggest children write their own books by using or modifying the pattern of the book.

Sibley developed a list of predictable books, which is located in the Teacher Resource Kit. (All books were in print at time of publication of this book.) These predictable books may be found as big books or can be used to make big books. Sibley has classified or categorized the books into topics and themes appropriate for students by age. Most are appropriate for non-English-speaking students as well.

Big Books. Big books are enlarged versions of original pieces of literature. The story line is usually very simple, often predictable. Big books can be made by teachers and children or are commercially available. When teachers enlarge stories suitable for doing shared reading, children may be involved in the projects by making illustrations for the book. Big books are particularly effective when multiple child-size copies of the book are available. The latter can be taken home and read, building children's self-esteem. Big books, according to Heald-Taylor (1989), not only introduce the English-language learner to English reading but to new syntax and vocabulary which support oral language development. In addition, big books are excellent motivators for personal writing.

In planning to make big books with children, Heald-Taylor (1987a) suggested that the teacher discuss the book format possibilities with the children; that is, should the book be an exact copy, have new illustrations, or be a totally new version of the story? This becomes an opportunity for the children to learn the format of a book from cover to cover. Heald-Taylor suggested that the text be written in large manuscript on the top of each page, providing ample space for illustrations. Various options for making the illustrations should be presented and children might select pages to do individually or in small groups. Children should be given opportunities to sequence the pages. The pages might be placed along the chart rail so the total book can be seen as it is sequenced. A page in the book is provided for reader comments and the book covers are laminated for durability. The binding of the book can be done simply with a heavy-duty stapler, metal rings, or dental floss stitchings. Stands are now available for big books, or wooden podiums and art easels can be used.

Literacy-Focused Books.   Children need to read books that have characters who read and write. Literacy-focused books provide opportunities for discussion of the importance of reading and writing. They provide purposeful literacy modeling for the young learner (Hall, 1984). One of the most delightful examples of these books is Allan and Janet Alberg's *The Jolly Postman* (Heinemann, 1986). Additional books that will give you a start in using these types of books include:

> Frank Asch, *Good Lemonade* (Franklin Watts, 1976)
> Steven Kellogg, *Pinkerton Beware* (Warne, 1979)
> Robert Kraus, *Leo the Late Bloomer* (Windmill Books, 1971)
> Graham Oakley, *The Church Mice in Action* (Atheneum, 1982)
> Jan Ormerod, *Moonlight,* a wordless book (Lothrop, 1982)
> Jan Ormerod, *Sunshine,* a wordless book (Lothrop, 1981)
> Beatrix Potter, *Yours Affectionately Peter Rabbit* (Warne, 1983)
> Vera B. Williams, *A Chair for My Mother* (Greenwillow, 1982)

Shared Reading

Big books and textual material printed on an overhead projector can be used in shared reading activities. Shared reading requires that student(s) be able to view the print as the book is read. The process is simple and involves repeated readings of the text using strategies that build contextual print awareness.

The suggested sequence for doing a shared reading activity is as follows:

1. Introduce the book to a group gathered around the big book (as suggested in "Procedure for Reading Aloud").

2. Use the following choral reading procedure to read the book the first time.
   a. The children listen as the book is read the first time.
   b. The children follow the teacher's hand or a pointer as the book is read the second time.
   c. The children read with the teacher the third time.
   d. The children read alone in a group the fourth time.
   e. The children are asked who can read each line or the total story. (The teacher assists as help is needed by fading in and out.)
3. Have the children retell the story using the pictures. Then ask who can retell the story individually. Assist as is appropriate to retain the general story content. Discuss what was liked and disliked in the story.
4. For future readings of the story use the following sequence as is appropriate to the needs of the group:
   a. Read only the parts that predict the refrain and have the children "read" the refrain.
   b. Ask the children to volunteer to read the text page by page.
   c. Have the children fill in the missing final word, rhyming word, or key word as the teacher reads and points to the text.
   d. Have the children read the total book as a group and then take turns for each single page.
   Accept the reading as produced by the children. Do not correct their text. Repeated reading is the key for success and word recognition fluency will increase with repeated reading (Samuels, 1979). Children will develop attention to pictures, then form oral stories, next use book talk, and eventually attend to print (Sulzby, 1991).
5. Plan to extend and expand the text with interpretative activities such as drama, puppets, art, music, or dance. Share other books on the topic or theme with the students.

Storytelling

"Storytelling from the worldwide oral tradition celebrates our cultural diversity" (Farrell, 1991, p. 10). If children are told and read many types of stories, they will realize that each type of literature has its own unique language, style, and format. Further, they will recognize culturally stylized methods of telling tales. When children are encouraged to retell stories after hearing them read, it also improves their recall and understanding of the major structural elements, especially if the listener prompts with supportive questions to bring out the structural elements of a story (Morrow, 1985). Oral storytelling is an important feature of many cultures. According to Farrell (1991) it can be a way to connect with the disconnected in the classroom.

Roney (1989) introduced printed versions of stories immediately after telling a story or engaged children in a shared writing activity using a pattern from a story such as Bill Martin's *Brown Bear, Brown Bear, What Do You See?* (Holt, 1983). Roney believed that storytelling helps children learn to read and write because it provides a framework for understanding the text.

Wordless Books.   Wordless books present excellent opportunities for children to develop storytelling skills while developing and increasing language. These beautifully illustrated materials provide opportunities to give attention to sequential thinking, story sense, visual discrimination, inferential thinking, and predicting conclusions (Lindauer, 1988). Because there are no words, only illustrations, the barrier of unfamiliar words is gone for the language-different child, and the illustrations communicate the story. These provide excellent opportunities for all children to tell stories.

Children can learn language through the use of wordless books as well as books with print. They will learn it in a safe and supportive environment if the temptation to correct grammar and sentence structure is resisted. Refinement of oral language can occur in countless other ways during the day through teacher modeling and demonstrations. L2 learning students will ask for vocabulary assistance as they recognize known and unknown concepts.

Lindauer (1988) suggested that although there are countless variations for sharing wordless books with children, they should be introduced by asking, Tell me what is happening here? or What do you see in the picture? When children want to preserve the story they have told with the book, it can be recorded. The listening center can also be converted for recording children's telling. Providing a bell for children to ring when the page changes will give an air of authenticity to the telling, just like a read-along book. Lindauer also suggested using wordless books to develop cooperative group stories. In cooperative stories children take turns, each telling a page of the story. Teachers of L2 students might decide to tape dictated sentences to each page of a wordless book. (This paper or tape should be easily removed without ruining the book.)

Experiences with wordless books can also assist students to minimize their fear of books and print. When children have limited experiences with books, they have limited schema for what is expected and limited knowledge of how to deal with books, let alone how to take from books. Wordless books reduce anxiety and provide a nonthreatening experience for learning how to experience print.

The following selections are excellent wordless book suggestions:

Mitsumasa Anno, *Anno's Counting Book* (Harper, 1977)
Raymond Briggs, *The Snowman* (Random House, 1988)
Margaret Wise Brown, *Goodnight Moon Room* (Harper, 1984)
Tomie de Paola, *Sing, Pierrot, Sing* (Harcourt, Brace, 1983)
Peter Spier, *Peter Spier's Rain* (Doubleday, 1982)
Ed Young, *Up a Tree* (Harper & Row, 1983)

Storytelling Favorite Books.   One day as a first grader was retelling her reading, the teacher realized how sketchy the retelling was. She said, "Pretend you are going to tell this story to kindergarteners, and tell the story again." The difference was significant. This led to developing an activity designed to contribute to improving children's understanding of story concept. In addition, oral communicative skills developed as well. Children were given opportunities to be creative through elaborating and extending a known story though storytelling, which is culturally relevant to many diverse cultures found in American communities. Further change was also noted in the children's story-writing quality. The storytelling strategy follows:

Day One.   The children are told a cumulative story with an excellent story line using a flannel board (Verna Aardema, *Bringing the Rain to Kapiti Plain* [Dial, 1981]). The children are encouraged to use the flannel pieces in retelling the story.

Day Two.   The book from which the story was taken is read, and the pictures are shared as the class progresses through the book. The written story is discussed and compared with the oral story. The children are asked if they would like to tell a story. It could be told to another class, perhaps a younger group.

The children are asked for ideas that would be helpful in selecting a good story to tell and write on a chart.

Locating stories and how to get ready for the telling are discussed. (The Sibley lists in the Teacher Resource Kit may be used for book suggestions.)

Day Three.   The children discuss what the storyteller must do to tell a good story. How should a story be told so that everyone will listen? Suggestions are elicited and written on a chart to be displayed in the room.

Materials are available for the children to make props or flannelboard pieces for telling the story. Children are encouraged to draw pictures for their stories. As children finish they are placed in pairs to practice telling their stories using the props, pictures, and flannel pieces. The class discusses how students can help a partner improve the telling. The children focus on talking so everyone can understand the story.

Day Four. The children discuss what they must remember in telling the story. When a story is told what must the listener learn? The children make suggestions which are recorded on a chart.

The children are divided into cooperative groups of three, with roles that will rotate between teller, responder, and helper. Responders are to help the teller in following the suggestions on the chart by asking questions not understood from the story. Helpers are to let the responder know if he or she is asking the right questions.

Day Five. The children tell their stories to small groups of children and time is provided for the children who wish to tell stories every day at a storytime.

Observations. As the children were observed telling their stories, the teachers realized that they had been practicing their stories at home. There was a general feeling of enthusiasm in the class, no one seemed reluctant to tell a story. The teachers were amazed at the length of some of the stories and how well the children told the stories.

Telling Folktales. Folktales are an important ingredient in learning about a culture. Teachers concerned about developing a multicultural classroom will want to use folktales as a means of building bridges to other cultures. Folktales are important for language-different students because they may not have the allusions, assumptions, and cultural context important for comprehension of the language found in materials used for other reading and listening. When children realize their rich cultural heritage they will be stimulated to learn to tell stories from their cultural tradition.

Folktales tend to be concerned with themes such as conflict between good and evil and strength and weakness. Folktales present struggles and suffering, but kindness, humility, and patience generally prevail. When listening to stories from other cultures, children learn certain expectations about the characters in the tales which build understandings about how a people perceive notions such as wickedness, bravery, cleverness, goodness, and wisdom embodied in the characters. Although the exact characters representing these notions may differ from culture to culture, language-different students probably expect these characteristics to be found and thus the concepts are more easily learned (Lunge-Larsen, 1981).

The following suggestions are for telling folktales:

1. Select a folktale you like, enjoy, and want to tell. It is best to select folktakes from among the universal catergories of tales—animal tales, cumulative tales, explanatory tales, numbskull tales, and hero tales—and to consider the age group of listeners (Lunge-Larsen, 1981). A list of appropriate folktales is suggested as one of the categories in Sibley's List of Predictable Books for Emergent Readers in the Teacher Resource Kit. Other sources of folktales include the following:

> M. R. MacDonald, *The Storyteller's Sourcebook. A Subject, Title, and Motif Index to Folklore Collection for Children* (Neal-Schuman Publishers, 1982)

> M. A. Jagendorf and Virginia Weng, *The Magic Boat and Other Chinese Folk Stories* (Vanguard Press, 1980)

> Emerson Coatsworth and David Coatsworth, *The Adventures of Nanbush: Objiway Indian Stories* (Atheneum, 1980)

2. Know the general idea and scope of the story. Stories should not be memorized; they are not meant to be the same each time. Farrell (1991) suggested blocking, structuring, or diagraming the story into content chunks for remembering. Every storyteller changes his or her story a bit (Lunge-Larsen, 1981). Practice telling the story aloud to learn it by heart but not word for word (Farrell, 1991).

3. Tell the story simply, directly, and sincerely with freedom and ease, involving natural body movement (Tooze, 1959). Get started by establishing the setting. Some people wear something special to establish a mood. Lunge-Larsen (1981) described the way in which Eskimos pass a rock around and let each person hold it for a second to warm it up and release the stories in it. The person holding the rock may tell a story.

4. Personalize the story by giving characters in the story children's names; give characters simple differences in voice, gesture, and expression. (For more information on storytelling see Farrell (1991).)

Activities That Facilitate the Emergence of Writing

Learning to write requires much more than just learning the alphabet and copying and tracing letters, words, and sentences. In fact, copying and tracing practices should probably be discouraged as a teaching strategy. If children want to copy or trace, it should originate from them. Copying exercises probably do not encourage writing to emerge. Instead, it may encourage children to rely on others for writing and thinking. Copying and tracing teach children that they can not write unless it is written correctly. This frame of mind inhibits development.

Dyson (1985) reported that not all children can monitor the message being copied—some may focus on forming letters not on composing. She stated that "one cannot break apart the writing act (separating meaning formation and mechanical forming of letters) and preserve the essence of the cognitive program of writing, which is, for young children, how intentions and read messages converge in written symbols" (p. 509).

Establishing a Classroom Environment that Encourages Writing

Writing, like reading and talking, should happen throughout the classroom. Consequently, there should be many locations where writing is ongoing. These locations might change as the classroom environment evolves with different themes and topics.

Most teachers who are successful in encouraging student writing have spots in the classroom where students are invited to write independently and in collaborative small groups. The independent writing areas are located in a quieter part of the classroom. They are stocked with writing paper, blank books, writing instruments, and art materials for illustrating. There may be a word processor or typewriter.

Practices that Facilitate Writing Emergence

Heald-Taylor (1984) found that when first graders were encouraged and supported in writing, children who scribble-wrote were able to use scribble to communicate a message, had developed appropriate directionality, had achieved manipulative control of their writing instruments, had developed sentence and spatial awareness, and had integrated their scribble with print to communicate a message.

Young learners learning English as a second language need to experience English print much as native speakers. They need to be immersed in print as a necessary condition for their development. Young children from literate non-English-speaking homes are observant of print that surrounds them in their environment. In the Manchester Writing Project in Manchester, Great Britain, indications of the first language in children's scribble-writing or mock writing were noted. The writing of children from culturally diverse homes demonstrated symbols from their first language as well as English. Print gradually began to resemble written language and conventional spelling, whether the children were learning to read and write in one or more languages. Children from all cultures in the community progressed through similar development.

Having literate community members demonstrate writing in a language other than English will impress upon children the need and importance for learning to write, even if the literacy program is only English. Community members need to be regular and welcomed members of the classroom. All children need the opportunity for exploration in the acquisition of written language. Schools are too often in a hurry to develop skills and make up for what is perceived as lost educational time for children learning English. All children must be allowed time to develop naturally.

A number of teaching practices hold promise in facilitating writing emergence for children from all cultures represented in the community. These practices include the following:

1. The learners must view the teacher writing. Learners need to observe letter formation, sentence and paragraph construction, as well as various forms of writing. Interaction with a teacher is important for facilitating the emergence of writing.

2. Plan experiences that develop a personal interest and need for learning to write.

3. Place ideas that will stimulate writing around the room—questions, a book, a letter to respond to, or a tape recorder to interview someone for getting information. When possible, post an alphabet from each minority culture represented in the classroom so children can use it.

4. Include writing activities that will support themes and topics or ongoing projects in the classroom—like making a menu for a café or writing a letter to apply for a job as a salesperson in a shoe shop.

5. Writing may be used when the teacher aids students to solve problems posed, respond to questions asked, or simulate real-life experiences.

6. Include writing in the classroom from the cultures of children in the classroom. Literate parents and community members from all language groups in the community should be invited to take dictation and assist in bookmaking activities.

Providing Variety in Writing Experiences for Emergence

McKenzie (1985) specified that there should be four types of opportunities and purposes for writing for younger children: shared writing, dictated texts, curriculum-related writing, and individual writing. Three additional writing experiences provide valuable teaching activities: dictated books, parallel stories, and key words.

Shared Writing.   Shared writing is a teaching strategy in which the teacher and students cooperatively develop and create writing. The teacher listens to children's ideas, and through questioning and comments assists in the production of text. The teacher's role is to suggest appropriate language, focus the writing, and, in general, guide the children's discussion toward a growing awareness and understanding of language and writing. The teacher helps students to develop more precise meanings and to expand and extend their language usage.

In shared writing the teacher plays a key role in shaping the writing through developing an understanding of the patterns of writing. The teacher's comments and questions focus attention on important aspects appropriate for this particular piece. This is especially important for culturally and linguistically different students who may need this directed attention. It is an opportunity to discuss how writing works, both the composing and transcribing processes.

Shared writing is a powerful tool because the teacher works with children in meaningful and relevant writing. In this strategy, children become apprenticed to a literate demonstrator—the teacher. During their apprenticeship they learn how ideas can be developed for stories or other texts and how to organize them into words, sentences, and longer forms of discourse (McKenzie, 1985). Most important, the children see a competent language user in collaboration with them, composing and transcribing. Consequently, community members in such a role make an important impression on the young learner.

Shared writing is an opportunity to use scaffolding to assist student writing. Scaffolding is a useful technique for students from all cultural communities. In scaffolding, experienced readers and writers elaborate and expand a learner's attempts to use language and facilitate effective communication beyond the learner's actual linguistic capability (Boyle & Peregoy, 1990). The experienced language user models graphic, syntactic, and semantic skills, as well as discourse, and models and demonstrates for the learners.

Students learning a second language can profitably engage in writing well before they have gained control over the cueing systems. Scaffolding supports students in comprehending and producing written language beyond their competence. As they gain control, their writing gradually begins to approximate standard English. Patterns from the books read to children act as effective writing scaffolding techniques. Many books found in Sibley's List of Predictable Books for Emerging Readers in the Teacher Resource Kit use language that will aid emerging writers. For example: Stan Mack's *Ten Bears in My Bed* (Pantheon, 1974) and two books by Charlotte Zolotow, *If It Weren't For You* (Harper, 1987) and *Someday* (Harper, 1965) provide excellent scaffolding writing patterns for both L1 and L2 learners.

Just about any writing can be done as shared writing—notices, signs, poems, verses for songs, news articles, stories, letters, reports, and classroom diaries. However, the following suggestions are centered around trade books:

1. Teach a song that has action words and a repetitive chorus. Then encourage children to make it into a story. Plan with the children where the illustrations will go, their size, and relation to the text. Expect to do a rough draft to assist children in developing the illustrations. (See Arnold Lobel, *Singing Bee!* (Lothrop, 1982) for songs and familiar nursery rhymes. Songs from American cultural groups have been collected and published. Some like Ashley Bryan's *I'm Going to Sing: Black American Spirituals* (Antheneum, 1982) are available for students. Sibley also lists songs in the predictable book list in the Teacher Resource Kit.)

2. Take a familiar story such as Pat Hutchins' *Rosie's Walk* (Macmillan, 1972). Remove all the content words leaving only the structure or functional words (Observed in Bill Pogge's first grade classroom, Probstfield School, Moorhead, Minnesota). Write the sentence frames on a chart and have the children discuss and compose new content for a story. Plan what and where the illustrations will be and where to place the print.

3. Use enjoyable nonsense rhyme patterns to develop books in large or small groups. Examples of patterns might be taken from books like *Oh, That's Ridiculous,* edited by William Cole and illustrated by Tomi Ungerer (Puffin Books, Viking Penguin, 1972) such as William Brightly Rands' poem *Godfrey Gordon Gustavus Gore.* Children love playing with names in language. Poems such as these provide opportunities to have good fun with language.

4. Write group takeoffs from traditional Mother Goose rhymes. These rhymes are excellent models for writing as well as for listening. Suitable Mother Goose books include:

> Marguerite de Angeli, *Marguerite de Angeli's Book of Nursery and Mother Goose Rhymes* (Doubleday, 1979)

> James Marshall, *James Marshall's Mother Goose* (Farrar, 1979) (wonderful cartoon illustrations!)

> Brian Wildsmith, *Brian Wildsmith's Mother Goose* (Oxford University Press, 1982)

McCracken and McCracken (1983) offered examples of suitable Mother Goose nursery rhymes for writing takeoffs. "Sing a Song of Sixpence" became (p. 73):

> Sing a song of Big Mac,
> Sesame Bun,
> Two all-beef patties,
> Very well done.
> Onions, pickles, lettuce
> . . . .

5. Use any seasonal topic or theme for writing. For example, John Burningham's *Seasons* (Bobbs-Merrill, 1969) is a book that has a simple pattern that would be easily emulated and is beautifully illustrated with very large print, visible to any group sitting around the teacher and listening. Each season begins the same. This model provides an excellent pattern for children to use in creating their own book and is another example of scaffolding. "Summer is (ripening corn, holidays, buzzing bees, heat waves, and thunderstorms). . . ." Such a book provides the opportunity for children to learn new concepts for each of the seasons.

6. Use counting books, alphabet books, and books about colors. Examples of counting books are Eric Carle's *The Very Hungry Caterpillar* (Putnam, 1989) and Molly Bang's *Ten, Nine, Eight* (Greenwillow, 1983). Examples of alphabet books are Edward Lear's *An Edward Lear Alphabet* ((Lothrop, 1983) and Cheryl Willis Hudson's *Afro-Bets ABC Book* (Justus Books, 1987). Such books provide fun activities for children in listening and then a basis for composing and illustrating. Many of these types of books, like the Lear book, use enjoyable language rhymes. Most counting and alphabet books are excellent models for doing some very creative illustrations with multimedia.

Dictated Texts.   Using dictated texts the teacher records student dictated information and ideas. Many teachers worry about using children's dictated material for reading and writing, fearing that children will not learn the key basal language essential for reading success. On the contrary, language used in the student-authored texts is sophisticated and has complete or nearly complete episodes (Sampson, Briggs & Sampson, 1986). The style generally provides sample practice of key language for reading and writing.

According to Froese, 1977 there are four types of dictating experiences:

1. Personal language
2. Narrative language
3. Functional language
4. Conceptual language

Personal Language. Personal language dictation provides learners with opportunities to see their speech written down for the purpose of transcription—the relationship between speech and writing. The teacher places no pressure on the children to read back the writing or copy. Personal dictation can be encouraged when a child has drawn a picture and is asked to tell about the picture. The child's response might only be a single word or phrase. As the teacher writes he or she tells the child the word and perhaps discusses the letters or letter formations. At this time the teacher might also expand on single responses and ask questions to elicit further information.

Narrative Language. Narrative language dictation involves recording a real experience or an imaginary experience for the narrator(s). These narratives are made into books, either regular size books or big books. When the narratives are made into books they are usually shared with other children by being read aloud and/or placed in the classroom or library. These stories may be read back using the choral reading procedure, or they may be prepared for "publication."

Functional Language. Functional language dictation involves having pupils dictate plans for activities, tasks, or ideas that the teacher and children decide should be remembered. These activities provide a vehicle for developing functional language. Examples of functional language experiences are rules dictated for a trip or the brick-making process observed in a trip to the brick factory.

Conceptual Language. Conceptual language dictation provides opportunities for children to develop new understandings or to conceptualize ideas held. In developing conceptual language the teacher elicits ideas and moves the children to a higher conceptual level, perhaps through classification or categorization of terms students have listed or compared. The students learn, through the teacher's intervention, new concepts or generalizations.

Dictated Books.   Herring (1989) provided an excellent suggestion for narrative language dictation. Parents, caregivers, and community members were involved in helping children write and publish a book. Children in Herring's reception (kindergarten) class in Manchester, Great Britain, developed books with parent volunteers, some bilingual, through the process of dictating, drafting, editing, and illustrating during four afternoon sessions. Herring's goal was to help children understand that authorship required certain kinds of responsibilities toward the text and reader. Herring's project was carried out as part of her school's involvement with the Manchester Writing Project, a part of the National Writing Project.

Since younger children were to be the audience for the books, Herring felt it essential that her students meet and talk to the child audiences. She invited parents to bring their preschool children to be the audiences for the books. Working with some local volunteers, Herring provided care for the younger children when the parents were involved with the students from her class. Parents were given a presession in which Herring explained the parents' role in making a book. It was hoped that they would go beyond being scribes and make suggestions, offer thoughts, and invite children to reflect upon what was written. Parents were shown books made by children, and Herring talked with them about how children authored and illustrated. Concerns were addressed, such as the amount of direction they were expected to give, their handwriting and spelling.

Parents in the study demonstrated sensitivity by keeping the children on track, rereading, encouraging children to go on composing, and quietly asking questions and prompting children to clarify what was being composed. Bilingual parents involved in the project chose not to work with their own children nor with other L2 children. This provided for a richer learning environment for all children involved in the project.

When one parent in the project was called away due to a family illness, one of the writing project staff worked with her writing team of two boys, one an L2 learner. Each youngster clearly had specific ideas for the story content, and after a story structure was established the adult facilitator and young writers finally worked out the authoring situation by having each child take responsibility for alternate pages in the book while the other served as reader and reactor. The facilitator was able to use some scaffolding in helping these boys with vocabulary and sentence patterns, but they clearly kept a tight control of the content and illustrations of their book. By the time they had finished the project both boys could read the total text without assistance.

The children did not give up their control of the text in working with the parent volunteers. Although they listened to what the parents contributed, in the end they made up their own minds about what they wanted to author. Herring (1989) stated that working with the parents increased the confidence of the children as authors. At the end of the project the children produced books which were passed on to the intended reader. Each book was unique, some were further adventures of favorite characters, others involved experiences of the students and consequently reflected their cultural community. Many were completely original creations of the students.

In dictated language narratives, a child's speech is written down exactly as the child expresses it. After it is transcribed, the language is read back, and the child is asked, "Is this right? Is it what you wanted to say?" The statement is worked on until it says what the child wants (Heald-Taylor, 1989). When the text satisfies the student, the teacher asks to have it read back. The aim in asking the children to read rather than tell the story is to encourage children to view themselves as writers (Martinez & Teale 1987).

Will the children be able to read the dictated texts they write? In the beginning, the children will probably remember what is in the stories. They may be able to recognize words that have special meaning to them. They will learn from dictation activities how writing and reading work, how to make meaning in writing, and how to take meaning from reading. They should read over and over again the stories they have composed, just as they reread or ask to hear favorite books countless times.

Children should be encouraged to use the charts, posted stories, and dictated books as supportive materials for writing. Gradually, students will develop vocabulary, word discrimination, and spelling competencies to become independent readers and writers.

Parallel Stories.   Gillet and Gentry (1983) suggested that a parallel story technique be used when the teacher wishes to model language in relation to that used by the children in a language experience approach (LEA) story. (LEA is an approach in which children learn to read and write by dictating real language to the teacher and composing stories and text.) The parallel story provides culturally diverse and language-different children with vocabulary and sentence structure they may not be able to produce but can comprehend. The teacher should use the vocabulary related to the sentence patterns and develop a story that parallels the children's story. In using parallel stories the teacher should tell the children that he or she had wanted to write a story about the topic, too. Next, the story should be shared using the choral reading procedure. This demonstrates language for the children and does not violate the retention of children's exact dictated language, which is needed to build a bridge between oral speech and print.

Key Words. A strategy that can be used by ESL/bilingual teachers is the key words procedure. The key words procedure is simple and begins as soon as a student has a minimum communicative oral language. The procedure, adapted from Veatch, Sawicki, Elliott, Flake, and Blakey (1979), is a variant of the approach popularized by Silvia Ashton-Warner (Blakey, 1983). Ashton-Warner developed this strategy while working with Maori children in New Zealand. The following procedure was adapted from Veatch et al. (1979):

1. Elicit the key words from each child by asking the child questions such as: What is the "best" word you can think of? What is the scariest thing you know? What is your favorite food? What is the nicest thing you can think of? What is your favorite animal?

2. Print the word, phrase, or sentence elicited from the child on a large piece of paper with a marker (Cochrane et al., 1984) or use filing cards. Ask the learner questions like, Do you know what letter this word starts with or ends with? Have the child assist in naming any known letter as the word is printed. When letters are unknown name them as the word is written (Cochrane et al., 1984).

3. Talk about the word, phrase, or sentence with the child—immerse the child in language, drawing out experiences the student has had with the word, why it was selected, and so on. This will increase the importance of the word and aid the child in retaining the visual representation.

4. Suggest that the student illustrate the word on the back of the paper or card. Discuss the student's ideas for the illustrations. Key words written on large paper might be bound into books that are shared with the class. Cards can be punched with a hole and kept on a ring (Cochrane et al., 1984). When the words are placed on cards they can be used for categorizing, sharing, writing, even a game of Concentration.

The key words strategy is a useful strategy but one that should not be extended for too long a period. Its value is in developing awareness of print and seeing a relationship between oral language and print. When children have not had extensive experience with the print of a language and have a limited oral language, the strategy may fill in gaps. It is especially helpful for bilingual students learning to read in their first language and transferring the learning to the second language. Children might also use the word cards much like a dictionary or a source for writing. However, key words should only be used in conjunction with the other holistic strategies suggested in the chapter.

Curriculum-Related Writing. When classroom literacy activities are planned, they must be tied authentically to the questions and interests of the children (Franklin, 1988). If children create their own text, they will respond to content materials in a more personal and interested manner. Students need opportunities to pursue their interests about life, the community, and nature. Themes and topics must be developed in the classroom that will interest, motivate, and stimulate children to want to read and write. Fact and fantasy can often be integrated in content writing. Fantasy can be based on learned facts.

Curriculum themes or topics that provide opportunities for extending imagination through fantasy and fiction while still concentrating on nonfiction are appropriate at any level. In addition, there is no reason why fiction cannot lead into nonfiction or fantasy to realistic study. John Steptoe's *Stevie* (Harper, 1969) can provide an excellent beginning for students learning to cope with their feelings. Ina R. Friedman's *How My Parents Learned to Eat* (Houghton, 1984) provides opportunities for studying how different cultures can exist side by side. These types of books can contribute to understanding the integration of diverse cultural elements in U.S. society. They serve as ideas and models for student writing. Children can respond in journals after reading or listening to such books.

Individual Writing. Various strategies and practices encourage individual student writing. Individual writing activities should be ongoing in the classroom along with other reading and writing activities.

Labeling. Dyson (1983) suggested that children's first representational writing serves to label their world. Children's talk should provide meaning for these labels. Children begin with a limited set of letters to label what they know in their world—their names, names of family members, perhaps labeled objects or places in their environments.

Labeling is a common type of individual writing. It is not surprising that labeling is important to the emergent reader and writer because labels and lists surround children in their environment. All food and clothing are labeled. Brand labels are important. Children learn this early by "helping" select groceries or buy clothing. Signs such as street and building names are really labels as well. To some extent menus, telephone directories, and calendars are also label-like.

Labeling is an effective teaching strategy for all children. Names of the objects in the classroom environment are written on each object or next to the object as they are learned or discussed. Putting the words in oral sentence patterns further expands language by visualizing speech. When teachers develop situations in which children dictate or independently list words they know, spoken language is related to written language.

Messages. Messages are an important part of children's daily lives. Children observe family members give and take messages from the telephone, leave other family members notes, and write messages to friends or coworkers. Teachers in the Manchester Writing Project in Great Britain, recognizing the functional value that messages had for encouraging writing and reading, provided notice boards (bulletin boards) in their classrooms for children to post messages for others. Classrooms with home centers had a notice board for children to leave messages on. These were covered with messages. There were messages in languages other than English. Play phones had message pads next to them for children to use in writing notes. These message boards and pads provided opportunities to use writing in a functional manner, and they provided teachers with information about the children's writing development. Teachers also left messages on the notice boards or attached one to a story a child had written to increase children's understanding of the importance of writing for communication.

Journal Writing. Journal writing is a form of writing that has gradually received more and more attention. Journal writing is a means for encouraging written expression from preschool through adult education. There are two different types of journals that can be used with children: dialogue and response. Dialogue journals are conversations in writing between the student and teacher (Gambrell, 1985). Response journals, a borrowed form from secondary school and adult experience, are used for research and writing ideas and reflections or reactions on reading. Response journals should be a source for personal educational growth. Journal writing is a powerful technique for the multicultural classroom because it is personal, develops interaction, and provides an opportunity to develop self-expression. It provides the teacher with an opportunity to increase student self-esteem while developing writing ability.

Dialogue journal writing provides an opportunity to integrate reading and writing. This makes the medium very powerful. Children are able to use their knowledge of the writing system to communicate in a meaningful manner. The response from the adult models conventional spelling and mechanics, elaborating on the child's entry. This exposes the learner to indirect editing in a manner that will lead to his or her internalizing the conventionalities (Bode, 1989). Another reason for the powerfulness of the medium is that the process actually provides a means for personalizing education for students at a most crucial period in their development. Bode (1989) found that this empowered teachers to respond at children's developmental levels.

Dialogue journals can be started with emergent readers and writers by encouraging children to select a drawing or draw a picture and dictate information about it. They can observe the teacher writing back a response (Bode, 1989; Kintisch, 1986). Children who are comfortable in using invented spelling may be encouraged to write first and then draw their pictures. Each entry should be very personalized and read aloud if necessary. If children are having trouble with a first-entry topic (Gambrell, 1985), they may discuss something they would like to do for a writing entry. This is an excellent way to get to know children and can lead to long sharing communications.

Response journals are often ignored by teachers of emergent readers and writers. However, response journals are a means of encouraging reading interaction. At this stage in children's development, teachers probably will not wish to use the strategy as a daily activity. They may wish to only use it as a way for personalizing instruction for those students who have already advanced in reading and writing.

The nature of these journals must be personal. Consequently, children must understand that their responses must be honest reactions. The teacher models this through his or her own responses to books liked or not liked very well. The use of sentence lead-ins can get students started in responding. For example:

> I really like/dislike . . .
> (Character in story) reminds me of . . .
> (Character in story) is like . . .
> If I were (name of character), I would . . .
> This book is very much like . . .

Follow these types of statements by inviting the students to respond by agreeing or disagreeing.

Responses should not be in the same journal as the dialogue journal. They might be done on separate pieces of paper and later bound for a record or kept in a bound book.

For teachers who have not had experience with journals before, Carline, Crawford, and Babb (1988) suggested the following six strategies:

1. Use bound composition books if possible. Gambrell (1985) suggested that children can make bound books by stapling together appropriate writing paper with a construction paper cover.

2. Begin the journal experience by relating it to letter writing. Build upon the personal aspects of the interaction and the privateness of the exchange.

3. The teacher can develop a rapport with the students in their journals by sharing his or her own experiences as well. His or her response is focused on getting students to express themselves. This will involve eliciting clarifying statements about their feelings, asking questions to expand their thinking and ideas, and relating their reactions to his or her own or perhaps to other children, a situation, or a character in a book they have read. The teacher's responses should always indicate understanding and contribute to a student's self-worth.

4. Do not correct or have students rewrite their entries. Think of ways to subtly model the correct form. Although this may not be immediately integrated by the student, it will eventually be more effective and will keep them responding.

5. Keep students writing by using responses that show interest in them, such as the following:

> Tell me more about . . .
> My that was really . . .
> What else . . .?
> How did . . .?
> When did . . .?

These responses show concern in them as a person.

6. Set aside a time every day for journals, either dialogue or response or both.

The great value of journals is that children write daily and receive daily responses. Strackbein and Tillman (1987) suggested that the time be a short period at the beginning and that setting a timer may have a positive effect. If children are worried about spelling, they should be encouraged to attempt the word or draw lines to indicate unknown words. (These would be the only words ever written for the children in their journals.) If the whole class is writing in journals at one time, the teacher may also wish to write as well. In this way the teacher will model for the children. If the teacher is writing or working with other children, he or she will not be able to help with words. Although some children may be frustrated without assistance at first, this does encourage them to work on speaking and writing relationships themselves. Children should know that writers usually get down their ideas first and worry about spelling later; this may help.

Dialogue and response journals are excellent strategies for L2 learners as well. Children should be encouraged to write in both languages. If the teacher is not literate in the student's first language, a parent or member of the child's language community may be located — one who is willing to assist by taking dictation, even establishing a journal or letter-writing relationship. (Another alternative is to locate an older literate student who might be able to provide some writing assistance and modeling for the child through letter-writing.)

Journals provide similar interactions as found in oral language, and they focus on known topics and interests of the student. This is particularly valuable for L2 students. Journals allow learners to bring meaning to the writing, receive increased contact time with the teacher, express themselves without fear of censure or embarrassment, and relate experiences that are happening in their daily lives with language (Peyton, 1986).

Letters, Cards, and Notes.   Other forms of personal writing that will functionally and meaningfully engage young children in classrooms are letters, cards, and notes. Two studies conducted in Great Britain with reception-age children gave some insight into the powerful nature of the letter as a dialogue (Rowcroft, 1989; Robinson et al., 1990). Rowcroft (1989) reported that children were reflective in the ways they approached crafting letters and were capable of operating on many different levels at one time. Although their work was not always recognizable in conventional terms, to "say that because children's work does not appear to be conventional means that authorship is too difficult for them is to miss the essential qualities of the things that children actually do" (Rowcroft, 1989, p. 37).

Robinson et al. (1990) concluded in their report of the first two years of a letter exchange that from the beginning young children functioned efficiently and appropriately as correspondents. They revealed an ability to handle dialogue and the relationships implicit in the dialogue, as well as being able to accommodate the social and spatial distance of exchanging letters with adults. They developed in their first letters from being able to tell about themselves, ask about the receiver of the letter, and refer to a shared experience to being able to generate novel topics, sustain topics, and close topics. The children were able to employ in their letter writing "interpersonal skills that they had developed through being socially, psychologically and linguistically proficient in their everyday lives" (Robinson et al., 1990, p. 116).

School-written language may actually require a narrow range of linguistic demands and deny children the right to use the language they know. As a result, they often have to write safely. Children in the Robinson et al. (1990) sample linked talk with literate language and demonstrated a move toward control over formal literate requirements. In both letters and dialogues children can draw upon their knowledge of oral discourse to be used in becoming literate.

Bill Pogge set up mailboxes in his first-grade classroom made from milk cartons a few weeks before the Christmas holiday to encourage letter writing. Children were encouraged to write to each other, to him, and to a researcher in the class twice weekly. (This was in addition to the dialogue journals.) The letters provided a medium for children to use their emerging and developing writing abilities in very personal and functional ways.

The teacher and researcher noted that many children practiced again and again variants of the same message in their letters. Letters allow this type of practice, just as oral language allows us to practice variants of the same message. Responding personally about the pleasure one has in seeing the development of a child is very affirming and seems even more convincing when the time is taken to write it in a letter. Letters also provide information about children's literacy development. When the researcher's mother died that year the children wrote unedited cards with notes. The following selection from an Asian American child shows the carryover from Bill's journal-dating procedure. It indicates the ability to relate a situation, be philosophical, give advice, and respond with a caring aspect in written form.

> She'll always be with you 2-15-88
> Dear _____
> I am sorry for your Mom because.
> everyone dies too an I am sad, for
> you too
> She'll always
> Love you
> Cheer up
> Love,

The child had been in the United States since infancy and attended a Head Start program and an ESL pull-out program in her kindergarten year and was not receiving any special English-language instruction at this time. The child's general behavior in the classroom was quiet and usually required being invited to speak in a group. The researcher received frequent letters and often had special artwork addressed to him in his mailbox. These were opportunities to write back to the child to sustain the letter exchange.

STRUCTURING LANGUAGE AND LITERACY DEVELOPMENT FOR L2 LEARNERS

Language learners will begin generating language as they acquire oral language. A strategy adapted from Moustafa and Penrose (1985) and Moustafa (1987) provided a means to assist students in generating language with literacy as the focus. Moustafa and Penrose developed an approach that combines an LEA with Krashen's (1982) and Krashen and Terrell's (1983) concept of comprehensible input (understanding through context). The Moustafa and Penrose strategy provided limited English speakers with extensive repetition of comprehensible input, including expanded vocabulary and syntax, preceding the dictating of text (LEA).

Moustafa (1987) later studied 58 limited-English-speaking students in grades four through six using comprehensible input plus LEA. These students had not had the opportunity of language arts instruction in their primary languages. When students had a 2.5 oral language age, as was measured by the Peabody Picture Vocabulary Test, they were given repeated comprehensible input plus LEA using a large study print or illustration. Children demonstrated transfer of learning by reading with ease and dictating stories based on the study prints of other groups. In addition, they were able to read print not taught through the literacy lesson.

The following strategy adapted from Moustafa and Penrose (1985) and Moustafa (1987) is suggested for emergent L2 readers and writers:

1. Choose an illustration that will expand the children's language, or plan a real experience. Any illustration should be related to children's real-life experiences. Include appropriate realia for the children to examine, if possible.

2. Elicit names of the setting, characters, objects, and actions in the illustration: Where are they? What are they doing? What is this? If it is

the recall of a common experience, ask: Where did we go? What did we do? Who did . . . ? If children fail to name or recall the event, object's name, or situation, supply the answer. Reaffirm correct answers. Work through every character and action in the picture or the event. Keep repeating the process until the relevant information has been learned.

Moustafa and Penrose (1985) stated that children "need to hear a message many times before they can commit it to long-term memory" (p. 640). Moustafa (1987) further indicated that this may take several sessions. Accept the student's response if mispronounced and expand usage by using it correctly. This step is crucial for the success of the strategy because comprehensible input is being developed. Consequently, it is important that the students have learned the terms in the sentence patterns that have been elicited and expanded (i.e., *Yes, that's right! The mechanic fixed the car.*). This is the oral scaffolding aspect of the strategy.

3. Next, have the children dictate sentences that retell the experience or tell about the illustration. Record the sentences on either an overhead projector, chart, or board. Continue until all the information is obtained. The teacher may have to suggest or ask questions to place the events in the correct order. If the teacher is writing on a board or chart, be sure that the children can observe as each word is written. Speak the words aloud as they are written down, keeping children's attention on the formation of the words. Have a child or children repeat the sentence after it has been written.

4. Follow the dictation with a modified choral reading procedure. Place a hand (or finger, if on a transparency) under the words as they are read to establish the oral language bridge to print.

5. Prepare sentence strips of the story. Have the students read the story. Then hand out the sentence strips and have the children match them with the story. Have the sentence read aloud and placed under the appropriate line in the story. (With some thought this can be done on the overhead projector.) Next, remove the chart versions and redistribute the sentence strips. Have children reassemble the story in the original order by reading their sentences and deciding who has the first, second, and so on. These can be placed in a sentence chart or on a board rail to ease selection.

6. Have children read the sentence on the strip through and each time cut off another word. Then pass the words around and have the children put them together in the correct order. Give the words to the children and have them match their words with words on the original

story chart. Next, select specific words and have the children identify them with objects, actions, characters in the illustration, realia, or items in the class.

7. Give the children duplicated copies of the story and have it first read in pairs, then individually as the other partner watches and assists.

Teachers of English as a second language who used the adapted strategy above, reported success for their students. After using the strategy for a time, students eventually started pointing out words that were alike, had similar spellings, and so on. They would ask, "What's this?" "Why did you do this?" Older students became very interested with the form and mechanics of written language, and they ask excellent questions.

LEARNING THE CONVENTIONS OF PRINT

For children to learn the conventions of print requires that they participate in a multitude of reading and writing experiences. Learning occurs because children are active participants in literacy experiences. Children infer through these experiences which principles are important, which apply when and how. They learn this when they experience language in real situations and in a whole context, not when bits and pieces of language are explained through rules. Instructional programs must be developed and organized that allow children to select their own reading materials and write about their own personal experiences or about topics that are of interest and are meaningful to them.

Allen et al. (1989) studied 180 children throughout their kindergarten year. Seven teachers taught writing as a process, integrated the language arts, immersed children in real books which included student-authored texts, and made songs, rhymes, and chants an integral part of the literacy environments they created in their classrooms. The instruction in these kindergartens supported the exploration and invention of language. This study demonstrated that children are not limited in their abilities to grow in writing by the alphabet, sounds, or words knowledge they bring to school, nor is their acquisition of reading-related behaviors limited by their levels of writing sophistication. Given the right classroom environments and literacy experiences, children can learn to become literate. Literacy is not only for the child from the literate home environment.

Allen et al. (1989) found that children improved their abilities to make connections between sounds and letters in words they were reading as they learned to represent words. Children entering school, however, with some knowledge of the alphabet and letter/sound correspondence were more likely to be using that knowledge to compose with invented spelling by the end of the year. All children can have equal opportunities to grow if teachers respond to what children can do and will facilitate what children are attempting to do. The teachers' philosophies in the study supported the emergence of literacy by building upon each child's understanding about literacy. This does not mean that teachers should not intervene or facilitate learning. Students need to be carefully observed, and when teachers know the children they should intervene to help them understand as often as they feel it is appropriate.

A wide range of individual differences in writing and reading/writing relationships should be expected in young learners. This conflicts with beliefs commonly held that young children are much alike at the beginning of their educational careers, with little knowledge of literacy. All children should not be expected to write long stories with invented spellings that are found in the teacher education literature. For example, in comparing the writing of two boys for two-and-a-half years, beginning when they were in reception (kindergarten) for the letter writing project reported by Robinson et al. (1990), one boy began writing long letters with invented spelling while the other used limited invented spelling from the beginning of his correspondence with one of the researchers. His letters were never very long, no matter how the researcher responded or what was suggested. Other children in the project began writing two- to three-page letters the first year of their correspondence.

The Allen et al. (1989) study confirmed that once children start hearing beginning sounds, teachers should expect that they will soon be ready to listen for ending sounds, then middle and vowel sounds. The teachers in the Allen et al. study found that children would make progress in writing without the required copying and handwriting exercises so common in schools. When given the opportunity, children provided their own practice using their own interests and concerns about learning. The study showed that children will probably develop rules about spelling or letter/sound relationships without direct instruction, and children will learn control over the syntactic and semantic system through their reading and writing.

Strategies Focusing on the Conventions of Print

Children's developing competence in observing and generalizing about the conventions of print can be facilitated. Many of the strategies mentioned previously will do just that. The following types of activities focus students on print in meaningful context:

1. As children are read to, focus their attention to note print, see similarities, and locate alike words, letters, and sounds. The teacher may use his or her hand to follow under the reading to help children develop speech-to-print relationships. Encourage them to note alliteration and speculate why they enjoy rhyming words.

2. Have children cut apart sentences from dictated stories and reorder. Later, as children reread each sentence, cut off the last word until the sentence is completely cut apart.

3. Brainstorm words that go in a topic to stimulate ideas for writing. Put these words on cards, let children illustrate them, then bind the cards together and label the cards with a classifying word. Store these in a convenient location for students to use for writing. These will serve as a picture dictionary specifically related to a topic.

4. Record familiar poems and songs on charts. When children can read these fluently, another chart can be made, first leaving out total words and later adding the beginning letter/sounds or only the ending, to focus children on the graphophonic cueing system. Bill Pogge had children contribute to a news chart every day. He used a cloze technique when the format was familiar to combine the use of prediction and the various cueing systems. He first focused on replacing whole words, then gave students clues with letters. For example:

Today is Th___day, th___ ___th of ___ ch.

5. Respond to what the child is trying to do by looking into the child's ideas and work. For example, *I see this says* my *because it starts with* m. Or ask the child what he or she hears as a word is slowly sounded out for the child. Always present information as it is needed for learning to take place (Freppon & Dahl, 1991).

Literacy Phases

An examination of the works of researchers, such as Cochrane et al. (1984), Temple, Nathan, Burns, and Temple (1988), Dobson (1989), and Weaver (1988), shows that all children progress from whole to part and from using schemas, information about the reading act, story structure, and prior information to gradually increase in their use of the semantic and syntactic cueing systems and graphophonic cueing systems. Sulzby (1988) further reported that learners move back and forth across stages of writing.

Learning does not appear linear or sequential but an evolving sophistication as children's strategies and concepts become refined, reflecting the conventions of written language (DeFord, 1980). Consequently, there is a lack of uniformity in their process (Weaver, 1988). They will not all learn to read and write naturally without specific interaction and intervention on the part of the teacher.

Teachers can develop a useful understanding of what children are attempting and thinking as they progress toward conventional literacy if they understand the literacy behaviors of children in the classroom and attempt to determine how they can facilitate their development. (See Chapter Eight for a brief description of the phases of literacy development.)

BECOMING AN INTERACTIVE DEMONSTRATOR

It is important for children's language and literacy acquisition to have a teacher who is an interactive demonstrator of language and literacy. One of the greatest opportunities for learning is through demonstration. Although the brain is learning all the time, children may not always learn from demonstrations, according to F. Smith (1982a, 1984). Learning requires learners to engage in the demonstration. An engagement is when the learner assimilates a demonstration and vicariously makes it his or her own. Children are engaging when they say, for example, "Oh, that's how that word is spelled," "I like how that is said!" or "Is that how that word looks?"

Interaction does not result from teacher-dominated and -controlled teaching/learning experiences in a classroom. Teachers in multicultural classrooms must make students active learners, learning whole to part. Norman (1990) suggested that the role of the teacher should, however, include the following four aspects:

1. *Scaffolding* occurs through dialogues with the child and extends the child's understanding through shared reading and writing, reading and writing conferences, and assisted reading.

2. *Modeling and demonstrating* occurs through supportive use of listening and talking or functional and relevant use of reading and

writing and thinking aloud to solve problems and to determine questions to be answered, points to be made, and situations to be analyzed.

3. *Listening and questioning* succeeds when children's statements and responses in personal and learning situations are accepted and the teacher uses open-ended questions sparingly to extend ideas, challenge assumptions, and require clear explanations. When a child knows that what he or she says is taken seriously, the child will think more carefully and communicate well.

4. *Taking part and becoming an audience* allows for planned intervention that will extend thinking; introduces some new aspect or provides information while being an audience; and provides an opportunity to help a child in restructuring and/or reorganizing. The teacher determines when to be the audience to assist in rehearsals of ideas, to be a critical friend in responding to a piece of work, and to give constructive advice.

Strategies that engage children in participating are interactive. Predictable books, big books, dictation, and journals, to name just a few, are strategies conducive to interactive demonstration. These strategies are extremely motivating and will engage children for learning.

However, according to F. Smith (1982a), motivation is no assurance of learning; motivation places people in situations where relevant demonstrations are likely to occur. Learners must engage. They are more likely to engage when the environment is nurturing, the learning situation is culturally relevant, and they are involved in language and literacy that have purpose. For example, situations for African American students that stem from their oral traditions would be motivating and would stimulate engagement (Scherer, 1992). Storytelling, dramatizing, and choral reading would fit this tradition.

Interaction between learner and teacher is also required for language and literacy learning. F. Smith (1982a) stated the need and importance of interaction best in the following:

> There is no evidence that any child ever learned to read and write without human interaction, nor is there any evidence that children who fail to learn from people will do any better with impersonal programs. Rather, it is the children who have the least success in learning who most need personal contact, to be reassured of their ability to learn and of the utility of what is to be learned. (p. 82)

F. Smith's (1982a) concern is that programs tend to take the place of teachers. He explains that programs appear to exist to make teachers redundant and that they emphasize facts and skills, not uses and attitudes. It is the teacher who is remembered for teaching, not the program or a text. Teachers have the opportunity to model language in all their language and literacy interactions.

The important aspect of demonstrating is what it does for the classroom environment. If a teacher takes part in activities and reads and writes with children, it changes his or her relationship with the class; both the teacher and the children become active in the learning process. The class then becomes a community of learners, members helping each other to learn.

SUMMARY

Teachers in multicultural classrooms can facilitate the emergence and development of language for all children in a multicultural school. Language emergence requires a communicative environment that would support and facilitate language development. Language emergence requires classrooms where social, communicative, and cognitive language are encouraged through culturally appropriate curricula and strategies by sensitive caring teachers who understand how language develops. Teachers must be aware of cultural characteristics of learners for their language and literacy success.

The emergence of literacy requires not only a literate classroom environment that immerses children in meaningful, relevant, and functional literacy learning experiences, but teachers who employ strategies that integrate listening, speaking, reading, and writing and apply a variety of scaffolding learning strategies. The need for parental and community participation and involvement in the curriculum and instruction of culturally diverse children in the classroom is an essential component for learning. Attention on speaking, reading, and writing experiences encourages children to engage in self-directed learning which leads toward the learning of conventional forms and structures of English language and literacy. Language and literacy learning develops when a learner interacts with an experienced language user or literate demonstrator.

Teachers become interactive demonstrators when they act as scribes for children, transcribing their language into print, or when they model reading and writing for children or demonstrate how they think through reading and writing as literate people. It is important for students to engage with the demonstrator. Children must be immersed in language, for talking and good literature, for reading and writing, to become speakers, readers, and writers.

IMPLICATIONS FOR INSTRUCTION

1. Develop the classroom environment, curriculum, and instruction that emulate key cultural features of the home environments of L2 students to facilitate L2 emergence. Children must be empowered to speak expressively and extensively.

2. Facilitate L2 learning by interacting with L2 learners in speech that is slower, more pronounced, syntactically shorter and simpler. Use imperative and interrogative structures related to student behavior. Integrate language learning across the curriculum that has a thematic focus, involves students in collaborative learning experiences, and provides learning experiences that are not fragmented or segmented.

3. Assist culturally diverse students to understand and learn implicit language and discover social and cultural behavior rules to function effectively in dominant and nondominant societies. Accept culturally diverse children's language and encourage its use and continued development.

4. Organize classrooms to contribute to listening and speaking emergence and development through listening centers, talk corners, and sharing centers and provide real reasons for listening and talking across the curriculum.

5. Facilitate literacy emergence by developing activities that immerse learners in meaningful, purposeful, functional literacy activities in a literate environment. Activities that contribute to literacy emergence include environmental print related to children's prior experiences and culture, book talk activities that include reading aloud to students, retelling, storytelling, shared writing, dictated writing, journals, letters, and labeling.

6. Assist L2 literacy learners to increase language and literacy by using learning experiences that structure language and literacy experiences and aid the student to generate language.

7. Focus children's attention on print to see words in sentences, note similarities in sentences and words, predict words in familiar contexts,

match alike words, locate like letters and sounds. Always respond to what the child is trying to do.

8. Become an interactive demonstrator by responding to the student through scaffolding, modeling and demonstrating, listening and questioning, and taking part and becoming an audience.

9. Involve parents and community members to assist students in language and literacy learning by being models and demonstrators, assisting with L1 and L2 and literacy learning when possible.

CHAPTER SIX

Developing Language and Literacy Through Multicultural Literature Themes

- *What factors affect comprehension of literature, and how can the teacher increase understanding?*
- *Why is multicultural literature essential to the language and literacy program?*
- *How should multicultural literature be integrated in daily programs?*
- *What are major strategies for developing language and literacy through multicultural themes and how are they developed?*
- *What are specific suggestions for teaching language-different students?*

INTRODUCTION

Children's literature can provide excellent sources for helping children understand their own cultural heritage and the heritage of other cultural groups in society. Multicultural literature further provides excellent sources for contrasting cultural perspectives. Since the problems faced by cultural groups in society are portrayed in literature, multicultural literature can produce models for students in decision making and social action. Good books are excellent starting places for studying issues in expository materials as well as narrative (Rasinski & Padak, 1990).

Classroom environments should immerse students in literature through listening and reading experiences. Students should be surrounded with books, art, and writing materials of all kinds for extending and interpreting their reading experiences (Huck & Kerstetter, 1987). Using excellent multicultural literature rich in interesting themes and topics that have meaning and relevance for children is an excellent way to encourage children's learning. Cullinan (1987) stated that "literature informs the imagination and feeds the desire to read" (p. 6). When children are immersed in excellent literature, they are engaged in language events that provide a storehouse of images, story patterns, and language that can be tapped for generating and composing language and writing.

A language and literacy program with a curriculum focused on multicultural literature fulfills the goals for a multicultural school in four ways. First, multicultural literature in the classroom provides students from diverse populations with reading materials, characters, themes, and plots that are more closely related to their life experiences. Second, multicultural literature provides students with reading materials that challenge misconceptions and stereotypes and develop awareness and understanding of cultures. Third, multicultural literature provides students from diverse cultures positive role models who have overcome problems dealing with life and society. Story role models assist culturally diverse students in developing better self-concepts; they provide dominant-culture students with images of people from diverse cultures that assist in overcoming stereotypical biases. Fourth, multicultural literature assists students to "walk in the shoes" of book characters from another culture to begin the process of gaining a new perspective.

Another way that literature can fulfill the goal for a multicultural school is through social action. Social action implies identifying problems and concerns, making decisions, and taking action to resolve problems (Banks, 1989b; Rasinski & Padak, 1990). Literature has great potential for moving people to action. Literature is the real stuff of human events and conditions. Multicultural learning inspires students to act upon their beliefs and values about people different from them. Literature conveys knowledge, helps develop a value system about multicultural events and issues, and provides an impetus for action on events and issues. "Literature does more than change minds; it changes people's hearts" (Rasinski & Padak, 1990, p. 580).

Multicultural goals, when applied in language arts programs focused around literature, can lead students to become more socially active and conscious of their society. Learning experiences resulting from good multicultural literature in the hands of a sensitive teacher can stimulate critical thinking about actions that may lead to resolving problems and, perhaps, eventually changing society's perception about culturally diverse people and how they are treated. As a result of a multicultural education, students may become more thoughtful, caring people who act on values and beliefs developed through thoughtful analysis (Rasinski & Padak, 1990). This can happen when learning in the language arts curriculum radiates from multicultural literature.

Good narrative multicultural literature helps to develop speaking, reading, and writing competencies. The construct story is important for learning to read and write. "In other words, stories become a vehicle for learning about the way in which language structures experiences, as well as about language structures themselves—both very important reading lessons" (Sawyer, 1987). In narrative literature content-oriented or expository writing may have a supporting role for extending and expanding learning in the curriculum.

FACTORS THAT AFFECT
READING COMPREHENSION

Students in multicultural classrooms may represent many diverse cultures and languages. Cultural language differences have been demonstrated to affect student success in reading (Andersson & Barnitz, 1984). Students may lack the cultural knowledge or schemas—values, attitudes, beliefs, and traditions—necessary for understanding what is read (Steffensen, 1987), especially for content, themes, and experiences alien to their cultural contexts. This is compounded when second-language (L2) students are less proficient in determining and using textual and contextual processes essential for understanding (Andersson & Barnitz, 1984). The use of multicultural literature poses a viable solution.

Importance of Prior Information

Readers use their view of the world or schema for transacting meaning. This world view may act as a hidden barrier to understanding when the author's text is incongruent with the reader's cultural context (Rivers, 1968). Comprehending reading is a transaction between a reader's background knowledge and schemas and the cues provided by an author's textual organization to construct an interpretation of the meaning of the text (Pritchard, 1990). Comprehension requires being able to relate textual material to one's own knowledge (Carrell & Eisterhold, 1983). Consequently, prior knowledge is at the core of reading comprehension (Lipson, 1984).

Schema theory contends that comprehension results when input is matched with preexisting background knowledge. When incoming data is found by the brain to be contradictory, one of two things happens. Either the schema is amended by the new information or the information is rejected in favor of the existing schema (James, 1987).

A reader learns the numerous types of schemas, or chunks of knowledge or experiences (Weaver, 1988), used to comprehend any piece of literature from prior life experiences and experiences listening to and reading literature. For example, in reading a story readers reference their knowledge about how to use a book and put into play their cultural knowledge of story structure and topic knowledge to develop, expand, or refine their schemas. However, sometimes prior information about a topic, particularly for young readers, is vague, ill defined, inaccurate, or built upon misinterpretations (Lipson, 1984). When this happens meaning is seriously affected.

Lipson (1984) suggested that even able readers might run into reading difficulties when the text either contradicts their factual knowledge or is contrary to their deeply held world perceptions. Readers cling to prior information, whether accurate or not, and manipulate the text information to fit their schema. Lipson (1984) reported that poor and average readers were better able to acquire new, conflicting information if they did not have prior inaccurate information.

Cultural Influences Affect Comprehension

Students from diverse cultures and groups may be literally barred from understanding when reading materials and themes and topics do not provide appropriate clues to activate their schemas and/or they do not possess appropriate schemas. Both of these instances are examples of mismatches between what the writer anticipates the reader can do in extracting meaning and what the reader can actually do (Carrell & Eisterhold, 1983). Andersson and Barnitz (1984) reported the effects of cultural differences between urban, working-class African American students and European American students from an agricultural area. Both groups of students read a letter sent from one African American male friend to another, who had moved away, describing an episode in the school cafeteria. The letter quoted a verbal exchange among students such as "You so ugly that when the doctor delivered you he slapped you in the face." The European American students interpreted the passage as involving physical aggression while the African American students generally interpreted the passage in relation to the verbal style common to their community.

Students fail to comprehend when they lack formal schemas to match the text's cultural information, are unfamiliar with content or topics, and have different or incorrect perceptions (James, 1987). The above situation is an excellent example of such a mismatch. Readers who have a match with the text's cultural information or story structure will find the text easier to read and understand, no matter how complex it is syntactically and rhetorically. Consequently, for understanding this African American exchange, readers must know and understand something of the dialogue communication style appropriate in the urban, working-class African American community between males.

In another study, Lipson (1984) chose an equal number of children from a private Hebrew day school and a Catholic school to read a culturally neutral passage about divers in Japan, and in counterbalanced order, passages entitled "Bar Mitzvah" and "First Communion." Children from both groups actually performed better on the completely unfamiliar neutral passage on Japan than when reading partially familiar passages from the other religious group that contained analogous information. Their religious content schema acted as a barrier rather than a bridge to understanding the other religious events. They did not realize when their prior information was a mismatch.

Analogous knowledge should not be assumed to help readers. It may raise spurious comparisons that can lead children to construct erroneous notions related to their own experiences as was shown above. When culturally unfamiliar materials are read, readers may lack relevant schemas for understanding, which results in fewer connections and greater ambiguity (Pritchard, 1990). Readers of unfamiliar cultural material will probably be reluctant to relinquish their present information in favor of text information or will distort the text information to align it with their previous information (Lipson, 1984).

What readers must learn to do is accept the fact that they are unable to make a cultural connection to the author's cues in the text and persevere and search for appropriate global understanding, not text-based connections (Pritchard, 1990).

Suggestions for Improving Reading Comprehension

The following five suggestions should improve reading comprehension in regard to multicultural material:

1. Assist students in developing appropriate schemas for gaining reading comprehension. Appropriate background information will be a bridge for what students know to what they do not know (McNeil, 1987; Roney, 1984; James, 1987; Pritchard, 1990). Students are likely to be more involved, interested, and successful when reading materials match their cultural backgrounds. The use of multicultural literature would appear appropriate. However, if students are to develop proficiency in reading unfamiliar material they need contexts and schemas that support developing understanding through the use of pictures, cultural experience discussions (Andersson & Barnitz, 1984), and first-hand experiences.

2. Provide ample reading materials around multicultural themes. This allows the students to become familiar with ample materials in an area, a genre, or from one author (Carrell & Eisterhold, 1983; James, 1987). Themes and topics should be developed using real books (children's literature), not short passages or adaptations found in reading books (James, 1987). Themes and topics also help students to develop sensitivity to dealing with cross-cultural vocabulary used to make distinctions and provide information (Andersson & Barnitz, 1984), especially when multicultural literature is included.

3. Introduce students to reading materials through prereading strategies that activate prior knowledge and ensure that students' prior information is checked out against the text (Lipson, 1984). Develop textual understandings about print and genre (fiction, nonfiction or expository, and so on) (Crawford & Carline, 1987; Roney, 1984) to help students deal with the unfamiliar organizational structures of texts. Address cultural aspects of the material prior to reading the material to increase understanding and analysis of the theme of the reading.

4. Aid students to learn how to focus on the transaction between the

reader and the work in reading literature (Squire, 1989). A transaction between the reader and text (or author) allows the reader to place prior knowledge at the core for understanding (Lipson, 1984; Squire, 1989; Pritchard, 1990) and does not impose a teacher model for interpreting the work (Squire, 1989).

5. Assist students to develop critical thinking skills that allow deep processing of text by aiding them to use mental imagery, draw inferences, and self-monitor understanding. Literature that students have sufficient personal experiences to understand is essential for developing critical thinking skills because it speaks to boys and girls today (Squire, 1989). Consequently, multicultural literature provides excellent solutions for culturally diverse students. Squire (1989) stated that in order to liberate the imagination, schools should provide students with a broad range of literature, that is, works past and present, reflecting cultures different from their own.

MULTICULTURAL LITERATURE: ESSENTIAL FOCUS IN THE LANGUAGE AND LITERACY PROGRAM

The values and ethics of multicultural literature are appropriate for developing understandings of other people and cultures that will contribute to comprehension. In multicultural literature there is greater opportunity to develop a match with students' prior information and to stimulate critical, imaginative, and ethical thinking.

Rationale for Using Multicultural Literature

Authors of good multicultural literature for children provide values and ethics that are universal in their writing, whether factual or fiction. "Honesty, kindness and compassion, faithfulness, discipline, respect for the law, perseverance, sharing and unselfishness, humility, proper ambition, forgiveness, courage, integrity, public service and democracy" (McMillan & Gentile, 1988, p. 877) are values and ethics found in children's literature. These can aid children in eliminating stereotypical biases and posing alternative societal solutions when students are assisted in contrasting cultures and peoples in a multicultural curriculum.

Norton (1991) stated that the goals for multicultural education are matched closely by values of multicultural literature. When culturally diverse children read about how people have solved their own problems or made social changes and notable achievements, their personal aspirations are raised (Norton, 1991). Children from a particular cultural heritage will realize that they can be proud that their culture has made significant contributions to the nation and the world. This improves their self-image and develops cultural identity.

Children learning about other cultures come to understand that other people are real, with feelings, emotions, and needs similar to their own. They can be assisted to focus their reading beyond the traditions, beliefs, and practices reported in the stories to deeper understandings of people and alternative solutions to the dilemmas facing society. However, educators in their desire to devlelop awareness for children of other cultures must take care not to treat many distinct cultures together under broad categories. *Hispanic,* for example, may have many meanings. People classified under this category may be distinctly different from one another with different heritages, values, and dialects (Reimer, 1992). Stereotyping may result when programs combine groups into cultural conglomerates.

Using real books gives the student the opportunity to gradually develop comprehension of an author as the book is read. Individual authors use a specific set of vocabulary, sentence structures, and ways of expression that lend themselves to developing prediction skills. If real books are self-selected, the reader is more likely to be interested and motivated to read the selection (Carrell & Eisterhold, 1983). Real books provide opportunities for students to develop critical reading skills and make affective responses. Literature provides the opportunity for facilitating imaginative thinking as well. If a student's imagination is caught through real purposes for learning, the chance for critical reading is increased.

Good children's literature as the basis for the language and literacy program allows the teacher to develop numerous themes each year that provide for narrow or intensive reading in a genre or topic or about an author, illustrator, or person. Literature develops four major understandings for children, according to Bishop (1987):

1. Literature helps students understand how people are connected to one another through common experiences of emotions, needs, and desires.
2. Literature helps students understand, appreciate, and celebrate the differences among cultural groups that enrich the larger society.
3. Literature helps students understand the effects of social issues and forces on the lives of ordinary people.
4. Literature helps students understand the values that are transmitted in a culture or society.

If U.S. society is indeed intent on making itself more humane and supportive—a better place for every child to live and grow—then good cross-cultural or multicultural literature must have a paramount position in a classroom. Literature is a powerful vehicle for developing understandings across cultures and societies with different histories, traditions, and beliefs. Each time children read or hear a good piece of literature from a culture different from their own, they can be changed by the experience because multicultural literature helps them see the world in a new way (Bishop, 1987). For example, Eve Bunting's *The Happy Funeral* (Harper, 1982), Virginia Hamilton's *Zeely* (Macmillan, 1967), or Vera B. Williams' *A Chair for My Mother* (Greenwillow, 1982) cannot be read without realizing the powerful statements that good multicultural literature makes in helping to understand the people of a culture.

Literature, according to Huck (1990), "helps us crawl inside the skins of persons very different from ourselves" (p. 3). Literature provides various experiences to journey through the world of other people, other children. Mildred Pitts Walter's *Justin and the Best Biscuits in the World* (Lothrop, 1986) lets the reader experience the world of the young African American boy who learns of the rich heritage of his people and himself as an African American male. This book unfolds for the reader the universality of gender-role problems and presents the struggles for self-identity that most children go through today. Yoshiko Uchida's *Journey to Topaz: A Story of the Japanese-American Evacuation* (Creative Arts, 1985) takes the reader into the life of a Japanese American girl whose family life was disrupted and whose family members and friends were separated through injustice committed by the U.S. government during World War II.

Reading good multicultural literature under the guidance of a sensitive teacher helps children deal with racist attitudes and behaviors that are destructive to society. Schools that are Eurocentric have an urgent responsibility for helping students accept and appreciate the cultural diversity present in the larger community. Themes and topics that focus around or incorporate multicultural literature provide ways to counter stereotypes, bigotry, and racist views. Literature can assist students to see life through another perspective. When students enter the world of the book, they engage their feelings to identify with characters and situations. Points of view can be felt and understood at no great personal risk, and the art of multiple perspectives can be learned and practiced (Oster, 1989).

In addition to multicultural literature presented in books, tapes and transcriptions can open windows to the rich cultural contributions of people recorded in music, songs, dances, poetry, and traditional oral literature. Further, language tapes for bilingual students will extend language usage and heritage understandings and give prestige to the students' languages (SCDC Agenda for Multicultural Teaching, 1986).

Ways to Include Literature in the Daily Program

Teachers must embed literature in their daily teaching and learning frameworks that involve three major language and literacy events: teacher daily reading aloud, student self-selected reading, and student daily writing.

Teacher Daily Reading Aloud

The teacher reads aloud significant pieces of literature daily. These pieces introduce children to authors, genres, and cultural, racial, and ethnic groups and should include readings of poetry, prose, and hearing music from these cultures. These readings and recordings should be authentic and, when possible, presented in the language and dialect of the culture. Time should be spent listening and talking about literature that will extend understandings of themes and topics under study as well as literature that will provide children obvious pleasure in listening. The discussion should lead to opportunities for exploring problems raised by the literature with possible social-action solutions.

Student Self-Selected Reading

Children select real books to read individually, in self-sustained silent reading, and books for reading and discussing in groups, which lead to responding to authors and ideas of others through discussion (literature circles and literature response groups), writing (journals), and other literacy activities and projects. Self-selected individual books should be shared by children in Reader's Chair or other types of sharing experiences. (In Reader's Chair, children select and choose to read aloud books they have read. Listeners respond and discuss the selection.) Students in group discussions should be empowered to respond to problems posed in their readings and to propose and act upon alternative social solutions.

Student Daily Writing

Children should write as a daily routine in dialogue and/or response journals and through self-selected activities in conjunction with their reading. Writing should be an integral part of the ongoing themes in the classroom. Written pieces are shared daily through Author's Chair or in other types of publishing activities, such as letter-writing exchanges, collected life experiences of community members, newspapers, and so on.

STRATEGIES FOR DEVELOPING LANGUAGE AND LITERACY THROUGH MULTICULTURAL LITERATURE THEMES

There are several communication areas and generic strategies appropriate for multicultural literature themes. These strategies are appropriate learning activities for most multicultural literature themes and generally integrate both language and literacy.

Listening and Speaking

Oral communication is integral to understanding, enriching, and expanding reading and writing experiences. Listening and speaking strategies should be included at all stages of development for use in developing literature themes. When children are encouraged to listen and talk with peers about what they are reading and studying, they can explore concepts, try out theories, or express opinions tentatively and receive immediate responses (Norman, 1990).

Oral communication is neglected in many schools and receives little attention. It is important that schools plan listening and talking experiences for all children. Oral language is a significant factor in cognitive growth. Children develop oral communication fluency when they use listening and speaking for relevant and functional reasons. When children are actively involved in getting and giving meaning, they learn language by using it with peers, teachers, and other adults in the classroom. "People develop most when they are trying to do things somewhat beyond their current ability" (K. S. Goodman, E. B. Smith, R. Meredith, & Y. M. Goodman, 1987, p. 258). Consequently, children must be encouraged to take risks and practice speaking in new and different contexts.

In speaking, reading, and writing, learners need to feel that it is all right to try something and make a mistake or to guess using the best information available to make a decision. The teacher's role is to provide a temporary framework that allows the student to develop competencies and build confidence (Peregoy & Boyle, 1990), whether it is in a first or second language. If there is a bilingual adult available in the classroom, children from the nondominant-language group can be encouraged to talk in their own language about the ideas being learned. This assists access to the curriculum and demonstrates for children that their language is acceptable in school (Norman, 1990). Once something is understood in a first language, it will be easier to talk about in another.

Creating Language Learning Contexts for Nonstandard Dialect Speakers

Speech for children is bound up with their cultural identities and self-concepts. School programs must be flexible to accommodate a range of languages, dialects, and language abilities children have when they come to school. The standard English (SE) dialect of any English-speaking country has the highest social prestige in the nation. While speaking a nonstandard dialect may have detrimental economic as well as educational and social consequences for a student, teachers still should accept, value, and appreciate a student's language. Becoming bidialectal is an individual decision.

Bidialectal Rational.   A child's language or dialect should not ever be eliminated. The home language must have its place and be valued. Instead, the child's language competencies should be broadened to include ranges of styles and cultural speaking behaviors (Rubin, 1985). To achieve this goal, children should hear an effective SE model. SE-speaking peers and teachers, as well as the use of good literature, provide such models. Nonstandard English–speaking children should be provided opportunities to learn how to communicate effectively in standard and nonstandard dialects. Reading material should include SE and community-language or dialect trade books whenever possible.

Teachers working with students from homes where English or SE is not the primary language or dialect must always respond to the communicative value of the language message, not the form. To do otherwise is to risk damaging or destroying students' self-confidence. Students learn better and faster when they have a strong self-image. Our role as teachers is to ensure that language learning is achieved without children losing cultural identity. The reality of the school language is that it provides the child with extended social and economic opportunities. Schools should make students aware of the political and social power of language in the wider community. How an individual utilizes SE and majority cultural practices is, and must always remain, an individual choice.

Schools should also assist SE-speaking students to develop an understanding of other dialects as well. Works of literature written in other English dialects provide excellent opportunities to develop such understandings as they are read and discussed. A number of works listed in Sibley's Recommended Books for Multicultural Teaching

Themes and Topics in the Teacher Resource Kit are appropriate for doing this in black English (BE). An example for younger readers is Patricia McKissack's *Flossie & the Fox* (Dial, 1986) or Gail E. Haley's *A Story, a Story* (Atheneum, 1970). Older readers will enjoy hearing and discussing Nikki Giovanni's *Spin a Soft Black Song* (Hill & Wang, 1985), Clayton Bess' *Story for a Black Night* (Houghton Mifflin, 1982), and Virginia Hamilton's *The People Could Fly: American Black Folktales* (Knopf, 1985).

Facilitating BE Speakers Learning SE.   BE as a dialect has a structure, a system, and a logic of its own and more similarities with SE than differences (Boseker, 1988). Not all children speaking BE produce the same number of SE or BE forms in their speech. Use of SE and BE will be dependent upon age, social situation, and prior experiences with either dialect. (BE should never be considered synonymous with the color of a child's skin. A large number of African American children may only speak SE.) Boseker (1988) suggested that teachers need training and practice in becoming accustomed to hearing BE and being able to identify real BE mistakes.

There are five recommendations, adapted from Boseker (1988), for working with BE speakers in language arts and reading. These suggestions are provided for teaching SE using literature examples from African American author Mildred Pitts Walter and have application for teachers working with children who have any dialect differing significantly from SE. The suggestions include the following:

1. Be able to distinguish between actual errors and speech characteristics of the dialect. Do not correct dialect characteristics. Success in reading, for example, is not dependent upon correct SE pronunciation (see Chapter Eight).

2. Put attention on the aspect of SE that is critical for learners' understanding. BE speakers may need to pay more attention to final endings of words in print activities. Emphasize this aspect through oral modeling and demonstration in speech and while reading aloud— *"Brandon, stretched out to read"* (*Two and Too Much*, Bradbury, 1990).

3. Introduce words in contexts that bring out the distinction between SE and the students' dialect in the most contrastive manner. BE speakers, for example, are likely to simplify consonant clusters before a pause and least likely before a vowel that follows. The teacher, wanting to focus on this aspect of speech, should place a vocabulary item in a sentence to give more distinction to the consonant item— *"He thought he would* burst *into tears"* (*Two and Too Much*). Reading aloud

such selections in the normal course of daily oral reading to all students will not handicap other students in the classroom. Ask questions for discussion that will elicit the use of these distinctions. Select choral reading and readers' theatre pieces that will provide students with opportunities to practice for greater clarity.

4. Use full forms of words to avoid contractions during early stages of reading and writing. This means avoiding reading aloud sentences such as *"She's always in my room"* in favor of *"She is always in my room" (Two and Too Much).*

5. Assist students to contrast contracted forms in relation to full forms to develop meaning and determine usage. For example, in discussing *Two and Too Much,* the teacher might bring out that Brandon's mother responds to Brandon about his sister, Gina—"She's only two." Assist the students to compare the meaning of the contracted and the full form by writing both on the board. Choral reading examples might be selected that provide practice with contractions.

Language Learning Activities and Strategies that Foster Speaking and Listening Development

The teacher will want to foster oral communication development by using many different teaching strategies. Many of these strategies are extensions of other activities and strategies.

Oral Storytelling and Story Retelling. In storytelling, the past can be retold, the present given form, and the future rehearsed. Children learn to organize experiences and respond to an event through story. Oral storytelling helps students move toward literary quality (Van Dongen, 1987). The need for storytelling is doubly important for students learning English. Storytelling provides opportunities to hear English modeled and to provide time for practice in a supportive environment. Children from culturally diverse and non-English-speaking homes should have opportunities to hear and tell stories from their cultural and ethnic backgrounds. For example, Juanita Havill's *Treasure Nap* (Houghton, 1992) provides children with a model for storytelling and a means for integrating important family events and traditions into original stories. Well-known stories provide opportunities to work on making the story meanings more precise for understanding. Consequently, plan to tell a story that children like numerous times and then encourage them to learn and tell it.

Teachers could provide students with a flavor of other cultures by using techniques and traditions from various cultures for telling stories. Norton (1991) provided strategies from literacy researchers of many cultures that will catch the imagination of children and encourage and enhance storytelling in the classroom. For example, many cultures use a traditional story starter. Norton (1991) reported the following as being used in Cameroon, Africa:

> *Storyteller:*   *Listen to a tale! Listen to a tale!*
> *Audience:*   *A tale for fun, for fun.*
> *Your throat is a gong, your body a locust;*
> *bring it here for me to roast!*
> *Storyteller:*   *Children, listen to a tale,*
> *a tale for fun, for fun. (p. 573)*

Norton (1991) reported the following from the Navajo people:

> *In the beginning, when the world was new*
> *At the time when men and animals were all the same*
> *and spoke the same language. . . . (p. 583)*

The latter certainly could be a very stimulating opening for telling stories while sitting in a circle in the classroom. A book such as Edward S. Curtis's *The Girl Who Married a Ghost and Other Tales from the North American Indian* (Macmillan, 1978) may be used. Even more authentic would be using the language of a people to begin a story. Try having children retell tales retold in book form; for example, Arlene Mosel's, *The Funny Little Woman* (Dutton, 1972) or Sumiko Yagawa's, *The Crane Wife* (Morrow, 1981), using the following starter (Norton, 1991):

> *Mukashi, mukashi (Long, long ago)*
> *Aro tokoro ni (In a certain place)*

D. Norton (1991) reported that West African storytellers carry fishinglike nets in which objects such as bones, feathers, or such are placed. An object is chosen by a listener and the storyteller tells a story about it. Gail E. Haley's *A Story, a Story* (Atheneum, 1970) or West African stories selected from Ashley Bryan's *Lion and the Ostrich Chicks and Other African Folk Tales* (Atheneum, 1986) would be excellent sources for selecting stories and objects to place in a net for this storytelling technique. As the net is passed around, whoever placed the object in the net would then tell the story to go with the object. Bryan's tape, *The Dancing Granny and Other African Stories* (Ashley Bryan, Caedmon, 1985), would be an excellent way to introduce storytelling styles as well as a further source of African literature.

Listening Center. There should be a range of listening materials both commercial and teacher- or child-made in the listening center. Use of authors or actors reading poetry both in SE and dialect is an excellent addition to any taped listening collection in the classroom. Parents should be encouraged to provide cultural materials for the centers as well and to tape books and stories from their communities for listening. These collections might include all languages and dialects spoken in society but especially those appropriate to the community. Tape recorders can also be placed here for recording stories for writing and oral reading that students want the teacher to hear prior to a conference.

The taped recordings allow students to listen to a message as many times as they would like to develop understanding and to record a message as many times as necessary to ensure it will be understood. The advantage of the latter is that students learn to monitor their own language for clarity and understanding. Students might develop tape exchanges. These can be between peers or with older students in the same community. Students might record works they have written in prose and poetry for a tape exchange. An exchange can provide a language community relationship for a student who is the only member of a cultural community in the classroom. Tape exchanges can be used as well to provide peer language models for students for developing clarity and understanding.

Creative Dramatics. All forms of dramatics are appropriate for children developing control over language and literacy. Dramatizing is one of the best ways for children to experience literature. It can involve responding to a poem read by the teacher or poetry set to music. It might involve a puppet play or dramatization of a piece of literature read aloud by the teacher or by the students. Scripts are not required and memorization is unnecessary. Drama brings new meaning to a piece of literature. It can help students understand concepts, face issues, clarify values, and grasp the central "truth" of a story, the basis of comprehension (Kukla, 1987).

When children role-play they become other people in other places and participate in events of a story different from their own lives (Kukla, 1987). This extends and expands understandings of other cultures, beliefs, and traditions. To develop the necessary background information to create plays of this nature requires reading in narrative, particularly historical fiction, as well as expository materials. This must be followed by opportunities for contrasting and activities that will enrich students' background knowledge about the culture.

One class studying the contributions from the Greeks and Romans read Greek myths and some excellent versions of *The Illiad* and *The Odyssey.* The teacher shared information on the Greek dramatic form and a short excerpt from a Greek drama in a film that demonstrated the use of the chorus. This resulted in writing Greek-style plays that were performed for the class. These plays caught the mood, structure, and tone of the Greek drama and provided examples that indicated the students understood racism and gender discrimination of that time.

Puppet plays are another excellent way to respond to literature. Sorenson (1981a) suggested using simply made puppets that covered the hand, and were attached to sticks, on strings, and made from odds and ends, and a puppet stage that was simply made and quickly assembled. Older children will find it fascinating to experiment with other puppet modes such as Hindu shadow puppets. One class put on puppet plays of folk stories, legends, and myths of India. The students located the literature, a film showing a Hindu puppet show, and directions for making puppets in their social studies research.

Choral Speaking and Readers' Theatre. Two forms of dramatic expression that are successful in developing language and literacy are choral speaking and readers' theatre. They can be used with children at all levels, rely on the use of excellent literature, and provide opportunities for children to use and practice language. The poetry and stories selected for choral reading and readers' theatre require a large component of words, phrases, and dialogue borrowed from oral language (Woodbury, 1979).

Choral Speaking. Using good poetry selections in doing choral speaking can make a celebration out of language. Choral speaking may be introduced with good, short, humorous readings prior to using more serious selections. Readings and speakings will evolve from being merely a vehicle for fun to an art form. Most children generally get caught up in the process of exploring ways to express feelings and emotions through rhyme and the rhythm of language that create the story line. They learn effective nuances when they do parts and make recordings to hear spoken selections. These are important experiences for L2 learners. Choral speaking provides meaningful, enjoyable repetition of verse that transfers easily to children's oral language and writing. Interpretive reading readily transfers to oral reading.

One class of intermediate-age children on the United States/ Mexico border became fascinated with choral speaking. This class of predominantly Mexican American students improved their English rhythm, syntax, and vocabulary through this medium. Further, it provided a pleasant way for opening and closing a day.

Suggestions for developing choral speaking include the following:

1. Select a simple piece of poetry or a short humorous jingle that the children will enjoy. Poems with fascinating sounds, contrasts, and moods will be winners with children (Woodbury, 1979). Selections that will catch children's imagination by title and content make for a most successful start. For example, *Nathaniel Talking* (Eloise Greenfield, Black Butterfly, 1990) allows children to use a rap format to express a range of emotional experiences.

2. Read or speak the piece for the students. Discuss the meaning. Have students participate in doing the piece. Practice doing the selection until the children have a feeling of the rhythm and syntax. Help children feel the rhythm by tapping the fingers of one hand on the palm of the other (Bryan, 1971). Increase the amount of time spent each time a selection is practiced. The first reading or speaking of the poem can also be effective when a flannel board is used. This visual representation of the piece is excellent for students learning English.

3. Have children discuss the mood and meaning of the poem and how their voices might bring this out. Ask children to suggest different ways to render various sections of the poems and have them decide which is most effective to fit mood and meaning. If possible, try out the various suggestions by recording them on a tape recorder and playing them back for children to hear and critique. Practice these changes with the children. Woodbury (1979) suggested various types of voice contrasts in choral speaking.

4. As the recitation quality develops, add sound effects, hand clapping, body movements such as standing in place and marching, even music that fits the recitation. For presentations, appropriate props made by the children can be very effective.

Heald-Taylor (1989) reminded teachers that limited-English-speaking children may not participate in all choral activities at the beginning. She pointed out that they will likely participate in the body movements before speaking. Consequently, it would be wise to select pieces that are appropriately filled with action at the beginning.

Use the following books to choose selections for choral speaking:

John Bierhorst (ed.), *The Sacred Path: Spells, Prayers and Power Songs of the American Indians* (William Morrow, 1983)

Toni de Gerez, *My Song Is a Piece of Jade* (Little, Brown, 1984)

Barbara Michels and Betty White (eds.), *Apples on a Stick: The Folklore of Black Children* (Coward-McCann, 1983)

Charlotte Pomerante, *If I Had Paka: Poems in Eleven Languages* (Greenwillow Books, 1982)

Jack Prelutsky (ed.), *The Random House Book of Poetry for Children, A Treasury of 572 Poems for Today's Child* (Random House, 1983)

Virginia Driving Hawk Sneve, *Dancing Teepees: Poems of American Indian Youth* (Holiday, 1989)

Readers' Theatre.   The readers' theatre art form differs from choral speaking in that the scripts are never memorized. It is a medium in which readers interpret literature for an audience. Through interpretations listeners receive and develop mental images through the readers' voices. Readers learn to suggest physical action or movement through their vocal interpretation. The selections usually are works that have a lot of narrative and may not be as appropriate for dramatizing. A narrator develops a relationship with the audience by directly speaking to the audience as theme, situation, and explanation are shared. Poetry, letters, diaries, and biographies are forms of literature that may lend themselves to readers' theatre (Woodbury, 1979) as well. Teachers doing readers' theatre with younger readers generally write the scripts from an actual trade book. Commercial scripts are now available.

Many pieces of literature are easily adapted to narrative (Woodbury, 1979). There are some pieces of literature that can immediately be used in that format. One example is Ossie Davis's *Langston: A Play* (Delacorte, 1982), about the life of Langston Hughes, the great African American poet. Readers' theatre might be done following the teacher's reading of an enjoyable story or as an activity connected with literature circles or direct reading intervention. Because of the amount of repetitive reading of the scripts, with children taking different parts, there are great opportunities for transfer of language, vocabulary, and syntax into the children's oral and written usage. A good opportunity for this is Bill Martin, Jr., and John Archambault's *Knots on a Counting Rope* (Bantam, 1987). This book beautifully demonstrates the oral storytelling tradition of the Navajo people and portrays the strong family relationship between a young boy and his grandfather.

Older children may enjoy making their own scripts for readers' theatre. This would certainly be an excellent opportunity for them to do some cooperative writing based on the book, perhaps huddled around a word processor. Try beginning with books like Julius Lester's *The Tales of Uncle Remus: The Adventures of Brer Rabbit* (Dial, 1987), Sumiko Yagawa's *The Crane Wife* (Morrow, 1981), Marcia Brown's *Backbone of the King: The Story of Paka's and His Son Ku* (University of Hawaii Press, 1983), or Scott O'Dell's *Sing Down the Moon* (Houghton, 1970). If children need more assistance in being able to elaborate on their reading, the teacher might become more involved in the writing, as suggested by the following (Shanklin & Rhodes, 1989):

1. After reading the story encourage students to retell the story and determine characters and the role of the narrator.

2. Have children dictate the script and record it on a chart. As the process proceeds discuss how to change the story line to dialogue. Work out comprehension problems as the script develops. Adapt the first part of the book into script.

3. Type up the script and have children read through it, discuss it, and make any revisions to keep to the intention of the author. Do any rereading of the book as is necessary. Emphasize that students must decide what to change, what to keep, and how the script should be read. This allows children to share their own personal meanings of the text and determine how meanings are to be represented in a script.

4. Assign students in pairs to adapt groups of pages and return to the teacher for typing (unless there are computers available in the classroom).

5. Finish typing the script and make copies for the students. Have the students practice the script as a group and then present it for the rest of the class. Give children feedback on language clarity and expression during the practice sessions.

Readers' theatre can be an excellent vehicle for students developing important information about the mechanics of reading and writing. When children understand how parts are determined, they can easily read from stories full of dialogue without special scripts. Harste, Woodward, and Burke (1988) reported how one student asked how other children knew when to read and when to stop reading. This led to a discussion of quotation marks, and the knowledge immediately transferred to writing stories full of dialogue. Another solution for introducing children to dialogue is to use actual plays. Published plays for early readers such as Paul T. Nolan's *Folktale Plays Round the World* (Plays, 1982) will develop the concept of play and provide children with a transition for developing their own dialogue based on the story line.

Sharing and Discussing. Sharing and discussing have both similar and different purposes and objectives. In sharing, the sharer receives satisfaction and pleasure in sharing an idea, a project, or an experience, while the listener may be learning from the information and stimulated to go on and learn. The speaker's role is only more visually active. The role of the listener is difficult to observe unless he or she is encouraged to respond or ask questions. Sharing can help a speaker organize his or her ideas. In a discussion, sharing of information and ideas is certainly an aspect of the event. In a discussion both speakers are also receivers. Discussions may be held as well to determine, compare, and contrast understandings or to change attitudes or solve problems. Discussion is essential to reading because it is the foundation for developing higher level reading skills (Alvermann, Dillon & O'Brien, 1987).

Sharing. Sharing contributes toward the development of language and literacy. When a child shares, he or she has the opportunity to talk about something important using language in a meaningful, relevant way. Sharing can also assist the learner in organizing his or her ideas for writing. In many sharing situations the sharer prepares for the activity and plans what is to be said, perhaps even how it is to be said. This provides L2 learners with opportunities to functionally speak about something known that has been thought through.

Sharing has particular value to the L2 and dialect speaker because of the feedback about the communicative quality of the utterances. When children work in small groups to complete a task they become aware of language patterns and differences. They can compare and contrast different aspects of the language they speak and share this knowledge and understanding with others (Barrs, Ellis, Hester & Thomas, 1990). Teachers should model active listening by responding and questioning speakers. Questions should aid the speakers and listeners to improve organization and content.

Sharing experiences can be embedded in the language and literacy curriculum by having students share books read and films viewed and through techniques for learning how to critique. These experiences provide teachers with opportunities for facilitating student reflective abilities. Children need to assess their strengths and think about ways for becoming more confident and effective as talkers and listeners. This assists them in becoming more responsible for their own progress and development. For example, the following questions might be asked: What did you like about Christina's sharing? What was the main point she shared? Are there other points she could have made? What did you like about how the group listened? How could the group improve as listeners?

English second language (ESL) speakers might develop sharing skills through oral dialogue tapes (MacDonald, 1989). The student would record his or her sharing about a book read or heard in a quiet environment, then revise and reorder the oral text. This setting presents no pressure for production. The student is able to listen in a nonintimidating environment to his or her response, as well as the response from the teacher, as frequently as necessary.

Listening centers could be used for sharing as well. Encourage children to tape a selected reading, retelling, sharing, or response to a book for conferencing with the teacher. These should be in addition to written journals. Teachers can also develop oral dialogue exchanges by pairing English-learning students with English speakers or dialect-speaking students with SE speakers, much like pen pal projects (MacDonald, 1989). These can revolve around commonly read books or other topics and can be exchanges between classes or schools in a city or even farther afield. They are opportunities for both groups of students to develop in understanding.

Discussion. Children will be assisted to expand and refine their understandings from listening and reading through discussion. As children share their ideas, new meaning is extended and developed. Discussion gives the teacher an opportunity to hear what children are thinking and help them move to higher level thinking through skillful questioning. Children generally enjoy interacting with one another. Teachers should enable children to rely on themselves as interpreters of what they read. When children discuss literature in literature response groups they are put in the role of experts or resource persons. The presenter has to decide what is important to reveal about the book and what to read aloud. Students have greater control over their talk and more opportunity to interact while the teacher takes the role of participant (Strickland, Dillon, Funkhouser, Glick & Rogers, 1989).

Different teaching strategies should be employed to fit the different types of discussions (Alvermann et al., 1987). When teachers want students to master information, the teacher should use probing questions that require the student to clarify, justify, or refocus or that prompt answers or foster greater student interaction. If the class is discussing issues in which students may have conflicting opinions, the teacher should promote understanding and empathy among the discussants. When there are problems to be solved, the teacher should aid the students in dividing the problem into parts and then work in small groups through the parts to develop solutions, perhaps seeking additional data and evaluating proposed solutions.

Discussion results should be analyzed by the students, not only in regard to solving the problem but in regard to communication effectiveness. For example, are all members of the group participating? Again, here is a way to use cooperative grouping effectively by assigning different roles to members. One student certainly could monitor input by members to ensure participation. Are there speakers dominating the group discussions? Teachers must be sensitive to cultural gender roles of societies that have strong taboos regarding male/female interaction. These may require extensive school and community dialogue for reaching a solution. How can group members better support one another in discussions?

Planning a Discussion. A number of considerations must be included in planning discussions. First, it is necessary to consider group size, group makeup, instructional purpose, and necessary student communication abilities for the discussion. Group size should depend on how many persons are necessary to carry out the task and the intended teacher role during the discussion. Group makeup should consider gender, cultural considerations, personalities, interaction patterns, and abilities of the children. Self-selection should be structured to require heterogeneity. Scott (1991) stated that students in heterogeneous groups will more likely stay on task and stretch their thinking because of the opportunities for controversy and creative thinking. Cooperative learning is a useful strategy for breaking down stereotypes and helping all students learn to think and work together. It can facilitate the leadership development of female students and students from diverse cultures.

A number of helpful suggestions, adapted from Scott (1991), may assist teachers to improve discussion in classrooms with culturally diverse students. These suggestions include the following:

1. Teach students to view controversy as positive, to remain issue-oriented, and to respond appropriately. Work toward involving all participants in the discussion, explaining their rationale and differentiating ideas before integrating them through consensus. Learning the language for successful discussion is a key. For example: I understand how you feel, but . . . What do you think about . . . Have you considered . . .

2. Teach students to participate in "12-inch" voices in a pleasant, relaxed manner and use paraphrasing language. A 12-inch voice can only be heard a foot away and maintains a better classroom learning environment. Assign a noise monitor. Develop classroom signals for getting attention and reward children periodically for responding quickly.

3. Teach students language that encourages others to take part in a discussion and feel they have a receptive climate for being heard. For example: What do you think? It's your turn. That's a good idea!

4. Teach language for paraphrasing and summarizing ideas heard to facilitate effective communication. For example: Are you saying that . . . Do you mean . . .

5. Assist students in understanding that successful dominant-culture communication requires providing for wait time, looking at the speaker or listeners, listening attentively, a pleasant look or smile. These behaviors help students learn sources for miscommunication between listeners and speakers in the dominant society. Also, help students learn the communication behaviors of other cultures represented in the classroom to facilitate cross-cultural communication and understanding.

6. Plan groups or structure self-selection to include children with mixed ability levels, with different learning styles, and of different genders. These groups work more cooperatively, and there is less chance of one or two children doing all the talking. Most of the time students benefit in achievement and attitude if they are in small groups of two to four members. Groups of two are excellent to start with and then can be combined into groups of four in an activity. A group of four allows each child to see any materials being used or written and make eye contact with one another.

7. Focus on the need for learning to communicate with anyone as an important life-long skill. Bright, highly structured students may need conferencing to impress upon them the importance of being able to participate in a group.

8. Structure discussion activities to develop interdependence. Give acknowledgment for reaching a preset criterion for evidence of good interaction and social skill competence. Make sure that the students perceive that they need one another to achieve the task. Roles of group members should be clear and concrete; assigned roles provide for individual accountability. Tell students ahead of time that you will call on them randomly to explain group work and results from discussions. This lets students know everyone is accountable.

Students need opportunities to become confident. They need time to respond without stressful time constraints. Some children need more think time than others to respond. They must develop independence and confidence in their responses. Students often look to their teachers for reactions to a response rather than trusting their interpretations.

Role of the Teacher in Discussion.

According to Alvermann et al. (1987), a teacher should have the facility to use several different teaching roles at different points in the course of a discussion.

The *instructor role* is one of a telling or clarifying position. When overused this role discourages active participation and students cease to take their own responsibilities seriously.

The *participant role,* a contributing position, is one in which the teacher may share information and freely express opinions. This role provides children with a role model but also might influence children because the teacher is seen as being more credible and less open to criticism.

The *consultant role* is an advising position in which the teacher directs students toward finding answers on their own. This role allows the teacher to move about between small groups and consult upon request. The teacher must be careful not to be the final word in solving disagreements. Instead, the teacher must turn the problem back to the students for solving by suggesting alternative routes.

The *neutral role* is a position that promotes independent thinking. In this role the teacher remains silent and places responsibility on the students. All questions directed at the teacher are redirected toward the students.

Teachers have to be sensitive to the responses, or lack of them, from culturally diverse children. Lack of response does not mean that the student does not know the material or understand it. It may mean that the student does not know how to express his or her understanding or does not feel able to take the risk of self-expression. It is very easy to underestimate students' abilities, especially children from non-English-speaking or culturally diverse homes. Lack of response is too often assumed to be caused by a child's inability when it is, instead, the result of cultural diversity.

Children from diverse cultures in the community may appear shy because the school situation and cultural practices are alien to them. They may not know how to relate to children and adults with different cultural styles and may need to be invited to participate without pressure. They may need more thinking time to respond. L2 children can be encouraged to respond nonverbally if they are insecure in English language production. This will help the teacher learn about their listening comprehension and understanding. Their responses may demonstrate a very high quality of thinking.

Reading

The aim in developmental reading is to develop readers who can and do read. It is particularly important in a multicultural classroom to provide access to literacy for students from diverse cultures.

Establishing a Sequence for Studying Multicultural Literature

Norton (1991) stated that educators now realize that the aim of multicultural reading should be "to encourage students to accept and be sensitive to cultural diversity, to understand that similar values frequently underline different customs, to have quality contact with people from other cultures and to role-play experiences in order to involve students with other cultures" (p. 571). Norton (1990; 1991) modified a model for studying multicultural literature into a sequence of five phases. The redesigned Norton model starts with a broad awareness of myths, legends, and folktales from one cultural group and narrows to myths and legends of a particular subgroup. It then proceeds to autobiographies and biographies. Students are directed to use the values and beliefs determined from these stories for reading historical fiction and contemporary literature.

The model, according to Norton (1990; 1991), requires that the teacher carefully monitor the development of the reading phases to ensure that students acquire adequate prior information for developing values and beliefs. These become the bases for evaluation of the authenticity of historical fiction and contemporary literature. Each culture is studied individually, and cross-cultural comparisons are made. Literature is provided for one culture across all five phases. The following is an example of Norton's five phases using multicultural literature sampled from various cultures (these books can be found in Sibley's Recommended Books for Multicultural Teaching Themes and Topics in the Teacher Resource Kit). This example should not be interpreted as suggesting this sequence but serve only to show ways in which multicultural literature would fit specific Norton phases.

Norton's Five Phases in the Study of Multicultural Literature

Phase I: Traditional Literature   (Generalizations and Broad Views). Phase I emphasizes the traditional genre of a culture of folktale, fable, myth, and legend and focuses on identifying the commonalities among cultures and oral traditions in the culture. Examples that would fall into this phase include the following:

AFRICAN

Gail E. Haley, *A Story, a Story* (Atheneum, 1970)

Ashley Bryan, *Lion and the Ostrich Chick and Other African Folk Tales* (Atheneum, 1986)

Clayton Bess, *Story for a Black Night* (Houghton Mifflin, 1982)

HAWAIIAN

Marcia Brown, *Backbone of the King: The Story of Paka's and His Son Ku* (University of Hawaii Press, 1983)

Vivian L. Thompson, *Hawaiian Mythology of Earth, Sea, and Sky* (University of Hawaii Press, 1988)

Phase II: Traditional Tales from One Area (Narrower View). Phase II emphasizes the analysis of traditional myths and stories that will be compared with understandings developed in Phase I. Values, beliefs, and themes of one region's traditional tales are analyzed. Literature examples that would be appropriate for this phase include the following:

AFRICAN AMERICAN

Patricia McKissack, *Flossie & the Fox* (Dial, 1986)

Steve Sanfield, *Natural Man: The True Story of John Henry* (Godine, 1986)

Julius Lester, *The Tales of Uncle Remus: The Adventures of Brer Rabbit* (Dial, 1987)

SIOUX INDIAN

Paul Goble, *Iktomi and the Boulder: A Plains Indian Story* (Orchard, 1988)

Olaf Baker, *Where the Buffaloes Begin* (Penguin, 1985)

Phase III: Autobiographies and Historical Nonfiction. This phase examines values, beliefs, and themes identified in traditional literature and compares information in historical sources with autobiographies and biographies. Examples of literature from the Sibley collection that would be appropriate for this phase include the following:

AFRICAN AMERICAN

Joyce Hansen, *Which Way Freedom?* (Walker, 1986)

Joyce Milton, *Marching to Freedom: The Story of Martin Luther King, Jr.* (Dell, 1987)

JAPANESE

Eleanor Coerr, *Sadako and the Thousand Paper Cranes* (Putnam, 1977)

Yukio Tsuchiya, *Faithful Elephants: A True Story of Animals, People and War* (Houghton Mifflin, 1988)

HISPANIC

Elizabeth Borton De Trevino, *El Guero* (Farrar, Straus & Giroux, 1989)

Phase IV: Historical Fiction. Phase IV examines fiction of a culture and evaluates it according to authenticity of setting, conflicts, characterization, theme, language, and traditional beliefs and values. These are compared with nonfictional autobiographies, biographies, and historical information. The theme is a search for the role of traditional literature. Literature examples that could be included in this phase include the following:

AFRICAN AMERICAN

Candy D. Boyd, *Charlie Pippin* (Macmillan, 1987)

Joyce Hansen, *Which Way Freedom?* (Walker, 1986)

JAPANESE

Yoshiko Uchida, *Journey to Topaz: A Story of the Japanese-American Evacuation* (Creative Arts Book, 1985)

HISPANIC

Paul Robert Walker, *Pride of Puerto Rico: The Life of Roberto Clemente* (Harcourt, 1988)

Phase V: Contemporary Fiction, Biography, and Poetry. Phase V focuses on how beliefs and values identified in traditional literature and biography continue in contemporary works. Emphasis is on characterization, conflicts, and themes across the various selections. Examples of books for this phase of study might include selections from the following various cultures:

AFRICAN AMERICAN

Valerie Flournoy, *The Patchwork Quilt* (Dial, 1985)

Virginia Hamilton, *Zeely* (Macmillan, 1967)

Mildred Pitts Walter, *Justin and the Best Biscuits in the World* (Lothrop, 1986)

CHINESE AMERICAN

Eve Bunting, *The Happy Funeral* (Harper, 1982)

Bette Bao Lord, *In the Year of the Boar and Jackie Robinson* (Harper, 1964)

Laurence Yep, *Dragonwings* (Harper, 1975)

ESKIMO AMERICAN

Jean Craighead George, *Julie of the Wolves* (Harper, 1972)

Scott O'Dell, *Black Star, Bright Dawn* (Houghton Mifflin, 1988)

Group Reading Strategies

Two strategies can be incorporated into the multicultural classroom. The first, literature circles, provides for developing student self-direction. The second, the directed reading intervention strategy, is applied when the teacher needs to provide students structure to assist them in making better predictions while reading.

Literature Circles. Literature circles, a powerful teaching strategy, provide opportunities for children to select, respond, and interact with peers about interesting, meaningful, significant, and enjoyable ideas they have encountered in their reading. In literature circles children focus on quality literature, and read books in a supportive environment. They are guided by teachers to respond critically, to explore their imaginations, and to use creative thinking abilities. Literature circles give children the opportunity to explore emerging ideas and expand their understanding. The teacher's role is to become a group discussion member or discussion moderator.

Developing Literature Circles.   The procedures outlined by Harste et al. (1988) are for developing and conducting literature circles. The following procedures have been adapted for a multicultural classroom using multicultural literature with children from all cultures represented in a community:

1. Select four to six good multicultural books around a theme that students will find interesting. Children should have had experiences

related to the book's content, and the books should represent the reading range of the children in a class. Five to six copies should be available. Children certainly can be invited to assist in selecting themes and books. (See locating and selecting books later in this chapter.)

Multicultural literature themes might include those adapted from E. J. Brown (1992). Brown's themes, although recommended for early adolescents, appear to have a universal adaptability for all childhood use. Her multicultural themes include emphasis on individual role models and self-esteem, characters in cultural and socioeconomic settings, characters dealing with values of a community, peer-group relationships, relationships of characters with families, and characters dealing with dominant world views and social change.

2. Introduce these books to the students by giving a short book talk about the title, author, plot, and characters of each (see book talks later in this chapter). Invite the children to browse through the books. Then ask the students to select their first and second choices. This can be done by having children sign up on a chart, sheets of paper, or the board and placing after their name a "1" for their first choice or a "2" for their second choice. Groups should be kept small, and books should be repeated as interest continues.

3. Initiate activities that establish the theme of the study and prepare the students for reading. Involve the students in decision-making tasks to determine how much of the book is to be read and by when. Have the children read the determined selections. The reading process will vary between very early readers and children who are more fluent readers.

For early readers the teacher might read aloud or use books with a high degree of predictability. These can be read through the shared reading strategy (discussed in Chapter Five). Have students predict what the book will be about and what will happen. As the story unfolds emphasize refutation by asking the students what they think at certain points during the story. Is the information that they guessed wrong? How will the students change their ideas of what will happen? What influenced their thinking? Children should justify their reasoning for maintaining their predictions or refutations (Garrison & Hoskisson, 1989).

More able readers should read the determined length or total piece of material prior to coming to the circle. Students might keep response journals and/or reading logs to have a longitudinal record of their reading. These responses can be used for beginning the next discussion.

4. Students might be trained for paired reading and retelling. A student needing help is paired with a slightly better reader. Difficult sections are read aloud together and repeated. The stronger reader reads along silently and then reads aloud when the peer needs help at an agreed signal. This is followed by retelling. Paired reading and retelling supports L2 learners very well. According to Topping (1989) same-gender, paired combinations appear to have the most positive effects for male students needing reading assistance.

5. Initiate student interactions about the book by asking students to share impressions, ideas, or problems in constructing meaning. Discussions and activities about the book might continue for a number of sessions. When books are read in parts, students can be encouraged to predict in writing what is going to happen for each grouping of pages and then record what happened (Macon, Bewell & Vogt, 1991). The group should be led to determine some issues of interest that they would like to discuss over the next few days, and the teacher might guide children's attention to the story structure.

E. J. Brown (1992) suggested that students need to learn a process for analyzing multicultural literature. They should learn to identify the theme, summarize the piece around the theme, become aware of their ideas and feelings about the piece, study the piece to determine how the cultural setting influences all aspects of the piece, and draw conclusions about how culture and background influence people.

6. Apply the book to other readings and experiences through discussion. Macon et al. (1991) suggested using a Venn diagram (two partially overlapping circles) to contrast the two books being compared. Each of the outside sections of the diagram sections would identify how the books are different while in the middle section of the diagram the teacher would elicit how the books are alike. This could be done on the board or on a large chart.

Another technique suggested by Macon et al. (1991) is webbing. The character's name is written in the center and then characteristics are placed in circles surrounding the name. These are attached by lines to the name, and the characteristics are bound by lines to examples from the text in an outer ring.

7. Suggest activities that the children can select for extending and expanding the book. These might include writing letters to the author, writing a sequel to the book, making the book into a play and acting it out, using readers' theatre, and doing related research at the library for a specific project.

Developing Critical Thinking.   Literature circles provide an opportunity to develop critical thinking because they offer the possibility of developing a community for learning. To develop critical thinking, students need to have opportunities to share and to interact with one another. They need to work with one another in a variety of arrangements that provides opportunities for sharing both informally and formally. Experiences in creating and sharing meaning through art, music, and oral and written language experiences are particularly appropriate.

Shanklin and Rhodes (1989) suggested a strategy that would be appropriate in all multicultural classrooms. Students are encouraged to ask questions about a text. When students ask questions and explore meaning they are in the position of making decisions about what is important. When answers require inferences, the responses will come from children's own background knowledge and experiences. This process encourages better student interaction and interaction with the reading material.

Responding to Text.   In a literature-based program activities that are used with the reading must not be artificial but rather have real communication opportunities that engage the readers' minds, interests, and feelings (Altwerger, Edelsky & Flores, 1987). Readers need to learn how to respond to literature to make judgments and relate what they have read to their own experiences (Cullinan, 1987). All activities should stem from students' prior experiences as active comprehension is developed (Macon et al., 1991). This is an important consideration for students from diverse cultures who may have different sets of schemas to bring to a reading. The teacher can guide the children to develop better responses to the text for both literature circles and literature response groups (discussed later in this chapter) by using the following strategies adapted from Carline, Crawford, and Babb (1988):

PANEL DISCUSSIONS
1. Have a panel of reporters interview a panel of readers about the theme, characters, plot, and setting of a book like Eleanor Coerr's *Sadako and the Thousand Paper Cranes* (Putnam, 1977).

2. Have students present pro and con points of view to the class when there are strong feelings for or against a book.

DRAMATIZATION
1. Have students take different roles from the story and tell the story from their point of view. A good book for this might be Mildred

Pitts Walter's *Justin and the Best Biscuits in the World* (Lothrop, 1986).

2. Have students pantomime the story for the class as a way to encourage other students to read it.

ORAL ACTIVITIES
1. Have students debate the decisions made by a character in a book like Jean Craighead George's *Julie of the Wolves* (Harper, 1972) as being appropriate or inappropriate to the character.

2. Have students prepare a talk from a list of questions. For example, Why was this book written? Would this be a good movie or television presentation? What did the students learn from this book? How are characters in this book alike or different from people the students know?

3. Have students present biographical sketches of the author and/or illustrator.

4. Have students write and present vivid descriptions of a character they enjoyed from the book. Other students are required to guess the character.

ART EXPRESSION
1. Have students develop a pictorial time line or story map for a historical fiction book like Scott O'Dell's *Sing Down the Moon* (Houghton, 1970) which they share with the class.

2. Have students make a poster of the book to attract others to read it.

3. Have students develop a scene from a book in a three-dimensional "stage" in a shoe box turned on its side; share and explain the importance of the scene to the book.

4. Have students develop murals from a book like Vivian L. Thompson's *Hawaiian Mythology of Earth, Sea, and Sky* (University of Hawaii Press, 1988). The planning should develop rationale for the illustrations, setting, characters, and behaviors of characters depicted.

WRITING EXPERIENCES
1. Have students develop and share a reference book of facts from books like Margaret Musgrove's *Ashanti to Zulu: African Traditions* (Dial, 1976) or Russell Freedman's *Indian Chiefs* (Holiday, 1987).

2. Have students write and share with the group a sequel to a book

like Bette Bao Lord's *In the Year of the Boar and Jackie Robinson* (Harper, 1984).

3. Have students write a book review to be published in a class newsletter or newspaper that they share and discuss with the group.

4. Have students make and illustrate book jackets for books they are reading. Include a blurb and a biographical sketch for each of the authors and illustrators. Have these shared and displayed.

5. Have students prepare radio broadcasts that include book talks, advertisements on books, a book review, and a reading from a section of a book. Plan for two students to read each book reviewed to provide for conflicting opinion.

ORAL READING

Have students participate in Reader's Chair. Brief ideas about the book are told to prepare the class for listening. The reader then reads the total book (picture-book variety) or a prepared section from the book. Students and teachers ask questions about the book which are answered by the reader.

Directed Reading Intervention Strategy. The Directed Reading-Thinking Activity (DRTA), originally developed by Stauffer (1969), is a strategy to encourage students to make predictions and check the accuracy of their predictions. Studies of the DRTA strategy, according to Stieglitz and Oehlkers (1989), determined that students receiving instruction using this strategy were superior in the quality of their responses. The strategy encouraged students to formulate questions and hypotheses, process information, and evaluate tentative solutions.

This strategy seems to be effective in guiding students from diverse cultures, especially L2 readers, to use their prior information to formulate questions and hypotheses for predicting reading. It is also helpful in assisting students to develop appropriate understandings when their prior information may be mismatches with textual content. Teachers may have to determine if students have appropriate background experiences and knowledge for reading the selection through questioning. When students lack adequate prior experiences, the teacher will have to assist students to develop these prior to reading. Discussion following reading should examine those crucial cultural mismatches that can cause misunderstandings.

The following is an adaptation of this strategy applicable for students needing greater assistance in predicting:

1. To develop prereading skills have students locate information to determine what the selection or book will be about. Call attention to the title, subtitles and chapter titles, pictures and illustrations. Ask the students if the piece has a specific ethnic or cultural focus. What do the students know about this topic? Who is the author? Have the students read any of the author's books or stories before? What might the theme of this piece be? Assist students with experiences and activities that will develop appropriate background. Conclude by having students predict what they think will happen in the selection and why.

2. To develop prediction skills have the students read the book or selection to a predetermined point and discuss their predictions. Did the students change their predictions about what the story was going to be about or what was going to happen? What do the students think now? What cultural information is the author providing? Have the students read to the next point, stop again, and discuss changing predictions. Elicit story structure points as the reading progresses. What story events are developing the theme? Is it real?

3. To develop postreading skills follow the reading with discussion (C. B. Smith, 1989b; E. J. Brown, 1992). Can the students retell the story? What is the theme? Compare this to other stories that • e similar or completely different. What conclusions can the students draw about this story? What did they learn about the cultural groups? How does this story make the students feel about the cultural group? Why? What would the students do if they were in this story? What does the author want the readers to understand about growing up in the world of these characters? The students' world?

Developing Independent Reading Habits

Independent reading is a major force for developing reading fluency (Anderson, Hiebert, Scott & Wilkinson, 1985). Practice should be easy and should provide students with feelings of success and enjoyment that encourage continued reading. Books for independent reading are those used beyond group reading activities. They are student selected from a collection that reflects the literacy communities so as to provide opportunities for students to engage in familiar reading (Barrs et al., 1990).

Students need a reading environment in which browsing (spending time among books to get to know them) is not only condoned but encouraged. Time must be provided in classrooms for this activity as parents and primary caregivers may not be able to take children to public libraries. If children are going to become readers, they must have ample access to good books.

Tunnell and Jacobs (1989) found that when children self-select their own reading materials they develop a positive attitude toward reading. In these studies students had a specific time when they were encouraged to browse, select books, and read. Consequently, book collections should offer students from diverse cultures ample materials appropriate to their culture. This does not, however, negate the teacher's responsibility for introducing children to different genres and interesting books or encouraging students to try new topics or authors in their voluntary reading.

Literature Response Groups. Literature response groups stimulate speaking, reading, and writing through the use of good children's literature. Response groups contribute to the development of both language and reading. This flexible strategy varies from teacher to teacher, thus providing for the individuality of teachers and the needs of students (Strickland et al., 1989). The basic procedures involved in using literature response groups include the following:

1. Student-read books are shared followed by a prepared reading of a passage from the book. Other students are invited to respond to the book with questions or comments. One variation is to occasionally have students blind choose a question from a set of teacher-prepared generic questions written on cards. These are asked of the student sharing. They should prompt other questions and discussion.

2. Response journals are completed and used for later sharing in group discussions.

3. The teacher holds one-to-one conferences with students about their reading and writing. Notes or entries in folders or portfolios might be kept on these conferences by both students and teacher.

4. Each day a book or selection is read aloud to the class by the teacher. Class discussions follow the reading. In addition, teachers might share their own student-level or adult-level reading.

Sharing and conferencing are essential elements to sustain literature response groups. In a conference focused on reading, the teacher might listen to a student read (or have listened to the reading the student taped the day before) and discuss the book with the student. Discussion might include talking about the characters and how the author developed them. Figurative language, imagery, and style of writing might evolve out of this discussion.

During the conference the teacher might also do informal teaching that helps a child develop a particular competency. For example, suppose that a younger reader is not using the cueing systems. The teacher might stop and have him or her read the context and guess what a covered up word is going to be and why. (This need not be a word that the student does not know.) Or, perhaps the student is unable to pronounce a proper noun. The teacher could demonstrate how to give the person a name close to the spelling and go on reading. Pronunciations can be refined later when there is more time to concentrate on the word. Reading requires concentration on comprehension.

Literature response groups provide opportunities for students to use and practice language integrated with literacy. Strickland et al. (1989) explored the use of literature response groups in four classrooms in Fairfax County, Virginia, and through observations in the New York/New Jersey area. Students in classrooms employing this strategy used talk more effectively and functionally and learned to interpret literature.

Book Talks. One helpful strategy that encourages voluntary reading is the use of book talks. Book talks give students a glimpse of what the book is about. In a book talk the speaker highlights the major characters, plot, setting, and theme. Enough is told to whet the students' interest for reading. Part of the book is read aloud, and information about the author might be shared. Book talks should reflect the fun and excitement to be found in good books. When a teacher knows the class well, he or she has an opportunity to select books for book talks that fit the interests of students. Therefore, the teacher in a multicultural room must be sure to include books that will interest the entire class as a way to capture the interest of students who are not reading independently and to provide students with books and themes that provide life models.

Students can also give book talks. This provides excellent practice in summarizing material read and organizing it to share with others. Student book talks are especially appropriate because students know the interests of their peers and are influenced by their peers. Many students also enjoy reading aloud, and this provides an opportunity to select a good spot in a book and practice reading it aloud. Book talks can be held in small groups by inviting children who want to share or listen to join the group.

Including the teacher's book talks when children are sharing every week makes the teacher a real participant in the group. The children will look forward to what he or she shares.

How effective are book talks for increasing students' reading and their attitudes toward reading? Dahl (1988), a librarian, studied the effects of book talks on the amount of independent reading done by adolescent students, and Berkey (1988), a classroom teacher of eight- and nine-year-old children, studied children's attitudes toward reading as a result of participating in book talks. Dahl found that participating in book talks increased the amount of reading done by the adolescents; Berkey's study indicated that reading attitudes improved for children receiving book talks. The use of book talks appears to be a valuable strategy for increasing independent reading.

Self-Sustained Silent Reading.   One strategy that provides time and incentives for students to practice reading in the language and literacy program is self-sustained silent reading (SSSR). During SSSR students and teachers read materials of their own choosing without interruptions. SSSR is a time set aside every day for students' silent reading and independent writing. Students experience pressures for other diversions in their after-school time, or they may not have home environments conducive to silent reading. Therefore, it falls to educators to facilitate student development of strong reading and writing habits. Since there is a positive relationship between time spent independently reading and reading achievement, Anderson et al. (1985) stated that time in school is well invested in students' future reading habits.

SSSR, if used appropriately, provides students with a teacher model who reads (McCracken & McCracken, 1978). For some students, teachers may be their only reading models. Morrow and Weinstein (1986) found that when teachers read in free-choice time in their reading and literature programs, children's use of the classroom library center increased.

There are many different ways to organize for SSSR. An SSSR program might be schoolwide—everything stops at a given time for reading and writing. Or, the program might be scheduled by teachers on an individual classroom basis. If SSSR is an individual classroom activity, the teacher should plan with the children when the daily reading and writing will take place and the amount of time it will last. It is wise to discuss the amount of time children think they can read without interruption and how they should work toward increasing their silent-reading time. Develop classroom rules for the SSSR time.

It might be best to use a timer at the beginning of these experiences to encourage the children not to watch the clock. Reporting or sharing from SSSR is not the intent of the program. Consequently, this reading is not included as part of literature circles, literature response groups, or a recreational reading program (see discussion below). The children's reading can be discussed with the teacher during conferencing, if the child chooses.

Recreational Reading Programs. Another classroom reading strategy that is used to develop independent reading is the recreational reading program. Morrow (1987) stated that most of the studies showing benefits for voluntary reading involved children from middle-class homes. She set out to change the recreational reading behavior and attitudes of 130 inner-city New York City children, aged 6–10, in recreational day-care centers with a summer program emphasizing literature.

Various teacher-directed literature activities lasting 30 minutes included reading a book aloud and then displaying it prominently. Discussions of authors, illustrations, or types of literature followed with activities that were related to the stories. Storytelling techniques, such as chalktalks, felt-board stories, roll(er) movies, sound stories, and prop stories, were used. Children were encouraged to make their own books, write to authors, and share books in group discussions.

The program increased the use of books, and children stated in interviews that this type of program should be carried out in schools during the year. Children's comments indicated that they liked opportunities to choose books and wanted to take books home to read and that they appreciated not being rushed while reading.

The three programs—literature response groups, SSSR, and recreational reading—vary as a result of basic objectives for each. Literature response groups involve children in sharing but includes journal writing and conferencing. SSSR is intended to facilitate the amount of time children spend reading and serves as a means for encouraging life-long reading habits. Morrow's (1987) recreational reading program is a broadly designed literacy program intended to extend reading for inner-city children by introducing them to books, providing time for them to motivate one another from their individual reading, and providing rich language and literacy activities. The recreational reading program would appear to transfer to most school situations and certainly should have a multicultural literature focus. Literature response groups and the recreational reading program have great similarities and might be integrated.

Locating and Selecting Books.   If children perceive the teacher as a person who knows good books, they will ask for suggestions. In turn the teacher must observe what children read to ensure that the students are provided options for reading that will expand their interests and increase their positive self-concepts. Girls, for example, need to be encouraged to read informational materials and boys to read fiction (Barrs et al., 1990).

Some sources of information on children's books that teachers can use in selecting and/or ordering good books include the following:

> Barbara Barstow and Judith Riggle, *Beyond Picture Books: A Guide to First Readers* (Bowker, 1988)
>
> Early Years, Inc., *Teaching K-8* ("Children's Books," reviews by Carol Otis Hurst)
>
> International Reading Association (IRA), *The Reading Teacher* ("Children's Books" by Lee Galda; "Children's Choices," published every year in the October issue – a joint project of IRA and Children's Book Council)
>
> Ginny Moore Kruse and Kathleen T. Horning, *Multicultural Children's and Young Adult Literature: A Selected Listing of Books Published Between 1980–88* (Cooperative Children's Book Center, University of Wisconsin-Madison, 1988)
>
> Carolyn Lima and John Lima, *A to Zoo: Subject Access to Children's Picture Books,* 3rd Edition (Bowker, 1989)
>
> National Council of Teachers of English (NCTE), *Language Arts* ("Bookalogues" by Miriam Martinez and Marcia F. Nash)
>
> Beverly Slapin and Doris Feale, Revised Edition *Books without Bias: Through Indian Eyes* (Oyate, 1988)
>
> Diana L. Spirit, *Introducing Bookplots 3: A Book Talk Guide for Use with Readers Ages 8–12* (Bowker, 1988)
>
> George Wilson and Joyce Moss, *Books for Children to Read Along: A Guide for Parents and Librarians* (Bowker, 1988)

Although only two of the above sources deal with multicultural literature explicitly, the other sources include some excellent multicultural literature as it is published or have topics in their collections including diverse cultures, gender issues, or disabilities. Teachers should be aware of the current reviews in the periodicals for newly published materials. Particular issues throughout the year will deal with multicultural books. For example, *The Reading Teacher*'s "Children's Books" section may include cultural diversity in at least one yearly issue. Unfortunately, only a small amount of multicultural literature is published yearly. Many new titles continue to be from authors writing about the experiences of people of color. What they present may be different from how a person of a particular heritage would view and express ideas (Reimer, 1992).

Writing

Writing helps improve thinking; it separates ideas from the person and allows him or her to examine, explore, and develop them (F. Smith, 1982b). As a reflective process in clarifying thinking, writing allows people to try out combinations of words, phrases, and clauses as they strive for expression (Morris & Stewart-Dore, 1984). Students need experience with different forms of writing for composing. Students from diverse and mainstreamed cultures need to experience good writing from a range of cultures for writing models. Experience comes from reading widely and being exposed to a varied diet of literature. Reading can inspire people to write; they certainly learn written models from what they read. Through reading and listening to good literature, children become aware of the functions of words, figurative expressions, and different sentence patterns (Kolczynski, 1978). Sensitive conferencing with teachers helps developing writers become aware of the functional and creative attributes of language as they attempt to use language expressively.

Linguistic Diversity and Writing

Children from nondominant languages need to develop writing abilities in their first language. Even after becoming fully competent in English language and literacy, nondominant languages should continue to be developed and refined. The *Bilingual Education Handbook* (T. R. Smith, 1990) specified that this is important for the following three reasons:

1. There are economic advantages for those who are able to communicate in two languages in today's job market.
2. Respect and value for the native language is affirmed.
3. Skills learned in the first language are quickly transferred to the second.

When schools through their programs demonstrate a valuing of the nondominant language, it contributes to the learner's self-esteem.

When writing demonstrates influences from a dialect, first language, or multilingualism, educators tend to be more concerned than when a student's oral usage shows the same types of influences. Written work appears to have more of a concrete nature than oral language; there is more of a stigma for error. Non-English forms in writing, like oral language, are not an evidence of weakness or language deficiency. Non-English forms, like reading miscues, provide the teacher with information about the student's developing abilities and strategies being used. They may be indications that the student is relying on the first language when the written aspect of language is unknown in the second language. For example, a Spanish-speaking literate student learning English who places *es* in front of English words beginning with *s* such as *spider,* or *ch* for *sh* in *short,* is using forms that are known from the first language (Nathenson-Mejia, 1989). These are not indications of any weakness but indications of the student's problem-solving abilities. They show how learners reconcile the difference between two systems and/or use their knowledge of pronunciation.

Students who have developed literacy in their primary language are at an advantage in learning literacy in the second language. What learners know about writing in the first language forms the basis for learning to write in other languages (Edelsky, 1982). Learners have more resources to draw upon when they have more than one language. "Their spelling shows a definite use of their own pronunciations along with their knowledge of letter/sound correspondence in negotiating the written form of what they intended to say" (Nathenson-Mejia, 1989, p. 517). Teachers need to recognize and celebrate a student's efforts to reconcile two language systems.

The ideal situation for students becoming bilingual or multilingual is to maintain all languages throughout their lives. (The same principle applies for adding a dialect.) All language functions in the primary language, including written language if there is a written language, should be continued. However, multiple-language learning and maintenance appears impossible in many sites in the United States. The sheer multitudinousness of language communities in some areas of the nation makes either teaching or maintaining a primary language for students seem a near impossibility. Society's value for English-only education governs the economics of the situation. The best programs for these students would provide a school environment rich in language and literacy experiences, first in the primary language and then in English. Without such programs, schools should expect to provide prolonged support for L2 learning, particularly in academic subjects.

Guidelines for the Writing Program

Harste et al. (1988) suggested six universal components as being essential for a successful developmental writing program. The following guidelines have been adapted with particular application to the multicultural classroom:

1. *Immerse students in quality multicultural literature across a wide*

range of genre. Multicultural literature will provide students with models and forms for writing from authors writing with a different world view. Students develop structure, format, syntax, vocabulary, motivation, and interest in writing from literature. Children see topics for writing fiction and fantasy from their everyday experiences. Books used in the classroom should provide students from diverse cultures opportunities to see life and experiences that have relevance to their lives. For example, Nikki Giovanni's *Spin a Soft Black Song* (Hill & Wang, 1985), Eve Bunting's *The Happy Funeral* (Harper, 1982), and Eve Bunting's *How Many Days to America? A Thanksgiving Story* (Clarion, 1988) may provide experiences that will have relevance to students, and they will realize that what they write becomes another person's reading.

2. *Focus writing on the message, not the form.* Students must first be concerned with the content of what they are writing. A student can be aided in clarifying his or her ideas through reorganization of ideas, using vocabulary or terms that will better inform the reader, or including other important descriptive content. One question a writer should ask is, *Does this say what I want and need to say?*

When a student is able to perceive the message through the eyes of a character, the message has clear intent and the writer is better able to express a message. For example, Taro Yashima's *Crow Boy* (Viking, 1955) provides an excellent example of a growing understanding of a character and a point of view in a book.

3. *Develop a purpose or reason for writing.* When writing is encouraged, based on a purpose and reason, the learner is more likely to decide to participate. The writer is less afraid to express a point of view in his or her own voice when he or she perceives that diverse points of view are accepted in the classroom.

4. *Develop a sense of ownership in writing.* When young learners take responsibility for their own learning, they are determined to succeed and generally will do so. Students need to write for themselves, not others. It is then that learners value their own work. Consequently, it is important that students have experienced literature that provides models for seeing life from another view, in another's eyes. These opportunities arise reading books such as Clayton Bess's *Story for a Black Night* (Houghton Mifflin, 1982), set in rural Liberia; Candy D. Boyd's *Charlie Pippin* (Macmillan, 1987), which provides a study of war and peace from the point of view of a peace group; or Dale De Armond's *The Seal Oil Lamp* (Little, 1988), which focuses on why Eskimos would leave a blind child to die.

5. *Provide work time, space, materials, and a supportive environment.* When students are given time to draft, conference, rewrite, publish, or share their writing in a supportive environment that values what they have to say as authors, their writing develops.

6. *Provide opportunities for developing writers to share their authoring efforts with other developing authors.* Students need to share their excitement in writing both informally and formally through doing peer evaluations, publishing, and activities such as Author's Chair, a time when the total work is read aloud to a small group or to the class.

In the developmental writing program the teacher will continue modeling and demonstrating with children through shared writing and will increase the emphasis on independent writing through the writing workshop discussed below.

The Writing Workshop

Authorship is expected in the developmental writing program. Authors make decisions, take responsibility for what goes on paper, and are sensitive to the contexts in which they write and to their audiences. Teachers who instruct children to copy, or insist on taking control of the children's writing in their classes, will not have children functioning as authors. These children will not be concerned with the meaning they write or learn from the experiences of generating written text (Hall, 1989).

Hall (1989) pointed out that children do not act randomly and without thought. Children may not act as adults because they have limitations of experience that lead them to conclusions different from those of adults. Consequently, as children author text educators must seek the intention behind the text and identify the children's interpretation of the task and view of how to work through the task. This requires a sensitive teacher conferencing as part of the writing process in a writing workshop. Students will learn concepts and ideas through experiences in making meanings with print.

The writing workshop should have long periods to allow students opportunities to feel comfortable in producing a piece of writing. Each student should have his or her own writing folder in which ideas or topics for writing and drafts of works-in-progress are kept. These should be located where students can conveniently add work and take work out of them. Children should be encouraged to ask teachers about their writing progress, but the privacy of children must always be respected; teachers must be sensitive to when children need to be alone or have something kept private.

Integral to the writing workshop is the writing process. Although various authorities classify differently the writing processes used for developing and organizing the writing (Graves, 1983; Calkins, 1986; Moffet & Wagner, 1983; C. B. Olson, 1984; DeGroff, 1989), most include similar aspects: prewriting, in which the writer rehearses (Graves, 1983) what is to be written about; drafting; and rewriting. The writing processes are components for a Writing Workshop and are discussed in relation to multicultural literature. (Not all the selections discussed are in Sibley's Recommended Books for Multicultural Teaching Themes and Topics in the Teacher Resource Kit.) The importance of interaction with multicultural literature is implied as the basis for developing writers.

Prewriting.   Writing develops naturally out of good literature experiences. Discussion of a book can lead directly into a writing experience. Many children's authors of multicultural literature demonstrate how to use real experiences or everyday events in fiction and fantasy. Ezra Jack Keats (*The Snowy Day,* King, 1962), Lucille Clifton (*Everett Anderson's Goodbye,* Holt, 1983), Vera B. Williams (*Cherries and Cherry Pits,* Greenwillow, 1986), and Virginia Hamilton (*Zeely,* Macmillan, 1967) are authors who use actual family experiences and events in children's lives in their books. Discussing these books can help children write about fantasy as well as personal experiences (DeGroff, 1989).

Selecting Topics.   Children with topics begin writing immediately. However, a student may sit, become frustrated, or perhaps misbehave when he or she does not know what to write. Children might decide on a topic from brainstorming ideas about a story. For example, Vera Williams' *Cherries and Cherry Pits* (Greenwillow, 1986) provides an excellent model for writing. Students can brainstorm activities that might be done that could be shared with other children or family members. A semantic web of ideas can develop from a brainstorming session by listing suggested ideas and connecting them with lines to show relationships.

Rehearsal.   Ideas are selected, developed, and organized during the rehearsal stage. Students should be encouraged to recall information about sights, sounds, feelings, and actions that are related to their experiences. These provide a sense of reality. As children read and discuss a book, assist them in noting information in books similar to their own experiences (DeGroff, 1989). Children might be assisted in writing by first drawing illustrations they will write about. This assists them in organizing their information.

Focusing.   Authors write for an audience. Children also need an audience. When children write for an audience, they have a source for reaction. The type of audience will determine how the book is written. Audiences have different interests, require different language (syntax and vocabulary). Students learn to focus when they write from their own experiences. Help them identify from a book what the author did not include in the story and why (DeGroff, 1989). For example, in Miska Miles' *Annie and the Old One* (Little, 1972), why did the author not tell what Annie's parents and grandmother did while Annie was at school? Why did the story focus on what Annie did in school and emphasize the weaving at home? Children must come to realize that the events in the story had to focus on Annie's responses to the grandmother's weaving. Focusing helps us determine what and what not to write.

Drafting.   During the drafting stage a writer gets his or her ideas down into print. The ideas might be quickly jotted down so that the developing meaning will not be lost. Anthony Browne's *Piggybook* (Knopf, 1986) provides an example of the importance of setting a tone or mood early in a work to make the story effective. Have the students discuss the first part of the book and see how the author carefully develops all the work that the mother does in the story. The mother's contribution to the lives of the husband and sons is not appreciated. When she leaves, have the children predict what they think will happen. Will her work get done? If it does not, what will happen? These aspects are realistic in the book. Then the book becomes a fantasy. Do the father and sons really turn into pigs or do they seem like pigs because of the way they live? The author chooses both realism and fantasy to effectively develop the idea he wanted the reader to gain from the book.

An effective strategy for aiding young authors after they have drafted a piece of writing is use of the authors' circle (Harste et al., 1988). As students have completed drafts they are considering for publication, have them meet in groups of three or four and read their pieces aloud to the group. Follow this with other authors telling what they heard and found most effective, raising questions about any parts that were unclear to them. As students become more proficient in working in the circle, encourage the author, after reading his or her piece, to identify any troublesome parts and ask for responses about certain areas. The group should then discuss and explore ideas on how to deal with the author's concerns. Finally, they should discuss parts of the piece they liked and raise questions about meaning.

The teacher's role is to model and set the tone for the type of exchange that should occur in the authors' circle. Children should be informed that they may have to read their pieces more than once for listeners to get the sense of the piece and the author's problem.

Conferencing. Writers can conference with both peers and teacher. There are natural similarities in the roles of teachers and peers as they conference. Conferences provide ways for students to extend their language development. Conferences involve explaining a point or clarifying an idea. The student receives input to extend his or her ideas in discussing and listening.

Teacher Conferencing. As he or she conferences with a student, the teacher will serve as interested reader or listener and editor and through questioning will assist the writer in developing independence (Kolczynski, 1978). Conferences need not be formal situations. They can be a kind of close-up observation in which the teacher pulls a chair over and talks for a few seconds to 10 minutes or more (Turbill, 1982). Weekly times for planned conferencing should be scheduled. The teacher must be available for an emergency conference when someone is "stuck" with some writing. Conferences should be held often, even for a few minutes as students request help. Although the writing workshop might be only scheduled twice weekly, if the program is successful, the children write and read every available time during school and at home. Teachers must talk with parents about their roles in working with the young writer. Children must retain their roles as the author.

Conference discussions should be modeled after the discussions teachers do with children in responding and reacting to books read. In the conference the writer receives comments and responses and he or she takes them into consideration for revising or rewriting (DeGroff, 1989). The writer's ownership of the work is always respected. Teachers want to create the kind of discussion about a student's work similar to that in discussing a piece of literature.

Students may leave the teacher pieces of work to look at prior to their conferences. The teacher writes notes on separate pieces of paper to share with the students, either at the conference or prior to it. When these are on separate papers they are easier to work with and they can be used or discarded by the young writers as they wish. Teachers should follow a particular formula: Make a positive statement about the piece, then ask some questions or make some comments about a section not understood or needing greater clarification.

A first conference on a piece of writing always focuses on meaning and the communication of the writer's ideas. The writer is always free to accept or reject the ideas suggested by teacher or peers. A conference should be started with some statement that will get the student to open up, such as the following: How's it going? How are you doing? Tell me about your piece. As the conference progresses the following types of questions probably will be helpful: As a reader, I do not follow this part. Can you explain? Can you think of a different way to say this? (Turbill, 1982, p. 35.)

In conferencing with students the teacher should at times emphasize the process aspect of their writing to encourage student self-examination of their writing. This helps the developing writer to become aware of what works for him or her. To encourage students to think ahead in their writing, the following questions might be asked: What is going to happen next in this story? Do you know what's going to happen very far ahead? What happens when you get to know your characters? Do they seem to take charge of the story? (Tway, 1984, pp. 13–14.)

Peer Conferencing.   Teachers may wish students to conference with one another prior to a conference with the teacher. The aim is to get the writer to read the piece to someone and get a reaction from the listener. This process encourages students to be more independent in their writing and come up with their own suggestions for revising their work. A clear distinction should be made on the nature of the conference, content, or editing. This provides for better peer relationships. Students will know that the content conference deals with making the piece of writing interesting and communicating to the reader. An editing conference is clearly one in which the writer is helped to get a piece ready for publication.

Preparing for Publication.   When students have a purpose for writing, they see a reason for revising and editing work. Publication is certainly a legitimate reason for revising and publishing. Publishing takes many forms from Author's Chair to making a book to displaying the work to sending the letter to writing a play.

Revision.   Revising means arriving at alternatives, trying them out, and evaluating their logic and effectiveness (DeGroff, 1989). When people read, they make revisions. They predict what will happen, how something will be used, what some character will do. As they encounter new information in the text, they revise to go along with the author's meaning. When teachers ask students to suppose this or that happened as the work is discussed they get students to activate their revising skills. Children's experiences with revising predicting in reading will transfer to writing revision. For example: Suppose that Chin (Ian Wallace, *Chin Chiang and the Dragon's Dance* [McElderry Books, 1984]) had not run away? Suppose he had not climbed to the roof of the library building? Through working out these potential revisions, students see that the author's focus was to help Chin Chiang overcome his problem and develop self-trust.

In the revision, the student rethinks and reshapes the writing to be more communicative. Work that is not revised should be kept in the writing folder. Beginning writers would not be expected to do revisions.

Editing. In the revision stage students focus on conforming their work to meet conventional use of written language. At this point, however, the writer may still be selecting word choices or ways to give the writing just the right meaning. Word choice is important to create the right mental image. In early editing children should be sensitive to using the right words.

In Toshi Maruki's *Hiroshima No Pika* (Lothrop, 1980), for instance, four days after the atom bomb has fallen, Mii is still holding the chopsticks she had in her hand when the bomb fell. Her mother tries to take them from her hand and "pried her fingers open one by one." The word *pried* is perfect for aiding the reader to understand the shock, the sense of loss of the child in the story. Editing is a process the author does that aids the reader to develop imagery, clarity, and empathy.

DeGroff (1989) pointed out that when children are assisted to read as editors they become more conscious of what authors do. For example, several words in Ezra Jack Keats' *The Snowy Day* (Viking, 1962) are compound and hyphenated. Keats emphasizes these with hyphens to indicate action in the word *s–l–o–w–l–y*. The choices that most authors make are choices open and available to children as well.

Some points from Turbill (1982) might be used to influence students to value editing:

1. All adult published writing is edited.
2. Commercially produced books are polished.
3. Readers expect clear ideas, appropriate sequence, correct spelling, and good punctuation.
4. Potential audiences for the writing are identified.

Teachers will undoubtedly want to have editing conferences, especially with young writers. The conference is an opportunity to informally instruct the student. Spelling and punctuation are concerns when students' writing comes to the publication stage. A decision has to be made regarding who is the audience for this writing in deciding if the invented spelling will need to be correctly written. Some prereading education of potential parental readers of early writing can help to eliminate the need to tamper with the unique charm of these pieces. Remember that invented spelling provides insight into the child's growth.

In any editing conference the writer should always be in control. If students are doing peer editing, only the writer holds the pencil. If the teacher wishes to demonstrate or suggest an idea, he or she should write it on another paper that can be copied, if the student wishes. Peers might be used to make suggestions that may be better understood than the teacher's. A student who used a particular technique or device may be asked to discuss the idea with the writer or to share his or her work.

Publishing. Publishing takes many forms. Although publishing might be thought of as making books, publishing can range from articles for a student paper to letters to authors. When a student writes a note, puts up a notice, or writes a report, these are forms of publishing. The sharing of writing in the Author's Chair is publishing as much as putting a piece on display.

Many teachers encourage beginning writers to publish book after book, and to write, write, write! This develops fluency and risk taking. This aids students to view themselves as authors. Teachers of these students often provide many quickly made blank books to stimulate the writing. These can be published through sharing in the Author's Chair and/or by displaying around the room for all children to read.

As students develop greater fluency in writing, more care is usually taken in the development of books so that students understand all the options open to them. Works that are longer go through more drafts and consequently take longer to produce. All the components of commercially published books should be included in these more fully developed books. The covers should be carefully constructed, perhaps laminated, or completed using other processes that have been made available in the room.

Students who are directed to illustrations in books, pay attention to these as they write themselves. Picture books often depend greatly on the illustration. An excellent example of this is John Steptoe's *Mufaro's Beautiful Daughters: An African Tale* (Lothrop, 1987). Without the illustrations, the reader would lose the understanding of flora, fauna, and architecture of Zimbabwe. As authors, students should explore how the illustrations are achieved. Art materials and techniques for doing various illustrations should be available in the class-room. Perhaps illustrators can be invited to the school to demonstrate how they illustrate books.

All aspects of books should be pointed out to the students. For example, books are often dedicated. Katherine Paterson dedicated *Rebels of the Heavenly Kingdom* (Lodestar/Dutton, 1983) "for Virginia Buckley," followed by Chinese words in Roman letters, Chinese char-acters (symbols), and "a thousand thoughts—ten thousand thanks." Dedications often make for some interesting speculations for insights to the author. For example, how does Katherine Paterson come to be able to write Chinese?

Children need to notice devices authors use in opening books and discuss how they assist the reader. Marion Dane Bauer's foreword to *Tangled Butterfly* (Houghton Mifflin/Clarion, 1980) appears to serve the same purpose as a blurb on a dust jacket. While Dick Roughsey's, *The Rainbow Serpent* (Gareth Stevens, 1975) has an introduction that informs the reader that the author/illustrator is an Aboriginal man and provides information to understand dreamtime in the Aboriginal culture.

Teachers can simulate aspects of real publishing houses in their classrooms and stimulate writing. Since all materials sent to a book publisher are not published, only the best work of children might be prepared for publication, generally one book out of three or four. The teacher acts as an editor and helps the writer evaluate the best of his or her work (children's work is not evaluated against others, only against their own). These books then get special attention with special pro-cedures taken for publishing the work. They may be typed or printed on a word processor or have extensive use of handwriting, such as Vera B. Williams and Jennifer Williams' *Stringbean's Trip to the Shining Sea* (Greenwillow, 1988). Special care is encouraged in the preparation of illustrations. Book covers are made with special bookbinding pro-cedures.

Teachers should call children's attention to the various ways that authors place text in books and how the illustrations are placed on the page. Some authors might have the text across from the illustration, some might have the print on the page with the illustration, or the print might be superimposed over unimportant aspects of the illustra-tion. For example, in Ezra Jack Keats' *The Snowy Day* (Viking, 1962), there are no borders for the text and the illustrations take up the total page and contribute to a feeling of openness.

Teacher time could certainly be a reason for limiting books brought to publication! As children mature in their writing, they pass through the period of writing an extensive amount of small books and their book production takes longer, generally going through more drafts as their stories become longer and more complex. Consequently, for these children the teacher may need a volunteer with typing or word-processing skills to assist in preparing texts for publication if there is not adequate student access to word processors.

Model Multicultural Literature Theme

The multicultural literature theme "People in Our Country, Cities, and Neighborhood: How They are Alike and Different" is provided in Section 1 of the Teacher Resource Kit. It is an example of a theme that attempts to assist students to discover the underlying values of the various cultural communities in the United States. It is based on the premise that multicultural literature has power to inspire students to act upon the interactions they have in reading literature. Interaction in this context refers to the opportunities students have to see and experience the life of another child through the characters in books.

This particular model was developed for children from 8–10 years of age. Focus books selected for the theme provide opportunities for children to read about a wide diversity of people in the United States. In developing this theme it was assumed that the children would not have had extensive experiences reading about cultural diversity. Consequently, the concern was to use literature that developed understandings for which the children might have adequate prior information. Focus books in the theme demonstrate strong family relationships. Speaking, reading, and writing are embedded in the theme.

This model theme demonstrates the use of a number of strategies provided in this chapter as well as in Chapters Three and Four. Only one of the selected communities is further focused in the model theme with an instructional web. It is developed around one of the books in Sibley's Recommended Books for Multicultural Teaching Themes and Topics: Miska Miles' *Annie and the Old One* (Little, 1972).This book is a highly recommended book. But, despite its high literary quality, readers might make incorrect conclusions from story and illustrations about the Navajo people. Consequently, it provides opportunities for students to research the culture and life of Navajo people to rectify any misconceptions. Since children would be involved in both the development of the theme and learning activities, their interests and ideas about the theme's focus and their transactions with the reading and interactions with other readers would significantly change the model given in the Teacher Resource Kit. The values and beliefs that children learn from such a study when considered with a caring and thoughtful teacher can inspire them to engage in social action.

SUMMARY

Children in classrooms across the United States have diverse heritages. All children need to experience the literary heritage of the many cultures found in their nation. It is through multicultural literature that students will be able to identify with the characters and the tellers of stories who are different. Stories represent the values and beliefs of people. Norton (1990, 1991) has provided a model that teachers should consider in developing a strong foundation for students for understanding their own culture and the cultures of others in society. To comprehend any culture's literacy heritage, students need to experience it from the aspects represented by the Norton model.

Children in schools across the country are sojourners together into the future. When each one is able to accept, value, and appreciate the traditions, values, and beliefs of others, they will all be enriched and in turn be able to secure their own values, beliefs, and traditions. In the process of accepting others, they will come to realize the great similarities that all people have, recognize their common needs and goals as well as differences. Further, this process will stimulate the development of common beliefs, traditions, and goals in society that will glue all people of the nation together.

The challenge of educators is to develop classrooms that make multicultural literature an integral part of the reading and language arts curriculum and integrate the teaching of language and literacy through multicultural literature themes. Oral language, speaking and listening, is an essential component in the multicultural classroom for the success of all children. The sensitive educator weaves rich experiences throughout the learning themes that increase children's self-esteem through supportive listening and speaking activities. Cooperative or collaborative learning activities support the empowerment and development of self learners and requires student interaction.

Reading and writing must be an integral part of any theme along with speaking and listening. For example, discussion is an essential part of most reading and writing strategies. Sensitive critical listening is required for students as an audience for writer's chair, oral storytelling, and readers' theatre. Reading and writing strategies such as literature circles, literature response groups, and writing workshop rely heavily on listening and discussing as vital components.

Reading and writing are vehicles for extending learning in literature themes when other curriculum areas are integrated in the study. This is particularly possible when the theme is the focus for learning, not reading and writing. Children should use reading and writing to discover what they want to learn about a theme. Literacy is learned as a process or by-product, not the focus of instruction. Children then see a purpose for learning to read and write because reading and writing are means for achieving what they want to learn.

Learning experiences in the multicultural classroom must be based on the strengths of learners, their culture, language, interests, and observed learning patterns. Strategies must be selected that consider the optimum learning experiences for all students. Students need opportunities to work together, challenge each other with their ideas, and support each other in their development. They need time as well to read and write individually. This should happen in a relaxed classroom environment in which the only stress is a student's drive for learning. Such an environment requires balance for learner success. The educator balances group and individual learning, the emphasis on each communication skill, teacher-directed and student-directed activities, and the content to ensure that a multicultural focus is integrated into the curricula.

IMPLICATIONS FOR INSTRUCTION

Implications for the instructional program that can be drawn from this chapter include the following:

1. Develop activities for all students that provide for their continued listening and speaking development. Children from diverse language backgrounds, non-English and dialect speaking, must have language models and interaction with teachers and peers. SE-speaking children should understand and appreciate other languages and dialects. Misunderstanding and miscommunication are often culturally related. Classroom experiences can be provided through the use of multiculturally appropriate literature and activities to encourage sharing and discussing.

2. Facilitate listening and speaking, reading, and writing in a multicultural classroom by carefully selecting, sequencing, and using mul-

ticultural literature. Multicultural literature can increase student self-esteem, language and vocabulary development, critical thinking, and understanding of other people, and it can provide situations that might lead to social change.

3. Select multicultural literature that has characters, situations, and themes that relate to students' personal experiences.

4. Use literature circles to empower students for learning. Literature circles provide opportunities for decision making through group interaction and integrate sharing, discussion, and writing.

5. Employ the directed reading intervention strategy to assist students who need added structure in developing prior information for understanding.

6. Select multiple strategies such as literature response groups, book talks, SSSR, and recreational reading to encourage the development of individual reading habits.

7. Encourage first-language (L1) literacy as an aid for developing writing for L2 students. Writing competencies have high transferability from one language to another.

8. Accept L2 writing miscues students make. They are not deficiencies. Non-English forms or interference from the first language probably are indicators of a student's ongoing learning process to reconcile two language systems.

9. Develop a writing program in the multicultural classroom by immersing students in good multicultural literature. Focus on the message by having students develop a purpose for writing and a sense of ownership. Provide a supportive environment and opportunities to share and communicate with other developing authors.

10. Create an environment for writing by providing ample time for writing. Empower students to make decisions, draft their ideas, and learn from their trials through conferencing and peer interaction.

11. Employ a writing workshop strategy that includes prewriting, drafting, and rewriting. Use multicultural literature for writing models.

12. Select multicultural themes that provide students with an understanding of the social and cultural systems and structures in a multicultural society.

CHAPTER SEVEN

Developing Multicultural Social Studies Topics for Language and Literacy Learning

- *What is the nature of the present elementary social studies curriculum?*
- *How can social studies infuse multicultural content?*
- *How do European American cultural values affect the learning of culturally diverse students?*
- *What language- and literacy-related strategies will facilitate social studies learning for all students in a multicultural classroom?*

INTRODUCTION

Although the United States is made up of people from diverse racial, ethnic, religious, and cultural groups, school curricula provide scant attention to these groups. The focus for the majority of curricula is the dominant cultural group in U.S. society—middle-class European Americans. A curriculum that ignores the histories, experiences, and views of the American experience of people from diverse racial, ethnic, religious, and cultural groups has negative consequences for students from both dominant and nondominant traditions and cultures.

Students from the dominant culture are denied an opportunity to view their history and culture from other perspectives. This reinforces a false sense of superiority, provides a misleading conception of racial and ethnic groups, and denies dominant-culture students learning experiences gained from knowledge, perspectives, and frames of references through studying other cultures and groups. Students from diverse ethnic groups and cultures are alienated when a curriculum does not reflect their cultural experiences, perspectives, dreams, and hopes.

Many studies establish the textbook as the main source for teaching, especially social studies, reading, and language arts (Banks, 1989b). For social studies, this means that reading expository material is the main source for learning. (Expository refers to subject matter, impersonal and likely written from a specific cultural perspective.) Language, literacy, and literature, however, can be important mediums for learning social studies. Content topics such as social studies provide opportunities to use language and literacy in authentic experiences in which students discover the past and weave the past with the present. When the experiences are authentic, language and literacy are used and learned in meaningful, relevant, and functional ways. Authentic experiences reflect the community and world through the eyes of the learners—their world views. Narrative literature provides an opportunity to enrich, supplement, reinforce, clarify, and relate expository content to the curriculum and lives of the students for greater in-depth understanding.

Further, narrative literature provides the teacher with materials that develop other cultural perspectives. For example, most elementary schools study Columbus and the discovery of the new world in the social studies curriculum. Certainly there are other points of view, other perspectives, about this explorer, his feats, and the effect of the so-called discovery on the inhabitants of the new world, than what is usually presented in most elementary textbooks. A book such as Jane Yolen's *Encounter* (Harcourt, 1992) presents such a perspective for children through the voice of a Taino Indian (American Indian nation), first as a young child and finally as an adult. Readers learn that Columbus took slaves and through a note from the author in the end piece, are informed that 50 years after being discovered by Columbus, in 1548 only 500 Taino people remained.

AN OVERVIEW OF THE SOCIAL STUDIES CURRICULUM

Social studies materials in use in elementary schools, traditionally have been developed based on the expanding universe theory—focusing on the child and family and expanding to neighborhood, city, state, nation and world neighbors. Many elementary school social studies programs are still packed with information presented in a global manner and highly illustrated to assist student understanding. Each grade level covers such a wide scope of content that there may be little opportunity for in-depth study.

Textbook Approach

Social studies texts used by most elementary schools provide some recognition, however subtly, that other cultures, races, and religions coexist in society and have made contributions to the European American society, culturally, intellectually, and politically. However, the importance of these cultures and traditions and their struggle for equality are generally given inadequate coverage. Most of the social studies curriculum material about the nondominant American people is additive at best and not written with a perspective that presents points of view of peoples from diverse cultures and ethnic groups. The important sociological and cultural anthropological aspects of these peoples have generally been neglected. Every ethnic and cultural group in the United States, however, has had a role in the development of the present society.

It is likely that children of European American backgrounds would not understand the significance of the events and information presented about peoples from diverse cultures without further background information. The additive materials do not support the nondominant student's need for adequate, in-depth sociological and historical information about his or her cultural, racial, ethnic, or religious group and may contribute toward the development of a poor self-concept. Certainly, most of the materials would not contribute to serious inquiry, decision making, and social action. Readers of these materials are apt to not fully understand the importance of the information in the development of democratic ideals for all people; nor are they apt to understand how cultural values, traditions, and beliefs have influenced the role of women.

Concerned curriculum developers, desiring to include multicultural perspectives in the social studies curriculum, have erred by including materials about how women and ethnic, racial, and religious groups have contributed to the mainstream U.S. society and culture. They should have focused on how the U.S. society and culture emerged from a complex synthesis and interaction of diverse cultures and racial, ethnic, and religious groups making up American society. This would also focus social studies on a very positive foundation: what people have in common.

Most social studies texts presently used at the elementary level dealing with the United States, for example, although differing somewhat from texts of a few generations ago, are generally organized for study by regions of the country. The focus of the study is, undoubtedly, the historical point of view of European Americans, with additive materials written from a particular point of view.

Restructuring Social Studies Teaching

The lack of any in-depth study of the interaction of diverse cultures and racial, ethnic, and religious groups making up American society can produce negative or, at the least, erroneous perceptions or concepts. The solution is certainly not adding more content to the texts. This would increase the already oversized texts and make their use even more prohibitive. The solution lies in restructuring the curricula, as is suggested by Banks (1989b), to provide a thematic organization. This would enable students to view concepts, issues, and events from the perspectives of diverse ethnic and cultural groups.

School curricula organized by social studies topics might supply teachers with educator-developed sets of learning materials with a range of resource materials. When educators are provided resource units or topics that have been developed by teacher committees, they feel more empowered and consequently better able to provide for the individual needs and interests of the students in the class. These curriculum-developing committees might reassess the content organization of their present materials to ensure that their social studies curriculum provides a multicultural focus and that it includes multicultural literature and informational books.

Thematic organization generally provides a solution for schools committed to textbook teaching. Each textbook unit or chapter is restructured in a problem-solving approach encouraging student inquiry. This is possible when every student is not required to cover every aspect of the topic. Instead, all aspects are covered by various groups of students through problem-solving inquiry with the textbook as a guide. Multicultural information books and literature are used as research references and findings based on the posed questions for the study are shared with the other inquiry groups. This provides an opportunity to extend and reorganize the content and leads to student collaboration in solving the larger overall study problem. It allows the teacher to involve students in self-selection and in-depth study of the narrower aspects of a topic. When a topic or problem is subdivided among the students without distorting it, students study aspects in depth, sharing their developing expertise. This solution works well for many social studies topics or problems.

Whether the social studies curriculum is restructured into teacher-developed topics or restructured into textbook topics, teachers must be concerned about educating students for social criticism and social change. Teachers can become agents for social change when they promote democratic values through themes and topics (Banks, 1989b).

Teachers should keep the following questions in mind as the curriculum is restructured in a program that integrates social studies, multicultural literature, and language and literacy:

1. Are students presented concepts, issues, events, and themes from the perspective of diverse ethnic and cultural groups?
2. Are students provided opportunities to make decisions about important issues and take action to help solve problems?
3. Are readers provided with adequate background experiences to understand and appreciate other world views?
4. Are the roles and contributions of women in history and society across diverse cultures, races, and traditions faithfully presented?

A Restructured Social Studies Model

If these questions are used to restructure the social studies curricula into topics, students can be focused on inquiry and problem solving, essential emphases for multicultural schools. Content can be more relevant and current and provide for students' background experiences, still including geography and historical aspects in the elementary social studies curricula. In the restructured social studies programs, students would be assisted in developing background understanding for focusing on the topics and purposes for learning. The teacher would facilitate and guide student research by organizing the learners for inquiry, research, and sharing of information. Both narrative and expository literature would be integrated into the studies. Students would be assisted in learning how to locate and use information books. The social studies textbook might be used to develop geographical understandings and to introduce a region or period for study. Content and learning experiences from across the class curricula would be integrated to increase learning.

Three examples in Table 7.1 are provided to demonstrate how social studies might be restructured without causing great changes in the overall social studies scope and sequence. The first, "Living in World Communities," is derived from a topic in which children learn about four or five world communities. Such studies often inadvertently develop stereotypical concepts for the North American child of European background. These are often empty of real content and provide little opportunity for problem solving and inquiry. For example, intended focus on Japan may lead students to infer that all Japanese dress in kimonas and look like geishas, while the study of Eskimos may result in a belief that all Eskimos live in igloos. It is suggested, instead, that a study of world communities might focus on the commonalities shared by people as well as the differences. Start by examining features of homes across the globe. Next, children can be led to compare their lives with children in other parts of the world through noting daily activities: school, play, participation in family and community. (The books suggested in Table 7.1 are not all in the Teacher Resource Kit, nor are they inclusive of all materials that should be used. Those listed by Sibley are either in the language development or multicultural collections.)

The second topic, "Living in North America," focuses on the Southwest and is derived from studies that focus on various sections of the nation and examine the geography, climate, major industries, and historical significance of an area. This topic is intended to illustrate how such a study can be restructured to focus either on diverse populations in the region or how the diverse populations can be a source for expanding and extending the study of the region to provide needed focus on other cultural groups in the population. The literature selections might be integrated as part of the topic if themes or topics are not the organizing focus for study in the classroom.

The third example, "I have a dream . . ." is derived from the ideals contributed to the nation by Dr. Martin Luther King, Jr. The study is intended to be centered around the celebration of Martin Luther King, Jr.'s birthday holiday and focus learners on the perceived world role of the United States as the haven for people seeking freedom from oppression. Consequently, the major contents of Dr. King's famous speech need to be examined and implications made that these ideals apply to all people in the United States, and people seeking admission to the country come here to achieve these ideals. Children should develop an understanding that the struggle against oppression is ongoing, although mileposts have been reached.

The literature response group strategy suggests various pieces of literature that students might be interested in exploring that can be shared with other learners. During these sessions, the teacher would refer students to making comparisons, answering purposes they have set up for their study, and expanding their interests in engaging in background studies of cultural and ethnic groups. For example, Eve Bunting's *How Many Days to America? A Thanksgiving Story* (Clarion, 1988) provides opportunities to analyze and compare reasons people continue to come to the United States. A study of people of the Caribbean, and how many have sacrificed their lives to flee their homes for freedom, democracy, and economic reasons, would provide excellent opportunities for inquiry from present to past periods of history.

Teachers need to be aware that any studies of peoples from diverse cultures can lead to stereotyping. This is particularly possible when studying a topic involving American Indians. Children must learn that this term and topic covers many American Indian nations with diverse languages and traditions. To guard against this, learners have to refer to many sources for in-depth information. Students might first be led to list typical features about themselves, their families, and familiar groups in the community to recognize ranges of differences. They then would expect to search for multiple traits, behaviors, values, and traditions in their research as a basis for developing understandings of other cultural groups. Activities need to be planned to assist students in developing generalizations about nations, cultures, people, and values. Charting information allows data to be listed and generalizations developed as the data are analyzed.

EUROPEAN AMERICAN CULTURAL VALUES: FACTORS THAT AFFECT THE LEARNING OF CULTURALLY DIVERSE STUDENTS

Values, mores, and traditions are essential to the study of any culture or community of people. Children need to be able to examine their own lives and understand how their cultural values influence their lives and their interactions with other people. Teachers need to understand how the values that govern their teaching behavior or pedagogy may be opposed to those of their students from other communities. Specific

TABLE 7.1 Sample Restructured Social Studies Topics

Topics	Organizing Issues	Initiation/Interactions	Related Literature
Living in North America	Commonalities and differences in homes and children's activities Effect of geography/climate on home construction and on how people live and dress Respect and appreciation of all citizens in multicultural society	• Read aloud/discuss: Byron Barton, *Building a House* (Greenwillow, 1981). • Focus: houses U.S. children live in compared with homes across the world. • Speculate: How are they alike/different? What causes differences? Extend to food, dress, etc. • Establish study areas of interest to students. List problems to be researched. • Use literature circles. • Create habitat shadow boxes for different world settings. • Compare habitats and develop likenesses/differences. • Locate pen pals for exchange of letters with children in a distinctly different culture/climate. • Study climate and topography of each area. • Research desert life, Ancient Native American culture, Spanish and Native American languages through cooperative research. • Use videos, films, recordings, and community speakers as references. • If possible interview people from various Southwest communities. • Simulate European explorers and keep a journal recording the findings of peoples, places, and cultures, and describing the languages. • Develop a time line of human life in the Southwest. • List attitudes that should govern interactions between people of different cultures/attitudes. • Write a story to indicate American Indian perceptions of their encounter with European Americans.	**LITERATURE CIRCLE BOOKS** Eva Boholm-Olsson, *Tuan* (Farrar, 1988) Riki Levinson, *Our Home is the Sea* (Dutton, 1988) Ann Cameron, *The Most Beautiful Place in the World* (Knopf, 1988) Jan Andrews, *Very Last First Time* (Macmillan, 1986)* **RESEARCH SOURCES** Byrd Baylor, *The Desert Is Theirs* (Scribner, 1975) and *They Put on Masks* (Scribner, 1974)
Communities	Topography of southwestern U.S. Lives, cultures, languages of Southwest peoples:	• Read/discuss: Byrd Baylor's *Desert Voices* (Scribner, 198¹ • Focus: lives/homes/environment and influence on life. • Speculate: origins of people. • Read/discuss: Byrd Baylor, *Before You Came This Way* (Dutton, 1969). • Set up problems to be studied.	**LITERATURE CIRCLE BOOKS** Joseph Krumgold, *And Now Miguel* (Harper, 1953) Bernard Wolf, *In This Proud Land: The Story of a Mexican*

Living in World

"I have a dream. . . ."

Mexican Americans, Native Americans

Appreciation of life styles: comparisons and influences on European Americans

Struggles for freedom in the United States

Focus on power concept

Democracy requires all people to live free without threats, prejudice, discrimination, and racism

Economic results of oppression. Social action responses

- Read as group or aloud: Joyce Milton's *Marching to Freedom: The Story of Martin Luther King, Jr.* (Dell, 1987) and/or "I have a dream. . . ." speech.
- Speculate: What was Dr. King's dream?
- Focus on importance in U.S. multicultural society.
- Emphasize the important role of the country as beacon for freedom to the oppressed.
- Determine problems for study centered on people who have suffered due to lack of freedom, prejudice/discrimination, racism, and determine what can be done in the community.
- Research struggles of various American communities for freedom from oppression.
- Use literature response groups and KWL strategies.
- Have children write and present plays or readers' theatre productions of communities or famous individuals who faced oppression.
- Listen to poetry and music of communites.
- Enjoy art and artifacts from communites.

American Family (Harper, 1978)

Byrd Baylor, *When Clay Sings* (Macmillan, 1972)

Tomie de Paola, *The Legend of the Bluebonnet: An Old Tale of Texas* (Putnam, 1983)

Byrd Baylor, *Moon Song* (Scribner, 1982)

LITERATURE RESPONSE GROUP SOURCES

Joyce Hansen, *Which Way Freedom?* (Walker, 1986)

Eve Bunting, *How Many Days to America? A Thanksgiving Story* (Clarion, 1988)

Paul Robert Walker, *Pride of Puerto Rico: The Life of Roberto Clemente* (Harcourt, 1988)

Scott O'Dell, *Sing Down the Moon* (Houghton, 1970)

Jean Little, *From Anna* (Harper, 1972)

*Help children locate reference and informational material related to the problems of the study.

values appear fundamental to European Americans and, although well-intended, can be inhibiting learning factors for students from diverse communities.

Learning is a personal event. A learner learns by creating a knowledge base about the world. Human perceptions of the world are rooted in experiences people have in their culture and society. Experiences shape their interactions and transactions in learning. Speaking, reading, and writing are processes people use in learning. These processes empower people to construct the rules and conventions they need to operate effectively and independently. In learning, learners must first determine what the problem is before they can find the answers to problems others have posed (Neilsen, 1989).

Teaching, on the other hand, "is the process of providing opportunities for learners to transact in as wide a range of consequential real-life circumstances or contexts as possible so that learners can continue to refine their world view and add to the repertoire of strategies that they need to become independent in the world" (Neilsen, 1989, p. 11). A teacher's behavior demonstrates for learners his or her beliefs about the purpose and nature of learning. When these demonstrations are contrary or alien to children, their learning is threatened. Educators must indicate by their behavior that meaning resides in the learner. They must demonstrate that speaking, reading, and writing are meaning-making processes and that meaning is a personal world view. Values, mores, and traditions many teachers hold about learning are not consonant with many learners in multicultural classrooms.

European American Cultural Values

Buchanan (1990) stated that everything a person says, does, or thinks is dependent upon his or her culture. One's culture can be thought of as a giant bubble surrounding him or her. Everything seen, all acts and evaluations, are perceived through the bubble. As a cultural being, the educator brings into the classroom his or her cultural values and mores. An educator's cultural values and mores strongly influence the nature of the classroom experience provided for students. While cultural values and mores may vary from person to person within a culture, Buchanan (1990) stated that competition, confrontation, and cooperation permeate the general context of American culture.

Competition
American educators generally operate from a cultural perception that competition is a powerful motivating method for instruction. European American students are taught how to compete academically through sports and games in schools.

This poses a problem for culturally diverse students when competition is alien to them. Southeast Asians, for example, may possess a strong affiliation with family and community that negates winning at the expense of others. Further, Hispanic American students may not wish to be singled out (Buchanan, 1990). Native American children may come from homes with cultural orientations that value group needs and goals (Sanders, 1987). Native American children may value the ability to get along with a group as important and probably would not do well in instruction that requires individual recitation (Cuch, 1987), because this focuses attention on them (Sanders, 1987).

Buchanan (1990) suggested that educators be aware that when competition is alien to children, they will find difficulty participating in competitive games and activities. In such a situation, a teacher can bridge the students' cultures through using mildly competitive tasks gradually leading to more competitive activities. This allows students to experience and develop an understanding of the European American value, not necessarily adopt or accept it. Competing must always be a choice, and students must have the right to reject the activity without any ill consequence.

Students from diverse cultures are best taught in an accustomed style when presented with new information. When material is familiar, a presentation may be focused or aimed at more diversification of learning modes (Fiordo, 1988). This allows a focus on process rather than content. However, always be observant to student reaction in these situations and adapt instruction so as not to alienate the student.

Confrontation

European Americans generally like to confront a problem directly. In some cultures direct confrontation is avoided as much as possible (Buchanan, 1990). Consequently, students in these cultures would not express dissatisfaction directly but have a third party act as a go-between.

Students are expected to respond and react to ideas and points in social studies as a part of the discussion and interaction activities. Students in multicultural classrooms may not feel comfortable in confronting a different point of view. Educators must be aware that such differences may exist in their students and find ways for self-expression through culturally appropriate means. Small-group responses and evaluation interactions might be tried.

Cooperation

Although appearing to contradict competition, Americans value cooperation as a means for achieving their own individual goals. Educators expect students to be cooperative. Cooperation is reinforced by the use of deadlines and the importance of getting things done (Buchanan, 1990). Many cultures will not cooperate on a task to achieve a group goal if it means compromising their own principles or if they sense they should be working individually in learning, not in groups. The best solution is to carefully select a variety of different types of tasks that deal with circumstances familiar and reassuring to students, and then gradually begin to challenge students with the unfamiliar (Buchanan, 1990).

European American Pedagogical Values

Buchanan (1990) warned educators that some pedagogically approved American expectations for children in classrooms are not always exhibited by children from other cultures. These may cause children difficulties as they are immersed in the culture of the school. The students' culturally learned behaviors may not necessarily be appropriate in the school environment. Behaviors valued by American educators that may cause difficulties in learning for children from other cultures are working independently and individually, taking turns, participating in group work, meeting deadlines and asking questions.

Independent and Individual Work

Collaboration during quizzes, tests, and assigned work is generally considered cheating in the European American culture and forbidden because it limits the teacher from collecting individual information. However, the sense of affiliation between individuals in some cultures encourages them to share and not value individual success.

A restructured social studies program would expect students to interact in all aspects of their study to stimulate critical thinking and problem solving. Students would be encouraged to work in teams, to collaborate and problem solve.

Turn-Taking

According to European American values children should take turns talking and be quiet and listen in class. This value is taught from the time a child learns to talk. When they are interrupted, parents instruct children that it is their turn to talk. Communication in American schools is based on the pedagogical principle that when the teacher is talking, he or she is giving important information or explanations and learners will best learn by paying attention and listening. Other cultures, however, may have other expectations for students, according to Buchanan (1990). Therefore, in any multicultural classroom there may be students who will not participate individually, may participate only when called upon, may talk to others at the same time as the teacher, or may attempt to respond to every question.

When classrooms contain students with very different expectations about turn-taking, the teacher should plan activities in social studies that provide opportunities for quieter students to speak without allowing the more assertive student to dominate the discussion. Buchanan (1990) suggested that this can be done by pairing students in a task in which the quieter child has to speak while the more assertive child writes. Activities that require students to respond actively in writing, charting, or graphing from a video or film, or during an interview or as the teacher talks, can work well for students having trouble with turn-taking.

Group Work

Teachers in European American schools place students in groups to allow children to share information, develop independence, and increase communication skills. Many of these activities in social studies are problem-solving activities and include cooperative or collaborative group work. This may be foreign to students who come from cultures that emphasize rote memorization. Teachers with children in their classrooms from these cultures should make the group tasks explicit and carefully explain the roles of each member of the group. Students should use notebooks in upper-intermediate social studies classes to record information developed in small groups and discussions and decisions from large-group sessions. This satisfies the needs of many students and parents that real learning is occurring.

Deadlines

Teaching and learning in European American schools is made up of deadline after deadline. These are given for reasons involving motivation and time. However, this value is not a commonly shared value in all cultures. The Native American cultures may not place importance on future goals except as is required to satisfy present needs.

Educational programs in other cultures may have flexible examination and extendable assigned work dates for tests and projects. Students from these cultures will need explicit directions and instructions if work must be due at a specific time to accommodate school schedules. As schools become more objective-minded and move toward more individual mastery learning, students from other cultures might be better served. Time should not be a variable for learning.

Questions

In European American schools students are expected to ask questions during class. This indicates to the teacher that they are intellectually involved in the learning and attempting to follow the material or discussion. Teachers generally believe that learners who ask provocative questions are good students. The American educational system emphasizes thinking based on inductive reasoning, while in other cultures the teacher may be perceived as one who imparts knowledge through lectures. Students would not be expected to question nor would their opinion be valued or sought.

An educator in a multicultural classroom environment should not assume students understand or agree because there are no questions. The educator should not assume lack of learning if students are not looking at the teacher or nodding agreement while the teacher talks. Instead, they need to plan strategies for checking understanding to ascertain learning. Having students turn to one another to explain an assignment or tell what was learned in social studies can be a helpful strategy that can identify misunderstandings.

STRATEGIES FOR FACILITATING SOCIAL STUDIES LEARNING IN A MULTICULTURAL CLASSROOM

Educators may use several strategies to help students become active participants in the learning process—people who generate hypotheses and build content-knowledge structures in the search for meaning. Other strategies contribute to the expansion and extension of language and literacy learning. Strategies taught to students must transfer to independent study and learning strategies.

Developing a Content Topic

Most social studies topics generally have subtopics or component aspects that make up the topic. These are generally studied part by part. However, this may be confusing to many students unless they are able to perceive the whole before it is studied in parts. Introductory learning experiences should focus on the whole: what is the topic, what does the student know, and what does he or she want to know. To study the topic, the teacher focuses the learner on examining the subtopics. As the study of the subtopic is completed, students are assisted in examining the topic as a whole again, this time with expanded understanding through their learning experiences.

Reading the text and listening to teacher information are often the major vehicles used for learning content materials. While both might still be used, students should spend more time reading self-selected materials and doing investigative research that requires reading, viewing media, writing and discussing, and listening in small groups during planning, sharing, and working. Art, music, and drama should be explored as they relate to a study area.

Strategies Specific to Social Studies Inquiry

A major focus in content-area teaching at the elementary level is to develop independent self-learning strategies as means for developing problem solving and inquiry skills. The following strategies, adapted from Kaplan (1990), should be carried out in meaningful, relevant, and functional social studies activities that address topics for inquiry.

1. In introducing the social studies topic, engage students by asking them what they already know about the topic. Write their answers on a chart for students to refer to as the study progresses. Additional questions include: What does this topic mean to the students? How can it be used in their lives? Is it relevant (important) to their communities? Why or why not?

2. In planning with the group, challenge students by asking questions or directing the discussion to elicit the purposes they should have for studying the topic. List these for the students as they develop. (Help students pose these as problems.) The students may also be asked how the purposes, goals, or tasks can be organized to be learned. What materials do they need for the assignment or task? (Is there a range of materials to get different information and viewpoints?) How much time do they need to accomplish each task? (Later ask the students to determine how good their estimate was and how they can improve it in the future.) How can the students work with others in accomplishing the assignment or task? Have the strengths of each person in a group been used appropriately? Are there people in the community who are knowledgeable about the topic? How should they be interviewed for information?

3. In studying the social studies topic, encourage students by suggesting they try new ideas or tasks, take risks, and take chances. Push their thinking in search of new ideas. Ask the students to think about what they are learning and see if it fits other ideas and known or located information. Why does it fit or not fit? The students may want to keep a record of information determined from the study.

Ask the students to listen to the thinking other people are sharing to understand their points before disagreeing. Can they state opposing points of view? Can they disagree in a way that does not discourage others from participating in the discussions? Can they present points of view clearly without offending others? Have the class determine whether there are other ways to solve the problem or task. Encourage the students to ask someone to listen to their solutions and suggest alternative ways. Students must determine whether they have done their best to solve the task or problem. Ask them to identify what they have learned from the situation.

4. In evaluating the work, suggest to students that they consider if their assignments and work have pleased them and satisfied their own interests and standards. Does it meet their goals and standards? Are they happy about what they learned? Ask the students if they respect themselves no matter how well they did on a task or assignment. Do they respect others no matter how well they did on any given task or assignment?

Strategies for Directed Reading of Social Studies Text

When students need to use texts for data gathering in their inquiry and problem solving, they may require assistance in learning how to effectively read expository materials. Teacher-assisted content reading strategies must facilitate students' development of their reading and study strategies to fit their individual reading styles. Any successful model must make comprehension an active meaning-seeking process, have direct application to independent reading, and involve writing. The model adapted from Crawford and Carline (1987) follows six steps.

Step One: Activate Prior Information. Students' recall of their prior information about the topic may be facilitated through a series of questions that will stimulate thinking. Students are encouraged to think about what they know about a topic as a means of preparing for reading. A self-questioning process for recalling may be suggested.

If the teacher determines that the students need better prior information for reading, he or she might show films, filmstrips, or videos. Although general background information may have been developed during the orientation stage of the study, recalling prior information is necessary at every step for developing new concepts. Students learning English may find text language in which the new concept is embedded overwhelming, and they may require careful identification and defining or clarifying of the term through pictures, realia, and/or concrete experiences.

Step Two: Survey the Reading Material. The readers should be guided to survey the reading. Students are directed to read the topic title, all subtopics, first lines, last lines, all introductory paragraphs, and concluding paragraphs and to study pictures, illustrations, and any graph material. The teacher demonstrates how to read around all words that are written in italics or bold print to speculate on meaning from context. This may help the students to develop a word-learning strategy (Nagy, 1988).

A teacher-guided survey aids the second-language (L2) and culturally different reader to recognize important terms and content organization for reading. Specific terms and concepts in content materials may present a greater problem for these learners because of their lack of prior information. L2 readers will also be unsure if they skip a word, if it will be needed later, and may not recognize relevant points (Vorhaus, 1984).

According to Nagy (1988) "students do not need to know all the words in a text to read it with a high level of comprehension" (p. 29). Readers are able to tolerate a certain proportion of unknown words in the text without disruption of comprehension. The exact proportion will depend on the nature of the text, the role of the term in the context, and the purpose(s) for reading. Student interest and knowledge about the topic is also a factor.

Social studies texts may use specific organizational patterns: cause and effect, comparison and contrast, time order, problem and solution, simple listing. If students recognize the organization of the text, they may read the content more effectively. The teacher can assist students to recognize a pattern by asking questions that will lead to the next step: What is the issue in the chapter (problem)? What information is provided to answer the problem? How is it provided? Are these answers appropriate for a multicultural society?

Step Three: Develop Purposes for Guiding the Reading. As introductions, conclusions, topics, and subtopics are being read in the surveying, direct the reader to consider reasons for reading the material and setting goals that should be achieved during the reading. This raises a state of doubt or curiosity for the readers from what they know or do not know or about what will be reported. Then involve readers in purpose-setting so as to develop self-commitment on intellectual as well as emotional levels (Stauffer, 1969). This powerful force compels and sustains the reader until an answer is found, which may be beyond the text and includes other world views. The answers become personal; they reflect personal experience, knowledge, association, projection, and a reader's ego. Further, self-generated questions improve recall (Frase & Schwartz, 1975).

Stauffer (1969) stated that the teacher must be an agitator by stirring the minds of the students. This is extremely important in a restructured social studies program concerned with inquiry and problem solving. Students should not be reading to find an answer to satisfy the teacher about what the author alone thinks. Instead, if students are to become effective critical thinkers, they must be able to formulate purposes, they must be aware of what the author(s) want to be understood, and they must be able to assess the quality of the learning in relation to personal knowledge and other world views, if not presented. Consequently, the model employed in guiding the students' reading must incorporate strategies that will actively have students practicing these processes.

Step Four: Reading to Prove, Verify, and Develop New Purposes.   Students read an initial section of the text to defend, refute, and affirm their purposes. Readers must be required to produce evidence from the material, much like a detective, lawyer, or scientist (Stauffer, 1969). Students who learn to read content in this manner are more aware of facts and selection of evidence used to prove a point.

Since most social studies texts are organized in topics and subtopics, the teacher might have the students focus on major points in each section and respond to their predictions and purposes. Honor the pupils' prereading thinking by asking them if they found the answers to their questions (Stauffer, 1969). To foster the attitude of demanding and providing proof ask the students to read the line(s) that prove they found the correct answers (Stauffer, 1969).

Encourage critical thinking by asking questions that relate the information to the students' previous experiences:

Should this have been done? Why or why not?
Do all people believe this way?
What was the problem that needed to be solved?
How would you solve it?

Step Five: Increase Comprehension Through Writing and Discussion.   Students need to develop abilities to monitor their reading. They should write about what they have read in relation to the established purposes (Smith-Burke, 1982). This process helps students to monitor what they know and do not know and leads to strategies that fix up comprehension. For example, direct students to define and write about any ideas that are confusing to them and to pose questions that need to be answered that will clarify the reading. Questions not only serve as bridges between thinking, reading, and writing, but they provide vehicles for other students to demonstrate how the answers to the questions were constructed from the textual material (Smith-Burke, 1982).

The class should reach consensus on their understanding of the ideas corresponding with the purposes of the selection. These may be written on a large chart for students to view, compare, and discuss. If there are numerous purposes, various groups can respond to purposes that particularly interested them, or the teacher may randomly select a limited number of purposes for response. These provide opportunities for some variety in interpretation and yet cover all the purposes. The groups must cite reasons for supporting or not supporting a particular point of view. If the data are inconclusive in the text, this is an opportunity for students to search for further information. If one point of view is flawed, the teacher should facilitate student thinking to make this interpretation.

It is a teacher's responsibility in a multicultural curriculum to facilitate the thinking of students about other cultures in society and the world. Many statements in social studies may seem harmless but actually do great harm in developing perceptions of other people. Bennett (1986) cited examples about nonindustrialized people being less civilized than industrialized people as examples of misinformation that can develop prejudice and a sense of superiority for students of European American backgrounds. Students need to be able to determine when materials are written from a particular viewpoint. Students can easily learn to spot specific viewpoints by being asked questions that require them to speculate about the information that would be provided if the denigrated group would have written it.

Step Six: Verify, Expand, and Elaborate Topic Meaning. To aid the reader in recognizing what is known and what is needed to be learned, partial aspects of the text may be reread to verify specific learning purposes of the study and to provide possible answers to these. Students need to learn two competencies for verifying text information.

The first competency, an ability for developing logical connections, is important in social studies content. McNeil (1987) suggested that the following learning activities will encourage students to determine how the content is presented as a means for determining what must be learned:

1. Have the student reread the selection to determine alternately cause or effect when this is the predominant pattern for presenting content material.

2. Have the students reread a specific section to determine the points that compare or contrast happenings or some effect.
3. Have the students use or develop a time line for sequencing events.
4. Have the students take a listing of statements given in no particular order and restructure them into patterns that demonstrate relationships appropriate to a particular content material.

The second competency, the ability to process a text with deep understanding, aids students to engage in elaboration—the embellishing of what is read (McNeil, 1987)—to improve learning and thinking. Deep processing occurs when the reader uses mental imagery, draws inferences, and summarizes the text in his or her own words. Suggestions for using mental imaging, inferencing, and summarizing include the following:

1. To encourage mental imaging assist students to make the information or events more personal. For example, have one group of students imagine that they are Japanese Americans, and read Executive Order 9066 authorizing the exclusion of all people of Japanese ancestry from the West Coast and their relocation into internment camps. Have them discuss how they would feel, and why they would feel this way. Have another group of students explain to the Japanese Americans why this is important for national security. Then assist students in furthering their understanding of racism by examining these reasons. Determine that all laws are not necessarily just, and discuss what actions might have been taken by citizens to protect the rights of all citizens (Bennett, 1986). Have students speculate if this type of action could happen again and, if so, what could be done to overcome it.

2. Using inferencing readers make assumptions and conclusions from reading when they use reasoning and personal experience. To increase inferencing abilities give students practice determining the conclusion for a topic or selecting a conclusion from several topics; ask students a series of statements that requires them to state which is consistent with the information provided in a paragraph; provide students with an incomplete series of steps and ask them to supply the missing step; and have students list details under generalizations.

3. To encourage summarizing techniques delve into what students think is the purpose of a passage or selection before a response is affirmed or they are assisted to reach another conclusion. Being able to summarize is probably the most difficult task for students (McNeil,

1987). Summaries are dependent on the purposes for reading; the same material read for a different purpose will have a different set of points for a summary. Consequently, students from diverse cultures can be expected to write or give summaries that may be different from students from European American backgrounds.

Strategies for Interpreting Texts

To aid the student in expanding and elaborating on text topics requires ensuring conceptual understanding and personalizing of the topic. This assists the student in interpreting passages and developing a greater understanding of the text. The following three strategies contribute to this ability:

Develop an Understanding of Key Concepts. Key concepts in social studies texts may be unfamiliar and require more attention to instruction for understanding the selection. A small number of terms with subordinate words should be given this emphasis (Nagy, 1988).

Semantic maps and hierarchical arrays (Figure 7.1) are excellent methods for organizing new information—a type of visual conceptual

FIGURE 7.1 Hierarchial Vocabulary Display

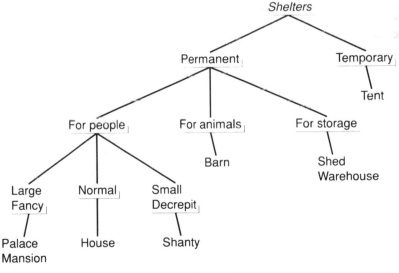

Source: W. E. Nagy, *Teaching Vocabulary to Improve Reading Comprehension,* ERIC Clearinghouse on Reading and Communication Skills, International Reading Association, and National Council of Teachers of English, Urbana, IL, 1988, p. 17. Reprinted by permission of the National Council of Teachers of English.

schema. As students add to the map or array, they may have to reorganize the information to better specify relationships. An important aspect of the process is determining which information should be included.

Thinking trees (Figure 7.2) are versions of the hierarchical array. The thinking tree can be used for both generation of vocabulary and developing term relationships. This process is most effective when cooperative groups (Nagy, 1988) are given a tree without the terms and asked to fill in terms that indicate appropriate relationships. Then decisions are compared and discussed in a large group.

List-Group-Label (Moore, Readence, & Rickelman, 1989) is another effective strategy. Have students brainstorm a list of terms from a topic under study and then group the terms and label them in small groups with a superordinate term.

Expand Thinking Through Writing. Encourage students to respond to what they have been reading as a way of using their own knowledge, experiences, and emotions to construct meaning in collaboration with the author. Writing encourages reflecting, and consequently it helps the reader or writer to recognize what is known.

Response journals can be used with content material to encourage students to concentrate on how they feel about the ideas stated, what the information means to them, what they think about the information, and their reactions as they studied the information. Suggest students write responses to their reading of the topic. Have them date each response and specify the section of their reading they are responding to in writing. Encourage them to ask questions as well as to share ideas. Respond in writing to each student to help them explore their personal ways of thinking. Be sure to ask questions about their reading that encourage students to explore how they read as well as what they read and think about it.

Rewrite the Text from Free Association. Have students rewrite the text from free association. This may be done by dictating the ideas to the teacher in a manner similar to the language experience approach (LEA), writing in cooperative groups, or writing individually. Have students leave space for information they would like to include but cannot remember, and ask other students if they have missing information. Let students reexamine their texts and make any changes they would like after they are finished. Have various writings shared in a large group and discuss different interpretations.

FIGURE 7.2 Incomplete Thinking Tree

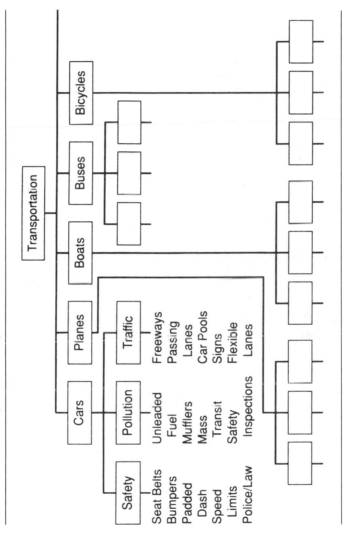

Source: D. Kirby and C. Kuykendall, *Thinking Through Language: Book One*, National Council of Teachers of English, Urbana, IL, 1985. Reprinted by permission of the National Council of Teachers of English.

Strategies for Developing
Reading Independence

Ideally, the strategies the teacher uses to help students transact meaning in the social studies text should transfer to their independent reading. Students, however, may require direct instruction and practice to connect relationships between teacher-assisted activities and independent reading. The teacher should provide instruction for students to become independent readers through practice. A number of strategies have been designed to assist students in practicing reading strategies applicable to independent strategies. These strategies provide a bridge between teacher assistance and independence. One strategy, the KWL Strategy Sheet, integrates key meaning-getting processes that require the learner to examine his or her prior information, and develop purposes for reading.

Ogle (1989) developed the KWL Strategy Sheet for transitioning readers from teacher direction to independence. The KWL (what we *k*now, what we *w*ant to find out, and what we *l*earned/still need to learn) Strategy Sheet is conceived to activate thinking before, during, and after reading. It recognizes the importance of prior knowledge and presents a process that develops how to think about expository material. In demonstrating the process, the teacher should work through the sheet with children using assigned readings. The teacher should record the information on an overhead copy of the KWL Strategy Sheet (see Figure 7.3). Gradually, the students should be encouraged to do aspects of the strategy sheet on their own, with the teacher discussing and affirming each aspect. A strategy sheet can be done for each reading selection in a chapter or for each chapter, depending on the length of the reading assignment, students' familiarity with the topic, and the difficulty of the material. The following suggestions teach students to use the KWL Strategy Sheet:

1. Before reading determine what students know and want to find out. Begin by encouraging brainstorming about the topic to be read. Record on the strategy sheet what the students know. Have the students copy the information on their copies. Encourage the students to anticipate what categories they expect to find in the reading. Write the categories on the strategy sheet. Help students focus on questions they would like to have answered. Questions that help students state ideas include:

> What do you mean by that?
> Can you tell more about that?
> How can we state these ideas?

FIGURE 7.3 KWL Strategy Sheet

What we know	What we want to find out	What we learned/still need to learn
A holiday is named after him.	Why was he famous?	He was a leader of the nonviolence movement that changed unfair laws—like Jim Crow laws.
He was a Black leader.	How did he die? How did he help people?	He made famous important speeches like "I have a dream today."
He was famous.		He was inspired by a brave woman, Rosa Parks, to work to overturn unfair laws and practices.
He was killed.		
He was a minister.		
He helped people get free.		He was killed by an assassin's bullet.
He did not like fighting.		
He had a wife and children.		He won a Nobel Prize.

Categories of information we expect to use.

A. Nonviolent actions: sit-ins, freedom rides, buying-power boycott

B. Segregation/integration

C. Open housing

Source: D. M. Ogle, "The Know, Want to Know, Learn Strategy," in K. D. Muth (ed.), *Children's Comprehension of Text: Research into Practice,* International Reading Association, Newark, DE, 1989, pp. 205–223. Reprinted with permission of Donna M. Ogle, K. D. Muth and the International Reading Association.

2. During reading determine what the students learned. Direct students to jot down new information under "What we learned" on the strategy sheet as they read.

3. After reading elicit information learned from the students. Have them share information appropriate to their own learning. Have students reexamine the purposes for reading and points of view students bring to the reading. Help students to categorize the new information and clarify meanings of concepts and terms. Have students review the strategy sheet to correct any misconceptions about the topic. Follow up with appropriate activities.

Comprehending and Composing Through
Writing Experiences

In the writing process, the writer converses with himself or herself as a highly responsive and reflective other person. Ideas are created that could and would not have otherwise existed in the mind except through writing, whether it is narrative or expository. Writers create thoughts and worlds for personal exploration and enjoyment. These may, in turn, change the writer.

Writing serves as an excellent vehicle for developing understanding of content. When students write about what they are studying, they can come to understandings or interpretations about a subject or topic. Interpretation may only be discovered by writing. As writing is undertaken by students, decisions are made from the reading, and decisions lead to a final interpretation, a realization. Writing clarifies thinking. It is not unusual for writers to realize that they were wrong about decisions they made. This may mean a significant change in a dearly held point of view. Writing about content allows students to explore ways to be explicit and exact in thought. This particularly happens when writers receive feedback from teachers and peers as readers.

Writing as a Cooperative Activity. F. Smith (1981) stated that the ability to write alone comes with experience. Writing probably should not begin as a solitary act but as a cooperative one. Sharan and Sharan (1990) reported studies indicating students involved in cooperative, group investigative studies developed higher level academic achievement and demonstrated positive social interaction with other ethnic groups. Further, cooperative groups increased participation in classrooms with culturally diverse students. Using cooperative writing groups supports cultural value systems (discussed earlier in the chapter). A five-step process for developing a cooperative group experience has been adapted from Sharan and Sharan (1990).

Stage One: Identify the Topic. The teacher assists students to develop a question about the content topic under investigation. Students brainstorm areas of interest to be researched. They are encouraged to explore multifaceted aspects of the topic and clarify the scope of the content. Next, the students classify and categorize the ideas to arrive at topics and/or themes that might be explored. The students are then guided in shaping each topic into a manageable size for the purpose of the investigative writing.

Stage Two: Plan the Investigation. Students select subtopics and form cooperative groups. Each group should appoint a recorder and other roles needed, such as a discussion leader for facilitating group contributions. The group should next develop ideas (questions) for investigating the subtopic and divide the subtopic among group members for investigation. The recorder should write down this information on a prepared card and share it at the end of the period with the whole class. The card containing the following information is then given to the teacher: topic, members, roles, research questions and assignments, and resources being used.

Stage Three: Carry Out the Investigation. The teacher makes suggestions on the cards and returns them to the students. The librarian is informed of the investigative study so as to elicit assistance in locating appropriate materials. The teacher prepares the students for carrying out the investigation by providing the necessary assistance for learning how to interview people and search for films, texts, picture books, magazines, and articles for information. Most students of this age will need instruction on how to make data searches in libraries. Having students locate their own sources in the library increases the quality of the learning. Plans should be made for carrying out interviews or for visits to other sites, such as museums, that are appropriate to the study.

Investigative studies are more successful if two procedures are followed:

1. Have a quick executive meeting at the start of each session. This provides a time for the teacher to direct, suggest, provide help, and touch base with students on any independent work they have done. Prior to this meeting return the note cards and any logs, on which students report progress, with suggestions.

2. Have the groups meet each day before the end of each period to share how their work is progressing and to prepare a very short progress report on their group card.

The students will probably discover new areas of interest as the study evolves. This may necessitate reorganizing the topic, adding other points, or redefining the major topic.

Stage Four: Prepare the Report. Reports can take a number of forms. For less experienced writers the teacher might focus on oral reports at the early stages of investigative writing having students support their work with displays, exhibits, and so on. When these students choose to write they provide important information about their development. If reports are first oral, it provides a basis for the teacher to note if the quality and quantity of reporting changes when they begin to write them. Students should be encouraged to include exhibits developed by the group, materials such as realia, and presentations of slides, filmstrips, films, illustrations, and books collected by the group for all studies.

The teacher meets with each group as plans are made for making the report. Organization of ideas is important at this point and students need a strategy. When research information is on cards, this process becomes easier. The following process may be helpful:

1. Direct students to write questions about the subtopic they researched. Have students lay out the cards that go with each question. The notes are then read to see if more investigative research is necessary. Try having the students put their questions and notes into an outline and identify someone responsible for each section. Give students appropriate feedback.

2. Help students move to higher order thinking (reaching inferences, conclusions, and generalizations, both cognitive and affective). Have students reread their cards. Question so as to lead students to insightful understandings.

3. The word processor provides a wonderful opportunity for students to work together as a team in writing the report from their notes. Students can take turns on the word processor writing sections they had done the original research for while peers provide feedback and editing. Drafting and editing flows together as students share, critique, and finally reach a hard-copy stage for editing. After this stage is reached, the teacher should get involved with the students in a group editing session.

4. Students might share their information by talking to the class about their topic, or the written report can be posted with illustrations and realia. Reports might also be collected and edited by a group of students into a book for publishing. When the reports are written on the word processor, publishing becomes a much easier job; the final product generally looks more professional. Most students will want copies to share at home. In addition, they may wish to share it with people interviewed or with those who contributed to their study.

Stage Five: Evaluate the Products and Process.   Evaluation has many facets to it. When students are working in group investigation, they are constantly evaluating their work because they are interacting with peers and the teacher. Their goal is to understand their self-selected topic and to seek out peers, the teacher, or the librarian to assist them in understanding what they are reading. Then during the writing they are in constant interaction about what is being written so that it will make sense to the readers. The process suggested above gives the teacher the opportunity to give feedback to students throughout the writing process to ensure continual growth.

Students should critique how they carried out the project as well as how much they learned. The evaluation might begin in the small groups and expand into large-group discussion. Try having students respond to statements such as the following:

> I learned in doing this project . . .
> What I liked about doing this project was . . .
> I would like to see changed the next time I (we) do a similar project . . .

Writing from Interviewing. Tway (1984) reported that interviewing is an important way of learning from knowledgeable people and provides a meaningful opportunity for doing content writing. As in writing reports, interviewing involves developing questions, taking notes, and organizing the information into a report, news article, or newscast. Students can be successful in interviewing from the beginning if they carry on the interviews in small groups assisted by a tape recorder. Interviewing is an important activity for the multicultural classroom because it provides the opportunity for engaging community members in classroom activities. These people are sources of information about an ethnic group, tradition, or culture that is otherwise difficult to tap.

Getting Started. Tway (1984) suggested excellent ways to help students learn how to interview that make the process meaningful, functional, and relevant:

1. Have students interview one another at the beginning of the year to get acquainted. Elicit information students are interested in learning about one another prior to the interviews. Have students participate in four roles: interviewer, subject, note-taker, and observer. This can provide information about the various cultural groups represented in the classroom.

2. Older elementary students might interview candidates campaigning for class or school offices. Notes from these can be written and reported in a class, school newspaper, or newscast.

Involving Parents. Parents and available family members may assist with the interviews. The teacher elicits generic questions that should be asked and does some simulated practicing in the classroom. Parents are asked to make arrangements for children to interview community people. As each project nears completion, the teacher arranges for the students to share their work with the class. Parents and interviewees are invited to the school for the event.

Writing Using Concrete Experiences.   Good content learning activities should include experiences that involve students in concrete learning experiences. The best experiences include hands-on concrete experiences, simulated experiences, and dramatized experiences. When students are personally involved, they are more interested in learning. Science and social studies provide vehicles for the students to learn through hands-on experiences. These experiences provide opportunities for integrating the language arts–speaking, reading, and writing. Field trips, visiting speakers, and experiences such as experiments and observations can be used for writing. Children learn better when they are actively involved in real experiences because they reflect real situations found in life.

Developing Aesthetic Response in Social Studies

Some teachers are reluctant to allow aesthetic response to content topics believing it may violate the content area. However, this is a grave error and results in the loss of an excellent learning opportunity. McClure and Zitlow (1991) explained that "concern for teaching facts has caused us to neglect forging an emotional connection between those facts and the lives of our children" (p. 28). The aesthetic dimension can be added through literature, poetry, and composition. When teachers do this they assist students in going beyond the facts to discover the depth of richness and beauty in a topic. McClure and Zitlow (1991) indicated that teachers can foster aesthetic experiences by providing guidance and time for contemplation and reflection.

Social studies provides opportunities for relating literature that will allow students to build upon what they already know. Multicultural literature provides opportunities for students to place themselves in literature and express their ideas about literature through writing, dramatizing, and responding through art. Social studies provides the opportunity to respond to the content through drama, art, and music. Historical topics, war, peace, and cultural differences provide motivation for response through writing, drama, art, and music that can go beyond aesthetic responses to the facts.

When teachers foster opportunities for students to make aesthetic responses to content issues and topics, as well as relate to literature, they foster reasoning and understanding. Thinking and questioning are essential to aesthetic response. It is through such experiences that the learner becomes actively and personally involved in a search for meaning. When students are guided to make connections between the facts and the aesthetic dimensions embedded in those facts, they realize how their own active thinking enriches their learning.

Developing Generalizations

Learning in social studies is founded on conceptualization and generalization. In the activities that were recommended above and in Chapter Three for development of the content of the topic, teachers were urged to involve students in learning that had them categorizing, classifying, and grouping located information.

Elementary students need a foundation of personal experiences with concrete realities before being expected to develop abstract or symbolic concepts. Concrete and simulated experiences aid students to develop essential characteristics of a concept. Generally, introductory materials should be simplified with essential characteristics to eliminate distractive elements even before students have direct involvement or actual observation.

Teachers need to aid students to classify and describe concepts. Discussing and writing about a concept helps a student develop a mental image of the concept, classify it, and describe it. When students interact with the teacher and other students, observation, classification, and descriptions are enhanced. This occurs when the teacher elicits and records ideas in a web, array, or some scaffolding technique or when the students discuss or brainstorm with peers.

Concept formulation is essential to the development of generalizations. Children of all ages can be assisted to develop social science generalizations. These can be very simple as well as complex. Generalizations are formed from the relationship of two or more concepts. Examples of generalizations, according to Banks and Clegg (1977), include the following:

1. The interaction of people with their physical and social environment changes both people and their environment.

2. Conflicts and inequities result when values are assigned to particular categories of differences such as dialect, language, or skin color.

3. Groups with different physical and cultural characteristics from those of groups in power are often victims of discrimination.

Students should develop generalizations through inquiry and problem-solving strategies. Teachers need to assist students through instructional strategies to reach these higher level ideas. This generally requires time for discussion among students and teachers in which the teacher facilitates the process through skillful questioning to stimulate and lead the students from elicited data to higher order thinking. Teachers have to be able to accept the thinking of the students and expand and carefully direct their ideas forward.

Culminating the Study

This aspect of the social studies topic deals with summarizing and interrelating all the major ideas that were studied. The teacher may, through the culminating activities, gain insight into student understanding and learning styles. Students should be involved in planning ways and means for culminating a study. These can include oral reporting, dramatic presentations, or preparing class books that summarize the study. School and community members certainly can be invited to culminating events, but the major focus of this stage of the study should be to review, highlight, and interrelate the major areas of the study for the students.

Sample Social Studies Topic

An example of a topic that demonstrates how the teaching strategies developed in this and previous chapters were used to plan and organize an upper intermediate–level multicultural social studies topic can be found in the Teacher Resource Kit. The example is entitled "The Development and Presentation of a Sample Content Topic."

The sample topic follows the format developed in Chapter Three and includes the curriculum framework, introductory experiences, the development of the topic (focusing only on one of the subtopics of the topic), the development of generalizations, and a summary and culmination of the study topic. In the topic, cooperative groups are used to do collaborative studies of subtopics through investigative writing and reading and studying multicultural literature. These subtopics are shared with the total group and generalizations are developed using strategies that develop critical thinking.

The topic was selected because many current elementary texts introduce infamous deeds perpetrated against minorities in the United States. These, however, needed further development to be understood. Children need to understand the contexts in which they occurred and how these deeds affected the people to whom the actions were directed. In this study students are to develop an understanding that racism and bigotry are not only harmful to the recipients, but also dehumanizing to the people who practice them.

The topic is organized in such a way as to allow students to develop either an in-depth study of the topic or to do in-depth studies of each minority as they were encountered in a text. The topic focuses on infamous deeds committed against nondominant cultural communities: the Japanese American internment during World War II; Bloody Sunday; an aborted freedom march in Selma, Alabama; and Wounded Knee, a Native American massacre. A particular deed against Hispanic Americans and Jewish Americans did not appear in the research; however, there is significant data covering bigotry against these two communities to make the study very relevant.

SUMMARY

Developing language and literacy in multicultural content topics is based on the dual premises that learning is personal and that teaching provides opportunities for students to transact a wide range of meaningful, relevant, and functional learning experiences to flush out their own world view and learn other world views while increasing their independent learning strategies.

Learners must learn how to learn. They learn through teacher modeling and demonstration and through meaningful learning experiences. They are more apt to learn when they are involved in decision making about their learning. In learning how to learn students come to know how to prepare for learning, how to monitor their learning, how to assess their learning, and how to develop generalizations from isolated and connected facts. However, students from culturally diverse backgrounds probably will not learn unless educators are aware of how the Eurocentric pedagogical practices in most American schools may prohibit learning. This requires that the teacher change, adapt, and/or modify many current practices that undergird classroom instruction.

Strategies for developing a content topic should place emphasis on expository materials supported by narrative literature for bridging understanding from children's prior information. The development of a topic includes reading and writing strategies that integrate the use of language for interaction in an inquiry problem-solving approach. Instructional strategies must increase student ability to read and write expository material. Instructional strategies must model successful independent reading and writing skills. Topics should provide avenues for students to express aesthetic responses to the content under study.

Finally, if students are going to learn how to learn, they must learn how to develop generalizations, big ideas, about their inquiry. Learning must start with the whole, move to the part, and return to the whole again. Students must perceive what it is that they are going to learn, be facilitated in how to break the whole into parts for inquiry, and return the parts to the whole through the development of generalizations about the topic.

IMPLICATIONS FOR INSTRUCTION

1. Restructure the teaching and learning of content material, particularly social studies, to develop a thematic or topic focus that facilitates an inquiry problem-solving approach. Topics should be subdivided to allow students to become involved in a collaborative process through cooperative groups in a problem-solving process.

2. Infuse perspectives, frames of reference, and content from various diverse cultural and ethnic groups and traditions in society into the social studies topics.

3. Use a problem-solving inquiry teaching model that provides for student involvement. Starting with the orientation, involve students to focus their learning and develop purposes for the study. Aid students to make generalizations from the topic information to conclude the study.

4. Develop an environment for teaching and learning that does not discourage or inhibit classroom learning for students from culturally diverse groups. The European American values of competition, confrontation, and cooperation should be carefully assessed as to how they are applied to instruction to ascertain that they do not discourage and frustrate learners from diverse ethnic groups and cultures.

5. Examine strategies used for instruction having direct cultural orientation to the European American culture to ascertain that they are not discouraging and inhibiting the participation and learning of students from diverse ethnic and cultural groups. Of particular concern are the pedagogical values that support and reward independent and individual work, turn-taking, group work, deadlines, and questions.

6. Focus instruction toward helping students learn how to learn independently.

7. Use teaching strategies such as the directed reading strategies and KWL strategy to assist students to read expository materials independently. The basic communication processes should be integrated in these strategies.

8. Use content writing strategies that develop study and organizational abilities. Begin content research writing in cooperative groups. Provide opportunities for students to write from concrete experiences and learn to collect data from interviews for community information.

9. Include opportunities for an aesthetic response from children in social studies to bridge factual information with personal reaction and interaction. Aesthetic response in writing, music, art, and drama can provide an emotional connection for students that simulates "walking in another's shoes."

CHAPTER EIGHT

Assessing and Evaluating Language and Literacy in a Multicultural Classroom

- *Should students from culturally diverse populations be given IQ and achievement tests?*
- *What guidelines should be employed for testing culturally diverse students?*
- *What is a model and strategies for assessing and evaluating all students in a multicultural classroom?*
- *What should be the role of parents or primary caregivers in assessment and evaluation?*
- *How can students be involved in assessment and evaluation?*

INTRODUCTION

Assessing and evaluating learners in a multicultural classroom requires a teacher who is observant of learners in the learning process, one who interacts with the learners in teaching and conferencing, documents observations and interactions, understands the relationship between culture and assessment, and analyzes and evaluates the processes, performances, and products of learning. The teacher must focus on what each student is demonstrating about his or her understanding of language and literacy to understand student growth.

Assessment and evaluation involves teachers, students, and parents working together to improve students' learning. Assessment and evaluation must grow out of the learning environment, involve learning processes and products, and consider the culture of the learner.

Often educators confuse assessment with testing. They speak of assessment as if talking about the instruments used to test learning. Teale, Hiebert, and Chittenden (1987) made a clear distinction between assessment and testing. "Assessment means gathering information to meet diverse needs . . . [while] testing, by contrast, refers to one particular method for obtaining information about learning" (p. 773). Assessment might be thought of as a continuum from informal on one end to formal on the other. Informal refers to having low constraints on the behavior being assessed, and formal refers to having high constraints. Informal involves the teacher as an observer of and interactor with the learner. Information will be gathered through observation and interaction and from the learner's own self-analysis and self-evaluation.

Assessment is also confused with evaluation. While assessment is clearly gathering data and developing forms or means to interpret it, evaluation is an interpreting process, and consequently the data is open to various interpretations (Chittenden, 1992). Evaluation will more fully reflect the learning of the student if data have been collected in multiple settings through multiple measures and observations. In addition, the greater the understanding by the teacher of the student and his or her culture, the better the interpretation or evaluation.

FORMAL TESTING OF CULTURALLY
DIVERSE STUDENTS

The performances of students from ethnic and racial cultures on norm-reference achievement and intelligence quotient (IQ) tests may not be accurate measures of their abilities. These tests are written from the perspective of the European American and actually measure cultural inheritance of the middle-class European American society (Grant & Sleeter, 1986). Many of the students being assessed are neither European American nor proficient in English. Both the nature of the tests' perspectives and the cultural backgrounds of the students are crucial reasons for the failure of culturally diverse students to do well on these tests.

Formal Tests: Poor Predictors of Ability

Students from culturally different homes will not generally fare well on achievement and IQ tests because the testing instruments are a poor match with their backgrounds. Although intended to give teachers information about students' learning, the tests act as sorting mechanisms (Nieto, 1992). Middle-class European American students doing favorably on these tests are placed in the best learning situations and taught appropriate information to do even better on the next battery of tests (Grant & Sleeter, 1986). Culturally diverse students receive instruction in phonics and vocabulary with little attention to developing higher order thinking skills. They are assigned to compensatory programs for skill training that have little cong·uence between the content of this instruction and their regular classroom instruction (Means & Knapp, 1991).

Most reading and language arts achievement tests at the elementary level focus on discrete skills, such as ability to distinguish sounds (phonics), aspects of grammar (third person plural), or ability to select the main idea or specific details of a paragraph or story. This information has little relationship to what students can actually do in the classroom. Prior (1990) referred to such information as inert knowledge. It does not evoke knowledge of a learner's current perceptions and thoughts or memories of people, events, and places. Certainly expectations, constructed imagery, beliefs, and emotional evaluations are not included in the tests.

In one elementary school, teachers found results discouraging when administering tests to children from their multicultural community. They wanted to establish baseline data on beginning letter/sound knowledge of their students. They stated that their students knew these relationships being tested, yet, the results did not indicate this. The students were being impeded by their inabilities to identify the culturally based illustrations used in the test. One test item was typical. It showed the back of a man in a tuxedo (assumed) with his arms outstretched and holding a thin stick. The illustration was to elicit the /k/ sound. Even teaching children how to take tests could not overcome the problem of not having had a prior experience for learning this.

Most curricula in the United States are held hostage by practices based on a philosophy that operates from a premise that learning is putting knowledge into the learners' heads like banking is depositing money in the bank (Freire, 1973). Like the bank, the tester determines learning assets based on discrete items. Using this theory it is assumed that the more discrete the items put in, the higher the figures or scores one should achieve. This results in curricula consisting of masses of arbitrary facts and discrete details with instruction delivered from teacher-proof manuals (manuals with discrete teaching directions for each aspect of the lessons). In these situations students become unmotivated, passive learners (Harman, 1991). Scores fall instead of rise.

The Argument Against Formal Testing of Culturally Diverse Children

Mercer (1989) presented some very convincing points about the nature of IQ and achievement tests as they are currently known and used. These points present convincing arguments for discontinuing the use of IQ and achievement tests, especially with students from diverse cultures. Mercer (1989) identified the following points:

1. There are no known tests to measure intelligence. All content in IQ and achievement tests measures learning about aspects drawn from a cultural pool of information.

2. Intelligence and achievement are not separate dimensions. IQ and achievement tests measure what a child has learned and are dependent upon opportunity for exposure to the cultural content covered in the test. Results will depend, as well, on motivation to learn, effective learning strategies, sensory acuity for learning, and the emotional state of the learner at the time of learning and testing.

3. Individually administered tests can reliably measure what has been learned about language and cultural content and can validly be used to compare one individual's learning to another's.

4. All factors affecting learning (exposure, motivation, learning strategies, sensory acuity, learning disability, language, cultural background, and emotional state), except intelligence, can never be equal or held constant, thus, it is impossible to use achievement testing to attribute differences in intelligence.

5. Positive correlation between IQ and achievement tests with grades does not indicate predictive ability of the tests. Instead, it indicates that the tests are measuring the same dimension of performance. These measures are based on cultural materials taught in the schools. Consequently, this is why different IQ tests and achievement tests correlate with one another.

6. Students from different linguistic and sociocultural backgrounds have lower mean scores on tests of intelligence and achievement than dominant-culture students because they come from different populations with different languages, cultures, and traditions. Clearly, the cultural factors influencing learning are not the same between dominant and nondominant populations; therefore, the tests are not legitimate measures of learning or intelligence. These tests are measuring what students know about the dominant culture.

Assessment and evaluation of achievement should reflect the multicultural curriculum. If a teacher wishes to know what a student knows about a social studies topic, for example, the student's proficiency in the English language, reading, and writing will have a great influence on what the teacher is testing. Understanding the student's cultural background, and knowing if the student is a second-language (L2) learner requiring more working time, necessitates using assessment strategies that will assess knowledge through multiple means and in multiple contexts which may or may not require the use of English.

If achievement and IQ tests continue to be used, they must be improved to be sensitive to cultural differences and fair in the testing conditions for all. Until then, their results must be interpreted with an honest awareness of the biases that are not weeded out (Worthen & Spandel, 1991).

Too many students are being taught based on the criteria and content of the achievement tests. To overcome this some states are working with test publishers to improve assessment and evaluation by the development of alternative assessment strategies. These joint projects strive to devise methods of assessing students that will provide useful information through interviewing processes, portfolio review, assessment of small-group work, and discussion of reading and writing (Maeroff, 1991). This requires, however, that teachers in these districts be well prepared to assess and evaluate students and document data gathered in a process-oriented, learner-referenced manner. The down side is the time required to carefully carry out such a program.

When Formal Tests Must Be Given

Formal testing should only be undertaken for good and sufficient reasons. Most tests will not give educators the important information they need for teaching. These tests do not indicate if students can integrate all the aspects of language in order to communicate in a particular social or academic setting. Language and literacy assessment call for a more holistic or integrative assessment (Hamayan, Kwait & Perlman, 1985).

If standardized tests must be used, Worthen and Spandel (1991) made the following suggestions to make sure that the tests are used appropriately:

1. Make sure that the test used is appropriate to the task it is supposed to do. When this is not the case, select others that are appropriate or supplement poor tests with measures selected or constructed specifically to measure what the school is attempting to do. For example, use the actual reading a child does daily and collect daily samples of his or her writing.

2. Remember that a student's score is rarely identical to what the student can actually do. Thus, do not use scores as if they are precise measures.

3. Supplement test scores with other information. Teacher knowledge of the student can be more accurate than any score. Observations and interactions with the student, although more subjective, can provide better insight regarding student ability.

4. Avoid using minimum standards to make critical decisions regarding grouping and classifying. This is one of the most damaging misuses of educational tests.

5. Do not assume that a test measures all the content, skills, or behaviors relevant to a particular topic. Different content sampling of the test could have different results with the same test-takers.

6. Be critical of claims made by the publishers of a test. The math achievement test given to Inuit Eskimo students, for example, probably tests English language more than math.

7. Remember that test scores tell educators nothing about why an individual scored as he or she did. Scores take interpretation, and different people may make different interpretations. Collect multiple data to assist in making interpretations.

8. Avoid making comparisons of individuals and schools using test

results. This practice can foster competition and can be used to label children, which can be extremely harmful.

9. Do not allow tests to drive the curriculum. Tests should not unduly influence what goes on in a school's curriculum.

Teacher-Made Tests

Teacher-made achievement tests provide an alternate to more formal standardized testing. The findings from teacher-made tests can be used in conjunction with information gathered about each student's use of language and literacy. Teacher-made measures can use language and literacy samples that are more closely related to a student's prior information and the school's curriculum. Tests involving student performance in talking, writing from dictation, actual reading of real books, and writing taken at intervals are better references for measuring language and literacy learning. Cloze-procedure formats (automatic deletion of specific words, letters, or items in a particular pattern) can be used to measure beginning letters, medial vowels, or ending letters as well as vocabulary. However, cloze techniques should be used with less rigid interpretation. For example, you can allow students to use their own words instead of exact words when testing comprehension.

Whenever any type of test is used, it is necessary that students have had practice in working in the format, not just the few examples given at the beginning of most normed achievement tests. When you must give L2 students tests, it is best to administer these tests in small groups. Small groups are more conducive to informality and provide an opportunity for the teacher to assist students by modifying instructions to get a better measure of ability.

Before undertaking to test students with teacher-made achievement tests, it is helpful to ask the questions adapted from Mary P. Diaz (1989), Minnesota Representative, Upper Great Lakes Multifunctional Resource Center. The answers to the following questions will help determine the validity of the test, what it is supposed to test, and the reliability of its findings to other information the teacher has about the learner:

1. Does this instrument assess what has been taught?
2. Is this the best way to determine this information for these learners?
3. How culturally appropriate is it to student learning styles? Will the teacher be able to use the information to improve the stu-

dent's learning? Does the content have direct application to the student's curriculum?

4. Is the student as at ease and as comfortable as possible? Is the testing situation similar to the usual learning and studying modality?
5. Has the teacher made the instructions clear to the students? Can they restate them in their own words?
6. Are examples appropriate to the tasks required in the test?
7. If the test is written or uses visual stimuli, is it easy to read and see?
8. If the test requires oral perception by the student, are the oral stimuli clearly understood and can they be consistently repeated?
9. Will the test allow the teacher to be consistent in his or her evaluation?
10. Will the testing instrument provide opportunities for the teacher to compare its results with his or her observations and interactions of the student?
11. Will the teacher be able to use the test to evaluate the success of his or her teaching as well as the student's learning?

If the answers to the above questions are not positive, then the teacher needs to either revise his or her instruments and process or use another means for gathering information. Stiggins (1991) stated that educators need to ask two questions about assessment of student achievement: What information does it give students about outcomes educators value? and What is likely to be the effect of the assessment on the student?

LEARNER-REFERENCED ASSESSMENT AND EVALUATION

A model for assessment and evaluation should be based on a concept that assessment and evaluation are extensions of curriculum and instruction. Central to the model must be the premise that language and literacy learning should be assessed as they occur and as they are used daily. This differs from traditional assessment—the paper-and-pencil test. In this model teachers need to be able to observe and interact with students as they are engaged in learning activities to be able to assess learning. To do this teachers must make numerous observations and interactions for gathering information about the student in many different settings across the curriculum.

Students must be observed individually and in small and large groups. Oral reading and writing interactions should be noted. Observations and interactions must be made over periods of time before good analysis, evaluation, or interpretation is possible. Most teachers require some record-keeping instruments to guide them in recording information and making analyses.

Classroom Settings for Data Gathering

Teachers can learn what students know about language and literacy through observing and interacting with students about what they say and write. They should note how they use and value books, writing, writing instruments, and materials in their daily school activities. This requires a learning environment in which students are empowered to learn, where they feel secure and comfortable sharing their intellectual and emotional connections (Watson, 1990), and where they are encouraged to grow through self-evaluation. The evaluation and assessment process, as is described here, occurs if the following situations are present (Watson, 1990; K. Goodman, 1989; Teale et al., 1987; Marek et al., 1984):

1. Students are involved in real learning situations.
2. Students are supported in developing a collaborative attitude with the teacher about learning.
3. Students perceive that their learning activities are focused on personal goals.
4. Students are assessed using real learning activities through observed behaviors and actual learning products as indicators of growth over a range of time.
5. Students are assessed and evaluated using processes and measures appropriate to their developmental levels and ethnic and cultural backgrounds.

In optimum assessment situations the teacher might determine at times to intervene during learning to determine what the student is thinking and what problem-solving processes the student is using. This may occur, for example, when a student is reading and thinking through a problem, composing meaning in writing, and searching for a solution to express a thought. Getting insight into these thinking processes enables the teacher to determine appropriate avenues for further instruction. Assessment then becomes a part of the curriculum and instruction, not separated from it. Assessment must always be developed to fit the curriculum, not vice versa. Learning activities that lend themselves as appropriate settings for assessment adapted from Chittenden (1992) include discussion and conversation, story time, self-selected reading, group reading, writing workshops, and conferences.

Discussion and conversation encourage responses to oral information and promote ability to share, respond, express opinion, support a point of view, and socially relate to others. Story time encourages language and comprehension responses to books and stories read by the teacher and classmates. A student who self-selects reading demonstrates skills relating to selection of material and references to content and language in discussion, writing, and interpretation in oral reading. Group reading promotes strategies demonstrating the use of cueing systems, comprehension of text, and responses to text in discussion, writing (journals and stories), and artistic media. Writing workshops allow students to use the writing process, express concern for an audience, and publish when appropriate. Conferences encourage discussion of printed and self-generated texts and focus on meaning from miscues, use of invented spelling, understanding of reading, and analysis of learning processes.

Involvement of Parents and the Extended Family in Assessment and Evaluation

Parents and caregivers need to be involved in assessment and evaluation of children in ways beyond merely receiving information. Parents and extended family members have important information to add to the assessment and evaluation jigsaw, and they need to become involved in the major decisions aimed at improving the instruction of their children.

Conferences with parents and/or caregivers are essential early in the year. Ideally, it would be helpful to have a conference even before the year begins and again after the first month to six weeks. Parents can provide information about how children respond to assessment measures. They should be involved in making instructional decisions about their children. They must be involved with teachers in setting learning directions for children and then consulted in assessing student progress in learning. Establishing good channels of communication with the home can aid an educator in respecting the cultural diversity and differing needs of children as well.

Wolf and Stephens (1989) recommended that children might be involved in parent/teacher conferences at times during the year. Involving children can take on different forms. It might be a preschool, three-way conference among family members, child, and teacher. In lieu of coming to a conference, children might prepare examples of their reading (taped), writing, and other work to share with their parents.

Children with some fluency as writers (even inventive spellers) might bring together all their work they wish to share with their home members, and then write a letter to tell the parent or caregiver what they had learned and what they thought they needed to work on further. A conference with each student prior to a parent/teacher conference will help the educator understand the student's point of view. This can be extremely effective. It involves the learner in the assessment and evaluation process and aids the student to be more focused in his or her learning. The learner becomes more involved with his or her learning process, eventually self-monitoring it. Generally, this will increase student self-concept.

One side effect of this is that the children will prepare the family members for the conference, discussing their learning progress before the conference. The conference time is then well spent in working on a plan to support the child's learning.

A home visit is a valuable aid in assisting the teacher in relating to the child and for finding cues for developing a suitable classroom environment and program for the student. Home visits let parents and family members know, too, that the teacher cares about the children he or she teaches. Check, however, before making these visits to make sure they are culturally acceptable and would not cause embarrassment for the parents and children. Bilingual aids or community social workers can be helpful in supplying this information and preparing and organizing for the visits.

Love (1989) suggested that home visits be done prior to school as a bridge between home and school. Insights gained in home visits can tell the teacher much about the culture and traditions of the home that will help him or her adjust curriculum, materials, and classroom environment as well as information about the language. Love (1989) took a photo of each child during the home visit for the child to look for on the first day in school. She believes that home visits ally parents to the school. She recommends a visit during the year as well. The home visit is an opportunity to begin to involve parents in the educational process of their children.

Bill Pogge, a first-grade teacher, starts each school year with a home visit. He gets to know both parents and children. Each child comes to school knowing him and the year begins on a personal level. Further, Bill follows up his visit with a letter to the child telling him or her that he is looking forward to the child being in the class during the year. For some of his young children, this may be the first letter they have ever had, and it makes a significant impression upon them. When bilingual teachers and aides are available, this is an opportunity to send the letter written in the child's first language. This can relieve stress the child might be experiencing about entering a world where adults and other children do not speak the child's language.

Learner-Referenced Assessment and Evaluation Model

Teachers should learn about their students by observing and interacting as children learn. Knowing and understanding how students learn and what students are learning are powerful tools for the development of instructional strategies for learners. Students can be learning in all activities involving language and literacy all the time, not just during direct instruction. A learner-referenced assessment and evaluation model should include the following three important processes (Marek et al., 1984; Y. M. Goodman, 1989):

1. Observation of the student that is designed to elicit specific information about language and literacy through watching and listening behaviors
2. Interaction with the student that provides knowledge of language and literacy flexibility, functions, and cueing systems as well as attitudes and values related to language and literacy
3. Analysis or evaluation of student development by teachers and students from chronological or visible records of language, reading, and writing development

Observations

According to Cunningham (1982) strategies for assessing and evaluating must be based on an accurate perception of students' language and literacy processes. This is acquired through observation of students over a period of time in real communication situations. Y. M. Goodman (1985) cautioned that because teachers screen their observations through their point of view and knowledge base, they must be aware of their biases. This is an extremely important point to remember, especially when dealing with children from cultures, traditions, and beliefs that differ from the teachers' own backgrounds. The more the teachers know about the cultural communities of the learners in their classrooms, the better able they will be to observe and interact with students as teachers.

When students are placed in classroom environments that focus on meaningful, functional, and relevant topics and themes, students take ownership for their learning. These situations provide rich language and literacy observations. Observing students in a multitude of learning settings can help teachers learn how learners are engaging in the learning process.

Suggestions for Observing Speaking and Listening in the Classroom. Children are speaking and listening all the time in the classroom. There should be a constant, overall pleasant hum of communication. This presents opportunities to observe how children are socially interacting and communicating using language. Consequently, an observant teacher will notice any quiet children, if children feel free to use another language, and if some children talk more than others, thus dominating the conversation in a group or classroom. These will be opportunities, as well, to note how students from various cultural communities are engaging in socializing.

Guidelines for Observing Speaking and Listening. Teachers can focus observation of speaking and listening by employing the following strategies, adapted from Norman (1990):

1. Plan to observe children throughout the day in different curriculum settings and learning experiences. Jot down notes about children: who is talking, who is being talked to, what is being said and what the response is, and so on.

2. Periodically tape-record a cooperative or collaborative group working together. Determine from the tape who is the leader, who is keeping students on task, and if children are listening to one another, learning from one another, and collaborating with one another. Are children using language that is appropriate to the topics they are working on?

3. Tape-record children telling a story, giving a report, explaining some information for a group. These can provide a basis for making an assessment and evaluation over a period of time when a number of samples are collected for each child on individual tapes.

4. When structured learning centers are being used in the classroom, this is an opportunity to collect language taped over a period of time that will indicate the developing nature of informal language and indicate, as well, if children are using concepts that are the focus of the center. This will provide the teacher with a sample of oral language that might provide information about the development of imaginative, practical, colloquial, and technical language.

Teachers should not be concerned to find that children are using home languages. Although the teacher may not understand the language, if he or she discovers through the tape-recording that children are using their first language, they are probably using it to assist one another in learning the content, skill, or concept.

Noting Development in Observing Speaking and Listening. Observations of speaking and listening should extend across all areas of the curriculum and in different types of interactional situations: in pairs, small working groups, with adults, and in large groups. These situations have implications for determining the developing understandings of oral usage and cultural understandings. The teacher will want to observe students regarding the following aspects of language use (Barrs, Ellis, Hestor & Thomas, 1988):

1. Does the student take part in planning an event, solving a problem, reporting some event, or finding and telling a story?
2. Does the student express a point of view or feelings?
3. Does the student initiate a discussion? Listen to the contributions of others? Encourage others to talk?
4. Does the student exhibit language influenced from reading? Listening to stories? Films, filmstrips, and videos?
5. What indications are there that the student's language is developing? Does he or she show appreciation for subtle nuances of words? Appreciation for different styles of spoken and written language? Interpretation of language from books, films, filmstrips, and videos?
6. Is the student able to take on roles in dramatic play and use the language of the characters and sustain the role during the play?
7. Is the student able to report on results from a study or investigation, describe how something was made or done?

When teachers have students learning English as their second language they will want to note how English is used. Do students smoothly switch from one language to another? When L2 students work in pairs and small groups do they take risks in speaking? Informal interactions should not generally require much silent rehearsal of talk for L2 learners. Consequently, these should be rich sources of information about the developing nature of the language.

Suggestions for Making Reading and Writing Observations. Reading and writing present unique situations for observing children's learning. Often the teacher may be noting both in a given sequence of learning events.

Reading.   The teacher can observe the three stages of the reading process—prereading, reading, after reading—by focusing on the unique aspects of each stage of the reading process.

In the prereading stage the teacher observes the ways in which the student chooses books. What kind of books is the reader choosing— range, variety, and how frequently selected? Does the student need help or urging in choosing material to read? As the student begins to read, the teacher observes if the reader does anything to become familiar with the text. (Many children erroneously believe it is wrong to look ahead in their reading, perhaps because they have been told that they will spoil the story. Some even think it is cheating!) Does the child choose to read alone or in pairs?

In the reading stage the teacher observes general reading behaviors while the student is reading. For example: How does the student handle the book? What indications are there that the student is comfortable about the reading and confident in making meaning? Are the reader's miscues high-quality or low-quality miscues, if reading aloud? Reading in the reader's mind is not the same as that in the writer's head but an imitation of it (K. S. Goodman, 1988). The reading process is dependent upon the reader's prior information and desire to seek meaning. Readers do not match the author's text; they only approximate it. The message the reader derives from the text is not identical to that written by the author because no two people have identical experiences, thoughts, and feelings (Weaver, 1988). Consequently, a reader will make miscues—deviations from the expectant response to the reading.

Miscues are not the result of careless reading. They present evidence of language and thinking integrating behaviors. They are not random but follow a pattern (Y. M. Goodman, Watson & Burke, 1987). Those that lead to loss of meaning are serious; others are not. Miscues occur as text is predicted. As students read, and the meaning sounds right and makes sense, they go on to integrate the reading in the meaning-making process.

The reader's miscues reflect the simultaneous inappropriate use of the three cueing systems: graphophonic, syntactic, and semantic. The following example and explanation of reading miscues was taken from Hammond (1982):

Text: Soon his three sisters and two brothers would come home.

Reading: "Sun, his third sister and two brothers would come home soon."

The reader of the example above was probably a good developing reader. However, during predicting, the first miscue caused the reader to attempt to make other miscues to make sense of the reading. Thus, when "Sun" was made subject of the sentence, "sisters" was made singular to make semantic and syntactic sense in confirming, and "soon" was added to bring closure to the idea. The important information determined about how this reader perceived reading words is that reading must make sense and sound right. Consequently, the reader has constructed a syntactic and semantic sentence.

Not all miscues deserve equal attention. Miscues that significantly change meaning are of most concern. Miscues indicate patterns representing strategies students are using in reading. Teachers must examine the miscues that appear to significantly change the meaning in relation to the student retelling of the story or passages to determine if the student is not understanding. Retelling provides an opportunity to ascertain the level of understanding. This will let the teacher know if the miscue is deliberate, happened as a result of a poor prediction, or is a problem with some cueing aspects.

The following information concerning oral reading miscues will aid teachers in learning about how learners are processing reading:

1. Substitution miscues, which are semantically and syntactically acceptable miscues, are important indicators of a reader's comprehension (Beebe, 1980).

2. Excessive self-correction of semantically and syntactically acceptable miscues are indicators of a possible reading meaning disruption.

3. Deliberate omissions (in the form of pausing or recognizing that the word is not known and then going on without attempting to determine or predict the word or meaning, even mentally) can be important indicators of a disruption of meaning (Goodman & Gollash, 1980).

4. Nondeliberate omission of important words can indicate meaning disruption.

5. Semantically and syntactically acceptable miscues and self-correction of unacceptable miscues tend to decline and a reader will rely more on graphophonic cues when the reading frustration level is reached (Christie & Alonso, 1980).

6. Proficient readers tend to rely less on graphophonic information and make more spontaneous self-correction of unacceptable miscues (Y. M. Goodman, 1976), while nonproficient readers tend to rely more on graphophonic information in reading.

In the after-reading stage, as the student retells the story or discusses and shares, the teacher observes the learner to see if he or she is comfortable in retelling, refers to the text, bring others into the discussion, and shows uncertainty by readily accepting conflicting points of view. How willing is the learner to share and discuss books read? Although these are legitimate concerns of the educator, they must always be considered in relation to the learner's cultural orientation and experiences.

The retelling technique is a very powerful technique, but one also requiring both teacher and student practice and preparation. Retelling will be an insight into how the student interprets. It will reflect a cultural orientation that may be different from the teacher's. However, if used in the right context, a student's ability to recall and make inferences can be determined from retelling. It can be used to assess comprehension both quantitatively and qualitatively (Morrow, 1987). Retellings are more easily analyzed for the teacher unfamiliar with the strategy if a story grammar format is developed. (This is discussed in section three, "Running Record, Miscue Analysis, and Retelling," in the Teacher Resource Kit.)

Writing.   Teachers need to observe the writer in two of the three major stages of writing—prewriting and writing. During the prewriting stage the student should be observed to determine the processes and activities the student uses to prepare or organize for successful writing and if there are specific problems the student generally has to overcome in getting started. In what self-chosen topics does the student achieve greater success? Does the student demonstrate willingness and pleasure in writing? The teacher will want to observe the student's understanding of the aspects of the writing stage by determining if the student is able to develop a good beginning, if the student is independent and confident when writing, and if the student is able to conclude with a good ending. Does the student get involved in the writing and sustain interest in the piece until it is finished? Is the student willing to share and learn from the work of others?

As students are ready to develop drafts, the teacher determines if the student is able to draft without concern about the mechanics and if the student is able to refine ideas through redrafting. Young writers need to learn how to make revisions without total rewriting. They must realize that revising means cross-outs, rearranging, arrows, or carets. Does the student change the piece to improve the meaning? Does the student recognize and attempt to change writing to improve sentence sense and cohesion? Do the editing changes reflect concern for the audience?

Suggestions for Making Multiple Observations. Educators might observe many aspects of learning at a time. Since speaking, reading, and writing are integrated in classroom activities, teachers can focus observation for each child on different processes in the same learning activities. The teacher might concentrate on content understanding for one student, a process orientation for another, and developing competency for a third. The following examples will focus on making language observations, demonstrating possible focuses for a teacher. L2 children might be observed to note how oral language is developing, while first-language (L1) children might be observed for demonstrations of learning of the topic. The teacher might note social, communicative, and cognitive language learning for both groups of learners.

Story Time or Following a Video, Film, or Filmstrip.   While most students are being observed to note the cognitive understanding of the experience and ability to communicate this information with others, L2 students might be observed on other dimensions; for example, in language fluency in retelling the story and events. Is the L2 student able to coordinate the ideas to express the essential core meaning? Is he or she using appropriate vocabulary? Are appropriate nonverbal communication skills being used?

Art, Music, Physical Education, or Recreation.   While the majority of the class might be observed to note specific learning about the content area, the L2 student might be observed for fluency and indications of ability to connect ideas used as he or she explains how to do, make, label, or describe something, seek permission, or give directions.

Social Studies and Science.   While other students are observed to determine their developing understanding of the content language, L2 students might be observed for demonstrations of emerging conceptual knowledge exhibited in vocabulary choices used about specific topics.

Cooperative Group Interaction.   While observing students for the effectiveness of their interaction in cooperative learning groups, the teacher might observe L2 students for indications of beginning conversing with other students in these settings. Are they able to receive content information? Can they provide the necessary interactions and responses to others in the group to make themselves understood? Are they able to begin sharing in the planning and decision making?

Suggestions for Observing L2 Students.   Observing L2 and culturally different students requires an orientation to the learners' specific backgrounds and cultures as well as an understanding about L2 learning to be successful. Foremost, the teacher will want to be sure that his or her world view does not influence the observation of the students' learning. Teachers generally have questions and concerns in analyzing the learning behavior of children from cultures and homes in which English is not the primary language. According to Genishi (1989) teachers need to know answers to questions about why a child seems competent in one setting and not in another and how much English a child uses outside the school.

Determine Language Preference.   Teachers need to determine a child's preferred language if the student is bilingual. How long has the child been learning English? Learning a second language takes time, especially language of a conceptually academic nature. Thonis (1990) suggested that teachers of language-different students ask the following questions about students from non-English-dominant homes:

1. *How well does the student understand and speak the home language?*
2. *Can the student read and write the home language?*
3. *How well does the student understand and speak English?*
4. *Is the student's achievement in either or both languages appropriate for the age and grade placement? (p. 8)*

Genishi (1989) reminded educators that observation is the key to discovering what students learning English as a second language know about English and how each child approaches L2 learning. Family members can be helpful with insights about this. Remember, it would not be unusual for children from language-different homes to be silent when first learning English. This silent period might go on for weeks, even months (Krashen & Terrell, 1983). These children may feel miserable if forced to speak and/or miserable because they cannot communicate. Some children required to learn English may demonstrate little language for the teacher to hear. However, this does not mean that they are not developing. Parents and extended family members are excellent sources for learning what the child is experiencing and feeling. One silent student, for example, went home every day to share all the new English vocabulary being learned without ever speaking one English word in class! The parents went to school to express their pleasure in how their child was learning English so quickly.

Observe for Language and Literacy Function. Each child's approach or style for learning to communicate in a new language or dialect must be recognized and the learner placed in situations where he or she has a large variety of ongoing activities for talk. The teacher must keep in touch with the English-language teacher and bilingual teacher. These professionals can assist in recognizing learning indications and progress.

Students learning a second language in the process of acquiring literacy should be observed to note progress in developing the language and literacy functions (Halliday, 1975). These functions can serve as helpful guides in specifically determining where to focus observations. The following questions might be asked:

1. To what degree is the student using speaking, reading, and writing to fulfill his or her needs? Examples to note are questions the child asks, such as:

> How do you say . . . ?
> What does this say?
> Does this say . . . ?
> How do you write . . . ?

2. To what degree is the student using speaking, reading, and writing to control his or her environment or life space in the classroom? Is the student gaining more self-reliance in classroom interactions? Examples of language that might be observed include:

> Stay out!
> Keep out!
> We want to talk about . . .

3. To what degree is the student using speaking, reading, and writing to share ideas with others? For example, does the student share an idea or illustration from a text, a piece of writing recently finished, or does he or she help another student who is struggling with a composition problem?

4. To what degree is the student using speaking, reading, and writing to express individuality and personality? For example, does the student select personal reading materials? Is he or she developing a personal speaking and writing style and selecting his or her own topics for discussing and writing?

5. To what degree is the student using speaking, reading, and writing to create fantasy, poetry, stories, and drama? For example, does the student participate in group dictations and dramatizations? Is the student writing and illustrating individual stories?

6. To what degree is the student using speaking, reading, and writing to investigate or acquire knowledge and understanding? For example, does the student ask questions of a visiting speaker for personal information, seek help from the librarian to find information about a topic, find a peer to work with on a joint topic of interest, write a letter to seek information, or leave a note on the teacher's desk requesting a conference?

7. To what degree is the student using speaking, reading, and writing to communicate information? For example, does the student share current events, books, or personal experiences?

Note Classroom Behavior. Because children from diverse cultural backgrounds may feel that they are placed in situations that are alien to them, they may experience a multitude of behavioral reactions from withdrawal to aggression. They should be observed with attention to how they are responding to the daily activities in the classroom. These students need an understanding and supportive teacher and environment. The teacher should determine the progress that these students are making through careful observation.

Questions that will guide the observation of culturally diverse and L2 students include the following:

1. Is the child attempting to communicate?
2. What behaviors does the child use to communicate?
3. Does the child understand and enjoy the stories read or told? How can the teacher tell?
4. What are the student's face and eyes telling you about how he or she feels about being in the classroom? (Remember that children of diverse cultures may have different communicative behaviors.)
5. How is the student interacting with other children? Who does he or she relate best to in the classroom?
6. What activities in the classroom are the most satisfying for the child? Are there some that are particularly more successful?
7. Is there some particular spot in the classroom where the child feels the most comfortable?
8. Under what conditions does the child appear to make the most progress?

Keep Careful Notes. Be aware of patterns that L2 learners may be using. This can be done by making anecdotal notes (discussed later in the chapter). When notes are kept on a child over a period of a month to six weeks, the teacher will have a record to determine if there are signs of growth and if any programs or practices are particularly successful. Parents or primary caregivers should be consulted to determine if they are noticing any growth and development.

Interactions

As the teacher works with a student over a period of time—individually, in small groups, and in large groups—the teacher should record information noted through his or her interactions. The teacher will want to discover what insights the student has about his or her learning and how the student problem solves and responds to the learning activities.

Notes from informal and formal conferencing should be kept. Some children might help with notetaking by dictating what they think the teacher should write down. This allows them to take responsibility for their learning and evaluation.

Speaking and Listening Interactions. In his or her interactions with students through talking and listening, the teacher should focus on the areas dealing with the development of responsive language and behavior and students' abilities to reflect on listening and language development. Norman (1990) reported that teachers in the National Oracy Project in Great Britain asked children what they thought about talking as a way of establishing a basis for assessment and evaluation in their classrooms. According to Norman the following kinds of questions were asked of the children in the project:

1. How did the students learn to talk? (This could be extended across both the first and second languages for bilingual children.)
2. Who taught the students to talk?
3. Do the students think they are good talkers?
4. Who do the students know who is a good talker?
5. What talking do the students do in school?
6. Who do the students like to talk to?
7. What do the students talk about?
8. When shouldn't the students talk?
9. Do the students talk differently in different places?

In responding to literacy, the teacher can note in reading and writing conferences the following language competencies that can be elicited that are indications of developing cognitive language:

1. The developing ability to retell a familiar story, such as a folktale, predictable story, or story from a book that the student has read
2. The developing ability to tell an event from real life with clarity

that involves identification of characters and setting and a reasonable sequence of events

3. The developing ability to create a story or a poem or to report an event through writing or dictation to the teacher
4. The developing ability to use language in role-playing with the teacher in creative drama and structured learning centers
5. The developing conceptual understandings about content topics in health, science, social studies, and mathematics

Finally, the teacher will want to explore students' developing skills in reflecting on what they have learned and ways of learning, working, and talking (Norman, 1990). Facilitating students' reflections aids them to develop better self-awareness and can provide the teacher with more information for assessment. Reflection is an important learning process if children are going to develop abilities for self-evaluation. Questions that might elicit reflection include the following (adapted from Norman, 1990):

1. What did the students like or dislike about the work they did or the group did? How could it be improved?
2. What did the students like or dislike about the way they worked or the group worked? (For example, focus on the ability of children to listen to one another, take turns in talking and sharing ideas, keep to the point, achieve a goal, and use time wisely.)
3. Were the students satisfied with what they learned or the group learned? How could their learning be improved?
4. What did the students like or dislike about the way they talked and listened? How could their abilities be improved?

Reading Interactions. In reading the teacher will want to interact with students before, during, and after reading. Watson (1985) suggested before-reading, during-reading, and after-reading strategies to keep in mind while interacting with students.

Before reading begins the teacher should find out what students know and let them look at the materials and predict what they expect. Particular attention should be paid to the thinking students use when asked what they expect to find in the text (story) and what they know about the topic. When doing this with a group, the responses should be listed on the board or chart, even listing the names of the students who did the predicting. Periodically the following information should be elicited:

1. What do the students do when they come to a word they do not know?

2. What do the students do when they do not understand something the teacher has read?
3. Do the students think they are good readers? Why or why not?

During reading the teacher may want to interact with the students by breaking the reading activity and discussing characterization, sequence, point of view, and so forth. Insights into student reading processes can be ascertained through the following procedures:

1. Encourage students to relate the reading to their own personal meaning by asking them if they have ever had anything similar happen to them or anyone they know.
2. Have students discuss how a word was figured out. This indicates which information was selected and used from the text to solve semantic, syntactic, or graphophonic problems. For example, How did you know how to pronounce . . . ?
3. Ask a student who has stopped reading aloud and says "That should have been . . ." to explain how he or she knows that information.

After reading the teacher will want to encourage and facilitate the students' retelling to determine how well each student is composing meaning. Y. M. Goodman (1989) suggested that carefully considered and appropriately stated questions be used to "gently push kids to consider greater, conflicting, or different information. Further, questioning should move students toward moments of disequilibrium so they have to reorganize their concepts and rethink their ideas" (p. 11). Determine the following information about readers after reading (Y. M. Goodman, 1989):

1. Abilities to retell the major aspects of the reading (For example, if it is a story, were character, setting, plot, events, and theme included?)
2. Inclusion of readers' background knowledge and imaginative speculation about the reading
3. Parts that gave trouble
   Was there anything you weren't understanding in the story/text?
   Have you ever heard the word before?
4. Abilities to examine statements critically
   Why do you think so?
   Is it possible?
   What if we tried this instead?

What if I said . . . ?

I wonder if . . . ?

Questions that can be used with students following the reading that encourage the student to focus on the reading process include:

How do you think you are doing?

Why?

Is there something you can improve?

How?

How do you decide the meaning of a word, a passage?

Writing Interactions. Interactions in writing need to occur in language activities focused on the writing process: planning what to write; drafting or dictation in language-experience activities; journal writing; publishing through sharing written stories, books, reports, and conferencing. The teacher can be guided in developing interactions with students at points in the writing process.

Brainstorming in groups or jotting down ideas on paper may precede writing as may individual conferences (Cochrane, Cochrane, Scalena & Buchanan, 1984). In a conference, the teacher may wish to interact with a student or small group, using the following question starters as an insight to the prewriting process:

What do you intend this piece to be about?

What do you know about this topic?

What do you do when you want to write about something you don't know much about?

Do you think you are a good writer? Why or why not?

In the writing stage drafts of a student's writing may be shared orally in an individual conference. The teacher should look over the piece only to assist when there is a request or need to help with the reading for the emerging writer. Responses should be made to hearing the piece, not visualizing it, and the writer should always remain in control of the piece (Cochrane et al., 1984). Interactions might develop around questions that provide insight into the writer's intentions in the piece, such as the following:

What part of the piece do you like best? Why?

What is going to happen next?

What did you find out about yourself as you wrote this?

For whom is this piece written?

Are you having any trouble with your writing?

Do you have any questions you want to ask your listeners?

Ask of me?

Information about the more experienced writer's understanding of revision can be elicited by asking the following questions suggested by Turbill (1983):

> *How successfully do you think you've revised?*
> *Why did you change that? (a specific point)*
> *Is anything still nagging—not quite right?*
> *Will you do another draft?*
> *Should it be published? In what form? (p. 65)*

The postwriting stage generally has some culminating activity. The student might read the piece to the teacher and/or prepare it for some type of publication or display. Generally, the teacher should determine how the student feels about the piece.

Interacting in Reading and Writing with Nondominant-Culture Students. Because nondominant-culture students may bring totally different perspectives or schemas to interpreting a topic, this does not necessarily indicate lack of prior background experience. Instead, it signifies different perspectives that must be respected. Topics and themes having cultural schemas unknown to the reader or writer may be confusing and frustrating to the student. Certainly these will not contribute toward understanding the learning of the student. Although these topics need not be avoided, nondominant-culture students might be expected to achieve better in topics that relate closer to their prior information.

Rigg (1986) suggested finding miscues that native-English speakers make reading a selection as helpful for locating syntactic traps that might naturally cause confusion for L2 students. Oral reading miscues that are probably mispronunciations should generally be ignored. English second language (ESL) students are still mastering the sound system of the language and consequently may not pronounce English words correctly due to phonemic problems, lack of understanding of syllabic change in English pronunciation, and confusion between pronunciation of similarly spelled words in English and their native language. This may not mean that meaning has been disrupted. When L2 students transfer from reading in one language to reading in another, it is not unusual to note the pronunciation of words using L1 rules especially when there is a syntactical and semantical meaning match, as there is in the Spanish/English *me/my*. Students have been noted to pronounce all English words ending in /y/ with the Spanish long /e/, but still have good comprehension of the reading.

Students learning English as a second language tend to be overly concerned with exactness and performance. Consequently, this concern can easily misinform the teacher about students' real competencies. Teachers must take care not to exacerbate the situation by focusing on exactness and performance over meaning. This happens when teachers insist on exact word-for-word reading of text and overemphasize correct spelling in writing.

Reading assessment should focus on silent reading comprehension. Language-different students need plenty of opportunities to read silently once past the beginning stage. It is through silent reading that fluency and speed develop. Students should read topics that are meaningful, relevant, and functional to them. Through retelling predictable reading materials and language books, teachers can assess emergent readers' progress and development. Emergent writing can be assessed from dictated stories, generated language stories, and teacher attention to content, not form.

Analysis

To aid in the analysis process, the teacher needs to develop a record-keeping system where the data gathered from observations and interactions can be summarized to provide the basis for making an analysis of learning. When this information is in place, the teacher analyzes it to make decisions about students' learning. There are a number of strategies and instruments that teachers can adapt, develop, or employ to aid in making analyses.

Developing a Data-Keeping System. Essential information must be recorded about each student to use in making decisions about instruction. Information must be available that will provide comparisons for an individual from one period to another to determine growth and development and to provide insight in determining how a student best learns. This information is necessary for instructional decision making and conferencing with students and parents. Teachers might choose to select or develop any number of combinations of data-recording instruments.

Anecdotal Records. Anecdotal statements collected from observations about the student at work, at play, individually, in groups, and from conferences provide a wide range of information for making decisions. They do pose a problem, however, when teachers wish to use them. How should the data be recorded as teaching and learning is in progress? One technique used in recording anecdotal information is to put cards out every day for recording anecdotal information for specific students. Students might be chosen for various reasons: an upcoming conference; a small group sharing some reading, a written paper or a project; or in looking over the records, the teacher may have realized that he or she had no current information on a specific child. Notes can be made from recording student discussions, reports, readings, or play. Dated anecdotal notes might be recorded in a journal with designated pages for each student.

Anecdotal records are a rich source of data that can be shared in conferences with students and parents. Because anecdotal records are made over a period of time, they require time for reading, rereading, searching back over the notes, and pondering about the child to think about language and literacy. A solution to this situation might be to record the notes in categories appropriate to the communication processes of speaking and listening, reading, and writing. Norman (1990) suggested recording and dating speaking and listening observations and interactions on one form. Figure 8.1 shows an anecdotal record form adapted from Norman (1990) and Barrs, Ellis, Hester, and Thomas (1990). Information on sheets like this, combined with actual samples of talk or reading and writing, will provide teachers with information for assessing and evaluating student development.

Checklists.   The use of checklists certainly is a viable strategy in assessing and evaluating the language and literacy program. The process of doing this for the teacher is as important as the record developed. The actual process contributes to understanding the developmental nature of language and literacy. One group of teachers, in attempting to gather specific information for assessing and evaluating the emerging language of their L2 students, developed a checklist in keeping with their philosophy (shown only partially in Figure 8.2). Included in the directions for the teachers' checklist was a guide for determining the appropriate column for checking emerging, present, or internalized behaviors. Their guide assisted them in determining if the student's speech was comprehensible, if the syntactic structures being used (one-word holophrases, telegraphic sentences, sentence fragments or clauses, and so on) were adequate, and if and to what degree the student used coherent language in instruction, selected topics, or conversationally to initiate discussion.

Hood (1989) developed a record-keeping form to document the

FIGURE 8.1 Speaking and Listening Anecdotal Record

Category:	Observation (Date)	Observation (Date)	Observation (Date)
Group speaking/ listening interactions			
Listening/speaking responses to stories/ poems/events			
Describing language and thinking for conveying real and imaginary events/ideas			
Giving, following and responding to directions/messages			
Asking and responding to questions			
Other language patterns noted			

Source: Adapted from K. Norman, *Teaching Talking and Learning in Key Stage One,* National Curriculum Council, York, Great Britain, 1990, and M. Barrs et al., *Patterns of Learning: The Primary Language Record and the National Curriculum,* Centre for Language in Primary Education, London, Great Britain, 1990.

progress of her Spanish-speaking students learning English and English literacy in her kindergarten classroom. She formally documented children's development a number of times each year, in addition to using anecdotal records and writing folders. Involved in the assessment and evaluation process were specific checklists used for observing. Hood's Kindergarten Growth Documentation Form is shown in Figure 8.3.

Turbill (1983) shared a checklist record-keeping form, Hughes' Individual Writing Record, that she suggested could be used for reporting about student development. This form consists of a list of things to watch in children's writing performance. She noted that such lists needed to be personalized and specific to each teacher and classroom.

FIGURE 8.2 Emerging Literacy Checklist

Observable Item	Not Observed	Emerging	Present	Internalized
Takes part in discussions				
Expresses needs effectively				
Communicates effectively with peers				
Describes personal experiences				

Below are some of the questions that might be included on this checklist:

> Does the student have a willing attitude toward writing?
> Can he or she select topics independently?
> Is the student able to collect information independently?
> Is the student able to write a first draft fluently?
> Is the student able to revise and rewrite?
> Does the student reveal a growing vocabulary?
> Can the student structure sentences correctly?
> Can the student form coherent paragraphs?
> Is the student improving his or her control over mechanics?

Eeds (1988) adapted an earlier work into the Checklist for Developmental Stages in Early Writing (Figure 8.4). Eeds's checklist spans the four stages of spelling prior to the final stage: correct spelling. It integrates writing development that would also typify each stage.

Profiles. D. Goodman (1989) developed a profile for recording information about her students that integrated important information about the reading process and the cueing systems (Figure 8.5). She arranged the information on a grid and developed questions in each section of the grid to reflect that particular aspect of the reading process. Then she analyzed the information to develop four or five instructional objectives for each student that she recorded on the form for easy reference.

FIGURE 8.3 Hood's Kindergarten Growth Development Form

Name _____ Language _____

  ✓ = does this   B = beginning to   E = English
                                         S = Spanish

	Date	Date	Date	Date
Recognizes name in limited contexts				
Recognizes name in many contexts				
Writes first/last name (indicate F/L)				
Approximates print in writing				
Relates print to pictures				
Uses invented spelling				
Selects writing as a choice				
Uses writing spontaneously				
Reads pattern books				
Knows print carries meaning				
Reads some environmental print				
Reads back own writing				
Selects reading as a choice				
Uses written resources				
Uses second language				
Counts to (#)				
1:1 correspondence to (#)				
Numberness to (#)				
Writes numbers to (#)				
Reads numbers to (#)				
Maths in play settings				
Solves problems				
Predicts outcomes				

Source: W. Hood, "If the Teacher Comes Over, Pretend It's a Telescope," in K. S. Goodman, Y. M. Goodman, and W. Hood (eds.), *The Whole Language Evaluation Book,* Heinemann, Portsmouth, NH, 1980, p. 37. Reprinted with permission from Kenneth S. Goodman, Yetta M. Goodman, and Wendy K. Hood, eds. *The Whole Language Evaluation Book* (Heinemann Educational Books, Portsmouth, NH, 1989).

FIGURE 8.4   Checklist for Developmental Stages in Early Writing

Name _____ Age _____ Grade _____

	I	II	III	IV

Precommunicative Stage   *Date*
1. Produces letters or letterlike forms to represent a message
2. Includes number symbols as part of message
3. Demonstrates left-to-right concept
4. Demonstrates top-bottom concept
5. Repeats known letters and numbers
6. Uses many letters and/or numbers
7. Mixes upper and lowercase letters
8. Indicates preference for uppercase forms

The Semiphonetic Stage   *Date*
1. Realizes letters represent sounds
2. Represents whole words with one or more letters
3. Evidence of letter name strategy
4. Demonstrates left-to-right sequence of letters
5. Puts spaces between words

The Phonetic Stage   *Date*
1. Represents every sound heard
2. Assigns letters based on sounds as child hears them (invented spellings)
3. Puts spaces between words
4. Masters letter formation

The Transitional Stage   *Date*
1. Utilizes conventional spellings
2. Vowels appear in every syllable
3. Evidence of visual as opposed to phonetic strategy
4. Reverses some letters in words

Comments _____

_____

_____

_____

_____

_____

Source: M. Eeds, "Holistic Assessment of Coding Ability," in S. M. Glazer et al. (eds.), *Reexamining Reading Diagnosis,* International Reading Association, Newark, DE, 1988, p. 546. Reprinted with permission of Mary Eeds and the International Reading Association.

FIGURE 8.5 Sample of Completed "Profile of Reading Strategies" Form

Name _Susan_   Date _10/16/87_

	Semantic	Syntactic	Graphophonic
P R E D I C T I N G	Minimal focus on making sense. Knows print carries message. Knows balloons carry dialogue. Predicts dialogue and boy's questions. Substitutes concept-ually related nouns: room/house	Knows book. Knows left to right. Knows sentence starters: This is/The Attempts to form questions: What? Tries to maintain story sense—cohesive ties. Uses grammatically accept-able nouns and non-words	Makes strong use of graphophonics: beginning, middle, ending, and vowels. Examples: town/t...end street/sees bad/box that, the/ this, there, the

| **C O N F I R M I N G** | *Does not attempt to regress to correct. Self-corrects across text: tries "the", returns to "there"; tries diff. words for "street", "door."* |||
| | Uses pictures. Looks up at teacher.

Needs to build self-confidence | Changes words across text, retains grammatical function. | Makes use of graphics pictures

Not able to recreate story. |

| **I N T E G R A T I N G** | Can give a retelling. Not reading enough. Enjoys hearing stories and discussing them. | Objectives
1. Focus on story meaning. Build confidence in use of semantics and meaning.
2. Support her use of language patterns and increase use of own language ability in reading.
3. Develop independent reading strategies to encourage self-correction strategies.
4. Build story sense; encourage story telling and retellings.
5. Improve opportunities for listening to focus on story sense. ||

Source: D. Goodman, "So Why Don't I Feel Good About Myself?" in K. S. Goodman, Y. M. Goodman, and W. K. Hood (eds.), *The Whole Language Evaluation Book,* Heinemann, Portsmouth, NH, 1989, p. 210. Used with permission from Kenneth S. Goodman, Yetta M. Goodman, and Wendy K. Hood, eds. *The Whole Language Evaluation Book* (Heinemann Educational Books, Portsmouth, NH, 1989).

Student Self-Evaluation. Students need to develop self-evaluation abilities to assist their development. Opportunities for self-evaluation should be provided in conferences and through oral discussion in large and small groups. To aid children to value themselves, teachers need to help them view their speaking, reading, and writing development in positive ways. These experiences will be facilitated if the teacher has learners writing response journals, keeping portfolios, and periodically sampling their writing and recording their reading on tape. This body of information becomes the data base students use in making comparisons of their development from one time to another. Portfolios (discussed later in this chapter) allow students to take ownership for their learning and assessment. When they are involved in developing and keeping samples of their work, there are greater opportunities for student growth.

Crowley (1989) made an important point about assisting students in self-evaluation. Instead of responding to questions students ask about what a teacher thinks, Crowley suggested turning the question around and asking the students for their opinions. This helps students become their own critics first. Questions that might be asked of the student that will aid in self-evaluation of writing include:

Why did you choose this topic to write about?

If this were someone else's piece and you were reading it, what questions would you ask?

What are some problems you experienced in writing this piece? How did you solve them? Are you satisfied?

Did you discover anything about yourself or your ability as you wrote this?

How would you describe yourself as a writer?

Another aid that could assist students in developing self-evaluation is to have each student begin a list of areas in listening, speaking, reading, and writing he or she thinks should be focused on during the year. These areas might be suggested from the first samples the student makes of his or her reading, writing, and speaking. The samples and student lists are then discussed by the teacher and the student during a conference. Care must always be taken to put the most positive light on the student's work. Teachers should not agree to any aspects for student improvement that will be far beyond a learner's present ability for achieving. This list should then be used by both to discuss progress, eliminate goals achieved, and add new learning goals as the year progresses.

Older students might use a series of questions to assist themselves in evaluating their progress. In writing, this might include the following.

Does the piece make sense to me?

Do I have a voice?

Am I aware of my audience?

Is the piece clearly and concisely written or does it require rereading of certain parts in order to understand the message?

Does the piece flow or are there parts that seem to be in the wrong order or left out altogether?

Will the readers find it interesting?

Portfolios. Paulson, Paulson, and Meyer (1991) stated that portfolios can become windows into the students' heads and can assist teachers to understand the educational processes at the level of the individual learner. A portfolio provides a complex and comprehensive look at a student's learning performance in a given context. If used properly, it can be a tool that facilitates a take-charge attitude by the student about his or her own learning. Portfolio assessment involves the student in collecting and documenting development and reflecting on the learning. Keeping portfolios should assist students in developing their self-evaluation abilities and encourage self-directed, independent learners (Paulson et al., 1991).

Portfolios can be inclusive, representing all aspects of language and learning, or they can include only one language or literacy aspect. They might include anecdotal records, checklists, profiles, and student evaluations in various forms and formats, individual or integrated. Portfolios are potentially powerful teaching and evaluation tools. In addition, they are excellent sources of data about students' learning for discussion with primary caregivers to enlist their collaboration in decision making. A portfolio, ideally, should go home prior to a parent/teacher conference for families to study the student's work. Or, it might go home periodically for reading and signature.

Many schools have employed student writing portfolios for decades. Examples of student writing are collected from many sources to be used for writing analysis. Turbill (1983) suggested that writing assessment and evaluation take place from the following sources:

1. The information the teacher carries around in his or her head as the result of conferences, observation, and insight into the learner

2. Anecdotal records kept in a book in which two pages are devoted to each child in the class (the teacher would date notations made about a child at each entry)

3. Checklists that the teacher devises to use on aspects of writing currently emphasized, such as the mechanics of writing, or some specific weakness that is currently a focus

4. A writing folder that includes a complete copy of all the student's dated writing samples, whether draft, revision, or finished pieces

5. Published or finished pieces of writing (such as books the student has written), class publications (such as class anthologies), and writing selected by the student to be finished

The idea of the writing portfolio would be to include examples of the student's progress and products over specific periods of time. This provides concrete examples for analyzing student development.

A writing sample would be taken from every child at the beginning of the year, again at the middle, and near the end of the school year. These could be compared and contrasted with one another to determine progress. Focus for the contrasts would differ according to the age and development of the writer—attention to "wordness and sentenceness" (emergence of words written in invented spelling, and extended text that has a sentence structure format), clause structure, clarity, and concern for audience understanding.

The writing portfolio might begin with a series of processes, suggested by Powlesland (1985), that finds out what students think and feel about writing. She conducted interviews with her students at the beginning of the year, guided by the information she wished to find out about them. Powlesland recommended no set order in eliciting the following types of information:

1. Establish a writing sample. Ask each student to write something to be kept in his or her portfolio. Following the writing ask the student to tell about what he or she has written.

2. Determine home writing experiences. Ask questions about experiences the student has had writing outside of school. For example:
Have you ever noticed your parent(s) writing?
Why do they write?
What do they write?
When?
Record this information.

3. Determine self-evaluation ability. Ask the student to show something he or she has written and find out what is thought about it— whether the student liked it, whether he or she thought it was good, and why (or why not). Have the student review and respond to this information at two or three other intervals during the year. Keep a record with each piece of writing.

4. Establish the role of the teacher. Ask the student to describe the sort of help he or she would like from the teacher. Record this information for later.

5. Determine the student's feelings about writing. Ask the student if he or she thinks writing is hard or easy, if he or she likes writing. (This might be included in the student self-evaluation.)

6. Elicit difficulties in writing. Ask the student what he or she does if he or she forgets what was going to be written, or ask what causes him or her the greatest problem in writing.

7. Determine the student's knowledge of writing. Ask an emerging writer to show or tell the teacher what a word is. Discuss concepts, such as sentence, paragraph, title, draft, and so on, with advanced writers.

In gathering this information the teacher must take good notes, develop a form for recording the information, or make a tape-recording to be listened to by both the teacher and the student prior to the next conference. Older students might respond in writing to questions about their writing. This activity should be followed with a conference.

Mathews (1990) suggested a reading/writing portfolio, developed by the Orange County Public Schools, in Orlando, Florida, that included: a reading development checklist, writing samples, a list of books read by the student, and a test of reading comprehension. The reading development checklist, for example, included statements regarding concepts about print, attitudes toward reading, strategies for word identification, and comprehension strategies.

This type of assessment record provides the teacher with a particular organizing focus to use in assessing and evaluating students. Examples of a student's audiotaped speaking and reading at different periods of the year, and writing at various junctures during the year, would be included. Certainly, the teacher could involve students in decision making about what is included in the portfolio and include student self-evaluation. Writing might be added from across the curriculum as well as examples of a work at various stages. Books read could include reactions and responses, even response journal pages in addition to mere lists.

Language/literacy portfolios include speaking, reading, and writing processes. These require more teacher involvement in the development and suggestion of information for data collection. However, the portfolio must always be seen by the student as his or her own: something of individual ownership and involvement in selecting what should be included. The data and documents in the portfolio should help the learner see himself or herself as successful as the learner engages in the process of developing and keeping the portfolio and as the teacher provides help in assessing and evaluating progress. It should also be a source for primary caregivers to become better informed about a learner's progress.

Suggestions for helping students to develop a language/literacy portfolio include the following:

1. Begin the portfolio process by discussing with the students what it is and how it will be used during the year. Develop a feeling of ownership for the portfolios with the children. Have them suggest what they might include. This might be done by having students inventory their interests or reading and writing self-assessment.

2. Include items, documents, and records that a student might wish to keep during the year in the portfolio. For example, there can be a place to record the books read during the year. The student might fill in an interest inventory by answering questions that will assist the student in recording ideas of interest. These can always be used later for possible writing topics. There can be spaces for some self-analysis about speaking, reading, and writing.

3. Be sure that the portfolio is kept in a location that is easily accessible for the students. Remember to keep suggesting items to keep in the portfolio during the year and to provide time for students to work on the portfolio. Be sure that the material in the portfolio is material that the students want there.

4. Use the portfolio as a valuable document in conferencing. Have a conference with the student prior to each parent/teacher conference. Have the student take the portfolio home periodically with a letter asking parents to spend time with their child discussing its contents. (See Tierney, Carter & Desai, 1991, for assistance in developing and using portfolios.)

Making Decisions Based on Data Gathered.   In exploring how to make decisions about learning, there are several points that teachers should consider about a student's development in listening and speaking, reading, and writing for decision making.

Listening and Speaking. Progress in listening and speaking is very difficult to determine because these communication competencies are not hierarchical, are highly dependent upon the experiences a student has (Norman, 1990), and assessment is best made during real situations. These are important factors to remember, especially as educators consider the diverse backgrounds and experiences of students in multicultural schools. A student's language, listening, and speaking would be expected to demonstrate indications of growth and development in at least six major areas: listening, world knowledge, sentence and vocabulary development, personal interactions, concern for others in communicating, and expansion of the speaking register (Norman, 1990).

Therefore, teachers need to examine student speaking and listening information gathered on the anecdotal records, checklists, and profiles, or in the portfolios for three areas of language use: social interaction, communicative ability, and cognitive applications. The following questions might be asked about each area (Norman, 1990):

1. Social interaction: What interaction patterns does the student demonstrate in a range of situations?
2. Communicative ability: Was the student able to express his or her ideas clearly to others? Did he or she understand what others were communicating? Did he or she use language that was appropriate to the topic and in a register appropriate to the context?
3. Cognitive applications: How well was the student able to express thinking-aloud solutions? Was the student able to learn from others? Could the student follow a line of thought?

Information gathered from such questions could form a grid of data for decision making about the student. Figure 8.6 illustrates how the data might be arranged. This process would develop a broad profile of the student and enable the teacher to make professional judgments about the development of the child.

Reading. In analyzing a student's reading development it is important to determine if the student is a proficient reader for his or her stage of development. Therefore, the teacher would examine the student's learning based on an evolving sophistication from whole to part. This assumes the increasing development of the conventions of the language system (DeFord, 1980). Reader proficiency would need to

FIGURE 8.6 Listening and Speaking Decision-Making Grid

Indications	Social	Communicative	Cognitive
Expanding active listening			
Growing knowledge/ experience			
Expanding language • Sentence structures • Vocabulary			
Growing ability to self-evaluate interactions (listening/talking)			
Growing sensitivity to communication needs of others			
Increasing range of language registers			

Adapted from K. Norman, *Teaching Talking and Learning in the Key Stage One,* National Curriculum Council, York, Great Britain, 1990.

be examined across a very fluid set of developmental phases in which indications of more than one phase may be identifiable at any given instant (Weaver, 1988; Temple, Nathan, Burris, & Temple, 1988; Dobson, 1989). These phases include the following:

1. A reading-writing-like phase in which the learner simulates reading and writing activities
2. An early symboling phase in which the learner matches oral language with written language to approximate reading and writing
3. A developing alphabetic principle phase in which the learner exhibits growing understanding of the letter/sound relationships but relies heavily on semantic and syntactic cueing systems for getting meaning from reading and communicating in writing
4. A graphophonic refining phase in which the learner combines understanding of letter/sound relationships with semantic and syntactic cueing for reading and writing
5. A conventional phase in which the learner demonstrates increas-

ing control over the text print and context as central to getting meaning for reading, while the learner's writing becomes more booklike in language and form

Against this framework the teacher would ask the following questions to ascertain developing learning in reading:

1. Is the learner interested in books? Does he or she choose to look at or read books independently? Or, if he or she is not a reader, does the learner enjoy being read to and request stories to be read aloud?
2. Is the learner able to predict events and usage that anticipates print?
3. Does the learner relate the reading context to prior information before, during, and after reading to increase understanding?
4. Does the learner demand meaning by trying context and meaning strategies to aid the development of meaning?
5. Does the learner demonstrate ability to organize ideas heard or read into thought units to compose meaning?
6. Are the predictions that the learner uses semantically and syntactically acceptable with the context of the reading?
7. Does the learner correct a miscue that disrupts the meaning of the reading?
8. Do the semantically acceptable miscues translate the print into the learner's own language patterns?
9. Does the learner exhibit the use of reading to solve problems and satisfy and increase interests?
10. Is the reader able to vary the rate of reading to suit the purposes of reading?

Writing. Writing is an interactive, recursive process that involves thinking, feeling, reading, and reflecting to make a message clear. There are differences between reading and writing that should not be minimized. In reading, the reader has the physical patterns or signs to relate to while the writer starts with a blank page and perhaps vague feelings and ideas to produce text (Rosenblatt, 1989). Decisions required about the development of writing will be better understood by analyzing writing in two categories: the emergent writer and the developing writer.

Emergent writers learn to attend first to the whole of writing and later to the parts. They discover and manipulate various principles to make their writing look like writing (Clay, 1975). They discover the gross differences about writing that separate it from the other types of visual or written graphic displays and gradually develop finer and finer distinctions (Temple et al., 1988).

Educators need to observe if these principles are emerging in the writing of young children. Temple et al. (1988) organized and documented five principles about the features of writing that can be used in analyzing the writing development of young children (Figure 8.7).

FIGURE 8.7   Writing Principles

---

1. **A Recurring Principle**
   Does the learner's writing consist of repetitions of the same moves again and again? This can be noted in recurring scribbles or repeated marks resembling letters. Below is an example from a four-year-old ESL Pakistani child.

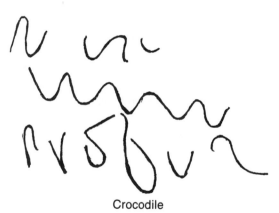
Crocodile

2. **A Generative Principle**
   Does the learner's writing consist of combining different combinations of a small set of symbols or letters to arrive at a variety of arrangements? For example, Jean at five years wrote:

   > I loves you.
   > Mommy loves you.
   > Daddy loves you. (Etc.)

3. **A Sign Principle**
   Does the learner's writing consist of relating the generic to the word, symbol, or sign? Meg, at two years, would identify every sign starting with M as being her name.

FIGURE 8.7 (Continued)

4. **A Flexibility Principle**

   Does the learner vary the writing forms to make other forms and use a variety of forms for the same letter? The orientation of the letter formation and organization give beginners trouble. Combinations of circles and sticks change the identity of a letter and word. The example below is from a five-year-old ESL Spanish-speaking child.

The lion is going to eat the boy

5. **A Directionality Principle**

   Does the learner demonstrate writing arrangement on a page to fit his or her culture? Young learners generally arrange the print in the space available. Their flexibility is extremely fluid. (Directional difficulty in writing may continue even after it is solved in reading.) The illustration below is from a five-year-old Caribbean child.

Adapted from C. Temple, R. Nathan, N. Burris, and F. Temple, *The Beginnings of writing* (2nd ed.), Allyn and Bacon, Boston, 1988.

Because writing is a developmental process, it evolves. Children appear to experiment with the ways in which writing represents ideas to test and develop their evolving knowledge. They use their knowledge of their speech sounds, the alphabet they have observed from their environments, and information about writing they receive from adults to reinvent the spelling system. They struggle to resolve the number of letters required for a word and represent syllables with single graphic letters. They experiment with a developing theory to discover the correspondence between writing and speech (Ferreiro, 1986). Ferreiro (1986; 1990) reported the work she and other researchers had done indicated children's development progresses through stages of understanding. These levels (see Figure 8.8) can be used to recognize the development of emergent writing. Emergent writers, however, may not exhibit clear distinctions between and among the stages.

In the analysis process the teacher should review the range of

FIGURE 8.8   Children Developing Understanding of the Writing System

---

Level 1.   The learner makes no distinctions between drawing and writing.

Level 2.   The learner makes clear distinctions between drawing and writing. Writing forms are arbitrary and are organized differently from drawing. Writing says what the writer intended whether there is any difference in the graphic representation.

Level 3.   The learner uses the culture's orthography in writing and arranging different strings of letters to have different interpretations. Learners think that there must be a minimum number of letters to represent a word and the same letter must not be used all the time.

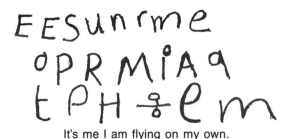

It's me I am flying on my own.

Level 4.   The learner indicates emergence of a syllabic principle: one symbol (graphic mark or letter) to one syllable. Learners write as many letters as there are syllables. Letter names may not be used, generally more consonants than vowels.

FIGURE 8.8 (Continued)

Level 5. The learner indicates the use of a combination of syllabic and alphabetic (graphic symbol to phoneme) representations.

The wolf was going to the pig's house.

Level 6. The Learner demonstrates the emergence of alphabetical principles.

I have been to a party we played games.

Adapted from E. Ferreiro, *Literacy Development: Psychogenesis,* paper given at the International Reading Association Eleventh World Congress, University of London, London, Great Britain, 1986, and published in *How Children Construct Literacy: Piagetian Perspectives* (pp. 12–25) Yetta M. Goodman (ed.), International Reading Association, Newark, DE, 1990.

---

writing the student has placed in the writing portfolio to determine the common writing characteristics of the student's work. Questions should be asked about the student's development in at least five categories concerned with writing development. The following categories list examples of questions for analyzing the growth of developing writers (Turbill, 1986; Cochrane, Cochrane, Cochrane, Scalena, & Buchanan, 1984; K. S. Goodman, Y. M. Goodman, & Hood, 1989):

1. Writing attitude
   a. Does the writer have a willing attitude to write?
   b. Is the writer willing to self-select topics?
   c. Does the writer search for and gather information for his or her writing?

2. Writing quality
   a. Does the writer's use of vocabulary indicate it is expanding?
   b. Does the writer demonstrate a growing use of a variety of sentence structures that creates interest?
   c. Do the samples indicate any experimentation with style?
   d. What indications are there of a developing ability to revise?
   e. Does the writer write clearly and concisely or does the work require rereading of parts in order to understand the message?
3. Writing devices
   a. Does the writer create interest for the reader in the opening of the piece?
   b. Does the writer create satisfying or dramatic endings?
4. Writing organization
   a. Does the piece have meaning?
   b. Does the piece have a sequenced development of ideas or are there parts that seem to be in the wrong order?
   c. Does the piece have a voice and awareness of audience?
5. Writing structures and mechanics
   a. Does the writer demonstrate a developing use of correct sentence structure?
   b. Does the writer demonstrate a growing understanding of paragraphing?
   c. Does the writer demonstrate an increasing control of the mechanics of writing?
   d. Is the writer's spelling becoming more conventional?

Developing an Individual Instructional Plan.   A process that teachers can find helpful involves developing an individual instructional plan for each student (Figure 8.9). A plan is developed after the teacher has made observations, interactions, and analyses of the student in a multitude of settings. It is used in draft form in parent/teacher conferences for instructional decision making. It may or may not be kept with the language/literacy portfolio.

In the parent/teacher conference, using the portfolio and/or other gathered data, the teacher shares with the primary caregivers specific learning strategies observed, accomplishments and strengths, and any learning needs. At this point the educator might suggest to the parents some specific long-range instruction goals and short-range objectives that the teacher believes would best assist student learning. These suggestions are presented as ideas for input, insight, and consideration. Primary caregivers must feel confident that they are being treated as partners and invited to assist in planning what is best for their child. For that reason, the teacher should be extremely cautious about writing specific information regarding goals, objectives, and instructions on the plan if, in doing so, parents perceive they have only token participation in the process. The focus of the conference must be an interchange of ideas resulting in an instructional plan for the student.

Finally, parents should have opportunities to provide specific considerations they wish remembered as the plan is implemented. The teacher should be alert and sensitive to parents and caregivers who may be nonliterate or who may have limited literacy ability. The teacher might offer to take dictation from the parent if the parent

FIGURE 8.9 Individual Instructional Plan

Student _____ School Year _____

Age _____ Grade _____ Languages Spoken _____

Community _____ Languages Written _____

Observed Learning Strategies:

Special Learning Needs:

Long-Range Instructional Goals:

Specific Short-Range Objectives:

Instructional Plan:

Parental Comment/Response:

_____
(Signature)

_____
(Teacher Signature)   (Date)

would prefer. Primary caregivers from some cultures may never have had a personal relationship with a school or teacher as an adult or parent. Consequently, they may be reticent to respond even through a translator in the beginning. Educators must realize that these caregivers are very concerned about their children and may be extremely frustrated with how their children are changing. This is particularly true for immigrant parents.

The individual instructional plan should be used in all future conferences to report on progress and to refine, adjust, or change goals. The plan, in addition, could be shared with the student before the conference for input and after the conference to assist the student in goal setting (if the student has not attended the conference). The plan must be seen by the teacher and the primary caregivers as a way to share responsibility for the child's social, emotional, physical, and academic development (Davies, 1991).

SUMMARY

Assessment and evaluation are an integral part of the program for students in a multicultural classroom. The philosophy and theory of the instructional program must be in concert with the assessment and evaluation program. If it is not, teachers will feel helpless, and their teaching will be totally governed by how they must assess and evaluate their students. This may paralyze them from making the changes in curriculum and instruction that they know are crucial for the success of their students. They may believe that unless their instruction fits the assessment and evaluation instruments, they and their students will be penalized. Consequently, change is held captive to the achievement test.

Effective assessment and evaluation components can be developed for multicultural classrooms that are learner referenced. Such components increase the importance of the teacher's role. When teachers put into practice learner reference assessment and evaluation, they become more knowledgeable about what students learn and how they learn than is ever possible through any battery of tests. Learner-referenced assessment and evaluation may, however, require educators to stretch beyond what they have done before. When educators become effective observers and hone their skills to analyze student learning patterns and behaviors, they will receive greater satisfaction from teaching. They will be able to see a closer relationship between student activities and learning.

Learner-referenced assessment and evaluation requires that teachers involve students and parents. Students need to be involved in their own assessment and evaluation. Through this process they will increase their self-evaluation. Parents need to be involved in their children's assessment and evaluation because they are so knowledgeable about how their children learn and how they respond. Parents are first line sources for collecting data about children and in providing educators valuable cultural information.

Finally, learner-referenced assessment and evaluation will enable teachers to develop assessment and evaluation tools that they will find more useful for decision making. It provides the opportunity to gather data that represents what the student does daily and to make frequent and regular comparisons of the data over a longer time span as the basis for decision making about children's growth and for planning instruction. Teachers should strive to develop and periodically update an individual learning plan for each student. Parents should be consulted and involved in the process from the beginning.

IMPLICATIONS FOR INSTRUCTION

1. Align the assessment and evaluation program with a holistic philosophy for teaching language and literacy.

2. Assess and evaluate real language and literacy, not fragmented aspects of language and literacy. Sample aspects of language and literacy as children are engaged in real language and literacy across the curriculum. Include samples of students reading real literature, writing for real purposes, and talking and listening from a multitude of settings where language is used for sharing, interacting, and solving problems.

3. Develop abilities to observe, interact, and make analyses about student language and literacy competencies. Create informal instruments to assist in keeping records about student growth. Invite and encourage students to become involved in the assessment process for their own self-learning, and involve primary caregivers as partners in data collection and decision making about children's learning.

4. Focus assessment and evaluation to become learner-centered. Evaluate learning from a point of view of student competence, not incompetence. Do not violate student values, beliefs, or cultural traditions or ignore student prior information and language orientation through the testing instruments used and the practices employed in assessing and evaluating learning.

5. Develop record-keeping forms and strategies for observation, integration, and analysis that consider each student as a unique individual and that are consonant with the student, his or her culture and language, and how he or she learns.

6. Examine and analyze data collected about the student at various junctures during the year. Develop and or use pertinent questions about the growth and development of the student in relation to the phase of learning.

7. Develop individual instructional plans that include primary caregivers and learners in the determination of long-range goals, short-range objectives, and instructional decision making.

Teacher Resource Kit

KIT # 1
A Model Multicultural Narrative Theme

Realistic fiction seems the appropriate genre to use for developing a model multicultural theme. This genre provides a large body of children's literature for selecting and developing multicultural themes.

The format for the theme selected was developed and explained in Chapter Six. The model theme, "People in Our Country, Cities, and Neighborhood: How They Are Alike and Different," will demonstrate the use of realistic fiction and the literature-circles strategy. This theme has a definite sociological focus that provides excellent opportunities for integrating expository or content area reading. An instructional web for Miska Miles' *Annie and the Old One,* illustrated by Peter Parnall (Little, 1972) is included. The web uses the format for teaching and learning taken from Goodman and Burke (1976): initiating, interacting, applying, and expanding/extending.

CURRICULUM FRAMEWORK

Theme: People in Our Country, Cities, and Neighborhoods: How They Are Alike and Different

Subtopics: Realistic fiction, values, beliefs, traditions, environment

Learning Intentions:
1. Realistic fiction describes life as it is currently.
2. People in families face problems and must search for solutions.
3. All people develop strong feelings of love and regard for their families and loved ones.
4. Death is a part of our life cycle. People wishing to be remembered and cherished after death prepare themselves and their loved ones to accept their deaths.
5. All people hold beliefs and have behaviors that they value.

6. Families have traditions that they pass from generation to generation.
7. Environment is a factor in determining how people live: homes, food, clothing, arts and crafts.
8. The United States can be divided into regions. Each region is often the home of particular populations and has a unique geography and climate.

Language and Literacy Functions: Expressing and sharing feelings, transmitting information

Multicultural Focus: People have universal needs and behaviors

Instructional Focus:
1. Develop an understanding that people have universal needs and behavior by comparing the characters in the fiction selected for the theme.
2. Increase independent decision making in literature circles through decisions regarding silent reading purposes, length of reading selection and activities for extending and enriching reading.
3. Encourage and extend sustained recreational reading time.
4. Identify values held by major characters in books being read.
5. Identify beliefs and traditions held by people that make them unique.
6. Encourage realistic writing.
7. Encourage interaction with reading through response journals.
8. Relate the study of the U.S. regional sections and populations to the characters in the books.

Instructional Strategies:

INTRODUCTORY EXPERIENCES
1. *Orientation.* Ask the children to make a list on paper of things they would tell about themselves and their families if they met a child their age from another area of the country.
   - Place the students in cooperative groups to share these and see if they can categorize them.
   - Have the children share their categories and develop a composite set of categories. Possible categories include physical, family, home language, housing, needs, interests, and problems. Have the students compare and discuss how they are alike and different. Graphs might be made for this purpose, for example:

Physical Family Language Home Needs Interests Problems

Min

Eric

Jose

Tanya

- Have the groups share their informational graphs and then elicit from the total group how the class is alike and different. List their contributions under the two terms.
2. *Focus the Study.* Tell the children that they will have the opportunity to read some books about children and families in their country, cities, and neighborhoods. Write the titles on the board.
3. *Themestorm.* Use the theme to develop ideas for the study with the children. List these on the board or perhaps develop a web. Develop a list of ideas that children think should be learned about the topic and have them brainstorm activities they would like to do during the study.

DEVELOPMENT OF THE THEME
1. *Introduce Books for Literature Circles.* Do a book talk on each book. Add to the web or list ideas that the children have after hearing the book talks. Suggested books for this study theme include the following:

Valerie Flournoy, *The Patchwork Quilt,* illustrated by Jerry Pinkney (Dial, 1985)
Doris Gates, *Blue Willow,* illustrated by Paul Lantz (Viking, 1948)
Deborah Gould, *Grandpa's Slide Show,* (Lothrop, 1987)
Miska Miles, *Annie and the Old One,* illustrated by Peter Parnall (Little, 1972)
Ian Wallace, *Chin Chiang and the Dragon's Dance* (McElderry Books, 1984)

2. *Self-Selecting Reading.* Have the students examine the books and select their first and second choices for reading. Set up the literature circles. If possible have the children develop their own reading schedules and take responsibility for selecting activities to accompany each book read.
3. *Reading of Books.* Have the students read the chosen books and participate in the activities for each book as long as there con-

tinues to be sufficient interest in each book, generally two to three rounds. Include suggestions from children in activities developed for each book. (Adapt the instructional webs for each book according to student interest and reading competencies.)

4. *Regional and Population Study of the United States.* The study provides an excellent opportunity to do a related study of various regions of the United States and populations represented in the literature circle books. Locate films, videos, and audiotapes to accompany the study.

5. *Recreational Reading.* Encourage reading books about this theme by setting out other books related to the theme at various spots in the classroom. Write a short blurb about each book and attach it to the book in some manner, or make a display of book jackets and respective blurbs and have the book nearby for selecting.

6. *Response Journals.* Encourage the children to use their response journals as they read each section of each book. Teacher responses should encourage children to interact with characters in the book:
   1. Would they do the same thing?
   2. What other options are there?
   3. What would have happened if the character had not done this?
   4. Would the students like the character for a friend? Why or why not?

(See the web for specific directions for introducing and developing *Annie and the Old One.*)

DEVELOPMENT OF GENERALIZATIONS

Have students who have read various books select groups that they will participate in during these next activities. These groups need not be the same groups in which they read or discussed the books. Children may wish to participate in a number of activities or all of them. The activities should facilitate the development of the generalizations about the theme. Involve the students in selecting and suggesting activities. Possible activities might include using murals, collages, and mandalas, or reading to the students; and using real-life stories, regional study summaries, and population studies.

1. *Murals.* Have the children develop a mural that portrays the life of the children in the books they read. Begin the activity by discussing how the children and families lived in the various books. Emphasize similarities and differences. Then discuss how these ideas might be portrayed in scenes. Have the children choose the book they would like to work on and to meet and make

their plans. The murals should be continuous. The following points could be developed in the murals:

- Environmental aspects that govern how we live
- Realistic aspects of the book
- Strong loving relationships between characters
- Behaviors of characters that demonstrate beliefs and values and reflect family traditions

When the murals are finished, they should be presented by each group and discussed with the class. Be sure that the names of the books, authors, and illustrators are given. These might be displayed in the school for all to enjoy.

2. *Collages.* Have the students develop collages from magazines, newspaper pictures, headlines, and short articles that portray values held by specific characters in a book. These should be developed on butcher paper. Begin by having students collect pictures and headlines, from magazines and newspapers, that represent beliefs and activities in their lives that they particularly value. Abstract values can be stressed by showing how to use a concrete item as a symbol for cooperation and fair play (Tiedt, Gibbs, Howard, Timpson & Williams, 1989). Individual collages can be shared and the abstract values discussed prior to beginning the collages for the people in each book read.

3. *Mandalas.* Have the children choose a book and work in cooperative groups to develop a mandala—a Tibetan artistic and symbolic circle that focuses a series of images in a circular pattern representing the harmony, wholeness, and continuity of life—that shares the traditions of the people in the book (Tiedt et al., 1989).

4. *Read to the Students.* The teacher should read aloud Paul Goble's *Beyond the Ridge* (Bradbury, 1989) if she or he wishes to expand the subtheme, death. The belief in afterlife as experienced by an elderly Indian woman from the Great Plains is one which students will find in traditional Native American literature (Norton, 1991). If the teacher wishes, instead, to focus on family relationships characteristic of the literature circle books for this theme, she or he might choose Virginia Hamilton's *The House of Dies Drear* (Macmillan, 1964). This book provides opportunity to discuss life styles and homes, and elicit from the class who is the teller (voice) of the story and discuss in what ways the teller demonstrates values and appreciation of his home. Children might respond to the book in writing by describing aspects of their home or life that they can write about with appreciation.

5. *Real-Life Stories.* Have the children compose stories based on some event that happened to them or a family member. These

should be a few incidents around a central event (they may involve how a family solved a problem they had). At the beginning of the writing workshop have the children briefly analyze the books read by discussing the central theme in each book and the specific events that told the theme. This can be graphically presented by making a web or doing a story map. For the web, write the theme in the center and then elicit the main events that explained or told the theme and write them around the center. Point out that all these events are plausible–they could have happened. Introduce the term realistic fiction if you have not done so.

6. *Regional Study Summaries.* Compare the study of the various regions of the United States by having students complete and share the following table in their study groups or with the total group:

Region	Geographical Features	Climate	Populations Located There
Atlantic Coast			
Pacific Coast			
Southwest			
Great Plains			
Rocky Mountains			

7. *Population Studies.* Have students select one ethnic or racial group or religious population in each region for study. Compare these in relation to the characters in the books read in the literature circles.

CULMINATION OF THE THEME

1. *Mural Sharing.* Have children put up the mural and choose a selection to read aloud from any book they have read that corresponds with the mural.

2. *Collage Sharing.* Have children display their collages and put a number on each collage. Provide time for children to view these. Each child should choose a character and determine the value held by that character. Record these by the appropriate number on a page. Discuss these when the children are finished. When there are conflicting decisions regarding the value, have each child provide his or her rationale to the class.

3. *Individual Writing.* Have the children prepare an illustrated book that includes their realistic writing. In addition, they might write about the values that they hold in their response journals.
4. *Comparing Needs and Behaviors.* Have children list all the major characters they read about through a group discussion. Have the students in small groups describe each character's behaviors; state if the characters had a problem or need. Share these with the class and then determine which characters behaved in similar manners and had similar needs.

ASSESSMENT
1. Do the students understand that realistic fiction describes life?
2. Do the students understand that families across cultures have feelings of love and regard for one another?
3. Do the students understand that all people have problems that must be solved?
4. Do the students understand and appreciate that all people have beliefs and behaviors that they value?
5. Do the students understand that the beliefs and behaviors of people are their traditions that are passed from one generation to the next?
6. Do the students understand that how people live is influenced by their environments?

Now examine the instructional web (Figure TRK 1.1) focusing on Miska Miles' *Annie and the Old One* (Little, 1972). The web demonstrates how one book in a literature-circle format might be developed for the theme. The book emphasizes three of the subthemes of the study: strong family relationships, beliefs and traditions, and environmental influences on life-style. As the book is read allow children to make decisions determining how much to read at a time.

Although this book provides a strong positive model of the Navajo people and how they strive to live in harmony with the earth and human life cycles of birth and death, it has some textual and illustration flaws that provide opportunities for students to research geographical materials and Navajo life-styles to correct misconceptions.

Students should be particularly focused to question if it is realistic to believe that Annie as a Navajo child would have responded as she did to the news from Grandmother. They should search for authentic pictures of Navajo people and where they live to verify how they actually look and what buildings are found at the sites of Navajo hogans. What do the hogans look like inside? What clothing would

FIGURE TRK 1.1   Instructional Web: People in Our Country

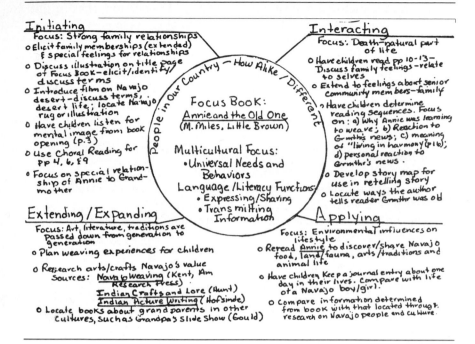

Navajo children and adults wear in daily life? What are typical Navajo rug and pottery designs? How do family members talk to each other and particularly how would they address a grandmother (Slapin & Feale, 1988)?

The model presented here provides moderate teacher direction. A group may need less or more direction.

KIT # 2
The Development and Presentation
of a Sample Content Topic

Many different elementary social studies series currently in use in the United States give limited attention to American culturally diverse populations. It is obvious that the focus of the programs is from a European American perspective. The versions presented in the texts often exclude the essential essence of the conflicts experienced by non-European Americans. These groups are not shown as having contributed to the development of the culture and society of the United States.

This sample topic is intended to provide the teacher with a model for use in conjunction with social studies materials telling only one version of history from one viewpoint.

CURRICULUM FRAMEWORK

Topic: Deeds of Infamy: Racism and Bigotry in the United States

Subtopics: Japanese Americans, African Americans, Hispanic Americans, Native Americans

Learning Intentions:
1. Racial and ethnic groups in the United States may have diverse life-styles.
2. Diversity is a valuable enriching factor in society.
3. Historical experiences have had both negative and positive influences on cultural patterns of ethnic and racial groups.
4. U.S. society and culture are a synthesis of the interaction of diverse cultures and racial, ethnic, and religious groups.
5. The history of the United States demonstrates a conflict between the ideals and values of freedom and equality.
6. One significant ideal in the United States is to judge persons as individuals, not on their ethnic or racial community membership.
7. Every citizen needs to recognize stereotypical, distorted, and biased information, as well as to identify personal values, to be able to process information, base interpretations, and make decisions relative to facts and knowledge.
8. A knowledge of racial and ethnic communities includes culture, historical experiences, contributions, and problems encountered in U.S. society.

Language and Literacy Functions: Expressing and sharing feelings and transmitting information

Multicultural Focus: Respecting and appreciating diversity and identifying and describing groups in a population

Instructional Focus:
1. Develop an in-depth understanding in a cooperative group of one specific racial or ethnic community that includes culture, historical experiences, contributions, and life-styles.

2. Carry out an investigative study of one racial or ethnic community involving reading, media, interviewing, and writing.
3. Read an expository text using the KWL strategy with teacher direction and assistance.
4. Summarize understandings and ideas about racial and ethnic communities gained through reading and discussion.
5. Interview available racial or ethnic community people and other community people for viewpoints.
6. Write letters to historical and art museums, public and private collections (papers), and libraries for data regarding a specific racial or ethnic community.
7. Read related historical fiction and autobiographies using a KWL Strategy Sheet independently.
8. Respond to related historical fiction and autobiographies through response journals, simulated diaries, or personal letters.
9. Compare and contrast racial or ethnic communities as to traditions, beliefs, and life-styles, significant historical experiences in the United States, contributions to American culture, and problems encountered in society.
10. Practice using the learning and thinking skills in cooperative study groups.
11. Develop social-action plans for the class.

LEARNING EXPERIENCES: DEEDS OF INFAMY

INTRODUCTORY EXPERIENCES
1. *Orientation.* Since students have been introduced to the racial or ethnic groups prior to this study through the social studies text, they will not need initial presentation. However, students should be aided in recalling and organizing prior information in the following manner:
   - Brainstorm with the students by taking five large sheets of chart paper and turn them horizontally. Write the name of one racial or ethnic community on each paper. Divide the class into five groups and instruct each group to freely associate what they know about one group. Have one person write these associations on the chart paper to develop a web of ideas surrounding the name. Tape these across the board. After each group has shared, elicit other ideas from the other students about what they know about each racial or ethnic community. If there are disagreements, put red question marks over the term or subtopic.

■ Write the term *infamy* on the board, and ask if anyone knows the word and what it means. (It is assumed that the term will be introduced in the classroom text and used in conjunction with the bombing of Pearl Harbor at the beginning of World War II.) Since the term may not be familiar, ask if any part of the word is familiar. Use the Piercey Talk Through Method (Piercey, 1976) to develop an association for the term by writing the following sentence on the board:

 − Adolf Hitler is *infamous* for the deeds he committed during World War II, while Winston Churchill is *famous.*
 − Ask the children to identify people they are familiar with who are infamous and famous. Make a list under each term from names that the students give you. Ask the students if things that people do, deeds, can be infamous and if they can think of some deeds. List any deeds that the students think would be classified as infamous and relate these as being infamies. Write "Deeds of Infamy" above the examples. This would be a good time for a few children to check dictionaries in the room to locate the term and read its definitions.

   Tell the students that they will be studying about deeds of infamy that have happened in the United States. Ask if they can think of any deeds they would think would be infamous. Discuss each mentioned and why they considered it infamous.

2. *Focus the Study.* Focus attention on the specific topic for the study by having students determine what they already know. Have the students examine the racial or ethnic webs to see if there are any deeds of infamy listed on the charts. If so, discuss what is known about them and why the students have classified them as infamous. Tell the students that the title of the topic they will be studying is "Deeds of Infamy: Racism and Bigotry in the United States." Add any ideas to the webs that the students might have that would be deeds of infamy as the meaning of the title is discussed. (It is assumed that racism and bigotry are known terms.)

   Undoubtedly this will lead students to mention Native American massacres of European American settlers, if it is not already on the web. Most students are familiar with massacres from fictionalized accounts on television or in films. They may perceive the Native Americans of the past as savages, as this is the term that is frequently used in so many of the older films dealing with conflicts between Native Americans and European Americans. This will provide an opportunity to question these perceptions and try to get them to begin questioning the sources of their information and beliefs.

Most elementary social studies series will briefly mention the Japanese internment and civil rights efforts led by Dr. Martin Luther King, Jr. and other African American leaders. Depending on the location and setting of the school, students may not be as familiar with Jewish Americans, and they may not understand why this ethnic group will be included in the study. If that is the case, share with the children the situation of Supreme Court Justice Brandeis, considered by many to be one of the greatest jurists in U.S. history. When Judge Brandeis was nominated by President Woodrow Wilson, there was a powerful movement nationally and in congress to keep him from being confirmed because he was Jewish (Meltzer, 1976).

The following examples, which can be quickly read or shared with the students, show deeds reflecting racism and bigotry in the United States:

- African Americans: Robert P. Ingals, *Hoods: The Story of the Ku Klux Klan* (Putnam, 1979)
- Hispanic Americans: Milton Meltzer, *Hispanic Americans* (Crowell, 1982)
- Japanese Americans: Daniel S. Davis, *Behind Barbed Wire: The Imprisonment of Japanese Americans During World War II* (Dutton, 1982)
- Jewish Americans: Milton Meltzer, *The Jewish American: A History in Their Own Words, 1650–1950* (Crowell, 1982)
- Native Americans: Peter Nabokov (ed.), *Native American Testimony: An Anthology of Indian and White Relations, First Encounter to Dispossession* (Crowell, 1978)

This aspect of the focus activities might culminate with the teacher asking if these racial or ethnic communities are still subjected to racism and bigotry. Allow time for discussing this.

Ask the students if they can name other racial and ethnic communities that live in the United States. Discuss where they live, if they are more regionally located. Direct the focus of attention to discussing why this country is made up of so many different racial and ethnic groups. Why is it important that all people be treated with equality, especially in the United States? Lead students into discussing the aspects of their lives and life-styles that can be attributed to various racial or ethnic cultural groups. This will include food, words, daily practices, yearly observation and celebrations, art, music, literature, modern conveniences, and so on. The purpose of the discussion is to stimulate interest and motivation for studying this aspect. Consequently, the teacher should not anticipate that the discussion will be extremely fruitful in eliciting information—it may be very superficial. The students probably will know little, for example, about Native Americans. Discussing the traditional Thanksgiving meal can indicate to students the extensive contribution from the first Americans to our diet.

Explain to the students that they will be choosing one racial or ethnic community to investigate. They are to make first and second choices of racial or ethnic groups to study. Give each student a note card and instructions for writing his or her name in the left-hand corner and then writing the numeral "1" or "2" after each selected racial or ethnic group. Allow time for students to write any rationale that they think should influence the teacher's decision.

3. *Setting Purposes.* Begin the purpose-setting session when it is perceived that the students have adequate background from the focus aspect for raising questions to guide the study. All the students should be involved in generating questions so as to give the students ownership for the entire study, not just the area they have elected to study. Aid students in generating broader questions by proceeding in the following manner:

- Place blank chart paper under or next to the web of each racial or ethnic community and tell the class that they are to develop some questions that can be used during their study of the racial or ethnic groups. Write student questions on the charts; try to get five or six important questions for each racial or ethnic community. The students may have to be asked questions about specific topic areas to elicit these. For example, do the students think they should find out if any important events influenced how the Native Americans felt about the European settlers?

- When the class has generated five or six questions on each racial or ethnic community, tell them to read all the questions over to themselves. Allow them time to consider each question. Ask the students to identify questions that are similar for each racial or ethnic community. Identify questions that could be adapted to other racial or ethnic groups. Lead the students to develop a general list of questions to guide the study of all racial or ethnic communities and specific questions that should guide the study of a specific community. Determine with the students how these will be used by each study group and if they want them on charts, typed and distributed, or both.

DEVELOPMENT OF THE TOPIC

1. *Investigative Writing.* Begin the topic by organizing the students for doing their investigative study. This will provide time and opportunity for the teacher to work with students in doing semi-independent reading in the text assigned for each racial or ethnic group. Since the topic has already been introduced and the sub-topics set out, the teacher can move directly to the next step: planning.

   Begin planning the investigative study with the class as a whole because the major questions and specific questions for each racial or ethnic community have already been developed. Depending on the amount of investigative research the students have been involved in prior to this study, introduce, review, and discuss references and resources. This may require a special session in the school library or a trip to the public library.

   In preparation for the small-group meeting, develop a sheet on which students list investigative questions, resources to be used, and responsibilities for the initial research questions. Include a place for students to list questions or problems. Help the students plan how groups are to be organized for cooperative learning. Provide the following instructions to members of the cooperative group:

   a. Review the questions that will guide the study of the racial or ethnic group and add others to be explored (this can be done throughout the study).

   b. Brainstorm resources the group could use in investigating this area, besides the basic text and required reading of an autobiography or biography or piece of historical fiction.

   c. Plan to interview available people in the community who are members of or knowledgeable about this racial or ethnic community.

   d. Write to area, regional, state, or national libraries and museums in search of publications and information.

   e. Determine how the task is to be divided to answer the questions.

   The planning sheet should be handed in at the end of their meeting. Circulate among the groups of students as the planning goes on to respond to questions and to make sure the groups are progressing.

   Direct the students to keep note cards on the research they are doing. Assist them as is needed in taking good notes. Make sure that the students have ample time to share in their cooperative groups as their work progresses. Keep in touch with the groups through conferences to assess progress and any problems. Require the group to keep their planning sheets current. Assist students with common problems noted from the planning sheet and/or through small-group conferences.

Writing business letters will not be discussed here. They are usually found in most language arts texts. Models of letters and adequate time for practice should be provided, along with appropriate discussion. The school or local librarian can help students locate sources for information where the letters should be addressed.

2. *Interviewing Members or Nonmembers of a Racial or Ethnic Community.* Interviewing will generally require some research on the part of the teacher to help locate people willing to be interviewed by the children. Whether this will happen in school or the children will do the interviewing after school with the assistance of a parent or aide, will depend on the school and community context. This part of the research can be a significant experience for the students, particularly if the teacher is able to locate racial or ethnic community members to interview. They can be excellent resources for explaining the life-styles of their communities and the range of differences found within a community.

To make this a successful experience the teacher will need to talk to each person being interviewed beforehand. If there are limited people available, try to locate at least one person to be interviewed by each racial or ethnic study group. When a racial or ethnic person is not available, try to find some person in the community who has had some significant positive experience with the racial or ethnic group. For example, older citizens, grandparents, or great-grandparents or residents of retirement homes can be sources who know about the Japanese internment. A veteran's group might be contacted to locate Japanese American veterans from World War II in their local groups or veterans who had experiences in World War II with these regiments. Requesting suggestions from parents for people who are knowledgeable about a topic is a fruitful way of locating people. In addition, an announcement might be made at a parent/teacher association meeting.

When children are interviewing nonmembers of a racial or ethnic community there is always the risk that children might experience racial or prejudicial comments, no matter how carefully the teacher might screen the adults to be interviewed. Students should be prepared and advised in ways to respond if this should happen. When this does occur, use the opportunity to make students further aware of the degree of racism and bigotry that still exists in society. Take care so as to not damage the reputation of the willing interviewee. Take the opportunity to discuss why an attitude might still be found in society. When the interviews are conducted in school, the teacher has more of an opportunity to roam among groups and interject in the interview, or diplomatically terminate one if necessary.

The class should develop general guidelines for questions to be asked in the interview, and each racial or ethnic study group should refine, modify, and augment the questions to fit their particular study areas. When possible, arrange to have students use a tape recorder. This will allow them to record the answers from the interview tape and be more accurate. If at all possible, arrange to have the students take photographs of the people interviewed. Often, resource people will share arts and crafts, costumes, or other realia that will be beneficial for the class to see.

Be sure that students have music, art, and drama experiences that are appropriate to each racial or ethnic community. This aspect will not be covered in this topic in the interest of space, but it is a vital aspect in the study of any people, their traditions, beliefs, and expressions. Films, videos, and recordings should be located to support this aspect of the study.

Students need to have at least one long session after the interview to listen to the interview and determine which points made by the person fit the questions they are investigating. These should be written as notes on cards, giving the person as reference with perhaps a notation of their qualifications as a resource person. Students will have to determine information they have heard that will answer additional points as well.

3. *Semi-Independent Reading.* Assign students to their selected groups. Prepare for each group a KWL Strategy Sheet (Ogle, 1989). Have each group fill in the sections "What we know," "What we want to find out," and "Categories of information we expect to use" before meeting with the teacher. Meet with each group separately to cover the following:

Introduce the materials they will be using.

- African Americans: Sheyann Web, Rachel W. Nelson, and Frank Sikora, *Selma, Lord, Selma: Girlhood Memories of the Civil-Rights Days* (Morrow, 1980)
- Hispanic Americans: Milton Meltzer, *Hispanic Americans** (Crowell, 1982)
- Japanese Americans: Daniel S. Davis, *Behind Barbed Wire:*

The Imprisonment of Japanese Americans During World War II (Dutton, 1982)

- Jewish Americans: Milton Meltzer, *The Jewish American: A History in Their Own Words 1650*–1950* (Crowell, 1982)
- Native Americans: Dee Brown, *Wounded Knee: An Indian History of the American West** (Holt, Rinehart & Winston, 1974)

Discuss student responses on the KWL Strategy Sheet and provide more time for them to add to their responses with the teacher's guidance. Particularly focus on the categories.

Determine with the students a tentative schedule for reading and studying the text. Meet at these deadlines, discuss the reading, and share ideas related to answering questions on the KWL sheet. Have students summarize each assigned reading part and bring to class. Open each discussion by asking students to share their summaries. Follow up the discussion by having students dictate the major points learned from the text, and suggest they add any of these points they did not include in their summaries.

4. *Independent Reading.* Select books available in the school library or public library that would be suitable reading for each particular topic. These should include autobiographies, biographies, and historical fiction. The number of available sources will dictate whether the pieces are to be read individually or if two to three students will read the same text. Examples of these for the Japanese American racial or ethnic community include:

Sheila Garrigue, *The Eternal Spring of Mr. Ito* (Bradbury, 1985)
Joy Kogawa, *Naomi's Road* (Oxford, 1986)
Yoshiko Uchida, *Journey to Topaz: A Story of the Japanese-American Evacuation* (Creative Arts Book, 1985)
Yoshiko Uchida, *Journey Home* (Atheneum 1978)

Students might be interested, as well, in learning about Dorothea Lange who captured the internment in photographs. Milton Meltzer's *Dorothea Lange: Life Through the Camera* (Viking Kestrel, 1985) would be interesting to young camera buffs.

5. *Simulated Journals, Diaries, or Letters.* As a way for students to interact and respond to their independent reading, have them do some role-playing and keep journals and diaries or write letters

---

*You may wish to have children select sections of each of the longer texts indicated by an asterisk (*), to read to make them more comparable to the size and amount of illustrations used in other texts. These books allow students to read common sections and divide various parts for reading and pooling.

as a character in one of the books being read. This requires students to respond to the information about the events and times in writing. It can also create a need for doing more research on the period or event. Ideas for simulations include the following:

- A journal or diary, using the reading as the source of information, is kept as if students are the main characters in the book or a friend of the main character. For example, Jamie and Ernie (*The Eternal Spring of Mr. Ito*) could write letters to Mr. Ito's son, George, and thank him for saving their lives. The letters would keep him abreast of what was happening in the war and in Vancouver.

- A series of letters may be written to someone who lived at the same time and who might be known by the main character or characters in the book. The student might write both the letter and the response, or another student in the class in the same group could be the receiver and respond by asking appropriate questions and telling what is happening in his or her life at the same time. For example, Yuki (*Journey to Topaz* and *Journey Home*) could write letters to her friends in Berkeley, such as Mrs. Jamieson, or to her brother who is in the famous 442 Regiment. Sara and Maggie (*The Eternal Spring of Mr. Ito*) could write letters to their mothers in England to tell what is happening in their lives in Vancouver and to tell about Mr. Ito, or they could write to their fathers who are in the armed services.

DEVELOPMENT OF GENERALIZATIONS

In this study the strategies for developing generalizations will be the same for each of the racial or ethnic groups. Students need experiences in sharing, discussing, and determining significant information before they can develop generalizations. These experiences are prerequisite activities for developing generalizations about the topic. The following discussion demonstrates how these activities might proceed with the Japanese American study group and how generalizations could then be developed.

1. *Relating Independent Reading to Content Text.* To aid students in relating their independent reading to *Behind Barbed Wire,* write or type out multiple copies of the following directions on slips of paper or cards, and have the students meet in their groups for discussion. Have each student blind-select one slip at a time and locate or determine the answer. Responses should be shared in the group. Encourage other group members to ask questions and,

if they disagree, give a rationale for a differing point of view. Students should share ideas and respond to the following discussion points:

■ Ask students to find an example in the independent reading book that agrees with a historical point or fact in *Behind Barbed Wire.*

■ Students may take a historical point or fact from *Behind Barbed Wire* and find a passage(s) in the independent reading that would personalize it.

■ Ask students to find an idea, happening, or event from the independent reading that cannot be verified in *Behind Barbed Wire.* Do the students think it is or is not based on possible events, happenings, or the feelings of the supervisors of the Japanese internment camps?

■ Students may state any idea, happening, or event in the independent reading that the students would not have understood without having read *Behind Barbed Wire.*

■ Ask students to state any idea, happening, or event the students read in their books that improved their understanding of what was read in *Behind Barbed Wire.*

2. *Sharing Independent Reading.* Assist students through one of the following activities to share their independent reading on the content topic:

■ Ask students to bring some news clippings to class to demonstrate how information about people is reported in newspapers or news magazines. Analyze the elements of a simple news article (using the five W's) along with beginning and ending paragraphs. Have the students write a news article about a character of interest in the book. These should be done using the writing process. They might be published by the students in a book about the topic.

■ Students may develop a simulated radio newscast. Elicit questions that characters from the book might be asked. Have students take turns as the reporter or interviewer. Each student would decide who he or she is and when the interview would take place—while the Japanese are interned or at the end of internment. One suggested idea is for students to pretend they are grown up and are explaining long after the internment what happened to them and how they felt. If they decide to be a non-Japanese character, they could tell why they agreed or did not agree with the internment.

■ Have students select and prepare one section from the book that was particularly meaningful to them to read aloud. Follow the reading with an explanation of why the reader selected it and have listeners discuss the types of impressions it made on them.

3. *Organizing and Preparing the Investigative Study Report.* Have students in groups share information they are locating from the investigative study as the topic progresses. The teacher should take part as frequently as possible to monitor progress and provide assistance. Sharing provides an opportunity for students to assist one another. Since the research should have been divided among them, they undoubtedly will be finding information that can be helpful to others in the group. Provide ample time for the group to work together as a whole. A short meeting at the beginning and end of each working session allows the teacher to keep on top of progress and to prepare how he or she can facilitate students in solving problems.

Initial directions for organizing the research and notes can be done with the total class before working with individuals and/ or groups. Demonstrate the process starting with a group of note cards and working until a summary statement is developed. The teacher must carefully talk through his or her thinking as the process is being carried out. Use either an overhead projector or chalkboard, or place the examples on charts when demonstrating the process for students. Making the process sequential and visible is the solution. This can be done in the following way:

A. Students having more than one question should list each question on a slip of paper and sort their note cards to fit under each question.

B. Next, students should sort through the cards identified for each question and find specific categories they have located from the research. Categories or specific ideas about the item should be organized into separate piles. Cards with similar ideas should be kept together. On top of each pile of cards should be placed a slip of paper or another card stating the idea that the cards are about.

C. Lead the students to see that the cards represent one of the following:

   a. The piles of cards represent questions and general answers. Read through each pile and decide brief points that will be answers for the question and important ideas to support each point.

   b. The piles of cards represent the elements of an outline. Remind students how to move from main topic to subtopic. Each pile of cards represents details about the subtopic.

D. Have the students write a summary using this information. This may be either one paragraph for the group of cards or a paragraph for each of the piles or subtopics. Traditionally, an introductory sentence begins the paragraph telling the idea the paragraph is about. If, for example, the students have more than one question and the answers are lengthy, a paragraph on each question is appropriate. If, on the other hand, each student has only one question, and the answer is not lengthy, they may write a small paragraph on each subtopic. If the students have worked in pairs on more than one question, divide the questions. If they have researched one question, they will do the activity together. Paired writing for beginning investigative writing is very successful.

E. Give each student rubber bands to put around each pile of cards. Have them put the question and all the piles together. Put a large rubber band around all until the teacher can meet with the students in a brief conference.

F. If students do not have sufficient data for all of their questions, they will need to search back through their sources for additional information or find new sources to respond to the purposes and questions they set out at the beginning of the study. For example, the topic "life-styles" can certainly be elusive. Be sure that students check with others in the group for information that is needed.

G. Check the questions, cards, and organization when meeting with each student or pair of students. Provide any help necessary for reorganizing the information and rewriting the summary. Particularly, pay attention to the content to make sure that students have interpreted the information correctly. Because the teacher has had students put sources of information on the back of each card, he or she may require the student to get the original source to verify information. The teacher may wish to review work before conferencing if class time is a problem.

4. *Preparing Students for Sharing Information.* With the whole class, look back and note what questions were to be answered by each racial or ethnic group. Have a large chart prepared that presents this information in table form: racial or ethnic groups down the left side of the table and major topics across the top. Give each cooperative group a duplicated form of the table. Have each group record the major points they will use in sharing and comparing their topic. Each group will provide the terms and phrases to be recorded but will expand on the major points under

each subtopic during the sharing using their note cards or outlines. If these are recorded on the chart before the sharing begins,
the groups will have more time to share what they learned. The
class will probably want to take notes on a student copy. (This
would be a good document for a book or study folder if the class is
making one.)

5. *Assisting Students to State Generalizations.* Have the class review
the subtopics. Discuss the information for each racial or ethnic
group as a whole, then discuss each subtopic across all racial or
ethnic groups. At this point ask the students to brainstorm what
the information is telling them about each topic. Elicit statements that will be written on the board or an overhead and get
the students to revise, modify, and restate the idea. For each of
the subtopics develop at least one statement. Record each on a
chart and keep it in the classroom for later use.

Developing appropriate generalizations may require the
teacher to do some very thoughtful probing. For example, the
students should note how the racial or ethnic communities have
survived in the United States, how they have changed over time,
the degree to which their languages continue, and how they
express their traditions and beliefs within a pluralistic society
despite the prejudice and bigotry they have experienced. These
determinations must serve as the basis for social-action measures
in the next part of the study.

SUMMARY AND CULMINATION
OF THE STUDY TOPIC

1. *Sharing Learning Experiences.* Students probably would like to
develop something particular for sharing that would truly provide an understanding of traditions, beliefs, and life-styles of the
racial or ethnic group. Examples might include a dramatic piece
representing or explaining something of significance to the racial
or ethnic community or musical selections or art from the racial
or ethnic group that demonstrate the beliefs and values of the
community. When members of each study group share something
of their own choice, the sharing tends to be varied and more
interesting. Much thinking will have gone into the selection.

2. *Time lines.* One interesting activity to carry on with the class
would be for each group to develop a time line of significant
events for their racial or ethnic community in the United States.
This would allow students to compare the histories of the peoples
who inhabit the North American continent, examine significant

events in the history of each community in relation to European American recorded history, and speculate on the history of the Native Americans prior to the arrival of the Europeans.

To make time lines, use rolled paper cut horizontally into 12–15-inch widths and tape them end to end to a desired length. Students should be given directions for the scale of inches to years. Significant historical occurrences should be located and placed along the continuum by each racial or ethnic group. For example, place along the time line Columbus's sighting of the North American continent; various colonizations by the Spanish, French, and English; the Revolutionary War, the Civil War, World War I, and World War II. Then each study group should place significant events in the history of their racial or ethnic community along their time line. An excellent teacher reference for these events is James A. Banks's *Teaching Strategies for Ethnic Studies,* fourth edition (Allyn and Bacon, 1987). The various time lines should be placed next to one another for comparison. Then each group should share their time lines and discuss the significant events they have placed along the continuum.

3. *Sharing Contributions From the Racial or Ethnic Communities.* Tell the children about a custom that some Native Americans used to build tribal and personal strength and camaraderie. Native Americans kept objects in a tribal bundle assembled according to the directions of the spirit power. These objects represented the origins of the myths of the tribe and were passed from one generation to another. Each member kept a personal bundle containing objects associated with important events in his or her life, such as a first hunt, an initiation rite, or a significant dream. Owners would tell each object's story around a campfire, and other members of the tribe would add their own thoughts (Toole, 1990).

Make a medicine bag for the students or have the Native American study group make a bag for the class. It might be beaded and/or simulated to resemble an authentic bag. Ask children to bring in special items that have significance to them that they would like to place in the bag and share. These items might be objects representing significant occasions in their lives. (Food can be shared and represented in the bag with some remembrance.) Turn out the lights on the day of this sharing ceremony, and have the class gather in a circle with the bag in the center. Have each child share his or her item and its history as it is placed in the bag. Make sure that class members have the opportunity to also respond to items placed by each person. (Of course, many items will be returned home but may be symbolized in the bag for remembrance.)

Next direct the racial and ethnic groups to meet and determine approximately three items or ideas about the racial or ethnic community they have been studying that they would like to go into the bag. These should have significance to the community. Brainstorm with the total group to get them thinking about significant contributions. Examples include the Native American community respect for the environment and the traditional Thanksgiving dinner items. Direct the study group to make some symbol of the contribution with its rationale for being selected for the bag. Plan a special day when this is to be done. If the children are not sharing foods, the teacher can add this dimension by having different items represent various racial or ethnic communities. The foods can be eaten in the circle as the sharing ceremony goes on. Parents, grandparents, and racial and ethnic community members can be of assistance in helping with this event.

Have students complete the event by writing why life in a pluralistic society is richer due to the make-up of the diverse communities represented in the society. Duplicate these writings, and put them in a study folder or on a chart.

4. *Social-Action Generation.* Have the students brainstorm what they can personally do to overcome prejudice and bigotry in U.S. society. List these on the board. Have each student write a social-action plan that he or she will personally carry out. Provide time for research or work on these in the class. Next, elicit what the class might carry on as a particular class activity to improve society. These might be focused to the particular community in which the children live. Examples include the following:
   - Letters to legislators about important social-action issues
   - Pen pals with students in another community to develop a relationship
   - Letters to local elected officials to change some aspect or practices
   - Posters in the school and local stores that remind and encourage change of behavior or support for some local issue that would enhance better relationships between ethnic, racial, and religious groups.

GENERAL TEACHING SUGGESTIONS
1. Sources for materials about racial and ethnic communities for the study might be located in Dianne L. Monson's *Adventuring With*

Books: A Booklist for Pre-K-Grade (NCTE, 1985). It is helpful for selecting current books in social studies, sciences, fine arts, historical and realistic fiction, and biography.

2. The multicultural book list prepared by Carol Sibley for Chapter Eight would also be of tremendous use for selecting books for this study topic. It would be well to have investigative writing, independent reading, and journal writing as aspects of the language and literacy curriculum. This provides an opportunity to fully integrate language and literacy in the study of this study topic, Deeds of Infamy.

3. Media should be included in the study of this study topic. The social studies teacher's manual should be a source for locating materials. Otherwise, the teacher should seek the aid of the school librarian in locating appropriate materials. Published books, record sets, or a series from Time/Life often is available in school libraries, as are complete sets of *National Geographic*. These materials, along with picture collections and taped music representing cultural and ethnic communities, can be sources for student research and learning. (The teacher may need to demonstrate how the class can analyze pictures for information for the study. The more information students have about a culture and a period before the study, the more able they are to make deductions from graphic materials.)

4. Research each racial or ethnic group studied to expose the students to authentic art and music experiences that will provide another dimension to the character of the people under study. Without this aspect of the culture, a significant gap is left in understanding and appreciating the racial or ethnic community. These activities can be done by the study group and shared and enjoyed by the entire class, or the total class might be involved in each art and music experience.

5. Have students begin and keep current a planning and progress guide. This can be kept in a folder and students should jot notes daily, leaving notes about questions or problems. The folder should allow the teacher to jot notes regarding conferences with the group, comments the students made that indicated growth, concerns the teacher has and wants to work on with the group, and notes the teacher makes to remind himself or herself about help needed for the group.

ASSESSING THE TOPIC LEARNING

Student Evaluation. Students should be involved in assessing and evaluating their learning as it aids in their developing self-assessment strategies. Involve students by first focusing on the learning of content information. Since the students have questions or purposes for learning already established, those questions become sources for their use in developing true/false questions, multiple choice questions, and fill-in-the-blank and short-answer questions. These provide the teacher with references for teaching students how to interpret and respond to each type of assessment technique.

College Bowl. Have each racial or ethnic study group write questions on note cards with the answers and rationale on the other sides. This provides a useful study model. These cards can be left in a central location for students to individually study or work on in pairs or small groups. The teacher will need to review each set with each study group before it is used by the class. After the cards have been available, a modified college bowl can be set up and played in the class. It would probably be best to play this in teams mixed from the original racial or ethnic study groups.

Cloze Procedures. The cloze procedure can be modified to provide an excellent check of knowledge about each racial or ethnic group. It can be done at the culmination of the total topic, or it might be done as each group finishes its report to the class. The students can give the class a summary they have developed with significant terms and vocabulary missing. (The teacher can decide if the vocabulary should be provided or not.) In addition, the students should determine what synonyms should be accepted for each blank. Further, they should be involved in the correcting process and explain why they are or are not accepting a specific word.

Observation. Important aspects in assessing learning are the teacher's observations throughout the study of the topic. Content learning is always more easily determined. Consequently, focus observations on aspects not as easy to assess. For example, What indications have the students given that relate to a growing respect and appreciation of the diversity in racial and ethnic communities? What indications have the students given about understanding the American ideal of freedom and equality? What indications have students given about understanding and appreciating the various life-styles of racial and ethnic communities? Information about these questions can be sought from comments you have heard students expressing in their informal cooperative group discussions, points they have made in sharing their reading about racial and ethnic communities, and in the simulated journals, logs, and letters they wrote as responses to their independent reading.

The teacher will also want to observe and note the development of the learning competencies by observing student participation in reading and studying information in the group text, researching group activities, sharing with the group located information, and making presentations to the class. For example, Are students able to summa-rize information collected from one source? Various sources? Are students able to compare and contrast information and develop generalizations? Are students able to work as a team in a cooperative group? Have students developed independent reading and study skills?

Self Evaluation. Students must have the opportunity to evaluate their learning from various aspects including strategies used for learning, achievement of the purposes of the study, and individual learning.

The first two aspects can be done through open discussions either in large or small groups. Small-group information then would be shared with the class, thus not identifying particular individuals but group perspectives. Or students could be provided with statements that they respond to by either marking a face that ranges from smiling to frowning or indicating degrees of change, learning, or satisfaction on a likert scale of 1–5, as shown below:

Strategies used in learning
My group worked cooperatively   1   2   3   4   5
         Very Well   Very Poorly
In my group everyone shared   1   2   3   4   5

Success in learning
I feel that I learned   1   2   3   4   5
       Great Amount   Nothing

As a result of this study, I
would treat racial and ethnic   1   2   3   4   5
communities   Very Respectfully   Without Respect

Students could evaluate their own progress in a conference with the teacher. Conferencing can be informal. Youngsters like the opportunity to have a personal talk. Have the student respond to a short list of statements developed around a particular instructional focus prior to the conference. For example:

I find reading social
studies   1   2   3   4   5
     Very Easy   Very Hard
I am able to summarize my
reading   1   2   3   4   5
     Very Well   Poorly

FIGURE TRK 2.1 Instructional Web: Deeds of Infamy: Racism and Bigotry in the United States

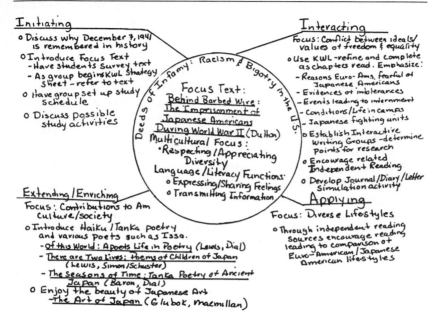

Initiating
- Discuss why December 7, 1941 is remembered in history
- Introduce Focus Text
  - Have students survey text
  - As group begins KWL Strategy Sheet - refer to text
- Have group set up study schedule
- Discuss possible study activities

Interacting
Focus: Conflict between ideals/values of freedom & equality
- Use KWL - refine and complete as chapters read. Emphasize:
  - Reasons Euro-Ams. fearful of Japanese Americans
  - Evidences of intolerances
  - Events leading to internment
  - Conditions/Life in camps
  - Japanese fighting units
- Establish Interactive Writing Groups - determine points for research
- Encourage related Independent Reading
- Develop Journal/Diary/Letter Simulation activity

Focus Text:
Behind Barbed Wire: The Imprisonment of Japanese Americans During World War II (Dutton)

Multicultural Focus:
- Respecting/Appreciating Diversity

Language/Literacy Functions:
- Expressing/Sharing Feelings
- Transmitting Information

Extending/Enriching
Focus: Contributions to Am culture/society
- Introduce Haiku/Tanka poetry and various poets such as Issa.
  - Of this World: A poet's Life in Poetry (Lewis, Dial)
  - There are Two Lives: Poems of Children of Japan (Lewis, Simon/Schuster)
  - The Seasons of Time: Tanka Poetry of Ancient Japan (Baron, Dial)
- Enjoy the beauty of Japanese Art
  - The Art of Japan (Glubok, Macmillan)

Applying
Focus: Diverse Lifestyles
- Through independent reading sources encourage reading leading to comparison of Euro-American/Japanese American lifestyles

Statements such as these can be given with faces describing degrees of pleasure, or students might be given a blank space for responding as follows:

When I read social studies _____

_____

An instructional web (Figure TRK 2.1) is developed for the Japanese American community previously discussed. Webs are useful in teaching and allow the teacher to visualize how well organized a study is.

KIT # 3
Running Record, Miscue Analysis, and Retelling

A more formal analysis of a child's reading might be done either when the teacher is concerned about a particular child's reading and is searching for further insight or when the teacher wishes to explore the extent of a child's reading ability. Many teachers may make more formal analyses of a student's reading at the beginning, middle, and end of the year. These analyses are based on a student's reading from trade books, not from the basal reading series. To do so, the teacher will need a number of books spanning reading range and a variety of interests. Data from these readings combined with observations of daily reading provide the teacher with background for curriculum decisions.

To prepare for this, collect books for the group of students with a range in reading topics and difficulty—differing vocabularies and predictability. Have fresh books, ones that have not been read by the students. When a child has read a book, ask the child if he or she would like to start with that book. This usually puts the child at ease. The following is a workable procedure for doing a more formal analysis of a student's reading development:

STEP ONE

Plan to tape the reading. This is an extremely useful record for comparison of growth and for use in conferencing. Each student might have an individual tape that can be added to as the year progresses. Make copies of the text selections to be used, preserving the lines of the story as they are in the book. Use this to record miscues as they occur. (Duplicate the copies of the texts for recording as needed.)

STEP TWO

Prepare the student for the oral reading by putting the pupil at ease. Start by gathering any information needed about the student's interest that can be related to reading. If it is the first session, ask him or her questions about the reading process using the student background information sheet (Figure TRK 3.1). Let the student know the purpose for the reading inventory and that he or she will be asked to retell the story when finished. Urge the student to do his or her best and to use any known way to figure out the words and meaning in the reading. If information on how a student perceives the reading process is unavailable, ask questions about how the student deals with unknown words and comprehension problems, if he or she is a good reader, and who he or she thinks is a good reader (Y. M. Goodman, Watson & Burke, 1987).

STEP THREE

Allow the student to look at the selection of texts and begin where he or she feels most interested and comfortable. When the student has overestimated his or her reading ability for the selection and the

FIGURE TRK 3.1 Sample Analysis

Student Background Information for Miscue/Telling Analysis

Student _____

Age _____ Sex _____ Grade Level _____ Date _____

Languages Understood: Languages Read:

Languages Spoken: Languages Written:

Cultural Community _____

Record of Conference with Parent(s)   Date _____

Vision, Hearing, or Physical Conditions Affecting Langauge/Literacy

Record of Assessment Conference with Student:

Interest Inventory

What do you like to do when you are not in school?

What places have you visited?

What TV programs/films do you like to watch?

Do you read books? What kind? Can you name one?

Do you own any books? Can you name some?

Is there one book that you have read or heard that is your favorite? What is it? Why?

Is there something you have written of which you are especially proud? What is it? Why?

Reading/Writing Process

What do you do when you come to something you don't know or understand when you are reading?

Can you think of someone who is a good reader? Who? Why?

Do you know what _____ does when he or she comes to something that is not known or understood when reading?

If someone were having trouble reading, how could you help?

What should a teacher do to help when someone is having trouble reading?

Are you a good reader? Why/why not?

FIGURE TRK 3.1   (Continued)

Reading/Writing Process (cont.)

Is there something you would like to do better as a reader? What?

Suppose you were writing and you came to something you had trouble writing. What could you do?

Do you know someone who is a good writer? Who? Why?

What do you suppose that _____ does when he or she is having trouble writing something?

If someone were having trouble writing something, what could you do?

What could a teacher do to help someone having trouble writing?

Are you a good writer? Why/why not?

Is there something you could do to become a better writer?

Can you remember how you learned to read? Write?

Adapted from Y. M. Goodman, D. J. Watson, and C. L. Burke, *Reading Miscues Inventory: Alternative Procedures,* Richard C. Owens Publisher, New York, 1987, pp. 219–222, and M. Barrs, S. Ellis, H. Hester, and A. Thomas, *The Primary Language Record: Handbook for Teachers,* Centre for Language in Primary Education, London, Great Britain, 1988, p. 10.

reading becomes labored, begin reading along as in assisted reading. When completed, have the student retell and discuss the text. Next attempt to get the student into a selection that will allow him or her to be more independent. Record the retelling data. Essentially, the teacher wants to move the student to a point in reading where the miscues provide the most information about the strategies the reader is using.

STEP FOUR

As the student reads, record the reading using a key the teacher developed or use the one below (Silvaroli, 1982). This constitutes a running record. (Replaying the tape later will help to record everything.) For example:

<u>Underline</u> repetitions

anyway, the

Cross out substitutions
and write miscue above

couldn't
~~could not~~

Mark insertions

                                     black

There is a bear in my bed

Circle omissions   (friend's)

Mark R for reversals   sᴿaw

STEP FIVE

When the student finishes reading ask him or her to retell the story. For the retelling, either use a simple story structure outline to aid in recording the retelling or develop a set of important ideas listed from the text based on the story structure.

    Points should be awarded for recall from the text by weighing recall items in reference to importance. By doing this the teacher will be able to achieve a comprehension percentage score. Elicit any aspect the student has omitted. Take care not to give the student any information not reported. When the recall has been aided, lower the points. A partially completed example incorporating story structure and important ideas based on the story of Red Riding Hood follows:

Story Structure Outline	*Important Ideas*
Characters:	_____ Mother (1)
	_4_ Red Riding Hood (4)
	_3_ Wolf (3)
	_1_ Ax Man (1)
	_1_ Grandmother (1)
	_9_ /10
Setting:	_2_ Grandmother's (2)
	_2_ Woods (2)
	_____ Home (1)
	_4_ /5
Plot:	_3_ She was taking food to her sick Grandmother (3)
	_3_ /3
Events:	_2_ In the woods whe met a wolf (2)
	and so on.
	_7_ /9

Theme/Message: __**3**__ She was told not to stop to talk to anyone. (3)

                                   __**3**__ /3

Total: **26** /30

Using the retelling records and the taped readings and retellings, complete the reading profile (Figure TRK 3.2).

STEP SIX

Select miscues beginning with what is judged the easiest section the student has read and continue to the frustration level for the miscue analysis. Order read is not important. Try for a minimum of 25 miscues for the decision making. The miscues most insightful for determining what processes the student is using are best selected from those the student makes at the level the materials become more difficult but before they become too difficult. Place these on the Modified Miscue Analysis Worksheet (Figure TRK 3.3). Care should be exercised in making decisions from the student sample. If there is an abundance of miscues from the frustration level, or if there are too few total miscues for analysis, these findings can be more questionable for decision making. Record identical miscues only once (Bauman, 1988).

STEP SEVEN

Code the miscues on the chart using the questions below as a guide. Omissions and insertions are also recorded. For omissions, place X's in the Miscue column. For insertions, place X's in the Word column.

1. *Repetition:* Did the reader repeat any word, phrase, or sentence? Place an X in the appropriate box on the worksheet.
2. *Omissions and Insertions:* Did the reader omit or insert a word? Did it retain the syntactical and semantical acceptability of the sentence? Place an X in the appropriate box under Yes or No.
3. *Self-Corrections:* Did the reader self-correct the miscue in the sentence to make it acceptable? Place an X in the appropriate box on the worksheet. If an attempt was made that did not make it acceptable, leave the box blank.
4. *Reversals:* Did the reader reverse any word (*saw/was*) or order of wording? Place an X in the appropriate box on the worksheet.
5. *Graphophonic:* What letter/sound relationship is there between the miscue and the printed word? Determine the percentage of

FIGURE TRK 3.2 Blank Form for Reading Profile

	Not Noted	Low Degree	Moderate Degree	High Degree
Comprehension				
Confidence and independence				
Essential information provided				
Directly stated information provided				
Inferred information provided				
Prior information included				
Language was appropriate to text				
Retelling organized				
Critical response included				
Reading Strategies				
Uses prior information to make sense of the reading				
Uses pictures or graphic cues				
Uses predicting				
Uses the graphophonic cueing system				
Uses the syntactic/ semantic cueing system				
Combines the use of several strategies				

Adapted from P. A. Irwin and J. N. Mitchel, "The Reader Retelling Profile: Using Retelling to Make Instructional Decisions," in L. M. Morrow, "Retelling Stories as a Diagnostic Tool," in S. M. Glazer, L. W. Searfoss, and L. M. Gentile (eds.), *Reexamining Reading Diagnosis: New Trends and Procedures,* International Reading Association, Newark, DE, 1988, pp. 140–141; M. Barrs, S. Ellis, H. Hester, and A. Thomas, *The Primary Language Record: Handbook for Teachers,* Centre for Language in Primary Language, London, Great Britain, 1988, p. 48.

each miscue's pronunciation that approximates the printed word (Pflaum, 1979). For example, "high" refers to a strong letter/ sound relationship between the printed word and the miscue. Mark the appropriate box:

High	Partial	Little
(75%)	(+50%)	(−50%)

FIGURE TRK 3.3 Blank Worksheet Sample

Modified Miscue Analysis Worksheet

L1: _____ Grade: _____ Name: _____

Book/Passage	Word	Miscue	Reading Production				Graphophonic Similarity			Syntactic/Semantic Acceptability		Meaning Change		Comment
			Repe-tition	Omission/Insertion	Self-Correct	Reversal	High	Partial	Little	Yes	No	Yes	No	

Retelling Summaries	Column Total
1st	No Analyzed
2nd	Percentage

Adapted from J. A. Baumann, *Reading Assessment*, Merrill Publishing, Columbus, OH, 1988, p. 151, and Y. M. Goodman, D. J. Watson, and C. L. Burke, *Reaching Miscues Inventory: Alternative Procedures*, Richard C. Owens Publisher, New York, 1987, pp. 98, 105, and S. W. Pflaum, "Diagnosis of Oral Reading," *The Reading Teacher*, 33(3), p. 281.

6. *Syntactic or Semantic:* Is the miscue in the sentence syntactically and semantically acceptable considering the preceding and succeeding portions of the passage? Place an X in the appropriate column under Yes or No on the worksheet.
7. *Meaning Change:* Did the miscue disrupt the intended meaning of the text? Place an X in the appropriate column under Yes or No. (Any aspect that sufficiently alters the intended meaning is yes.)

STEP EIGHT

Compute the miscues by totaling the miscues for each column under "Reading Production" (repetition, omission/insertion, self-correction, and reversal). Place the number in the "Column Total" box and divide each column's total by the total number of reading production miscues there are in all the "Reading Production" columns to achieve the percentage score. Place the percentage in the "Percentage" box in the appropriate column.

Total the miscues for each column under "Graphophonic Similarity" (high, partial, little). Place the number in the "Column Total" box and divide each column's total by the total number of miscues there are in the "Graphophonic Similarity" columns to achieve the percentage score. Place the percentage in the "Percentage" box in the appropriate column. (Remember that these columns will not have any reading production miscues included.)

Total the columns under "Syntactic/Semantic Acceptability" (Yes, No). Place the number in the "Column Total" box and divide each column's total by the total number of X's there are in the "Syntactic/Semantic Acceptability" columns to achieve the percentage score. Place the percentage in the "Percentage" box in the appropriate column.

Total the columns under "Meaning Change" (Yes, No). Place the number in the "Column Total" box and divide each column's total by the total number of X's there are in the "Meaning Change" columns to achieve the percentage score. Place the percentage in the "Percentage" box in the appropriate column.

STEP NINE

Analyze your findings. Combine percentages for high and partial graphophonic similarities. How well is the student using this cueing system? Compare with the syntactic/semantic acceptability. Were

most of the omissions/insertions syntactically and semantically acceptable? How well is the student retaining the author's intended meaning? How well is the student using the cueing system? Is one aspect
being used in place of all three? The worksheet gives a graphic picture
of the processes the student is using. Record the summary of this
information on the reading profile under Reading Strategies.

Compare these findings with the results of the retellings (Step
Five). If there is any doubt about any items (pronunciation, etc.) let the
retelling serve as a guide in the final decision. The retelling is always
the final word because the data indicates how the reader processed the
reading for understanding.

SAMPLES

As an aid in completing a more formal analysis of reading, a modified
running record (Figure TRK 3.4) of a student's reading has been included in the kit with a sample retelling (Figure TRK 3.5) and a
reading profile (Figure TRK 3.6). In addition, a modified miscue worksheet (Figure TRK 3.7) has been completed for the reading selection.
This analysis is based on the reading of a third-grade, bilingual Hispanic child. The sample should only be used for studying the reading
analysis as a process, not for making any other interpretation regarding the student since the data provided is incomplete. It is only based
on a single reading without any additional observations or interactions
with the student.

FIGURE TRK 3.4 Reading Analysis Sample

Reading Analysis

Running Record: Excerpts

Book/Selection: <u>A Kiss for Little Bear</u>   *Author:* <u>E. Holmelund Minarik</u>

His p—
"~~This picture~~ makes me happy,"

said Little Bear.

"Hello, Hen."

paper
This ~~picture~~ is for grand~~mother.~~

for
It is ~~from~~ his grandmother.

pool
But Frog saw a ~~pond.~~

Came
~~Come~~ and get the kiss.

get
But he came and ~~got~~ the kiss.

R ā (not)
But then he saw another little skunk.

give
He ~~gave~~ the kiss to her.

alone
And then Hen came ~~along.~~

How
"~~Who~~ has it now?"

paper she
"It is for the ~~picture you~~ sent her.

Everybody
~~Everyone~~ came.

Adapted from (data in sample) Sandi Anda, "Teaching Reading to Second Language Learners," graduate assignment, Moorhead, MN, Moorhead State University, 1990.

FIGURE TRK 3.5 Retelling Guide Sample

Retelling Guide

Book/Selection: A Kiss for Little Bear   *Author:*   E. Holmelund Minarik

Characters: ____✓____ Little Bear   _____ Frog ⎤
                 _____ Hen   _____ Cat   ⎬ **aided**
                 ____✓____ Grandmother   ____✓____ Skunks ⎦
                                                    ____**4**____ /6 pts.

Plot: ____✓____ Little Bear makes a ~~picture~~ **paper** for Grandmother.
         _____ When Hen brought the picture to Grandmother she asked
                         Hen to take a kiss back to Little Bear.
         _____ The Kiss gets mixed up when being passed around.
                                                    ____**I**____ /3 pts.

Events:
____✓____ Little Bear paints a   _____ The skunks pass the
              picture for Grandmother.   kiss back and forth.
_____ Hen takes the picture   _____ Hen says, "Too much
              to Grandmother.   kissing."
_____ Grandmother asks Hen   _____ Hen gets the kiss back
              to take a kiss back to   and gives it to Little
              Little Bear.   Bear.
_____ The Hen gives the kiss   _____ Little Bear asks Hen to
              to Frog.   take a kiss back to
_____ The Frog gives the kiss   Grandmother, she says
              to Cat.   ____✓____   no.
_____ The Cat gives the kiss   _____ The two skunks ~~get~~
              to Skunk.   ~~married~~. **got together**
_____ The Skunk gives the   _____ Little Bear is the best
              kiss to another skunk.   man.
                                                    ____**2**____ /12 pts.

Theme: _____ When things are passed between several people or
                         animals, they get all mixed up.
                                                    ____**O**____ /3 pts.
                                        Total ____**7**____ /24 pts.

Source: Sandi Anda, "Teaching Reading to Second Language Learners," graduate assignment, Moorhead, MN, Moorhead State University, 1990. Used with permission from author.

FIGURE TRK 3.6   Completed Reading Profile Sample

Reading Profile

	Not Noted	Low Degree	Moderate Degree	High Degree
Comprehension				
Confidence and independence		X		
Essential information provided		X		
Directly stated information provided		X		
Inferred information provided		X		
Prior information included		X		
Language was appropriate to text		X		
*Retelling organized		X		
Critical response included		X		

    *Retelling indicated 25% with aid

	Not Noted	Low Degree	Moderate Degree	High Degree
Reading Strategies				
Uses prior information to make sense of the reading		X		
Uses pictures or graphic cues	X			
Uses predicting		X		
Uses the graphophonic cueing system				86% X
Uses the syntactic/ semantic cueing system		54% not acceptable X		
Combines the use of several strategies		X		

Adapted from P. A. Irwin and J. N. Mitchel, "The Reader Retelling Profile: Using Retelling to Make Instructional Decisions," in L. M. Morrow, *Retelling Stories as a Diagnostic Tool* in S. M. Glazer, L. W. Searfoss, and L. M. Gentile (eds.), *Reexamining Reading Diagnosis: New Trends and Procedures,* International Reading Association, Newark, DE, 1988, pp. 140–141; M. Barrs, S. Ellis, H. Hester, and A. Thomas, *The Primary Language Record: Handbook for Teachers,* Centre for Language in Primary Language, London, Great Britain, 1988, p. 48; and Sandi Anda, "Teaching Reading to Second language Learners," graduate assignment, Moorhead, MN, Moorhead State University, 1990.

FIGURE TRK 3.7 Completed Worksheet Sample

Modified Miscue Analysis Worksheet

L1: __Spanish__ Grade: __3__ Name: __M.__

Book/Passage	Word	Miscue	Repetition	Omission/Insertion	Self-Correct	Revised	High	Partial	Little	Yes	No	Yes	No	Comment
			Reading Production				Graphophonic Similarity			Syntactic/Semantic Acceptability		Meaning Change		
	This	His					X			X		X		
	picture	p—							X		X	X		difficulty
	picture	paper						X		X			X	pronouncing
A Kiss for Little Bear by Else Holmelund Minarik	Grand-mother	Grandma					X			X			X	"r"
	chat	k—							X		X	X		esp. in
	from	for					X			X		X		vowels
	pond	pool						X		X			X	
	come	came					X				X		X	sometimes
	got	get					X				X		X	tried in
	saw	was				X		X			X	X		beginning
	another	a not					X				X	X		
	gave	give					X				X	X		then
	along	alone					X			X			X	abandoned
	Indeed	Ind—						X			X	X		
	Who	How					X				X		X	
	him	her						X		X		X		
	you	she							X	X		X		

FIGURE TRK 3.7 Continued

Book/Passage	Word	Miscue	Reading Production				Graphophonic Similarity			Syntactic/Semantic Acceptability		Meaning Change		Comment
			Repetition	Omission/Insertion	Self-Correct	Revised	High	Partial	Little	Yes	No	Yes	No	
	mixed	mixd					X				X	X		
	decided	ideas						X			X	X		
	married	married			X									
	they	then					X				X	X		
	lovely	long						X		X				
	Every-	Every-												
	one	body						X		X			X	
	best	the best												
	man	man		X						X			X	
	like	like	X											
	Retelling Summaries	Column												
		Total	1	1	1	1	10	8	3	11	13	14	8	
1st 25%		No Analyzed	4	4	4	4	21	21	21	24	24	22	22	
2nd		Percentage	25%	25%	25%	25%	48%	38%	14%	46%	54%	64%	36%	

Adapted from J. A. Baumann, *Reading Assessment*, Merrill Publishing, Columbus, OH, 1988, p. 151; Y. M. Goodman et al., *Reading Miscue Inventory: Alternative Procedure*, Richard C. Owen Publisher, New York, 1987, pp. 98, 105, and Sandi Anda, "Teaching Reading to Second Language Learners," graduate assignment, Moorhead, MN, Moorhead State University, 1990.

KIT # 4
Sibley's Recommended Books for
Multicultural Teaching Themes and Topics

AFRICAN CULTURES

Grades K–2

Aardema, Verna. *Bringing the Rain to Kapiti Plain.* Illustrated by Beatriz Vidal. Dial, 1981 (9–8037–0807–6); paper, 1983 (9–8037–0904–8). This Nandi tale, originally collected from two young boys in Kenya, reminds listeners of the cumulative rhyme, "The House that Jack Built." Ki-pat, who watches his herd of cows as they graze on Kapiti Plain, brings an end to a severe drought when he shoots an arrow into "the big, black cloud, all heavy with rain." The full-page gouache paintings show the abundance of plants and wildlife living on Kapiti Plain. Compare the plains environment to that of the forest in Helen Cowcher's *Rain Forest* (Farrar, 1988). Discuss how both environments are threatened, one by nature itself, the other by humans with machines.

Aardema, Verna. *Who's in Rabbit's House?* Illustrated by Leo and Diane Dillon. Dial, 1977 (0–8037–9551–3); paper, 1979 (0–8037–9549–1). With pastels and tempera paintings, Leo and Diane Dillon present this Masai tale as a play. Masai actors wearing masks that change expressions as the drama builds perform for their fellow villagers. After a series of animals, such as the jackal and elephant, tries to solve the mystery of who is in rabbit's house, frog cleverly solves the problem. After hearing the story, children may enjoy creating masks to use in their own performance of this tale.

Daly, Niki. *Not So Fast Songolo.* Macmillan, 1986 (0–689–50367–9); paper, Penguin, 1987 (0–14–050715–9). Malusi, a South African boy, helps his granny, Gogo, shop in the city. They ride a bus, window-shop, and cross busy streets to buy the items in Gogo's shopping list. Malusi feels surprised and pleased when Gogo buys him new red shoes. Illustrations in watercolor and marker show the affection between the boy and his grandmother, as well as scenes in a South African city. Compare Malusi's shopping experience with that of Rosa in Vera B. Williams's *A Chair for My Mother* (Greenwillow, 1982) and *Something Special for Me* (Greenwillow, 1983). Compare Malusi's happiness over his new shoes with Momo's over her rubber boots in Taro Yashima's *Umbrella* (Viking, 1958).

Greenfield, Eloise. *Africa Dream.* Illustrated by Carole Byard. Harper, 1977 (0–381–90061–4). Full-page, black-and-white paintings and a poetic text reflect the experience of an African American child who dreams that she crosses the Atlantic Ocean "in a slow, smooth jump" and lands in "long-ago Africa." In this soothing dream, she shops in a marketplace, meets her long-ago granddaddy, and dances to the drums of her uncles. Compare this vision of Africa with Leila Ward's *I Am Eyes: Ni Macho* (Greenwillow, 1978), where a young girl of Kenya introduces the reader to the beauties of her native land. Extend young children's understanding of African cultures with Claudia Zaslavsky's *Count On Your Fingers African Style* (Crowell, 1979).

Haley, Gail E. *A Story, a Story.* Atheneum, 1970 (0–689–20511–2); paper, Macmillan, 1988 (0–689–71201–4). An African storyteller tells the tale of how Ananse, the Spider man, brought stories to the people on earth. Ananse completes three impossible tasks for the Sky God and thus earns the Sky God's golden box of stories, which Ananse scatters to all the corners of the world. Gail E. Haley's colored woodcut illustrations, resembling Batik patterns, depict the beautiful African setting. Compare Ananse's capture of the fairy Mmoatia with other versions of the "Tar Baby" story. Extend the unit to other pourquoi tales, such as Verna Aardema's *Why Mosquitoes Buzz in People's Ears* (Dial, 1975) or Mwenye Hadithi's *Greedy Zebra* (Little, Brown, 1984).

Grades 3–4

Bryan, Ashley. *Lion and the Ostrich Chicks and Other African Folk Tales.* Atheneum, 1986 (0–689–31311–X). This collection of folktales introduces children to four African cultures – the Hausa, Angolan, Masai, and Bushmen. Each story, whether about animals or humans, demonstrates a triumph over a powerful figure in that particular culture. Children will enjoy learning the repeating verses in each of the tales. Compare the tale "The Foolish Boy," about Spider Ananse, with the spider tales in Joyce Cooper Arkhurst's *The Adventures of Spider: West African Folk Tales* (Little, Brown, 1964). Extend the study of African folklore to Nigerian tales in Ashley Bryan's *Beat the Story-Drum, Pum-Pum* (Atheneum, 1980).

Musgrove, Margaret. *Ashanti to Zulu: African Traditions.* Illustrated by Leo and Diane Dillon. Dial, 1976 (0–8037–0358–9); paper, 1980 (0–8037–0308–2). Through an alphabetical arrangement, readers learn about the customs of 26 African tribes, including initiation rites, religious practices, and marriage customs. Paintings in pastels, watercolor, and acrylics clarify and extend the text. Each illustration usually includes a man, woman, child, artifact, living quarters, and animal. A map of Africa at the end of the book shows the location of each culture. Extend children's understanding of African cultures with Muriel Feelings's *Jambo Means Hello* (Dial, 1974) and *Moja Means One* (Dial, 1971).

Stelson, Caren Barzelay. *Safari.* Photos by Kim A. Stelson. Carolrhoda, 1988 (0–87614–324–9). The author invites the reader to join her on a safari to Tanzania, where one meets members of the Masai tribe and sees animals living in national wildlife parks. Photographs capture the beauty of the wild animals, including zebras, wildebeests, and pink flamingos. Children may enjoy learning more about the animals seen on the safari. Compare to Jeannie Baker's *Where the Forest Meets the Sky*, (Greenwillow, 1987), about an Australian wilderness also threatened by encroaching civilization.

Steptoe, John. *Mufaro's Beautiful Daughters: An African Tale*. Lothrop, 1987 (0–688–04046–2). Mufaro's two beautiful daughters, bad-tempered Manyara and kind Nyasha, both travel to the city where the king will choose a wife. Names of characters come from the Shona language. The flora and fauna, as well as the architecture of the city, reflect the Zimbabwe region of Africa. The text and illustrations together create a richly layered picture book that children will enjoy again and again. Compare motifs in this folktale with those in variants of "Cinderella."

Walter, Mildred Pitts. *Brother to the Wind*. Illustrated by Diane and Leo Dillon. Lothrop, 1985 (0–688–03812–3). Emeke dreams of finding Good Snake, who might grant him his wish to fly. Emeke learns that to achieve his dream he needs faith, especially to endure the taunts of others. This original tale, written in the style of folklore, uses many symbols of African cultures. The Dillons' framed paintings capture Emeke's real world as well as the world of his dreams. Compare Emeke's dream of flying to Rudy Soto's, in Byrd Baylor's *Hawk, I'm Your Brother* (Scribner, 1976), or Louis Bleriot's, in Alice and Martin Provensen's *The Glorious Flight* (Viking, 1983).

Grades 5–6

Bess, Clayton. *Story for a Black Night*. Houghton Mifflin, 1982 (0–395–31857–2). Momo tells his son of his own childhood, when two strangers spending a night in his family's hut leave behind a baby ridden with smallpox. This story, set in Liberia and told in dialect, forces readers to confront the nature of good and evil. The book, recommended for advanced readers or for reading aloud, will lead to serious discussions about the beauties and tragedies inherent in being human.

Chiasson, John. *African Journey*. Bradbury, 1987 (0–02–718530–3). Color photographs and text provide readers with an ethnographic account of six African cultures. Chiasson pays particular attention to how the environment influences the lives of the people from the nomadic herders of Niger to the fishermen of Touba Diallaw, Senegal. A map of Africa locates each of the six cultures. A postscript draws attention to the need for proper technology to tap the rich natural resources of this continent. Extend this study of East and West Africa with Constance Nabwire and Bertha Vining Montgomery's *Cooking the African Way* (Lerner, 1988).

Courlander, Harold. *The Crest and the Hide and Other African Stories of Heroes, Chiefs, Bards, Hunters, Sorcerers and Common People*. Illustrated by Monica Vachula. Putnam, 1982 (0–698–20536–7). These 20 tales will increase children's understanding of primitive African cultures, such as the Ashanti, the Zulu, or the Tswana. Through Courlander's retellings, readers will hear the voices of African storytellers, narrating tales with themes that apply as much to contemporary society as they did to these ancient African societies. The author's notes give the sources for each tale, comments on the themes, or suggestions of other African tales for comparison. A black-and-white drawing sets the scene for each tale.

AFRICAN AMERICAN CULTURE

Grades K–2

Clifton, Lucille. *Everett Anderson's Goodbye.* Illustrated by Ann Grifalconi. Holt, Rinehart & Winston, 1983 (0–8050–0235–9); paper, 1988 (0–8050–0800–4). Poetry and expressive black-and-white drawings show Everett Anderson struggling to come to terms with his father's death. Compare to other books of children accepting death, such as Eve Bunting's *The Happy Funeral* (Harper, 1982), Miska Miles' *Annie and the Old One* (Little, 1972), or Tomie dePaola's *Nana Upstairs, Nana Downstairs* (Putnam, 1973). Extend the unit to other stories of loss and acceptance, such as divorce in Jeanette Caines' *Daddy* (Harper & Row, 1977); or moving away, as in Aliki's *We Are Best Friends* (Greenwillow, 1982).

Flournoy, Valerie. *The Patchwork Quilt.* Illustrated by Jerry Pinkney. Dial, 1985 (0–8037–0098–9). When Grandma becomes too ill to continue working on the quilt of family memories, young Tanya and other family members continue to cut and piece together the quilt squares. The book shows the love among three generations of a family and the importance of shared memories. Compare to other books which evoke family memories, such as Eloise Greenfield's *Grandmama's Joy* (Collins, 1980), Sharon Bell Mathis' *The Hundred Penny Box* (Viking, 1975), Angela Johnson's *Tell Me a Story, Mama* (Orchard, 1989), or Elizabeth Fitzgerald Howard's *The Train to Lulu's* (Bradbury, 1988).

McKissack, Patricia. *Flossie & the Fox.* Illustrated by Rachel Isadora. Dial, 1986 (0–8037–0251–5). While on an errand through the woods to deliver eggs, young Flossie outsmarts a fox. The watercolor paintings dominated by shades of yellow show a confident and brave Flossie. Compare Flossie's walk through the forest with that of "Little Red Riding Hood." Study the characteristics of the fox in other stories: the fox as trickster in Aesop's "The Fox and the Crow" or the folktale "Chicken Little"; or the fox outsmarted in Aesop's "The Fox and the Stork" or the "Tar Baby" tale.

Steptoe, John. *Stevie.* Harper, 1969 (0–06–025764–4); paper, 1986 (0–06–443122–3). Robert remembers how he felt when his mother took care of Stevie all week while Stevie's mother worked. He felt jealous about the attention Stevie got and angry when Stevie played with his toys or got him into trouble. After Stevie moved away, Robert's jealousy turned to love: "He was kinda like a little brother, Little Stevie." The six full-page paintings with heavy black outlines fit the emotional tenor of the text. Extend the unit to other books in which children's jealousy turns to acceptance, such as Eloise Greenfield's *She Come Bringing Me That Little Baby Girl* (Lippincott, 1974) or Ezra Jack Keats' *Peter's Chair* (Harper & Row, 1967).

Williams, Vera B. *Cherries and Cherry Pits.* Greenwillow, 1986 (0–688–05146–4). A narrator tells a story about her friend Bidemmi, who draws pictures and makes up stories about people sharing cherries with those special to them. Striking watercolor paintings show Bidemmi drawing the pictures for her stories with her favorite colors. This story-within-a-story serves as an excellent model for children to draw and tell their own stories. For another example, see Crockett Johnson's *Harold and the Purple Crayon* (Harper & Row, 1955). Compare Bidemmi's story about planting cherry pits to stories about Johnny Appleseed, such as Steven Kellogg's *Johnny Appleseed* (Morrow, 1988).

Grades 3–4

Giovanni, Nikki. *Spin a Soft Black Song.* Illustrated by George Martins. Revised edition Hill & Wang, 1985 (0–8090–8796–0). Poems written especially for black children capture the universal feelings of childhood. There are poems about children interacting with mommies and daddies and with friends, such as Lydia and Shirley in "Two Friends." There are poems about individual children, such as "Yvonne," "on her way to becoming a good Black woman" or capable "Mattie Lou at Twelve." There are poems that describe life in the ghetto, such as "Sleep" and poems that celebrate black unity, such as "Dance Poem." The black-and-white illustrations scattered throughout the book offer visual interpretations of selected poems. Extend the unit with additional poetry collections that capture the essence of black children's thoughts and feelings, such as Eloise Greenfield's *Honey, I Love* (Crowell, 1978) or *Daydreamers* (Dial, 1981).

Hamilton, Virginia. *The People Could Fly: American Black Folktales.* Illustrated by Leo and Diane Dillon. Knopf, 1985 (0–394–96925–1). A collection of 24 representative black folktales told in "reasonably colloquial language or dialect" invites readers to listen to "voices from the past." This carefully designed book, with numerous framed, black-and-white illustrations in soft shades, includes slave riddles, trickster tales, tall tales, and slave narratives. Notes at the end of each tale give valuable background information, including origins or variants. Extend to other collections of black folklore, such as Julius Lester's *The Knee-High Man* (Dial, 1972).

Milton, Joyce. *Marching to Freedom: The Story of Martin Luther King, Jr.* Paper, Dell, 1987 (0–440–45433–6). This easy-to-read biography of Martin Luther King, Jr. highlights the major events in his life as he led his people toward the dream of freedom and equality for all races. Seven pages of black-and-white, captioned photographs give readers a closer look at Dr. King and others involved in the civil rights movement. Compare to other biographies of Dr. King, such as David A. Adler's *Martin Luther King, Jr.: Free at Last* (Holiday House, 1986). Extend the unit to novels about African Americans facing racial prejudice, such as Mildred Taylor's *Song of the Trees* (Dial, 1975), *The Friendship* (Dial, 1987), or *Gold Cadillac* (Dial, 1987). Compare Dr. King's vision for world peace with Georgie's in Jane Langton's *The Fragile Flag* (Harper & Row, 1984).

Sanfield, Steve. *Natural Man: The True Story of John Henry.* Illustrated by Peter J. Thornton. Godine, 1986 (0–87923–630–2). The legendary John Henry, a natural-born steel-driving man, dies in triumph after beating the steam drill, a machine destined to take the place of railroad steel drivers. The lyrical text and soft charcoal drawings combine to show John Henry's inner and outer strength. The books ends with a John Henry ballad compiled by the author. Children might compare other versions of the ballad and the legend, such as Ezra Jack Keats' *John Henry* (Pantheon, 1965). Extend the unit to a study of other tall tales, such as Steven Kellogg's *Pecos Bill* (Morrow, 1986) or Adrien Stoutenburg's *American Tall Tales* (Viking, 1966).

Walter, Mildred Pitts. *Justin and the Best Biscuits in the World.* Illustrated by Catherine Stock. Lothrop, 1986 (0–688–06645–3). While spending time on his grandfather's Missouri ranch, 10-year-old Justin learns much about himself and his African American heritage. Compare Justin's attitudes toward gender roles with those in Anthony Browne's *Piggybook* (Knopf, 1986). Extend the reader's understanding of the west with Russell Freedman's *Children of the Wild West* (Clarion, 1983) or *Cowboys of the Wild West* (Clarion, 1985), Murray Tinkelman's *Rodeo* (Greenwillow, 1982), or William Katz's *Black People Who Made the Old West* (Crowell, 1977).

Grades 5–6

Boyd, Candy D. *Charlie Pippin.* Macmillan, 1987 (0–02–726350–9); paper, Penguin, 1988 (0–14–032587–5). For a sixth grade project, Charlie Pippin joins the war-and-peace group and specifically studies the Vietnam War and its aftermath in hopes of better understanding her rigid, bitter father, who returned from the war injured both physically and emotionally. Compare to Katherine Paterson's *Park's Quest* (Lodestar, 1988). Extend the unit to Langston Hughes's poem "Dream Deferred" or Jane Langton's *The Fragile Flag* (Harper & Row, 1984).

Davis, Ossie. *Langston: A Play.* Delacorte, 1982 (0–385–28543–4). Within the format of a play, Langston Hughes becomes the main character, acting out his life story for a group of young admirers. Hughes began his literary career during the Harlem renaissance movement, and by the end of his life in 1967 he had written poems, plays, and his own auto-biography. Especially known for his poetry, which was deeply rooted in experience, Hughes became known as the poet laureate of the folk. The dramatic format integrates much of Hughes' poetry into his life story. Compare with biographies such as Alice Walker's *Langston Hughes, American Poet* (Crowell, 1974). Extend the unit to collections of Hughes' poetry, such as *The Dream Keeper and Other Poems* (Knopf, 1932), and to collections of poems by poets he admired, such as Paul Laurence Dunbar and Carl Sandburg.

Hamilton, Virginia. *Zeely.* Illustrated by Symeon Shimin. Macmillan, 1967 (0–02–742470–7); paper, 1986 (0–689–71110–7). While spending the summer on her uncle's farm, 11-year-old Elizabeth realizes that understanding oneself means appreciating the beauty and dignity within. Through Zeely, a slender woman over six feet tall, who Geeder (Elizabeth) imagines to be a Watusi Queen, Geeder learns that dreaming and imagining are fine as long as they're tempered by self-understanding and inner strength. Compare to other stories about characters who make self-discoveries, such as Eloise Greenfield's *Sister* (Crowell, 1974). Extend the unit to creation myths, such as those retold in Virginia Hamilton's *In the Beginning: Creation Myths from Around the World* (Harcourt Brace Jovanovich, 1988).

Hansen, Joyce. *Which Way Freedom?* Walker, 1986 (0–8027–6636–6). With the help of an aged African American, two teenage slaves, Obi and Easter, flee the Jennings farm in South Carolina with the hope of gaining freedom. When caught by Confederate soldiers and forced to work for them, Easter decides to remain while Obi runs away and joins a black Union regiment to become one of the 200,000 blacks who fought in the Civil War. This vivid, fictionalized account based on historical facts should be included in Civil War units. Extend the unit to other accounts of slaves seeking freedom, such as Dorothy Sterling's *Freedom Train: The Story of Harriet Tubman* (Doubleday, 1954) or Virginia Hamilton's *Anthony Burns: The Defeat and Triumph of a Fugitive Slave* (Knopf, 1988).

Lester, Julius. *The Tales of Uncle Remus: The Adventures of Brer Rabbit.* Illustrated by Jerry Pinkney. Dial, 1987 (0–8037–0272–8). Using "modified contemporary southern black English," Julius Lester retells 48 of the Uncle Remus stories originally collected and published by Joel Chandler Harris. Children will enjoy reading or listening to these tales of Brer Rabbit, the trickster, as he outwits his fellow animals and even Mr. Man. They will also enjoy Lester's play with language as he uses literary allusions, imagery, and other figures of speech. Pinkney's black-and-white drawings and occasional full-page watercolor paintings add to the humor of the text. Continue the tales about Brer Rabbit with Julius Lester's *More Tales of Uncle Remus* (Dial, 1988). Extend to other cycles of trickster tales, such as those about Ananse or Jack or Native American tricksters, such as Coyote, Raven, or Nanabozho.

ASIAN CULTURES

Grades K–2

Boholm-Olsson, Eva. *Tuan.* Illustrated by Pham Van Don. Translated by Dianne Jonasson. Farrar, 1988 (91–29–58766–2). Based on the author's own experiences while living in northern Vietnam, Eva Boholm-Olsson tells about five-year-old Tuan, who lives with his mother in a small house with clay walls and a roof of palm leaves. While his mother works in a nearby factory, Tuan spends the day with Grandma. The full-color illustrations, painted on silk, capture Tuan's world as he and a friend ride a water buffalo and swim in a water hole. Compare to other stories of the everyday lives of children, such as Riki Levinson's *Our Home is the Sea* (Dutton, 1988).

Friedman, Ina R. *How My Parents Learned to Eat.* Illustrated by Allen Say. Houghton, 1984 (0–395–35379–3); paper, 1987 (0–395–44235–4). A young girl tells a warm and humorous story of her parents' courtship—how her father, an American sailor, secretly tried to learn to eat with chopsticks, while her mother, a Japanese schoolgirl, tried to handle a knife, fork, and spoon. The full-color illustrations and text show how the young girl has successfully integrated the two cultures into her life: "In our house, some five days we eat with chopsticks and some days we eat with knives and forks. For me, it's natural." Extend the unit to other books of families retelling stories about their own cultural backgrounds, such as Camille Yarbrough's *Cornrows* (Coward, McCann & Geoghegan, 1979) or Riki Levinson's *Watch the Stars Come Out* (Dutton, 1985).

Levinson, Riki. *Our Home Is the Sea.* Illustrated by Dennis Luzak. Dutton, 1988 (0–525–44406–8). School is out for another year and a young boy feels a sense of freedom as he hurries home through the city of Hong Kong to his family's "house on the water." Through text and impressionistic oil paintings, the boy takes the reader on a tour of Hong Kong to visit the market, see the tall apartment houses, walk through the park, and finally arrive at the wharf on the water's edge. Although his mother wants him to be a schoolteacher, the boy declares: "I will be a fisherman, like my father and grandfather. Our home is the sea." An excellent book to initiate a unit on families in various parts of the world.

Mosel, Arlene. *The Funny Little Woman.* Illustrated by Blair Lent. Dutton, 1972 (0–525–30265–4); paper, 1986 (0–525–45036–X). In a tale originally told by Lafcadio Hearn in *Japanese Fairy Tales* (Boni and Liveright, 1924), a funny little woman outwits the wicked, supernatural oni and runs away with their magical wooden paddle, which turns one grain of rice into a potful. Although the tale can be told without the pictures, Lent's illustrations add another dimension to the story. Children will enjoy returning to the book again and again to note the many details and symbols, such as the chrysanthemum at the book's beginning and end. Especially noteworthy is Lent's use of the double narrative to visually tell two stories at the same time, one underground and one aboveground.

Compare these illustrations to others by Blair Lent, such as those in
Margaret Hodges's retelling of *The Wave* (Houghton Mifflin, 1964). Ex-
tend the unit to other Japanese tales, such as those in Florence Sakade's
Japanese Children's Favorite Stories (C. E. Tuttle, 1958).

Yashima, Taro. *Crow Boy.* Viking, 1955 (0–670–24931–9); paper, Penguin,
1976 (0–14–050172–X). A painfully shy Japanese boy, given the deroga-
tory nickname of Chibi by his classmates, feels lonely and ostracized at
school until his sixth-grade teacher discovers and appreciates Chibi's
special talents. When Chibi imitates the voices of crows in the school
talent show, adults and children alike are moved to tears and honor
Chibi with a new name–Crow Boy. Yashima, through his expressionistic paintings, uses the artistic elements of space and shape to show Crow
Boy's metamorphosis from despair and loneliness to acceptance and
hope. Extend the unit to other school stories of lonely, isolated children
who finally gain acceptance, such as Tomie dePaola's *Oliver Button is a
Sissy* (Harcourt Brace Jovanovich, 1979) or Eleanor Estes's *The Hundred
Dresses* (Harcourt, Brace, 1944).

Grades 3–4

Bunting, Eve. *The Happy Funeral.* Illustrated by Vo-Dinh Mai. Harper, 1982
(0–06–020894–5). A young Chinese American girl describes her feelings
as she experiences the funeral rituals of her grandfather. The family
gives him gifts for his journey to the spirit world and shares special
memories about Grandfather. The black-and-white illustrations show
scenes of Chinatown and increase the reader's understanding of Chinese
customs. Extend the unit to Helen Coutant's *First Snow* (Knopf, 1974),
which shows a young Vietnamese girl struggling to understand her
grandmother's impending death, or to Jane Resh Thomas's *Saying Goodbye to Grandma* (Clarion, 1988), which shows a typical American funeral.

Chang, Heidi. *Elaine, Mary Lewis, and the Frogs.* Crown, 1988 (0–517–56752–
0). When Elaine Chow, a young Chinese American girl, moves from San
Francisco to Iowa, she feels lonely in her new school until she begins
working on a science project with Mary Lewis Thorp. With the help of
Elaine's father, they build a frog kite and at the same time learn from
Mr. Chow some history and symbolism about Chinese kites. Extend the
unit to informational books about kites as well as folklore, such as Jane
Yolen's *The Emperor and the Kite* (World Publishing Company, 1967) or
Nancy Luenn's *The Dragon Kite* (Harcourt Brace Jovanovich, 1982).

Clark, Ann Nolan. *In the Land of Small Dragon.* Illustrated by Tony Chen.
Viking, 1979 (0–670–39697–4). Ann Nolan Clark retells this Cinderella
variant with verses in traditional metric form, sprinkled with proverbs.
The text and illustrations in pen and ink and watercolor tell the tale of
Tam, who, despite her stepsister's trickery, captures the heart of the
Prince with the help of a magical fish and a fairy. Compare to other
versions of Cinderella, such as the Chinese variant in Ai-Ling Louie's

Yeh-Shen (Philomel, 1982). Extend the unit to other Vietnamese tales, such as those retold in Lynette Dyer Vuong's *The Brocaded Slipper* (Addison-Wesley, 1982).

Coerr, Eleanor. *Sadako and the Thousand Paper Cranes.* Illustrated by Ronald Himler. Putnam, 1977 (0–399–20520–9); paper, Dell, 1979 (0–440–47465–5). Because of radiation exposure from the atomic bomb dropped on Hiroshima, 12-year-old Sadako dies of leukemia 10 years after the bomb fell. During the last months of her life, she folds cranes with the hope that when she has folded one thousand she will regain her health. A statue of Sadako holding her golden crane now stands in Hiroshima Peace Park as a symbol of the wish for peace in the world. Sadako's story, told in a straightforward, unsentimental style, will touch the hearts of readers. Discuss with children the symbolism of the crane and extend their understanding through Japanese folklore, such as Sumiko Yagawa's *The Crane Wife* (Morrow, 1981).

Yagawa, Sumiko. *The Crane Wife.* Translated by Katherine Paterson. Illustrated by Suekichi Akaba. Morrow, 1981 (0–688–00496–2); paper, Macmillan, 1987 (0–688–07048–5). After Yohei, a poor peasant, saves the life of a crane, a beautiful woman comes to his hut and begs to become his wife. When Yohei breaks his promise to never look in on his wife as she weaves her exquisite silken cloth, she turns back into a crane and flies away. Akaba beautifully illustrates this picture-book version of one of Japan's favorite tales with water-thinned ink on paper that looks like silken cloth. Compare with other Japanese tales about animals, such as Momoko Ishii's *The Tongue-Cut Sparrow* (Lodestar, 1987) or Davis Pratt and Elsa Kula's *Magic Animals of Japan* (Parnassus, 1967). Extend the unit to variants of the "Crane Wife" tale, such as Molly Bang's *Dawn* (Morrow, 1983).

Grades 5–6

Huynh, Quang Nhuong. *The Land I Lost: Adventures of a Boy in Vietnam.* Illustrated by Vo-Dinh Mai. Harper, 1982 (0–06–024593–X); paper, 1986 (0–06–440183–9). In an autobiographical account, Huynh shares memories of his childhood in Vietnam where he lived on the central highlands in a small hamlet near a riverbank. His experiences with Tank, his pet water buffalo, and his encounters with wild animals, including wild hogs, crocodiles, and snakes, will especially fascinate readers. After reading the book, children may enjoy learning more about the Vietnamese culture through such books as Gail B. Graham's *The Beggar in the Blanket & Other Vietnamese Tales* (Dial, 1970) or Chi Nguyen's *Cooking the Vietnamese Way* (Lerner, 1985).

Lord, Bette Bao. *In the Year of the Boar and Jackie Robinson.* Illustrated by Marc Simont. Harper, 1984 (0–06–024004–0); paper, 1986 (0–06–440175–8). This story takes the reader through a year in the life of Shirley Temple Wong, a young Chinese girl, who moves from Chungking, China, to Brooklyn, New York. Shirley feels lonely at school until she's befriended by a classmate who introduces her to baseball and to Jackie Robinson, who becomes Shirley's hero. Even though she's immersed in American culture, Shirley understands the importance of maintaining her Chinese heritage and language. Compare the experiences of Shirley to those of Jean, who grows up as an American girl living in Hankow, China, in Jean Fritz's *Homesick* (Putnam, 1982). Compare Shirley's love of Jackie Robinson and the Brooklyn Dodgers to that of Sam and Davey in Barbara Cohen's *Thank You, Jackie Robinson* (Lothrop, Lee & Shepard, 1974).

Tsuchiya, Yukio. *Faithful Elephants: A True Story of Animals, People and War*. Translated by Tomoko Tsuchiya Dykes. Illustrated by Ted Lewin. Houghton, 1988 (0-395-4655-9). In this story, first published in Japan in 1951, a zookeeper tells of John, Tonky, and Wanly, elephants at the Ueno Zoo in Tokyo, who, along with other animals, were killed during World War II for fear a bomb would fall on the zoo and the animals would run wild. Expressive watercolor paintings show the frustration and sadness of the zookeepers as they watch the elephants slowly die. This book, along with Toshi Maruki's *Hiroshima No Pika* (Lothrop, Lee & Shepard, 1982) or Marion Dane Bauer's *Rain of Fire* (Clarion, 1983), will create a forum for discussing issues related to war and peace.

Uchida, Yoshiko. *Journey to Topaz: A Story of the Japanese-American Evacuation*. Illustrated by Donald Carrick. Paper, Creative Arts, 1985 (0-916870-85-5). After the Japanese bombing of Pearl Harbor, 11-year-old Yuki and her family are among the 110,000 Japanese Americans evacuated from the West Coast. In this fictionalized account of the author's own experience, readers learn about the tragic evacuation and internment of loyal U.S. citizens. Uchida's sequel, *Journey Home* (Atheneum, 1978), continues the story after the family's release from Topaz. Readers may extend their understanding through Joy Kogawa's *Naomi's Road* (Oxford, 1986) or Sheila Garrigue's *The Eternal Spring of Mr. Ito* (Bradbury, 1985), both novels of the evacuation and relocation of Japanese Canadians. Daniel S. Davis' *Behind Barbed Wire* (Dutton, 1982) will provide readers with factual information.

Yep, Laurence. *Dragonwings*. Harper, 1975 (0-06-026738-0); paper, 1977 (0-06-440085-9). In 1903 eight-year-old Moon Shadow leaves his home in China to join his father in San Francisco's Chinatown. Finally, father and son leave the security of Chinatown and the company to live among the white "demons" so Father can pursue his dream of flying as the Wright Brothers had. Compare Father's act of painting eyes on his plane, Dragonwings, to that of Ch'en Jung painting eyes on his dragon in Margaret Leaf's *Eyes of the Dragon* (Lothrop, Lee & Shepard, 1987). Compare Windrider's Eastern view of dragons to the Western view depicted in Margaret Hodges' retelling of *St. George and the Dragon* (Little, Brown, 1984). Compare Moon Shadow's life in San Francisco with Casey's in Laurence Yep's *Child of the Owl* (Harper & Row, 1977).

ATLANTIC AND PACIFIC ISLAND CULTURES

Grades K–2

Adoff, Arnold. *Flamboyan.* Illustrated by Karen Barbour. Harcourt Brace Jovanovich, 1988 (0–15–228404–4). Beautiful, full-color paintings in watercolor and gouache depict the Caribbean island world of Flamboyan, a young girl named after a tree with flame-red blossoms. The text and illustrations combine to depict Flamboyan's activities, such as gathering eggs, selling oranges and coconut candies with her mother, or resting under her Flamboyan tree. Best of all is Flamboyan's dream of flying like the birds. Readers may enjoy focusing on Flamboyan's appreciation of her natural world, comparing their environments with hers.

Feeney, Stephanie. *Hawaii is a Rainbow.* Photos by Jeff Reese. University of Hawaii Press, 1985 (0–8248–1007–4). The rainbow symbolizes Hawaii – through the vivid colors of the environment and the diversity of its people. This book highlights each of the colors of the rainbow. For example, the word "red" appears in white letters against a red page followed by seven pages of photographs highlighting the color. The pictures emphasize different cultural elements, such as hula dances, the hibiscus (Hawaii's state flower), or the celebration of Kamehameha Day, honoring the king who united the islands. The book's introduction and closing sections offer additional information for adults who share this book with children. For more information about Hawaii, see Stephanie Feeney's *A is for Aloha* (University Press of Hawaii, 1980).

Pomerantz, Charlotte. *The Chalk Doll.* Illustrated by Frané Lessac. Lippincott, 1989 (0–397–32319–0). After tucking her daughter, Rose, into bed for a nap, Mother tells Rose stories about her Jamaican childhood. These include Mother's preference for chalk dolls over rag dolls, her birthday party when she turned seven, and high heels made from mango pits. The book ends with Rose not taking a nap at all but working with her mother to make a rag doll. Full-page, naïve-style paintings beautifully capture scenes from Mother's Jamaican childhood.

Grades 3–4

Bunting, Eve. *How Many Days to America? A Thanksgiving Story.* Illustrated by Beth Peck. Clarion, 1988 (0–89919–521–0). Told from the point of view of a young boy, this picture storybook shows how people from a Caribbean island flee from their homes to seek refuge in America. During their journey they face the perils of being shot at and robbed, as well as running out of food and water. When they come to America, people welcome them and invite them to share in the Thanksgiving feast. Compare the reasons that contemporary refugees such as these seek freedom in America with those of the original Pilgrims through Maricia Sewall's *The Pilgrims of Plimoth* (Atheneum, 1986).

Greenfield, Eloise. *Under the Sunday Tree.* Illustrated by Amos Ferguson. Harper, 1988 (0–06–022257–3). Brightly colored, childlike paintings and accompanying poetry introduce children to life in the Bahamas. Both artist and poet celebrate the people and their island environment, from fishing or sailboat racing to weddings or families together "under the Sunday tree."

Grades 5–6

Berry, James. *A Thief in the Village and Other Stories.* Orchard Books, 1988 (0–531–08345–4). Set on the island of Jamaica, these nine short stories capture the longings and fears of the young protagonists. Becky longs for a bike so she can be part of "The Wheels-and-Brake Boys," while Delroy wants a harmonica so he can be accepted by the "Mouth-Organ Boys." In a more serious story, Elias, a handicapped boy, fears for his own safety and for the life of his pet mongoose as the village boys relentlessly harass him. Readers will feel transported to Jamaica with the author's use of authentic language and sensory details.

Brown, Marcia. *Backbone of the King: The Story of Paka's and His Son Ku.* University of Hawaii Press, 1983 (0–8248–0963–7). In this Hawaiian legend, Ku helps his father regain his rightful place as "backbone of the king." Readers will increase their understanding of early Hawaiian culture, especially the relationship between the people and the environment. A glossary provides definitions and pronunciations for Hawaiian words and phrases. The illustrations in linoleum blocks, based on sketches made on the scene, deepen the emotional response to the story. Compare this story to hero tales from other cultures. Extend the unit to other Hawaiian tales, such as those in Padraic Colum's *Legends of Hawaii* (Yale University Press, 1937).

Thompson, Vivian L. *Hawaiian Mythology of Earth, Sea, and Sky.* Illustrated by Marilyn Kahalewai. Paper, University of Hawaii Press, 1988 (0–8248–1171–2). Through these 12 myths, ancient Hawaiian or Polynesian people share their views of the world with contemporary children. The creation myth describes Kane, god of creation, tossing a calabash to create the earth and sky and finally making the first man out of the rich, red soil. Subsequent stories explain why there is a rainy season or how the Milky Way evolved. Compare these myths to those of other cultures, such as those in Virginia Hamilton's *In the Beginning: Creation Stories from Around the World* (Harcourt Brace Jovanovich, 1988). Also, compare Kamapuaa, the mischief maker, with Loki from the Norse tradition.

HISPANIC CULTURES

Grades K–2

Brown, Tricia. *Hello, Amigos!* Photos by Fran Ortiz. Holt, 1986 (8–8050–0090–9). Black-and-white photographs and text describe the birthday of Frankie Valdez, who lives in the Mission District of San Francisco.

Frankie details the events leading up to his birthday party, then describes the party itself with his favorite Mexican food, traditional music, birthday cake, and piñata full of candy. For background information on birthday celebrations, see Lila Perl's *Candles, Cakes, and Donkey Tails: Birthday Symbols and Celebrations* (Clarion, 1984).

Griego, Margot C., Betsy L. Bucks, Sharon S. Gilbert, and Laurel H. Kimball. *Tortillitas Para Mama and Other Nursery Rhymes.* Illustrated by Barbara Cooney. Holt, 1981 (0–8050–0285–5); paper (0–8050–0317–7). A bilingual selection of nursery rhymes collected from Spanish Americans includes rhymes about chocolate, tortillas, and the moon. Accompanying most of the rhymes are instructions for finger plays or other movement activities. Compare to other nursery rhymes, such as Robert Wyndham's *Chinese Mother Goose Rhymes* (World, 1968) or *Tomie dePaola's Mother Goose* (Putnam, 1985). Extend to Charlotte Pomerantz's *The Tamarindo Puppy and Other Poems* (Greenwillow, 1980), which introduces Spanish words in context.

Maury, Inez. *My Mother the Mail Carrier; Mi mamá la cartera.* Illustrated by Lady McCrady. Translated by Norah E. Alemany. Paper, Feminist Press, 1976. (0–912–67023–1). Five-year-old Lupita tells readers about the special relationship with her mother as well as about her mother's job as a mail carrier. Black-and-white line drawings with touches of brown and yellow support the bilingual text. Further explore jobs in the postal service with Gail Gibbons' *The Post Office Book: Mail and How It Moves* (Crowell, 1982). Extend the unit to the varied careers of mothers with Joe Lasker's *Mothers Can Do Anything.*

Williams, Vera B. *A Chair For My Mother.* Greenwillow, 1982 (0–688–00915–8); paper, Morrow, 1988 (0–688–08400–1). This story about a Hispanic family centers around Rosa. After a fire destroys everything they own, relatives and neighborhood friends help Rosa, her mother, and grandmother start over. In order to buy the luxury of an easy chair, they all save coins in a big glass jar. The book's expressionistic illustrations are particularly noteworthy, especially the borders which symbolize important events in the story. Children may continue to read about Rosa in *Something Special For Me* (Greenwillow, 1983) and *Music, Music for Everyone* (Greenwillow, 1984), which complete Vera B. Williams' "Bread and Roses Trilogy."

Grades 3–4

Cameron, Ann. *The Most Beautiful Place in the World.* Illustrated by Thomas B. Allen. Knopf, 1988 (0–394–99463–9). Seven-year-old Juan tells readers about his life in San Pablo, Guatemala, where he lives with his grandmother and three unmarried uncles. Grandmother earns her living selling *arroz con leche* in the market, while Juan contributes to the household expenses by earning $1 per day shining shoes. At the end of the story, Juan realizes his dream of attending school. Compare Juan's experiences to Lito's in David Mangurian's *Lito the Shoeshine Boy* (Four Winds, 1975).

Mohr, Nicholasa. *Felita.* Illustrated by Ray Cruz. Dial, 1979 (0–8037–3144–2). Felita Maldonado, the youngest in a Puerto Rican American family, narrates this story about growing up in an urban neighborhood. When the Maldonado family moves to a new neighborhood with better schools, they face racial prejudice and finally, out of fear for their own safety, move back to the Puerto Rican community. The author's use of details to describe Felita's neighborhood and the sprinkling of Spanish words in context create an authentic story. Compare Felita's reaction to rejection by peers with Wanda's in Eleanor Estes's *The Hundred Dresses* (Harcourt, Brace, 1944).

Williams, Vera B. and Jennifer Williams. *Stringbean's Trip to the Shining Sea.* Greenwillow, 1988 (0–688–07162–7). Each day, as Stringbean and his brother Fred travel from Kansas to the Pacific Ocean, they send their family a postcard. The postcards, along with photographs and drawings, describe their trip in detail, including visits to a buffalo ranch, silver mine, and circus. Children might use this unique book as a model for writing postcards about their own journeys, real or imaginary.

Grades 5–6

De Trevino, Elizabeth Borton. *El Guero.* Illustrated by Leslie W. Bowman. Farrar, 1989 (0–374–31995–2). From memories shared with the author, De Trevino weaves this story about the boyhood of her father-in-law, El Guero. When Mexico's new president exiles the De Trevino family to Baja, California, they face a harsh life, especially when outlaws imprison the father, a judge. Because El Guero has learned many survival skills from two new friends, he successfully treks over the mountains to La Paz to save his family. Authentic details woven into the narrative help create an exciting example of historical fiction about Mexico in the late 1800s.

Krumgold, Joseph. *And Now Miguel.* Illustrated by Jean Charlot. Harper, 1953 (0–690–04696–0); paper, 1984 (0–06–440143–X). Twelve-year-old Miguel is a member of the multigenerational Chavez family, who own a sheep ranch near Taos, New Mexico. Caught between childhood and adulthood, Miguel struggles to prove to his father that he is a competent sheep man. Compare Miguel's account of sheep raising with Dorothy Hinshaw Patent's in *The Sheep Book* (Dodd, Mead, 1985).

Walker, Paul Robert. *Pride of Puerto Rico: The Life of Roberto Clemente.* Harcourt, 1988 (0–15–200562–5). This fictionalized biography captures the life of Roberto Clemente, one of Puerto Rico's greatest heroes. The account begins with eight-year-old Roberto playing baseball on a muddy field and continues with his rise to stardom as an outfielder for the Pittsburgh Pirates. The author includes Clemente's feelings of frustration over racial discrimination as well as the pride he felt in representing Puerto Rico. Extend this unit to other nonfiction books, such as Harvey Frommer's *A Hundred and Fiftieth Anniversary Album of Baseball* (Watts, 1988) or Lawrence S. Ritter's *The Story of Baseball* (Morrow, 1983).

Wolf, Bernard. *In This Proud Land: The Story of a Mexican American Family.* Harper, 1978 (0–397–32268–2). Text and large, black-and-white photographs describe several months in the lives of the Hernandez family of Pharr, Texas. Part of this documentary describes how the family unites to earn money as migrant workers during the summer on a sugar beet farm in Minnesota. Wolf effectively shows the courage and strength of this proud Hispanic family, even in the face of prejudice, inequality, and poverty.

NATIVE AMERICAN CULTURES

Grades K–2

Aliki. *Corn is Maize: The Gift of the Indians.* Harper, 1976 (0–690–00975–5); paper 1986 (0–06–445026–0). Through this nonfiction book, children will learn about the discovery of corn, how Indian tribes planted and used corn, and how corn continues to be an important crop. Aliki also describes uses for husks and cobs, including directions for making a cornhusk wreath.

Andrews, Jan. *Very Last First Time.* Illustrated by Ian Wallace. Macmillan, 1986 (0–689–50388–1). Young Eva Padlyat, who lives in a village on Ungava Bay in northern Canada, undergoes initiation into her Inuit culture when she walks alone on the bottom of the sea for the very first time. In the winter when the tide is out, women lower themselves below the ice and walk on the seabed collecting mussels. Wallace's watercolor paintings, which effectively capture the eerie landscape under the ice, also depict life in a contemporary Inuit community.

Baylor, Byrd. *When Clay Sings.* Illustrated by Tom Bahti. Macmillan, 1972 (0–684–18829–5); paper, 1987 (0–689–71106–9). In poetic language, Byrd Baylor describes how pottery, molded and painted by prehistoric Indian groups of the American Southwest, "sings" about the culture that made it. The illustrations in shades of brown, tan, and gray are designs from actual prehistoric Indian pottery preserved in museums. Extend the unit to other Byrd Baylor books, such as *The Desert is Theirs* (Scribner, 1975) or *I'm in Charge of Celebrations* (Scribner, 1986).

dePaola, Tomie. *The Legend of the Bluebonnet: An Old Tale of Texas.* Putnam, 1983 (0–399–20937–9); paper, 1983 (0–399–20938–7). This pourquoi tale, based on a Comanche Indian legend, explains the origin of the bluebonnet, the Texas state flower. When She-Who-Is-Alone learns that the Great Spirits demand a sacrifice of the tribe's most valued possession, the young girl burns her warrior doll. This burnt offering ends the drought and, as a sign of forgiveness, the blue flowers grow where the doll's ashes had been scattered. Full-page paintings capture the hardship caused by the drought, as well as the beauty of the hills covered with bluebonnets. Compare this tale with Tomie dePaola's *The Legend of the Indian Paintbrush* (Putnam, 1988), a Plains Indian tale about the origin of another state flower.

Goble, Paul. *Iktomi and the Boulder: A Plains Indian Story.* Orchard, 1988 (0–531–08360–8). In a story about Iktomi, a Sioux Indian trickster, a storyteller explains why rocks are scattered around the Great Plains and why bats have flat faces. The format of the book invites participation. Iktomi's thoughts, scattered around the India ink and watercolor illustrations, add an additional dimension to the text, while italic text encourages listeners to comment on Iktomi's antics. Continue to read about Iktomi's adventures in *Iktomi and the Berries* (Orchard, 1989).

Grades 3–4

Baker, Olaf. *Where the Buffaloes Begin.* Illustrated by Stephen Gammell. Paper, Penguin, 1985 (0–14–05060–1). This Plains Indian legend tells about the mystical lake where the buffaloes began. When young Little Wolf goes to gaze at this lake, the buffaloes finally emerge and follow the young boy back to his camp where they save his people by trampling the approaching enemy. Gammell's soft, black-and-white paintings effectively capture the mythical quality of the text. Compare this tale about the buffalo to Paul Goble's *The Great Race* (Bradbury, 1985) or *Buffalo Woman* (Bradbury, 1984). Learn more about the importance of the buffalo to the Plains Indians in Russell Freedman's *Buffalo Hunt* (Holiday House, 1988) or Cary B. Ziter's *The Moon of Falling Leaves: The Great Buffalo Hunt* (Watts, 1988).

Bierhorst, John. *Doctor Coyote: A Native American Aesop's Fables.* Illustrated by Wendy Watson. Macmillan, 1987 (0–02–709780–3). Twenty fables, which Aztec Indians adapted in the 1500s from a Spanish translation of Aesop, describe the antics of Coyote, a common Native American trickster. The tales are interconnected, showing Coyote growing a little wiser with each new adventure. Watson's watercolor illustrations depict Coyote in a contemporary setting. Compare these fables to those of Aesop, or compare Coyote's experiences with Nanabush's in *The Adventures of Nanabush* (Atheneum, 1980), compiled by Emerson and David Coatsworth.

Curtis, Edward S. *The Girl Who Married a Ghost and Other Tales from the North American Indian.* Macmillan, 1978 (0–02–709740–4). Originally published in Curtis's *The North American Indian* (Johnson Reprint Corporation, 1970), these nine tales represent Indian tribes in the United States and Canada. The tales include myths, a ghost story, a trickster tale, and a campfire yarn. Curtis's soft, brown-toned photographs greatly enhance the text of each tale. Compare Monster-Slayer and Child-of-the-Water's search for their father in "How the World Was Saved" with Gerald McDermott's *Arrow to the Sun* (Viking, 1974). Extend the unit to George Bird Grinnell's *The Whistling Skeleton: American Indian Tales of the Supernatural* (Four Winds, 1982).

De Armond, Dale. *The Seal Oil Lamp.* Little, 1988 (0–316–17786–5). An Eskimo man and his wife rejoice in the birth of their son, Allugua. When the people of the village discover that the boy is blind, they force the parents to follow Eskimo law and leave the boy behind to die. However, Mouse Woman and the other mouse people bring the boy food and keep him safe until his people return. Mouse Woman's last gift to the boy is a magic hunting song through which he can attract animals who will allow themselves to be killed. He then can support himself and his village by becoming one of his people's greatest whalers. The text and black-and-white wood engravings will help children appreciate Eskimo culture. Extend the unit to Terry Tempest Williams and Ted Major's *The Secret Language of Snow* (Sierra Club/Pantheon Books, 1984).

Miles, Miska. *Annie and the Old One.* Illustrated by Peter Parnall. Little, 1972 (0-316-57117-2); paper, 1985 (0-316-57120-2). When Grandmother tells her family that she will die when the weaving is taken from the loom, young Annie tries to hold back time by removing strands of yarn from the woven rug. Annie finally accepts the fact that her grandmother will die when she sensitively explains that the cycle of nature always includes life and death. The illustrations in black, white, and gold show the expanse of the surrounding desert. Compare Annie's relationship with her grandmother with that of Tommy in Tomie dePaola's *Nana Upstairs & Nana Downstairs* (Putnam, 1973).

Grades 5–6

Freedman, Russell. *Indian Chiefs.* Holiday, 1987 (0-8234-0625-3). This collective biography, enhanced by many photographs, portraits, and paintings, describes the lives of six chiefs who led their people in the latter half of the 1800s when European Americans were advancing toward Indian hunting grounds. As European American hide hunters slaughtered millions of buffalo, the Indian leaders and their people were forced onto reservations. Freedman discusses how each Indian chief, including Red Cloud, Satanta, Quanah Parker, Washakie, Joseph, and Sitting Bull, chose to resist or cooperate with white officials. Extend the unit to Paul Goble's *Red Hawk's Account of Custer's Last Battle* (Pantheon, 1969) or Dee Brown's *Wounded Knee: An Indian History of the American West* (Holt, Rinehart and Winston, 1974) adapted by Amy Ehrlich.

George, Jean Craighead. *Julie of the Wolves.* Illustrated by John Schoenherr. Harper, 1972 (0-06-021944-0); paper, 1974 (0-06-440058-1). Thirteen-year-old Miyax, whose English name is Julie Edwards, runs away from her husband and becomes lost on the North Slope of Alaska. Because her father had taught her many of the survival skills of the Eskimo culture, Miyax survives with the help of a wolf pack which finally accepts her and offers her food and protection. When Miyax returns to civilization, she has to choose between giving up her heritage or adapting to the ways of the contemporary Eskimo. Compare Julie's search for self with Russel Susskit's in Gary Paulsen's *Dogsong* (Bradbury, 1985). Extend the unit to Scott O'Dell's *Black Star, Bright Dawn* (Houghton Mifflin, 1988), where the hero gains a better sense of self through her competition in the grueling Iditarod dogsled race.

O'Dell, Scott. *Sing Down the Moon.* Houghton, 1970 (0–395–10919–1); large-print edition, ABC CLIO, 1989 (1–55736–142–8). Bright Morning of the Navajo tribe narrates her own story of how the Long Knives (European American soldiers) drove thousands of Navajo from their homes to Bosque Redondo, a gray flatland near Fort Sumner. Many people died on the Long Walk and others died during captivity of smallpox and other diseases. Pregnant and longing for freedom, Bright Morning prods her young husband to escape and return to their home at Canyon de Chelly. Trace the Navajo and other tribes' struggle to retain their cultural identities from the turn of the century to the present in Brent Ashabranner's *To Live in Two Worlds: American Indian Youth Today* (Dodd, Mead, 1984) or Arlene Hirschfelder's *Happily May I Walk: American Indians and Alaskan Natives Today* (Scribner's, 1986).

O'Dell, Scott. *Streams to the River, River to the Sea: A Novel of Sacagawea.* Houghton, 1986 (0–395–40430–4). Sacagawea, a member of the Shoshone tribe, tells her own story from the time she was captured by the Minnetaree tribe through her dangerous journey exploring the Louisiana territory with Lewis and Clark. At the end of the journey, Sacagawea must choose between her Shoshone heritage and life in European American society with her beloved Captain Clark. Compare this version of the Lewis and Clark expedition with Charles Bohner's *Bold Journey* (Houghton Mifflin, 1985) or Rhoda Blumberg's *The Incredible Journey of Lewis and Clark* (Lothrop, Lee & Shepard, 1987).

Sneve, Virginia Driving Hawk. *Dancing Teepees: Poems of American Indian Youth.* Illustrated by Stephen Gammell. Holiday, 1989 (0–8234–0724–1). The reader of this poetry anthology hears many Native American voices, including that of Black Elk of the Lakota Sioux in "The Life of a Man Is a Man Is a Circle" or a Paiute mother in "Coo . . . Ah . . . Coo!," a cradle song. Gammell's paintings add to the authenticity of the text, whether he's re-creating the sand paintings of the Navajo or the bead work of the Sioux. Extend this unit to additional poetry in *The Sacred Path: Spells, Prayers and Power Songs of the American Indians* (Morrow, 1983) edited by John Bierhorst.

A SAMPLING OF EUROPEAN CULTURES: ITALIAN, GERMAN, POLISH, AND SCANDINAVIAN

Grades K–2

Cauley, Lorinda Bryan. *The Pancake: An Old Norwegian Folk Tale.* Putnam, 1988 (0–399–21505–0). After the pancake jumps out of the frying pan and rolls away from Goody Poody's hungry family, it continues rolling by others who want to eat it, such as Henny Penny, Cocky Locky, and Ducky Lucky, until it meets clever Piggy Wiggy. Children will be attracted to the cumulative text and brightly colored illustrations. A recipe for sweet-milk pancakes precedes the story. Compare this tale to other variants, such as the "Gingerbread Man," "Johnny Cake," or "Wee Bannock."

dePaola, Tomie. *Big Anthony and the Magic Ring.* Harcourt, 1979 (0–15–207124–5). After Big Anthony sees Strega Nona use a magic ring and a special song to transform herself into a beautiful lady, Big Anthony waits for a chance to borrow the ring. As in other Strega Nona books, Big Anthony soon learns that magic, at least when he uses it, brings unexpected results. The naïve-style illustrations and sprinkling of Italian words help readers appreciate the Calabrian setting. Continue to read about the adventures of Strega Nona and Big Anthony in *Strega Nona* (Prentice-Hall, 1975), *Strega Nona's Magic Lessons* (Harcourt Brace Jovanovich, 1982), and *Merry Christmas, Strega Nona* (Harcourt Brace Jovanovich, 1986).

Hertz, Ole. *Tobias Has a Birthday.* Translated from Danish by Tobi Tobias. Carolrhoda, 1984 (0–87614–261–7). This story is set in a small village in Greenland, a province of Denmark. Twelve-year-old Tobias has a traditional birthday celebration. His father hoists the flag onto their house and Tobias and his sister invite the entire village to the party. When the guests arrive, they take turns drinking coffee, eating cake, and listening to Grandmother's stories. Black-and-white line drawings with touches of watercolor and a map of Tobias' village help orient readers to Greenlandic culture. Learn more about Tobias' way of life in *Tobias Goes Ice Fishing* (Carolrhoda, 1984) or *Tobias Catches Trout* (Carolrhoda, 1984).

Sandin, Joan. *The Long Way to a New Land.* Harper, 1981 (0–06–025194–8); paper, 1986 (0–06–444100–8). After a severe drought in Sweden during the summer of 1868, Carl Erik's family decides to emigrate to the United States. The easy-to-read text and watercolor illustrations detail the family's journey from their farm in Sweden to New York. A sequel, *The Long Way Westward* (Harper & Row, 1989), traces the family's journey from New York to Anoka, Minnesota. Each book includes a map of the journey as part of the title page.

Zelinsky, Paul O. *Rumpelstiltskin.* Dutton, 1986 (0–525–44265–0). Zelinsky has referred to the 1819 Grimm version to retell this tale of the miller's daughter who bargains with a strange little man to spin straw into gold. The luminous oil paintings show landscapes and interiors of a late-medieval setting. Compare this version to other variants, such as "Tom Tit Tot," "Duffy and the Devil," or "Trillevip." Extend the unit to other picture book editions of German tales, such as *Hansel and Gretel* (Dodd, Mead, 1984) retold by Rika Lesser, *The Bremen-Town Musicians* (Doubleday, 1980) retold by Isle Plume, or *The Pied Piper of Hamelin* (Lippincott, 1987) retold by Barbara Bartos-Hoppner.

Grades 3–4

De Gerez, Toni. *Louhi, Witch of North Farm.* Illustrated by Barbara Cooney. Penguin, 1986 (0–670–80556–4); paper, 1988 (0–14–050529–6). This tale, taken from the Finnish national epic, the *Kalevala,* centers on Louhi, the Witch of North Farm. Louhi, bored by the thought of everyday tasks, steals the sun and the moon when they come down from the sky to listen to Vainamoinen's beautiful music. Vainamoinen and Seppo, the smith, find a way to convince Louhi to give light back to the world. Beautiful, full-page paintings show many details of the Finnish setting. Compare to the Greek myth "Persephone and Demeter."

dePaola, Tomie. *Tony's Bread.* Putnam, 1989 (0–399–21693–6). With his invention of panettone, Tony realizes his dream of becoming the most famous baker in northern Italy. Angelo, who helps set up Tony in his own bakery in Milan, also gets his dream when he marries Tony's daughter, Serafina. Full-color illustrations and Italian words and phrases enhance this literary folktale. Extend the unit to other Tomie dePaola stories with Italian settings, such as *The Prince of the Dolomites* (Harcourt Brace Jovanovich, 1980) or *The Mysterious Giant of Barletta* (Harcourt Brace Jovanovich, 1984).

Estes, Eleanor. *The Hundred Dresses.* Illustrated by Louis Slobodkin. Harcourt, 1944 (0–15–237374–8); paper, 1974 (0–15–642350–2). Because a Polish American family feels unwelcome in a small community, they move to a big city where their name, Petronski will not be such an oddity. Wanda Petronski's classmates do not see her as a person with her own feelings and talents until she wins the school color contest with her 100 drawings of beautiful dresses. By then, it is too late; Wanda has moved away. The story will encourage children to confront their own prejudices.

Nilsson, Ulf. *If You Didn't Have Me.* Translated by Lone and George Blecher. Illustrated by Eva Eriksson. Macmillan, 1987 (0–689–50406–3). A young boy and his baby brother spend a summer at their grandma's farm in southern Sweden while Mama and Papa build a house in town. The story, tightly focused around the boy's point of view, tells of the boy's adventures with the farm animals, his special relationship with Edwin, the hired hand, and his imaginative play. Extend the unit to another story of a young Swedish boy with Maria Gripe's *Elvis and His Secret* (Dell, 1979).

Vogel, Ilse-Margaret. *Tikhon.* Harper, 1984 (0–06–026329–6). After World War I, many Russian soldiers, stranded in Germany without discharge papers or identification, had to rely on the generosity of the German people, their former enemies. When Inge's father brings home Tikhon, a Russian "illegal alien," young Inge befriends him. Together they learn each other's language, write and draw, and most of all admire the Zobten Mountain, which reminds Tikhon of his native Russia. This sensitively written book shows how a special friendship can overcome cultural differences.

Grades 5–6

D'Aulaire, Ingri and Edgar. *D'Aulaire's Norse Gods & Giants.* Paper, Doubleday, 1986 (0–385–23692–1). This collection of 30 myths, based on the ancient *Poetic* and *Prose Eddas* texts, brings to life the Norse gods, giants, and monsters. The stories, telling of the nine worlds of Odin, begin with the creation of the world and end with the gods' destruction on Ragnarokk, the day of reckoning. The illustrations add to the reader's understanding and enjoyment of the text. A reader's companion gives phonetic pronunciations as well as literal and ancient definitions of Norse words. Compare the Norse myths to the Greek with *D'Aulaire's Book of Greek Myths* (Doubleday, 1962).

Hartling, Peter. *Crutches.* Translated by Elizabeth D. Crawford. Lothrop, 1988 (0–688–0799–1). A homeless boy and a one-legged man befriend each other during the chaos in Austria and Germany after World War II. The touching relationship between Thomas and Crutches grows from companionship to friendship and finally to love as they struggle to survive. Drawing from his own experiences as a child, the author has written an authentic story woven around historical events and full of the details of daily life.

Little, Jean. *From Anna.* Illustrated by Joan Sandin. Harper, 1972 (0–06–023912–3); paper, 1973 (0–06–440044–1). In 1933 when the German government increasingly denied its citizens personal freedoms, the Solden family emigrated from Frankfurt to Toronto, Canada. This sudden change becomes an important turning point in nine-year-old Anna Solden's life. Anna, whose awkwardness has been a mystery to her parents, is diagnosed as being visually impaired. Anna goes to a special school where she has time to learn English, relate to peers, and gain self-confidence. Through this story, readers will gain insight into the challenges of adjusting to a new culture, as well as to the problems faced by a child with a disability.

Lowry, Lois. *Number the Stars.* Houghton, 1989 (0–395–51060–0). In 1943 Danish citizens helped nearly 7,000 Jewish Danes escape to Sweden. This novel centers around 10-year-old Annemarie Johansen and her Jewish friend, Ellen Rosen. Annemarie, who feels that she'd never be called upon for courage, saves the Rosen family as they are being smuggled out of Denmark. Compare to Carol Matas' *Lisa's War* (Scribner's 1987), which tells the story of Jewish teenagers involved in the Danish Resistance.

Pellowski, Anne. *First Farm in the Valley: Anna's Story.* Illustrated by Wendy Watson. Putnam, 1982 (0–399–20887–9). This story, set in a Polish settlement near Arcadia, Wisconsin, in the late 1870s, captures the daily life of Anna Pellowski. Anna grows up in a large Polish American family where English is not learned until the children enter school. The author, who has based the book on the childhood experiences of her great aunt, includes many details of rural life, including the special ways these Polish Americans celebrate holidays. Stories based on later generations of this family may be read in *Winding Valley Farm: Annie's Story* (Philomel, 1982) and *Willow Wind Farm: Betsy's Story* (Philomel, 1981).

KIT # 5
Sibley's Selected Trade Books
for Language Development Activities

LEARNING LANGUAGE FOR SURVIVAL–
IN AND OUT OF THE CLASSROOM

Aliki. *My Five Senses.* Harper, 1962 (0–690–56763–4); paper, 1984 (0–06–445009–0). A young boy describes the five senses with examples for each. Then he plays a mental game which involves guessing how many senses he uses. For example, playing with his puppy, he uses four senses–seeing, hearing, smelling, and touching. The simple words and childlike pictures will encourage readers to appreciate their immediate environment.

Anno, Mitsumasa. *Anno's Counting Book.* Harper, 1977 (0–690–01288–8); paper, 1986 (0–06–443123–1). Children count more details on each spread as the time, seasons, and years change. To reinforce the counting, a large numeral on the right side corresponds to the same number of multicolored blocks on the left. This sophisticated book invites children to create their own stories for each page.

Aylesworth, Jim. *One Crow: A Counting Rhyme.* Illustrated by Ruth Young. Lippincott, 1988 (0–397–32175–9). A 0 to 10 counting rhyme presents animals and children on a farm in two seasons–summer and winter. For example, 10 children play games on a grassy meadow; later the same number sleigh down a snow-covered hillside. Large numerals stand beside the text.

Bang, Molly. *Ten, Nine, Eight.* Greenwillow, 1983 (0–688–00907–7); paper, Penguin, 1985 (0–14–050543–1). By using the objects in her bedroom, a young African American girl and her father count down from 10 to 1. Children will soon memorize this rhyming text illustrated with warm domestic scenes in full color.

Barrett, Judith. *Animals Should Definitely Not Wear Clothing.* Macmillan, 1970 (0–689–20592–9); paper, 1974 (0–689–70412–7). With animals modeling clothing, this hilarious story introduces children to the bizarre. When children laugh at the comic inappropriateness of a giraffe wearing a neckful of ties, they demonstrate their understanding of the appropriate uses of clothing.

Brenner, Barbara. *Bodies.* Photos by George Ancona. Dutton, 1973 (0–525–26770–0). Black-and-white photographs of numerous human bodies highlight the special qualities of individuals. The text introduces terms that make us similar–*bellybutton* and *flesh*–as well as ones that make us unique–*fingerprints* and *cells.* The book reminds children that each human body possesses a unique mind.

Brenner, Barbara. *Faces.* Photos by George Ancona. Dutton, 1970 (0–525–

29518–6). Black-and-white photographs and a poetic text celebrate human faces seeing, hearing, smelling, and tasting. Once again Brenner emphasizes diversity of detail while presenting common human characteristics.

Burningham, John. *John Burningham's Opposites.* Crown, 1986 (0–517–55963–3). A young boy introduces opposite words in humorous situations. For example, on a page labeled *dry,* the boy and a cat hold pails of water; on the facing page labeled *wet,* they throw the water at each other. Children might create their own antonym pairs after reading this book.

Burton, Marilee Robin. *Tail, Toes, Eyes, Ears, Nose.* Harper, 1989 (0–06–020874–0). Using eight familiar animals, the pictures and text playfully teach important body parts. Children solve puzzles by guessing what animals they should visualize from the parts. The book concludes with a mystery puzzle bringing all eight animals together.

Carle, Eric. *The Grouchy Ladybug.* Harper, 1977 (0–690–01392–2); paper, 1986 (0–06–443116–9). After first watching the sun rise and fall in the sky, children turn die-cut pages to discover the grouchy ladybug at different hours of the day. A tiny clock in each right hand corner marks the hour and the repeating pattern of the text encourages children to participate in the unfolding story.

Goor, Ron and Nancy. *Signs.* Harper, 1983 (0–690–04355–4). Fifty signs commonly found in a city appear in black-and-white photographs. Concluding games either match signs with appropriate pictures or signs with their opposites. Other excellent books are Tana Hoban's *I Read Signs* (Greenwillow, 1983), *I Read Symbols* (Greenwillow, 1983), and *I Walk and Read* (Greenwillow, 1984).

Hoban, Tana. *Is It Red? Is It Yellow? Is It Blue?* Greenwillow, 1978 (0–688–84171–6). City photographs of people and objects varying in shape, size, and color can teach geometric patterns and shades of color. Children might count objects, match colors, or describe city activities.

Hughes, Shirley. *Alfie's Feet.* Lothrop, 1983 (0–688–01660–X); paper, Morrow, 1988 (0–688–07812–5). In a story all about feet and the fun children can have in rubber rain boots, young Alfie buys new yellow boots but puts them on the wrong feet. Despite this he enjoys splashing and stamping until his father discovers why he is so uncomfortable. Children will identify with Alfie's enjoyment and learn about his mistake.

Maestro, Betsy and Giulio. *Harriet Reads Signs and More Signs.* Crown, 1981 (0–517–54167–X); paper, 1984 (0–517–55305–8). As Harriet the elephant skates through the city on her way to Grandma's house, she reads many signs. For example, she stops before the crosswalk when she sees the sign "don't walk," skates around the hole in the road labeled "danger," and mails her letter at the box labeled "U.S. Mail." Large-size print, simple text, and bold colors will attract beginning readers.

McMillan, Bruce. *Becca Backward, Becca Frontward: A Book of Concept Pairs.* Lothrop, 1986 (0–688–06283–0). Large, color photographs of a young girl illustrate antonyms basic to a child's vocabulary. For example, one page shows Becca jumping above her bed and the opposite page shows her playing below it. Some of the other concept pairs introduced include bottom and top, whole and half, and small and big.

McMillan, Bruce. *Growing Colors.* Lothrop, 1988 (0–688–07845–1). Photographs of common fruits and vegetables in their natural environmerts introduce colors. Each spread contains a large photograph of the fruit or vegetable, a smaller photograph showing how the plant grows, and the name of the fruit or vegetable printed in capital letters. A chart in the back of the book identifies the name of each fruit and vegetable included in the book. Refer also to Lois Ehlert's *Eating the Alphabet: Fruits and Vegetables From A to Z* (Harcourt Brace Jovanovich, 1989) for its alphabetical format.

Parnwell, E. C. *The New Oxford Picture Dictionary.* Oxford University Press, 1988 (0–19–434199–2). Through 2,400 words on 82 topics, students are introduced to basic vocabulary needed for getting along in an English-speaking country. On each page words appear below the full-color illustrations and are numbered to correspond to the items in the picture. An index lists all the vocabulary words and includes a pronunciation guide. Some of the topics in the dictionary are the human body, the supermarket, rooms of the house, and items in a classroom. Illustrations show people of many ethnic groups and women and men in nonstereotypical roles.

Roy, Ron. *Whose Hat Is That?* Photos by Rosemarie Hausherr. Clarion, 1987 (0–89919–446–X). The text and black-and-white photographs invite readers to participate. A photograph shows a child wearing a hat and asks a question such as "Who wears a hat shaped like a turtle's shell?" Readers then turn the page where a photograph shows builders at work, and the text briefly describes why they wear hard hats. The book introduces children to 18 types of hats and encourages role playing about careers. For a more humorous look at hats, see *Martin's Hats* (Morrow, 1984) by Joan W. Blos.

Serfozo, Mary. *Who Said Red?* Illustrated by Keiko Narahashi. Macmillan, 1988 (0–689–50455–1). A young boy who likes red searches the countryside for his lost kite with his sister. A predictable question/answer sequence and watercolor paintings introduce children to many colors.

Sis, Peter. *Waving: A Counting Book.* Greenwillow, 1988 (0–688–07160–0). On a multiracial city street Mary's mother waves for a taxi. A counting sequence begins when two bicyclists wave to Mary and her mother. Three boys wave to the bicyclists, four girls wave to the boys, until we reach "fifteen taxi drivers waving at everybody waving at them."

Winthrop, Elizabeth. *Shoes.* Illustrated by William Joyce. Harper, 1986 (0–06–026592–2); paper, 1988 (0–06–443171–1). In this humorous, rhyming text, children wear many kinds of shoes in different seasons and circumstances. The concluding rhyme–"made especially for the heat –your very own skinny-boned, wiggly-toed FEET"–will surely delight readers.

SCHOOL EXPERIENCES

Ahlberg, Janet and Allan. *Starting School.* Viking, 1988 (0–6707–82175–6). Large-size text integrated with small color pictures depict the activities of eight children during their first four months at school. Readers encounter every aspect of school—from bathrooms and book corners to exercises in the gym and units on rabbits. Whether happy or sad, puzzled or sleepy, the children survive until Christmas vacation.

Burningham, John. *The School.* Harper, 1975 (0–690–00903–8). With matching text and cartoon-style pictures, this book may prompt children to read on their own. While at school, a young boy learns to read and write, paints pictures, makes friends, and plays games.

Cohen, Miriam. *Starring First Grade.* Illustrated by Lillian Hoban. Greenwillow, 1985 (0–688–04029–2); paper, Dell, 1987 (0–440–48250–X). A multiethnic first-grade class experiences the whole process of play production. After the teacher chooses the cast for "The Three Billy Goats Gruff," the students learn to cooperate as they rehearse, write an advertisement, and prepare for opening night.

Cohen, Miriam. *Will I Have A Friend?* Illustrated by Lillian Hoban. Macmillan, 1967 (0–02–722790–1); paper, 1986 (0–689–71141–7). Although Jim's pa assures him he will make a friend on his first day of school, Jim doubts he will. As Jim shyly watches, the other children work and play among themselves. Finally Jim finds his friend when Paul shows him his tiny truck.

Crews, Donald. *School Bus.* Greenwillow, 1984 (0–688–02808–X); paper, Penguin, 1985 (0–14–050549–0). Bold, color illustrations show different kinds of school buses sitting in the parking lot, picking up students, and delivering them safely home.

Schwartz, Amy. *Annabelle Swift, Kindergartner.* Orchard Books, 1988 (0–531–08337–3). Annabelle Swift starts kindergarten eager to follow her older sister's advice, but almost everything goes wrong. When Mr. Blum holds up a light blue color, she calls it an eye shadow shade—blue desire. She finally succeeds because her sister taught her to count money. Amazed that she can correctly count the milk money, Mr. Blum sends her to the cafeteria to bring back milk for the whole class.

CHILDREN AT HOME

Barton, Byron. *Building a House.* Greenwillow, 1981 (0–688–80291–5); paper, Penguin, 1984 (0–14–050470–2). Full-color illustrations show all the steps of house building from bulldozing to painting. Children see bricklayers, carpenters, plumbers, and painters all working on the house.

Jonas, Ann. *Where Can It Be?* Greenwillow, 1986 (0–688–05246–0). This predictable text invites readers to help a young girl search for her lost blanket. By opening flaps children look in a closet, cupboard, kitchen cabinet, and even inside the refrigerator.

Rockwell, Harlow. *My Kitchen.* Greenwillow, 1980 (0–688–84236–4). A young boy leads readers on a tour of his kitchen. By labeling the refrigerator, the cupboards, and the stove where he warms some soup, he explains how he makes his lunch.

Rogers, Fred. *Moving.* Photos by Jim Judkis. Putnam, 1987 (0–399–21383–X); paper (0–399–21384–8). Large, color photographs help TV's Mister Rogers discuss all aspects of moving from one home to another. In particular, he reassures children about the sad feelings and fears that often accompany moving.

Van Der Meer, Ron and Atie. *Pigs at Home: A Picture Word Book.* Macmillan, 1988 (0–689–71232–4). Labeled cartoon illustrations follow a pig family during a busy day at home. Within the large spreads showing the pigs eating dinner or tinkering in the garbage, readers wind small flaps covering tiny items in cupboards, closets, and drawers. Richard Brown's *100 Words about My House* (Harcourt Brace Jovanovich, 1988) is also recommended.

ACTIVITIES WITH FAMILY MEMBERS

Caines, Jeannette. *Daddy.* Illustrated by Ronald Himler. Harper, 1977 (0–06–020924–0). This book discusses the loving relationship between an African American girl and her remarried father. When she visits Daddy and her stepmother Paula, they color, read books, or play dress-up together; but when she returns home she worries until he comes for her again.

Clifton, Lucille. *Everett Anderson's Nine Month Long.* Illustrated by Ann Grifalconi. Holt, 1978 (0–8050–0287–1). Still adjusting to a new stepfather, Everett must now cope with his mother's pregnancy. At times he looks forward to the new baby, but sometimes he fears his mother will not have enough love to go around. A poetic text enhances the subtle emotions of this African American family. Other excellent books are Eloise Greenfield's *She Come Bringing Me That Little Baby Girl* (Lippincott, 1974) and Mildred Pitts Walter's *My Mama Needs Me* (Lothrop, Lee & Shepard, 1983).

Douglass, Barbara. *Good As New.* Illustrated by Patience Brewster. Lothrop, 1982 (0–688–51983–0). After Grady's spoiled cousin completely ruins his favorite stuffed bear, his grandpa offers to remake the toy completely. He must remove all the stuffing, scrub the bear in a sinkful of suds, and sew all the parts together while Grady anxiously watches. Happy about his grandfather's success, Grady says, "I thought you could fix anything. But this bear isn't good as new. . . . It's better than new!"

Hayes, Sarah. *Eat Up, Gemma.* Illustrated by Jan Ormerod. Lothrop, 1988 (0–688–08149–5). Although Mom, Dad, and Grandma repeatedly exclaim "Eat up, Gemma," she will not. Only her brother can figure out an ingenious way to entice her to eat. Finally this loving black family watches Gemma devour a whole bowl of fruit.

Johnson, Angela. *Tell Me a Story, Mama.* Illustrated by David Soman. Orchard, 1989 (0–531–08394–2). An African American girl and her mother enjoy storytelling together about the mother's childhood. Since the child enjoys retelling the very stories she asks to hear, both can share the pleasures of listening and telling. Beautiful watercolor paintings also distinguish this first book for author and illustrator.

Long, Earlene R. *Gone Fishing.* Illustrated by Richard Brown. Houghton, 1984 (0–395–35570–2); paper, 1987 (0–395–44236–2). Easy-to-read text and watercolor illustrations contrast big and little as a young boy and his father spend a day fishing. "Big daddy" and "little me" have a "big breakfast" or use a "little fishing rod." The adventure ends in equality as daddy and son each catch a "big" and a "little" fish.

Ormerod, Jan. *Sunshine.* Lothrop, 1981 (0–688–00553–5); paper, Penguin, 1984 (0–14–050362–5). Awakened by the sunshine, a young girl goes into her parents' bedroom and kisses her father awake. She eats breakfast, dresses for school, and finally walks into the bright sunshine with her mother. Watercolor illustrations convey these morning rituals without words. Also see Jan Ormerod's *Moonlight* (Lothrop, Lee & Shepard, 1982) for its depiction of evening routines at home.

Rockwell, Anne. *I Like the Library.* Dutton, 1977 (0–525–32528–X). A mother and son pay their weekly visit to the public library. While she browses in the adult department, he attends a story hour, watches a filmstrip in the children's room, and selects his own material to check out.

Scott, Ann Herbert. *On Mother's Lap.* Illustrated by Glo Coalson. McGraw-Hill, 1972 (0–07–055897–3). In a small Eskimo village, Michael loves to sit on his mother's lap and rock "back and forth, back and forth." As he adds doll, boat, reindeer blanket, puppy, even baby sister, they discover there's always room on mother's lap.

ACTIVITIES WITH FRIENDS

Aliki. *We Are Best Friends.* Greenwillow, 1982 (0–688–00823–2). Extensive use of dialogue and letters makes this story about two best friends, who each must make new friends when one moves away, an excellent stimulus for readers' theatre. The childlike illustrations perfectly complement the boys' disappointments, anticipations, or joys.

Blegvad, Lenore. *Anna Banana and Me.* Illustrated by Erik Blegvad. Macmillan, 1985 (0–689–50274–5); paper, 1987 (0–689–71114–X). Fearless, carefree Anna Banana encourages a timid young boy to overcome fear. Full-color cityscape paintings present Anna Banana swinging high in the park, braving shadowy dark hallways, or telling scary goblin stories until her friend finds his courage: "I'm just as brave as Anna Banana!"

Keats, Ezra Jack. *A Letter to Amy.* Harper, 1968 (0–06–023109–2); paper, 1984

(0–06–443063–4). Peter worries more about whether his friend Amy will attend his birthday party than about whether the boys will tease him for inviting a girl. With watercolor and collage, Keats shows Peter accidentally causing Amy to fall into a slippery, watery scene the moment before he mails her invitation. The party succeeds when Amy arrives just in time for his blowing out the candles.

Keller, Holly. *Goodbye, Max.* Greenwillow, 1987 (0–688–06562–7). Only Zach, Ben's loyal friend, can help him express the grief he feels when his dog Max dies. Together they share stories about Max and cry about his loss. Only then can Ben accept the new dog his parents brought home.

Rogers, Fred. *Making Friends.* Photos by Jim Judkis. Putnam, 1987 (0–399–21382–1); paper, 1987 (0–399–21385–6). With color photographs and instructive text, Mister Rogers advises children about friendship and the activities friends can share. He urges them to seek adult advice in case problems among friends become overwhelming. In an introduction, he reminds parents that children often learn to interact among themselves by imitating adults.

Williams, Vera B. *Music, Music for Everyone.* Greenwillow, 1984 (0–688–02604–4); paper, Morrow, 1988 (0–688–07811–7). Williams concludes the Rosa trilogy by having the young girl form the Oak Street Band with her friends. Rosa on accordion, Leora on drums, Mae on flute, and Jenny on fiddle celebrate the anniversary of the neighborhood store. Rosa's music helps this multicultural neighborhood have fun together.

EARLY CHILDHOOD EXPERIENCES

Ahlberg, Janet and Allan. *The Baby's Catalogue.* Little, Brown, 1983 (0–316–02037–0); paper, 1986 (0–316–02038–9). Readers follow six babies through a catalog of daily routines. The babies play with toys and games, take baths, or interact with other family members. Labels accompany each humorous scene.

Ahlberg, Janet and Allan. *Peek-a-Boo!* Viking, 1981 (0–670–54598–8); paper, Penguin, 1984 (0–14–050107–X). This picture book ingeniously turns a question-and-answer format into a game of peek-a-boo. Predictable text and illustrations invite readers to peek at a scene on the next spread through a cutout circle. After turning the page, they answer a question about the scene, which depicts the daily activities of a baby and his busy family.

Caines, Jeannette. *Abby.* Illustrated by Steven Kellogg. Harper, 1973 (0–06–020922–4); paper, 1984 (0–06–443049–9). Abby's big brother Kevin helps her read and enjoy her own baby book. Together they remember the day she was adopted and grow so close that he wishes to bring her to school for show-and-tell. Kellogg's black-and-white illustrations create a cozy city apartment for this African American family.

Rogers, Fred. *The New Baby.* Photos by Jim Judkis. Putnam, 1985 (0–399–

21236–1); paper, 1985 (0–399–21238–8). Focusing on an African American family and a white one, Mister Rogers assures children they will still be loved when a new baby arrives. Color photographs show children growing accustomed to the new babies in several situations.

Rylant, Cynthia. *Birthday Presents*. Illustrated by Susie Stevenson. Orchard Books, 1987 (0–531–08305–5). Large watercolor paintings with small family snapshots create a birthday memory book. Through her parents' stories, a five-year-old relives her past birthdays, even the day she was born.

CHILDREN'S GAMES

Brown, Marc, ed. *Finger Rhymes*. Dutton, 1980 (0–525–29732–4). Marc Brown and his son Tucker select their 14 favorite finger rhymes to share with children. On a double-page spread, tiny diagrams demonstrate each finger play. A large, black-and-white drawing illustrates a scene for each rhyme, familiar ones such as, "Five Little Pigs," and "The Eensy, Weensy Spider" and less familiar ones, such as "Fish Story," and "Ten Little Candles," both counting rhymes.

Brown, Marc, ed. *Hand Rhymes*. Dutton, 1985 (0–525–44201–4). A companion to *Finger Rhymes,* this collection offers readers 14 rhymes accompanied by hand games. Clear diagrams give directions for animating each poem. Full-color illustrations add to the fun and humor. Many of the rhymes could be incorporated into seasonal or holiday units, such as "Jack-o'-Lantern" for Halloween, "Snowflakes" for winter, and "The Caterpillar" for spring.

Hoguet, Susan R. *I Unpacked My Grandmother's Trunk: A Picture Book Game*. Dutton, 1983 (0–525–44069–0). Full-color illustrations present this alphabet game. From Grandmother's trunk on the far right side of each spread come objects, people, or animals. Children will enjoy noticing the antics of the people and animals interacting with one another and with the objects emerging from the trunk.

Rockwell, Anne. *Games (and How to Play Them)*. Harper, 1973 (0–690–32160–0). A collection of 43 games offers children hours of entertainment both at school and at home. Humorous watercolor illustrations accompany straightforward directions for each game. Each picture includes visual puns adding to the fun of the book; for example, rabbits play "Hopscotch" in Scottish garb. Many games, including "I Love My Love," "Forfeits," or "Gossip," support language learning. Also recommended is Marc Brown's *Party Rhymes* (Dutton, 1988).

HOLIDAY AND PARTY ACTIVITIES

Adler, David A. *A Picture Book of Jewish Holidays*. Illustrated by Linda Heller. Holiday House, 1981 (0–8234–0396–3). A poetic text and soft, color illustrations emphasize the feelings of Jewish people celebrating their holidays and traditions—including the Sabbath, Yom Kippur, Hanukkah, and Passover. A glossary at the end of the book defines terms unfamiliar to non-Jewish readers.

Brown, Tricia. *Chinese New Year.* Photos by Fran Ortiz. Holt, 1987 (0–8050–0497–1). Readers learn how families in San Francisco's Chinatown celebrate the Chinese New Year, a spring festival over 5,000 years old. Black-and-white photographs depicting the arrangement of spring flowers, a New Year's Eve family banquet, or the dragon parade present some of the customs connected with this holiday. Children could discuss how the Chinese New Year combines elements associated with other American holidays. Especially because of the authentic paper cutout illustrations, readers should experience Hou-Tien Cheng's *Chinese New Year* (Holt, Rinehart and Winston, 1976).

Brown, Tricia. *Hello, Amigos!* Photos by Fran Ortiz. Holt, 1986 (0–8050–0090–9). This photo essay describes the birthday of Frankie Valdez, who lives in the Mission District of San Francisco. Although Frankie's family speaks Spanish at home, he learns English at school. The book dramatizes Frankie's day at school, his after-school activities at the Boy's Club, and finally his long-awaited birthday party. Family, friends, and neighbors enjoy eating their favorite Mexican food, listening to ethnic music, and watching Frankie break the piñata. The glossary will aid pronunciation and define Spanish words.

dePaola, Tomie. *The Family Christmas Tree Book.* Holiday House, 1980 (0–8234–0416–1); paper, 1984 (0–8234–0535–4). Both text and naïve-style paintings will inform readers about the tree decorating customs of mid-eighteenth-century German immigrants. A family chooses their own Christmas tree, decorates it at home, and describes Christmas lore. The book provides an excellent opportunity for discussing holiday customs of ethnic groups.

dePaola, Tomie. *Things to Make and Do for Valentine's Day.* Watts, 1976 (0–531–01187–9); paper, Scholastic, 1985 (0–590–11821–8). This book provides children with directions for numerous Valentine's Day activities—designing and printing Valentine's cards, making sandwiches and desserts for a party, or having a relay race. The text and childlike illustrations will not only help children plan a Valentine's party but also give them practice in following directions.

Friedrich, Priscilla and Otto. *The Easter Bunny that Overslept.* Illustrated by Adrienne Adams. Lothrop, 1983 (0–688–01541–7). Because the Easter Bunny oversleeps one cloudy, rainy Easter, he delivers no eggs to the expectant children. Finally, waking up on Mother's Day in May, he finds no one wants his Easter eggs. Readers follow him through other holidays until he meets Santa Claus and helps him make and deliver Christmas toys. Through a unique and humorous story, the book provides readers with an excellent overview of many holidays important to Americans.

Gibbons, Gail. *Thanksgiving Day.* Holiday, 1983 (0–8234–0489–7); paper, 1985 (0–8234–0576–1). Simple text and bright, full-color illustrations introduce children to the Thanksgiving holiday. The book provides historical background about the first Thanksgiving feast between the Pilgrims and

Native Americans and compares present and past Thanksgiving celebrations.

Hayes, Sarah. *Happy Christmas, Gemma.* Illustrated by Jan Ormerod. Lothrop, 1986 (0–688–06508–2). A family of Jamaican origin prepare for their family Christmas celebration. While the brother makes pudding, puts up decorations, and wraps presents, his baby sister makes messes, pulls off Christmas tree decorations, and tears up gift labels. Full-color illustrations enhance this humorous story about a closely knit family.

Rice, Eve. *Benny Bakes a Cake.* Greenwillow, 1981 (0–688–84312–3); paper, Morrow, 1988 (0–688–07814–1). On his birthday, Benny helps his mother bake his cake. The large-size text and illustrations show the steps of cake baking, including the recipe, ingredients, and utensils needed. Another fine book is Anne and Harlow Rockwell's *Happy Birthday to Me* (Macmillan, 1981).

SEASONAL AND WEATHER-RELATED ACTIVITIES

Gibbons, Gail. *Weather Forecasting.* Macmillan, 1987 (0–02–737250–2). Through text and carefully labeled illustrations, readers learn about the instruments used in forecasting weather and the work people do at a weather station. Common weather terms, such as "chilly," "drizzle," or "blizzard," highlight the forecasts for each season. Children will learn weather terms heard on radio and television.

Gundersheimer, Karen. *Happy Winter.* Harper, 1982 (0–06–022173–9); paper, 1987 (0–06–443151–7). A child describes the outdoor and indoor pleasures she and her sister enjoy during the winter season. At times they dress in bulky clothes, play in the snow, and make snow angels. Sometimes they read books, make up nonsense rhymes, or help mother bake a cake. The book includes the recipe for Happy Winter Fudge Cake.

Hughes, Shirley. *When We Went to the Park.* Lothrop, 1985 (0–688–04204–X). On a crisp autumn day, as a young girl and her grandfather walk through the park, they enjoy the beauty of the fall-colored trees and the scrunching sound of the leaves. They count the things they see; the end sheets give the reader a chance to count all of the people and animals met in the park.

Keats, Ezra Jack. *The Snowy Day.* Viking, 1962 (0–670–65400–0); paper, Penguin, 1976 (0–14–050182–7). Peter, a young African American boy, enjoys the wonders of fresh snow. The simple text and collage-style illustrations show him making tracks, smacking a snow-covered tree, building a snowman, making snow angels, or sliding. The book will complement science lessons, creative dramatics, and art activities. Also recommended is John Burningham's *The Snow* (Crowell, 1975) about a mother and child at play.

Skofield, James. *All Wet! All Wet!* Harper, 1984 (0–06–025752–0). On a rainy day a young boy dressed in yellow slicker and boots explores a nearby meadow and woods. Cutaways show foxes in their burrows or rabbits snuggling underground until the rain stops and the boy heads home.

Spier, Peter. *Peter Spier's Rain.* Doubleday, 1982 (0–385–15485–2); paper, 1987 (0–385–24105–4). A brother and sister in rain gear splash through their neighborhood and discover the wonders of a rainy world. They see a spider web dripping with water, birds huddled in their nests, and wave at their own reflections in a mud puddle. After the wind comes up, they spend the rest of the day playing inside. Children will enjoy creating their own text for this wordless book.

Tresselt, Alvin. *Hide and Seek Fog.* Lothrop, 1965 (0–686–77907–X); paper, Morrow, 1988 (0–688–07813–3). Summer activities in a seaside village change when a heavy fog rolls in and engulfs the village in grayness for three days. First sailboats creep home, swimmers trudge back to their cottages, and the lobsterman heads for shore. Then villagers mend buoys and lobster pots, play hide-and-seek, or read at home. Expressionistic gouache paintings help readers see the fog and feel its dampness.

Udry, Janice M. *Moon Jumpers.* Illustrated by Maurice Sendak. Harper, 1959 (0–06–026145–5). On a moonlit summer night, children play tag, tell ghost stories, and jump higher and higher trying to reach the "balloon of a moon." Sendak captures the mood of these scenes through alternating black-and-white drawings with text and full-color spreads without words.

Yashima, Taro. *Umbrella.* Viking, 1958 (0–670–73858–1); paper, Penguin, 1977 (0–14–050240–8). Momo, a Japanese American child, receives red rubber boots and an umbrella on her third birthday but must wait a long time before the rain makes wonderful music on her umbrella. When she walks in the rain, she feels grown up for the first time. Expressionistic paintings and authentic Japanese characters distinguish this story.

SHOPPING AND BUYING

Freeman, Don. *Corduroy.* Viking, 1968 (0–670–24133–4); paper, Penguin, 1976 (0–14–050173–8). While shopping with her mother in a large department store, a young African American girl wants to buy a small bear, even though he has lost a button from his corduroy overalls. The next day she buys Corduroy with the money from her own piggy bank and makes him very happy when she sews a new button on his overalls.

Hoban, Tana. *26 Letters and 99 Cents.* Greenwillow, 1987 (0–688–06362–4). Color photographs of soft-touch numbers and letters dominate this "double" book. Children learn to recognize both sides of coins and to count pennies, nickels, dimes, and quarters. The alphabet photographs match familiar objects with each upper- and lowercase letter.

Rockwell, Anne and Harlow. *The Supermarket.* Macmillan, 1979 (0–02–777580–1). A young boy and his mother grocery shop for many items including the ingredients for his birthday cake. Pastel illustrations show advertisements, prices, and labels. Children will also enjoy John Burningham's *The Shopping Basket* (Crowell, 1980) for its humorous look at a boy's grocery shopping experience.

Williams, Vera B. *A Chair for My Mother.* Greenwillow, 1982 (0–688–00915–8); paper, 1984 (0–688–04074–8). After a fire destroys most of what they own, a Hispanic daughter, mother, and granddaughter save enough coins to buy a new easy chair. When their money jar is full, they shop in four different stores before they find the perfect chair. Borders, which frame the watercolor illustrations, highlight the events on each page.

Williams, Vera B. *Something Special for Me.* Greenwillow, 1983 (0–688–01807–6); paper, Morrow, 1987 (0–688–06526–0). In this sequel to *A Chair for My Mother,* Grandma and Mama let Rosa buy a special present for her birthday. After a whole day of shopping, Rosa spends her money on a used accordion. Children will share Rosa's frustration and excitement as she tries to decide what to buy.

Ziefert, Harriet. *A New Coat for Anna.* Illustrated by Anita Lobel. Knopf, 1986 (0–394–97426–3); paper, 1988 (0–394–89861–3). After World War II, Anna's mother barters several of her beloved possessions to get her daughter a new coat. She trades Grandfather's watch for the wool, a lamp for the spinning, a necklace for the weaving, and a porcelain pot for the sewing. For its depiction of bartering, refer to Elsa Beskow's *Pelle's New Suit* (Gryphon House, 1979).

TRAVEL AND TRANSPORTATION

Barton, Byron. *Airport.* Harper, 1982 (0–690–04169–1); paper, 1987 (0–06–443145–2). Bold, color illustrations and a boldface text present a group of people arriving at an airport, checking in, going through security, and finally boarding an airplane. Also see Donald Crews' *Flying* (Greenwillow, 1986), which shows a flight from takeoff to landing.

Brown, Richard. *100 Words About Transportation.* Harcourt, 1987 (0–15–200551–X). Illustrations and labels teach children 100 different terms about transportation. Themes such as "in the city" or "in an emergency" introduce the words subway, taxi, ambulance, and fire truck. The back cover of the book alphabetically lists all 100 words.

Caines, Jeannette. *Just Us Women.* Harper, 1982 (0–06–020941–0); paper, 1984 (0–06–443056–1). Aunt Martha and her young niece take an automobile trip to North Carolina all by themselves. Along the way they stop at roadside markets, walk in the rain, and eat in a fancy restaurant. Readers share the journey through worm's-eye or bird's-eye views.

Cole, Joanna. *Cars and How They Go.* Illustrated by Gail Gibbons. Harper, 1983 (0–690–04262–0); paper, 1986 (0–06–446052–5). A simple text, labeled diagrams, and cutaway illustrations teach children the terminology for the moving parts of a car. The picture on the back of the book jacket labels all the parts—such as crankshaft, rear axle, piston—previously discussed.

Gibbons, Gail. *Fill It Up! All About Service Stations.* Harper, 1985 (0–690–04440–2); paper, 1986 (0–06–446051–7). Readers get a close-up look at a busy service station. They see customers pumping gas, mechanics doing repairs, and even a hydraulic lift operating. A concluding diagram labels many of the tools used by station workers.

Maestro, Betsy and Giulio. *Traffic: A Book of Opposites.* Crown, 1981 (0–517–54427–X). Readers follow the journey of a little pink car through a city into the countryside to its final destination. Both the simple text and bold color illustrations introduce words with opposite meanings, such as slow and fast, empty and full, and far and near.

Robbins, Ken. *City-Country: A Car Trip in Photographs.* Viking, 1985 (0–670–80743–5). From a child's backseat perspective, readers participate in a car trip, leaving behind the city skyscrapers on the way to the country back roads and small towns, finally arriving at the sea or up in the mountains. The text and hand-colored, black-and-white photographs encourage children to relive their own vacation journeys made by automobile.

Sattler, Helen R. *Train Whistles: A Language in Code.* Illustrated by Giulio Maestro. Revised edition, Lothrop, 1985 (0–688–03980–4). Onomatopoetic language teaches the importance of train whistles. Readers learn about freight and passengers trains, various railroad jobs, and special equipment, such as cranes and forklifts. In addition, the book ends with a list of common railroad signals.

HEALTH, ILLNESSES, AND EMERGENCIES

Brown, Marc and Stephen Krensky. *Dinosaurs, Beware! A Safety Guide.* Little, 1982 (0–316–11228–3); paper, 1984 (0–316–11219–4). This book provides children with safety tips in 14 different situations. As the text offers straightforward advice, the illustrations show dinosaurs humorously dealing with each predicament. For instance, they cope with fire emergencies, visits from strangers, and playground mishaps.

Gibbons, Gail. *Fire! Fire!* Harper, 1984 (0–690–04416–X); paper, 1987 (0–06–446058–4). Children see fire fighters saving apartments, forests, and waterfronts. Illustrations label the different types of fire-fighting equipment. Charts at the end of the book suggest ways to prevent fires and rules for fire safety.

Rockwell, Harlow. *My Dentist.* Greenwillow, 1975 (0–688–84004–3). A young girl gets her teeth checked and cleaned at the dentist's office. Illustrations and a simple text introduce the dentist's equipment to the reader. Children will see much of the equipment dentists use.

Rogers, Fred. *Going to the Doctor.* Photos by Jim Judkis. Putnam, 1988 (0–399–21503–4); paper, 1988 (0–399–21530–1). Color photographs show health care facilities and doctors examining young patients. The text encourages children to ask questions about the doctor's instruments and the examination itself. Italics emphasize important terms, such as waiting room, examination table, and stethoscope. Another fine book is Harlow Rockwell's *My Doctor* (Macmillan, 1973), for its even closer look at a doctor's instruments.

KIT # 6
Sibley's List of Predictable Books
for Emerging Readers

ADVENTURES WITH ANIMALS

Brooke, L. Leslie. *Johnny Crow's Garden.* Warne, 1986 (0–7232–3429–9).

Brown, Margaret Wise. *Where Have You Been?* Illustrated by Barbara Cooney. Hastings, 1952 (0–8038–9292–6); paper, Scholastic, 1984 (0–590–71408–2).

Brown, Ruth. *A Dark, Dark Tale.* Dial, 1981 (0–8037–1673–7); paper, 1984 (0–8037–0093–8).

Carle, Eric. *Have You Seen My Cat?* Picture Book Studio, 1987 (0–88708–054–5); paper, Putnam, 1988 (0–399–21597–2).

Carle, Eric. *The Very Busy Spider.* Putnam, 1984 (0–399–21166–7); paper, 1989 (0–399–21592–1).

Conover, Chris. *Six Little Ducks.* Harper, 1976 (0–690–01037–0).

Ets, Marie Hall. *Play With Me.* Penguin, 1955 (0–670–55977–6); paper, 1976 (0–14–050178–9).

Gag, Wanda. *The ABC Bunny.* Putnam, 1933 (0–698–20000–4); paper, 1978 (0–698–20465–4).

Gerstein, Mordicai. *Roll Over!* Crown, 1984 (0–517–55209–4).

Ginsburg, Mirra. *The Chick and the Duckling.* Illustrated by Jose and Ariane Aruego. Macmillan, 1972 (0–02–735940–9); paper, 1988 (0–689–71226–X).

Ginsburg, Mirra. *Good Morning, Chick.* Illustrated by Byron Barton. Greenwillow, 1980 (0–688–84284–4); paper, Morrow, 1989 (0–688–08741–8).

Hill, Eric. *Where's Spot?* Putnam, 1987 (0–399–21478–X).

Hogrogian, Nonny. *One Fine Day.* Paper, Macmillan, 1974 (0–02–043620–3).

Hutchins, Pat. *Good-Night Owl.* Macmillan, 1972 (0–02–745900–4).

Hutchins, Pat. *The Surprise Party.* Macmillan, 1986 (0–02–745930–6).

Inkpen, Mick. *If I Had a Sheep.* Little, Brown, 1988 (0–316–41888–9).

Kalan, Robert. *Jump, Frog, Jump.* Illustrated by Byron Barton. Greenwillow, 1981 (0–688–84271–2).

Langstaff, John. *Over in the Meadow.* Illustrated by Feodor Rojankovsky. Harcourt, 1957 (0–15–258854–X); paper, 1973 (0–15–670500–1).

Matthias, Catherine. *I Love Cats.* Illustrated by Tom Dunnington. Children's Press, 1983 (0–516–02041–2); paper, 1983 (0–516–42041–0).

McGovern, Ann. *Too Much Noise.* Illustrated by Simms Taback. Houghton
 Mifflin, 1967 (0–395–18110–0); paper, Scholastic, 1992 (0–395–62985–3).
Stadler, John. *Cat at Bat.* Dutton, 1988 (0–525–44416–5).
Tafuri, Nancy. *Have You Seen My Duckling?* Greenwillow, 1984 (0–688–
 02798–9); paper, Penguin, 1986 (0–14–050532–6).
Tafuri, Nancy. *Spots, Feathers, and Curly Tails.* Greenwillow, 1988 (0–688–
 07537–1).
Wells, Rosemary. *Noisy Nora.* Dial, 1973 (0–8037–6638–6); paper, 1980 (0–
 8037–6193–7).

CONCEPTS

Carle, Eric. *The Grouchy Ladybug.* Harper, 1977 (0–690–01392–2); paper,
 1986 (0–06–443116–9).
Carle, Eric. *The Very Hungry Caterpillar.* Putnam, 1989 (0–399–21933–1).
Domanska, Janina. *Busy Monday Morning.* Greenwillow, 1985 (0–688–03834–
 4).
Duke, Kate. *The Guinea Pig ABC.* Dutton, 1983 (0–525–44058–5); paper, 1986
 (0–525–44274–X).
Eichenberg, Fritz. *Ape in a Cape: An Alphabet of Odd Animals.* Harcourt, 1952
 (0–15–203722–5); paper, 1988 (0–15–607830–9).
Giganti, Paul. *How Many Snails?* Illustrated by Donald Crews. Greenwillow,
 1988 (0–688–06370–5).
Mack, Stan. *Ten Bears in My Bed.* Pantheon, 1974 (0–394–92902–0).
Martin, Bill. *Brown Bear, Brown Bear, What Do You See?* Illustrated by Eric
 Carle. Holt, 1983 (0–8050–0201–4).
Ormerod, Jan. *Young Joe.* Lothrop, 1985 (0–688–04210–4).
Sendak, Maurice. *Chicken Soup with Rice.* Harper, 1962 (0–06–025535–8);
 paper, Scholastic, 1986 (0–590–41033–4).
Sendak, Maurice. *One Was Johnny.* Harper, 1962 (0–06–025540–4).
Shaw, Charles G. *It Looked Like Spilt Milk.* Harper, 1988 (0–06–025565–X);
 paper, 1988 (0–06–443159–2).
Ward, Cindy. *Cookie's Week.* Illustrated by Tomie dePaola. Putnam, 1988 (0–
 399–21498–4).
Watanabe, Shigeo. *How Did I Put It On?* Illustrated by Yasuo Ohtomo. Put-
 nam, 1980 (0–399–20761–9); paper, 1984 (0–399–21040–7).

FOLKLORE, POETRY, AND SONGS

Ahlberg, Janet and Allan. *Each Peach Pear Plum.* Penguin, 1979 (0–670–
 28705–9); paper, 1986 (0–14–050639–X).
Domanska, Janina. *If All the Seas Were One Sea.* Macmillan, 1987 (0–02–
 732540–7).
Galdone, Paul. *The Gingerbread Boy.* Houghton, 1979 (0–395–28799–5); **paper,**
 1983 (0–89919–163–0).

Galdone, Paul. *The Little Red Hen.* Houghton, 1979 (0–395–28803–7); paper, Ticknor, 1985 (0–89919–349–8).

Galdone, Paul. *The Three Bears.* Houghton, 1979 (0–395–28811–8); paper, Ticknor, 1985 (0–89919–401–X).

Galdone, Paul. *The Three Billy Goats Gruff.* Houghton, 1979 (0–395–28812–6); paper, Ticknor, 1981 (0–89919–035–9).

Galdone, Paul. *Three Little Kittens.* Ticknor, 1986 (0–89919–426–5); paper, 1988 (0–89919–796–5).

Galdone, Paul. *The Three Little Pigs.* Houghton, 1979 (0–395–28813–14); paper, Ticknor, 1984 (0–89919–275–0).

Hale, Sarah. *Mary Had a Little Lamb.* Illustrated by Tomie dePaola. Holiday, 1984 (0–8234–0509–5); paper, 1984 (0–8234–0519–2).

Heilbroner, Joan. *This is the House Where Jack Lives.* Illustrated by Aliki. Harper, 1962 (0–06–022286–7).

Ivimey, John W. *The Complete Story of the Three Blind Mice.* Illustrated by Paul Galdone. Ticknor, 1987 (0–89919–481–8); paper, Houghton, 1989 (0–395–51585–8).

Langstaff, John. *Oh, A-Hunting We Will Go.* Illustrated by Nancy Winslow Parker. Macmillan, 1974 (0–689–50007–6).

Martin, Sarah. *The Comic Adventures of Old Mother Hubbard and Her Dog.* Illustrated by Tomie dePaola. Harcourt, 1981 (0–15–219541–6); paper, 1981 (0–15–219542–4).

Nerlove, Miriam. *I Made a Mistake.* Macmillan, 1985 (0–689–50327–X).

Ormerod, Jan. *The Story of Chicken Licken.* Lothrop, 1986 (0–688–06058–7).

Pearson, Tracey Campbell. *Old MacDonald Had a Farm.* Dial, 1984 (0–8037–0070–9); paper, 1986 (0–8037–0274–4).

Spier, Peter. *London Bridge is Falling Down.* Doubleday, 1985 (0–385–08717–9); paper, 1989 (0–385–08025–5).

Westwood, Jennifer. *Going to Squintum's: A Foxy Folktale.* Illustrated by Fiona French. Dial, 1985 (0–8037–0015–6).

Zemach, Margot. *Hush, Little Baby.* Dutton, 1987 (0–525–44296–0); paper, 1987 (0–525–44297–9).

GOOD TIMES

Bayer, Jane. *A My Name is Alice.* Illustrated by Steven Kellogg. Dial, 1984 (0–8037–0124–1); paper, 1987 (0–8037–0130–6).

Brown, Ruth. *The Big Sneeze.* Lothrop, 1985 (0–688–04666–5).

Burningham, John. *Mr. Gumpy's Outing.* Holt, 1971 (0–8050–0708–3); paper, Penguin, 1984 (0–14–050254–8).

Burningham, John. *Would You Rather . . .* Harper, 1978 (0–690–03917–4).

DeRegniers, Beatrice Schenk. *What Can You Do with a Shoe?* Illustrated by Maurice Sendak. Harper, 1955 (0–06–024850–5).

Ets, Marie Hall. *In the Forest.* Penguin, 1944 (0–670–39687–7); paper, 1976 (0–14–050180–0).

Hawkins, Colin and Jacqui. *How Many Are in This Old Car? A Counting Book.* Putnam, 1988 (0–399–21565–4).

Hoguet, Susan Ramsay. *I Unpacked My Grandmother's Trunk.* Dutton, 1983 (0–525–44069–0).

Martin, Bill and John Archambault. *Up and Down on the Merry-Go-Round.* Illustrated by Ted Rand. Holt, 1988 (0–8050–0681–8).

Raffi. *Down by the Bay.* Illustrated by Nadine Bernard Westcott. Crown, 1987 (0–517–56644–3).

Raskin, Ellen. *Ghost in a Four-Room Apartment.* Paper, Macmillan, 1978 (0–689–70446–1).

Scheer, Julian. *Rain Makes Applesauce.* Illustrated by Marvin Bileck. Holiday, 1964 (0–8234–0091–3).

Segal, Lore. *All the Way Home.* Illustrated by James Marshall. Farrar, 1973 (0–374–30215–4); paper, 1988 (0–374–40355–4).

Seuss, Dr. *Green Eggs and Ham.* Beginner Books, 1960 (0–394–90016–2).

Silverstein, Shel. *Giraffe and a Half.* Harper, 1964 (0–06–025656–7).

Slobodkina, Esphyr. *Caps for Sale: A Tale of a Peddler, Some Monkeys and Their Monkey Business.* Harper, 1947 (0–06–025778–4); paper, 1987 (0–06–443143–6).

Westcott, Nadine Bernard. *I Know an Old Lady Who Swallowed a Fly.* Little, 1980 (0–316–93128–4); paper, 1980 (0–316–93127–6).

Westcott, Nadine Bernard. *The Lady with the Alligator Purse.* Little, 1988 (0–316–93135–7).

Wood, Audrey. *King Bidgood's in the Bathtub.* Illustrated by Don Wood. Harcourt, 1985 (0–15–242730–9).

Wood, Audrey. *The Napping House.* Illustrated by Don Wood. Harcourt, 1984 (0–15–256708–9).

MYSELF, MY FAMILY, MY FRIENDS

Ahlberg, Janet and Allan. *Peek-a-Boo!* Penguin, 1981 (0–670–54598–8); paper, 1984 (0–14–050107–X).

Aliki. *At Mary Bloom's.* Greenwillow, 1983 (0–688–02481–5); paper, Penguin, 1978 (0–14–050278–5).

Aliki. *My Five Senses.* Harper, 1962 (0–690–56763–4); paper, 1984 (0–06–445009–0).

Bang, Molly. *Ten, Nine, Eight.* Greenwillow, 1983 (0–688–00907–7); paper, Penguin, 1985 (0–14–050543–1).

Bauer, Caroline Feller. *My Mom Travels a Lot.* Illustrated by Nancy Winslow Parker. Paper, Penguin, 1985 (0–14–050545–8).

DeRegniers, Beatrice Schenk. *May I Bring a Friend?* Illustrated by Beni Montresor. Macmillan, 1964 (0–689–20615–1); paper, 1989 (0–689–71353–3).

Ets, Marie Hall. *Just Me.* Paper, Penguin, 1978 (0–14–050325–0).

Gerstein, Mordicai. *William, Where Are You?* Crown, 1985 (0–517–55644–8).

Gomi, Taro. *Coco Can't Wait!* Paper, Penguin, 1985 (0–14–050522–9).

Hoff, Syd. *Who Will Be My Friends?* Harper, 1960 (0–06–022556–4); paper, 1985 (0–06–444072–9).

Hutchins, Pat. *Happy Birthday, Sam.* Greenwillow, 1978 (0–688–84160–0); paper, Penguin, 1985 (0–14–050339–0).

Hutchins, Pat. *Titch.* Macmillan, 1971 (0–02–745880–6).

Isadora, Rachel. *I Hear.* Greenwillow, 1985 (0–688–04062–4).

Isadora, Rachel. *I See.* Greenwillow, 1985 (0–688–04060–8).

Isadora, Rachel. *I Touch.* Greenwillow, 1985 (0–688–04256–2).

Jonas, Ann. *Where Can It Be?* Greenwillow, 1986 (0–688–05246–0).

Kellogg, Steven. *Can I Keep Him?* Dial, 1971 (0–8037–0989–7); paper, 1976 (0–8037–1305–3).

Krauss, Ruth. *The Carrot Seed.* Illustrated by Crockett Johnson. Harper, 1945 (0–06–023351–6); paper, 1989 (0–06–443210–6).

Levinson, Riki. *I Go with My Family to Grandma's.* Illustrated by Diane Goode. Dutton, 1986 (0–525–44261–8).

Martin, Bill and John Archambault. *Here Are My Hands.* Illustrated by Ted Rand. Holt, 1987 (0–8050–0328–2); paper, 1989 (0–8050–1168–4).

McDaniel, Becky Bring. *Katie Couldn't.* Illustrated by Lois Axeman. Children's Press, 1985 (0–516–02069–2); paper, 1985 (0–516–42069–0).

McDaniel, Becky Bring. *Katie Did It.* Illustrated by Lois Axeman. Children's Press, 1983 (0–516–02043–9); paper, 1983 (0–516–42043–7).

McKissack, Patricia C. *Who is Who?* Illustrated by Elizabeth M. Allen. Children's Press, 1983 (0–516–02042–0); paper, 1983 (0–516–42042–9).

Neasi, Barbara J. *Just Like Me.* Illustrated by Lois Axeman. Children's Press, 1984 (0–516–02047–1); paper, 1984 (0–516–42047–X).

Ormerod, Jan. *This Little Nose.* Lothrop, 1987 (0–688–07276–3).

Scott, Ann Herbert. *On Mother's Lap.* Illustrated by Glo Coalson. McGraw, 1972 (0–07–055897–3).

Simon, Nora. *I Know What I Like.* Illustrated by Dora Leder. Whitman, 1971 (0–8075–3507–9).

Simon, Norma. *What Do I Say?* Illustrated by Joe Lasker. Whitman, 1969 (0–8075–8823–7).

Viorst, Judith. *Alexander and the Terrible, Horrible, No Good, Very Bad Day.* Illustrated by Ray Cruz. Macmillan, 1972 (0–689–30072–7); paper, 1989 (0–689–71350–9).

Waber, Bernard. *Ira Sleeps Over.* Houghton, 1973 (0–395–13893–0); paper, 1975 (0–395–20503–4).

Wells, Rosemary. *A Lion for Lewis.* Dial, 1982 (0–8037–4686–5); paper (0–8037–0096–2).

Zolotow, Charlotte. *Do You Know What I'll Do?* Illustrated by Garth Williams. Harper, 1958 (0–06–026940–5).

Zolotow, Charlotte. *The Hating Book.* Illustrated by Ben Shecter. Harper, 1969 (0–06–026923–5); paper, 1989 (0–06–443197–5).

Zolotow, Charlotte. *If It Weren't For You.* Illustrated by Ben Shecter. Harper, 1987 (0–06–026943–X).

Zolotow, Charlotte. *Someday.* Illustrated by Arnold Lobel. Harper, 1965 (0–06–027016–0).

NEIGHBORHOODS AND COMMUNITIES

Crews, Donald. *School Bus.* Greenwillow, 1984 (0-688-02808-X); paper, Penguin, 1985 (0-14-050549-0).

Hutchins, Pat. *Don't Forget the Bacon!* Greenwillow, 1976 (0-688-06788-3); paper, Morrow, 1989 (0-688-08743-4).

Maestro, Betsy and Giulio. *Traffic: A Book of Opposites.* Crown, 1981 (0-517-54427-X).

Petrie, Catherine. *Joshua James Likes Trucks.* Children's Press, 1982 (0-516-03525-8); paper, 1982 (0-516-43525-6).

Raffi. *One Light, One Sun.* Illustrated by Eugenie Fernandes. Crown, 1988 (0-517-56785-7).

Raffi. *Wheels on the Bus.* Illustrated by Sylvie Kantorovitz Wickstrom. Crown, 1988 (0-517-56784-9).

Rice, Eve. *Goodnight, Goodnight.* Greenwillow, 1980 (0-688-84254-2); paper, Penguin, 1983 (0-14-050386-2).

Rice, Eve. *Sam Who Never Forgets.* Greenwillow, 1977 (0-688-84088-4); paper, Morrow, 1987 (0-688-07335-2).

Sis, Peter. *Waving.* Greenwillow, 1988 (0-688-07160-0).

THE YEAR ROUND: SEASONS, WEATHER, AND SPECIAL EVENTS

Aardema, Verna. *Bringing the Rain to Kapiti Plain.* Illustrated by Beatriz Vidal. Dial, 1981 (0-8037-0807-6); paper, 1983 (0-8037-0904-8).

Aylesworth, Jim. *One Crow: A Counting Rhyme.* Illustrated by Ruth Young. Harper, 1988 (0-397-32175-9).

Brett, Jan. *The Twelve Days of Christmas.* Putnam, 1986 (0-396-08821-X).

Brown, Margaret Wise. *Home for a Bunny.* Illustrated by Garth Williams. Western, 1983 (0-307-10388-9).

Charlip, Remy. *Fortunately.* Macmillan, 1964 (0-02-718100-6).

Flack, Marjorie. *Ask Mr. Bear.* Macmillan, 1932 (0-02-735390-7); paper, 1986 (0-02-043090-6).

Martin, Bill and John Archambault. *Listen to the Rain.* Illustrated by James Endicott. Holt, 1988 (0-8050-6682-6).

Merriam, Eve. *The Christmas Box.* Illustrated by David Small. Morrow, 1985 (0-688-05256-8).

Tresselt, Alvin. *Rain Drop Splash.* Illustrated by Leonard Weisgard. Lothrop, 1946 (0-688-51165-1).

Zolotow, Charlotte. *Mr. Rabbit and the Lovely Present.* Illustrated by Maurice Sendak. Harper, 1962 (0-06-026945-6); paper, 1977 (0-06-443020-0).

References

Allen, J., Clark, W., Cook, M., Crane, P., Fallon, T., Hoffman, L., Jennings, J. K. & Sours, M. A. (1989). Development in whole language kinder-gartens. In J. M. Mason (Ed.), *Reading and writing connections* (pp. 121–146). Boston: Allyn and Bacon.

Altwerger, B., Edelsky, C. & Flores, B. M. (1987). Whole language: What's new? *The Reading Teacher, 41*(2), 144–154.

Alvermann, D. E., Dillon, D. R. & Brien, D. G. (1987). *Using discussion to promote reading comprehension.* Newark, DE: International Reading Association.

Anda, S. (1990). *Teaching reading to second language learners.* Graduate assignment, ED 480(g), Moorhead State University, Moorhead, MN.

Anderson, R. C., Hiebert, E. H., Scott, J. A. & Wilkinson, I. E. G. (1985). *Becoming a nation of readers: The report of the commission on reading.* Washington, DC: National Institute of Education.

Andersson, B. V., & Barnitz, J. G. (1984). Cross-cultural schemata and reading comprehension instruction. *Journal of Reading, 28*(2), 102–108.

Applebee, A. N., Langer, J. A. & Mullis, I.V.S. (1988). *Who reads best? Factors related to reading achievement in grades 3, 7 and 11* (Report No. 17-R-01). Princeton, NJ: Educational Testing Service.

Arias, M. B. (1986). The context of education for Hispanic students: An over-view. *American Journal of Education, 95*(1), 26–50.

Asher, J. J. (1977). Children learn another language. A developmental hypoth-esis. *Child Development, 48*(3), 1040–1048.

Asher, J. J. (1981). Comprehension training: The evidence from laboratory and classroom studies. In H. Winitz (Ed.), *The comprehension approaches to foreign language instruction* (pp. 49–68). Rowley, MA: Newbury House.

Atwell, N. (1989). Bringing it all back home. *The New Advocate, 2*(1), 21–35.

Augustine, D. K., Gruber K. D. & Hanson, L. R. (1990). Cooperation works. *Educational Leadership, 47*(4), 4–7.

Baker, G. C. (1983). *Planning and organizing for multicultural instruction.* Reading, MA: Addison-Wesley.

Baker, N. D., & Greenfield, P. M. (1988). The development of new and old information in young children's early language. *Language Sciences, 10*(1), 3–34.

Banks, J. A. (1980). *Teaching strategies for ethnic studies.* Boston: Allyn and Bacon.

Banks, J. A. (1987). *Teaching strategies for ethnic studies* (4th ed.). Boston: Allyn and Bacon.

Banks, J. A. (1988). *Multiethnic education: Theory and practice* (2nd ed.). Boston: Allyn and Bacon.

Banks, J. A. (1989a). Multicultural education: Characteristics and goals. In J. A. Banks & C. A. M. Banks (Eds.), *Multicultural education: Issues and perspectives* (pp. 2–25). Boston: Allyn and Bacon.

Banks, J. A. (1989b). Integrating the curriculum with ethnic content: Approaches and guidelines. In J. A. Banks & C. A. M. Banks (Eds.), *Multicultural education: Issues and perspectives* (pp. 189–207). Boston: Allyn and Bacon.

Banks, J. A. & Clegg, Jr., A. A. (1977). *Teaching strategies for the social studies: Inquiry, valuing and decision-making* (2nd ed.). Reading, MA: Addison-Wesley.

Barrs, M., Ellis, S., Hester, H. & Thomas, A. (1988). *The primary language record: Handbook for teachers.* London: Centre for Language in Primary Education.

Barrs, M., Ellis, S., Hester, H. & Thomas, A. (1990). *Patterns of learning: The primary language record and the national curriculum.* London: Centre for Language in Primary Education.

Baskwill, J. (1988). Themestorming. *Teaching Pre-K-8, 19*(1), 80–82.

Bauman, J. F. (1988). *Reading assessment: An instructional decision-making perspective.* Columbus, OH: Merrill.

Beebe, M. J. (1980). The effects of different types of substitution miscues on reading. *Reading Research Quarterly, 15*(3), 324–336.

Benderson, A. (Ed.). *Focus 22* (1988). Minority students in higher education. Princeton, NJ: Educational Testing Service.

Benderson, A. (Ed.). *Focus 20* (1987). ETS Research: Assessment, Instruction and Equity. Princeton, NJ: Educational Testing Service.

Bennett, C. I. (1986). *Comprehensive multicultural education: Theory and practice.* Boston: Allyn and Bacon.

Berkey, S. M. (1988). *The effects of booktalking on reading attitude.* Unpublished master's thesis, Moorhead State University, Moorhead, MN.

Bishop, R. S. (1987). Extending multicultural understanding through children's books. In B. E. Cullinan (Ed.), *Children's literature in the reading program* (pp. 60–67). Newark, DE: International Reading Association.

Bissex, G. L. (1985). Watching young writers. In A. Jaggar & M. T. Smith-Burke (Eds.), *Observing the language learner* (pp. 94–114). Newark, DE: International Reading Association.

Blakey, J. (1983). Ashton-Warner's reading instruction strategy and Piaget. *Education and Society, 1*(2), 95–101.

Bode, B. A. (1989). Dialogue journal writing. *The Reading Teacher, 42*(8), 568–571.

Boseker, B. J. (1988). Bidialectalism in the United States. In A. Holmen, E. Hansen, J. Gimbel & J. M. Jorgenson, (Eds.), *Bilingualism and the individual* (pp. 133–158). Clevendon, GB: Multilingual Matters.

Boyle, O. F., & Peregoy, S. F., (1990). Literacy scaffolds: Strategies for first-

and second-language readers and writers. *The Reading Teacher, 44*(3), 194–200.

Bridge, C. A. (1986). Predictable books for beginning readers and writers. In M. R. Sampson (Ed.), *The Pursuit of literacy: Early reading and writing* (pp. 81–96). Dubuque, IA: Kendall/Hunt.

Brown, A. L. (1982). Learning how to learn from reading. In J. A. Langer & M. T. Smith-Burke (Eds.)., *Reader meets author/bridging the gap: A psycholinguistic and sociolinguistic perspective* (pp. 26–54). Newark, DE: International Reading Association.

Brown, E. J. (1992, Winter). *HAMLit: A strategy for analyzing themes in multicultural literature.* Paper presented at the Manhattan Council Conference on Parents and Reading, Fordham University, New York.

Brozo, W. G., & Tomlinson, C. M. (1986). Literature: The key to lively content courses. *The Reading Teacher, 40*(3), 288–293.

Bryan, R. (1971). *When children speak: Original choral verses for the primary grades.* San Rafael, CA: Academic Therapy Publications.

Buchanan, L. (1990). Some effects of culture in the ESL classroom and their implications for teaching. *Minnetesol Journal, 8,* 73–87.

Burke, C. L. (1980). The reading interview: 1977. In B. P. Farr & D. J. Stricker (Eds.), *Reading comprehension: Resource guide.* Bloomington, IN: School of Education, Indiana University.

Burstein, N. D., & Cabello, B. (1989). Preparing teachers to work with culturally diverse students: A teacher education model. *Journal of Teacher Education, 40*(5), 9–16.

Butler, D. (1980). *Cushla and her books.* Boston: The Horn Book.

Calkins, L. M. (1983). *Lessons from a child: On teaching and learning of writing.* Portsmouth, NH: Heinemann.

Calkins, L. M. (1986). *The art of teaching writing.* Portsmouth, NH: Heinemann.

Cambourne, B. (1984). Language, learning, and literacy. In A. Butler & J. Turbill (Eds.), *Toward a reading writing classroom* (pp. 5–9). Rozelle, NSW, Australia: Primary English Teaching Association.

Cardenas, J. A. (1984, January). The role of native language instruction in bilingual education. *IDRA newsletter,* 1–6.

Carline, D. E., Crawford, L. W. & Babb, J. (1988). *The answer book: A guide to literacy in reading, language arts and mathematics.* Bismarck, ND: Department of Public Instruction.

Carrell, P. L., & Eisterhold, J. C. (1983). Schema theory and ESL reading pedagogy. *TESOL Quarterly, 17*(4), 553–563.

Chan, K. S., & Tsang, S. L. (1983). Overview of educational progress of Chinese Americans. In D. T. Nakanish & M. Hirano-Nakanish (Eds.), *The education of Asian and Pacific Americans: Historical perspectives and descriptions for the future* (pp. 39–48). Phoenix, AZ: Oryx.

Chittenden, E. (1992). Authentic assessment, evaluation and documentation of student performance. In V. Perrone (Ed.), *Expanding student assessment* (pp. 22–31). Alexandria, VA: Association for Supervision and Curriculum Development.

Chrispeels, J. H. (1991). District leadership in parent involvement: Policies and action in San Diego. *Phi Delta Kappan, 72*(5), 367–371.

Christie, J. F., & Alonso, P. A. (1980). Effects of passage difficulty on primary grade children's oral reading patterns. *Educational Research Quarterly, 5*(1), 41–49.

Clark, S. (1983). Into the classroom: Reading of the young ESL learner. *Reading, 17*(3), 171–178.

Clay, M. (1975). *What did I write?* Portsmouth, NH: Heinemann.

Clay, M. (1982). *Observing young readers.* London: Heinemann.

Cochrane, O., Cochrane, D., Scalena, S. & Buchanan, E. (1984). *Reading, writing, and caring.* Winnipeg, Canada: Whole Language Consultants, Ltd.

Cohen, D. (1968). The effect of literature on vocabulary and reading achievement. *Elementary English, 45,* 209–213, 217.

Cohen, E. G. (1990). Continuing to cooperate: Prerequisites for persistence. *Phi Delta Kappan, 72*(2), 134–138.

Collier, V. P. (1987). Age and rate of acquisition of second language for academic purposes. *TESOL Quarterly, 21*(4), 617–641.

Collier, V. P. (1989). How long? A synthesis of research on academic achievement in a second language. *TESOL Quarterly, 23*(3), 509–531.

Crawford, L. W., & Carline, D. E. (1987). *A guide for reading in the content areas* (3rd ed). Bismarck, ND: Department for Public Instruction.

Cressy, D. (1983). The environment for literacy: Accomplishment and context in seventeenth-century England and New England. In D. P. Resnick (Ed.), *Literacy in historical perspective* (pp. 23–42). Washington, DC: Library of Congress.

Crowley, P. (1989). "They grow into 'em": Evaluation, self-evaluation, and self-esteem in special education. In K. S. Goodman, Y. M. Goodman & W. J. Hood (Eds.), *The whole language evaluation book* (pp. 237–247). Portsmouth, NH: Heinemann.

Cuban, L. (1984). *How teachers taught.* New York: Longman.

Cuch, F. S. (1987). Cultural perspectives on Indian education. *Equity and Excellence, 23*(1–2), 65–76.

Cullinan, B. E. (1987). Inviting readers to literature. In B. E. Cullinan (Ed.), *Children's literature in the reading program* (pp. 2–14). Newark, DE: International Reading Association.

Cummins, J. (1981). The role of primary language development in promoting educational success for language minority students. In California State Department of Education, Office of Bilingual Bicultural Education, *Schooling and language minority students: A theoretical framework* (3–49). Los Angeles, CA: California Evaluation, Dissemination and Assessment Center.

Cummins, J. (1986). Empowering minority students: A framework for intervention. *Harvard Educational Review, 56*(1), 18–36.

Cunningham, P. (1982). Diagnosis by observation. In J. J. Pikulski & T. Shanahan (Eds.), *Approaches to informal evaluation* (pp. 12–22). Newark, DE: International Reading Association.

Dahl, P. (1988). *The effects of booktalks of self-selected reading.* Unpublished master's thesis, Moorhead State University, Moorhead, MN.

Davies, D. (1991). Schools reaching out: Family, school and community partnerships for student success. *Phi Delta Kappan, 72*(5), 376–382.

Deeds, B. (1981). Motivating children to read through self-concept. In A. J. Ciani (Ed.), *Motivating reluctant readers* (26–34). Newark, DE: International Reading Association.

DeFord, D. E. (1980). Young children and their writing. *Theory into Practice, 28*(3), 157–162.

DeGroff, L. J. (1989). Developing writing processes with children's literature. *The New Advocate, 2*(2), 115–123.

Diakiw, J. Y. (1990). Children's literature and global education: Understanding the developing world. *The Reading Teacher, 43*(4), 296–300.

Diaz, M. P. (1989, Winter). *Assessing ESL language learners.* Oral presentation, Moorhead State University, Moorhead, MN

Dillon, D., & Searle, D. (1981). The role of language in one first grade classroom. *Research in the Teaching of English, 15*(4), 311–328.

Dobson, L. (1989). Connections in learning to write and read: A study of children's development through kindergarten and first grade. In J. Mason (Ed.), *Reading and writing connections* (pp. 83–103). Boston: Allyn and Bacon.

Dulay, H., Burt, M.E & Krashen, S. (1982). *Language two.* New York: Oxford University Press.

Dyson, A. H. (1983). The role of oral language in early writing processes. *Research in the Teaching of English, 17*(1), 1–23.

Dyson, A. H. (1985). Three emergent writers and the curriculum: Copying and other myths. *Elementary School Journal, 85*(4), 497–512.

Early, M. (1990). Enabling first and second language learners in the classroom. *Language arts, 67*(6), 567–575.

Eckard, R. D., & Kearny, M. A. (1981). *Teaching conversation skills in ESL.* Washington, DC: Center for Applied Linguistics.

Edelsky, C. (1982). Writing in a bilingual program: The relation of L1 and L2 texts. *TESOL Quarterly, 16*(2), 211–228.

Educational Testing Service (1985). *The Reading Report Card.* Princeton, NJ: Educational Testing Service.

Edwards, C., & Stout, J. (1990). Cooperative learning: The first year. *Educational Leadership, 47*(4), 38–41.

Eeds, M. (1988). Holistic assessment of coding ability. In S. M. Glazer, L. W. Scarfoss, & L. M. Gentile (Eds.), *Reexamining reading diagnosis* (pp. 48–66). Newark, DE: International Reading Association.

Elley, W. B. (1981). The role of reading in bilingual contexts. In J. T. Guthrie (Ed.), *Comprehension and teaching research reviews* (pp. 227–254). Newark, DE: International Reading Association.

English for ages 5 to 11 (1988). Proposals of the Secretary of State for Education and Science and the Secretary of State for Wales. London: Department of Education and Science and the Welsh Office.

Enright, D. S. (1986). Use everything you have to teach English: Providing useful input to young language learners. In P. Rigg & D. S. Enright (Eds.), *Children and ESL: Integrating perspectives* (pp. 113–162). Washington, DC: Teachers of English to Speakers of Other Languages.

Enright, D. S., & McCloskey, M. L. (1985). Yes talking! Organizing the classroom to promote second language acquisition. *TESOL Quarterly, 19*(3), 431–453.

Farrell, C. (1991). *Storytelling: A guide for teachers.* New York: Scholastic Professional Books.

Ferreiro, E. (1990). Literacy development: Psychogenesis. In Y. M. Goodman (ed.), *How children construct literacy: Piagetian perspective* (pp. 12–25). Newark, DE: International Reading Association.

Ferreiro, E. (1986, Summer). Literacy development: Psychogenesis. Paper read at International Reading Association Eleventh World Congress. University of London.

Fiordo, R. (1988). The great learning enterprise of the four world development project. *Journal of American Indian Education, 27*(3), 24–34.

Fishman, A. R. (1987). Literacy and cultural context: A lesson from the Amish. *Language Arts, 64*(8), 842–854.

Flatley, J. K., & Rutland, A. D. (1986). Using wordless picture books to teach linguistically/culturally different students. *The Reading Teacher, 40*(3), 276–280.

Franklin, E. A. (1988). Reading and writing stories. Children creating meaning. *The Reading Teacher, 43*(3), 184–190.

Frase, L. T., & Schwartz, B. J. (1975). Effect of question production and answering on prose recall. *Journal of Educational Psychology, 5,* 628–635.

Fredericks, A. D., & Rasinski, T. V. (1990). Involving parents in the assessment process. *The Reading Teacher, 44*(4), 346–349.

Freeman, D. E., & Freeman, Y. D. (1988). Bilingual learners: How our assumptions limited their world. In K. S. Goodman & Y. M. Goodman (Eds.), *Language and literacy for bilingual learners: Two papers* (Report No. 18) (pp. 2–15). Tucson, AZ: College of Education, University of Arizona.

Freire, P. (1973). *Education for critical consciousness.* New York: Seabury Press.

Freppon, P. A., & Dahl, D. L. (1991). Learning about phonics in a whole language classroom. *Language Arts, 68*(3), 190–197.

Froese, V. (1977). Diagnostic teaching of composition. In C. Braun & V. Froese (Eds.), *An experience-based approach to language and reading* (pp. 63–88). Baltimore MD: University Park Press.

Gambrell, L. B. (1985). Dialogue journals: Reading and writing interaction. *The Reading Teacher, 3*(5), 512–515.

Gardner, H. (1989, December). Learning, Chinese-style. *Psychology today,* 54–56.

Garrison, J. W., & Hoskisson, J. W. (1989). Confirmation bias in predictive reading. *The Reading Teacher, 42*(7), 482–486.

Gay, G. (1989). Ethnic minorities and educational quality. In J. A. Banks & C. A. McGee Banks (Eds)., *Multicultural education: Issues and perspec-*

tives (pp. 167–188). Boston: Allyn and Bacon.

Gay, G. (1990). Achieving educational equality through curriculum desegregation. *Phi Delta Kappan, 72*(1), 56–62.

Genesee, F. (1986, Spring). The baby and the bath water, or what immersion has to say about bilingual education. *NABE Journal, 10,* 227–254.

Genishi, C. (1989). Observing the second language learner. An example of teachers' learning. *Language Arts, 66*(5), 509–515.

Gillet, J. W., & Gentry, J. W. (1983). Bridges between nonstandard and standard English with extensions of dictated stories. *The Reading Teacher, 36*(4), 360–364.

Gingras, R. C., & Careaga, R. C. (1989, Spring). Limited English proficient students at risk: Issues and prevention strategies. *New focus: The NCBE occasional papers in bilingual education.* Silver Spring, MD: National Clearinghouse for Bilingual Education.

Glazer, S. M., & Searfoss, L. W. (1988). Reexamining reading diagnosis. In S. M. Glazer, Searfoss, L. W. & Gentile, L. M. (Eds.), *Reexamining reading diagnosis: New trends and procedures* (pp. 1–11). Newark, DE: International Reading Association.

Goldberg, M. F. (1990). Portrait of James P. Corner. *Educational Leadership, 48*(1), 40–42.

Gollasch, F. V. (1982). *Language and literacy: The selected writings of Kenneth S. Goodman (vols. 1 and 2).* London: Routledge and Kegan Paul.

Goodlad, J. I. (1984). *A place called school.* New York: McGraw-Hill.

Goodman, D. (1989). So why don't I feel good about myself? In K. S. Goodman, Y. M. Goodman & W. J. Hood (Eds.), *The whole language evaluation book* (pp. 189–212). Portsmouth, NH: Heinemann.

Goodman, K. S. (1989). Preface. In K. S. Goodman, Y. M. Goodman & W. J. Hood (Eds.), *The whole language evaluation book* (pp. xi–xv). Portsmouth, NH: Heinemann.

Goodman, K. S. (1986). *What's whole in whole language.* Richmond Hill, Ontario, Canada: Scholastic.

Goodman, K. S. (1988). *The process of reading and writing: An updated transactional model.* Paper presented at the 12th World Congress on Reading, Gold Coast, Australia.

Goodman, K. S., & Gollash, F. V. (1980). Word omissions: Deliberate and nondeliberate. *Reading Research Quarterly, 16*(1), 6–31.

Goodman, K. S., & Goodman, Y. M. (1977). Learning to read is natural. In L. Resnick & R. Weaver (Eds.), *Theory and practice in early reading: Vol. 1* (pp. 137–154). Hillsdale, NJ: Erlbaum.

Goodman, K. S., Smith, E. B., Meredith, R. & Goodman, Y. M. (1987). *Language and thinking in school: A whole-language curriculum.* New York: Owen.

Goodman, Y. M. (1976). Miscues, errors and reading comprehension. In J. E. Merritt (Ed.), *New horizons in reading* (pp. 86–93). Newark, DE: International Reading Association.

Goodman, Y. M. (1980). *The roots of literacy.* In M. P. Douglas (Ed.), *Reading: A humanizing experience,* 43rd Annual Reading Conference. Claremont, CA: Claremont Graduate School.

Goodman, Y. M. (1984). The development of initial literacy. In H. Goelman, A. Oberg & F. Smith (Eds.), *Awakening to literacy.* Portsmouth, NH: Heinemann.

Goodman, Y. M. (1985). Kidwatching: Observing children in the classroom. In A. Jaggar & M. T. Smith-Burke (Eds.), *Observing the language learner* (pp. 9–18). Newark, DE: International Reading Association.

Goodman, Y. M. (1988). *Developing literacy: Facilitating reading and writing connections for middle-graders.* Paper presented at the Ninth Annual Fall Red River Literacy Conference, Moorhead State University, Moorhead, MN.

Goodman, Y. M. (1989). Evaluation of students: Evaluation of teachers. In K. S. Goodman, Y. M. Goodman & W. J. Hood (Eds.), *The whole language evaluation book* (pp. 3–14). Portsmouth, NH: Heinemann.

Goodman, Y. M. & Burke, C. (1976). *Reading strategies: Focus on comprehension.* New York: Owen.

Goodman, Y. M., Watson, D. S. & Burke, C. L. (1987). *Reading miscue inventory: Alternative Procedures* (2nd ed.). New York, Owens.

Grant, C. A. (1989). Equity, equality, teachers and classroom life. In W. G. Secada (Ed.), *Equity in education* (pp. 89–102). New York: Falmer.

Grant, C. A. (1990). Desegregation, racial attitudes, and intergroup contact: A discussion of change. *Phi Delta Kappan, 72*(1), 25–32.

Grant, C. A., & Sleeter, C. E. (1986). *After the school bell rings.* Philadelphia: Falmer.

Grant, C. A., & Sleeter, C. E. (1989). *Turning on learning: Five approaches for multicultural teaching plans for race, class, gender and disability.* Columbus, OH: Merrill.

Graves, D. (1983). *Writing: Teachers and children at work.* Portsmouth, NH: Heinemann.

Hakuta, K. (1986). *Mirror of language: The debate on bilingualism.* New York: Basic Books.

Hakuta, K., & Gould, L. J. (1987). Synthesis of research on bilingual education. *Educational Leadership, 44*(2), 38–45.

Hall, N. (1984). *Making literacy meaningful: A list of books suitable for helping children understand the nature and purpose of literacy* (No. 1). Unpublished Monograph. The Language and Reading Centre, Manchester Polytechnic, Manchester, GB.

Hall, N. (1987). *The emergence of literacy.* Portsmouth, NH: Heinemann.

Hall, N. (1989). Introduction. In N. Hall (Ed.), *Writing with reason: The emergence of authorship in young children* (pp. vii–xvi). London: Hodder & Stoughton.

Hall, N., May, E., Moores, J., Shearer, J. & Williams, S. (1987a). The literate home-corner. In P. Smith (Ed.), *Parents and teachers together* (pp. 134–144). New York: Macmillan.

Hall, N., Jones, L., & McCaldon, S. (1987b). *Literacy and play in early year's classrooms.* Paper presented at the Reading Association of Ireland Annual Conference, Dublin, Ireland.

Hall, N., Robinson, A. & Crawford, L. W. (1989). Letter writing with young children. *Dialogue, 6*(1) 3–4.

Halliday, M. K. (1971). *Language acquisition and initial literacy.* Paper presented at the 38th Claremont Reading Conference, Claremont, CA.

Halliday, M. K. (1975). *Learning how to mean: Explorations in the functions of language.* London: Edward Arnold.

Halliday, M. K. (1977/1973). *Explorations in the functions of language.* New York: Elsevier North-Holland.

Hamayan, E., & Pfleger, M. (1987). Developing ESL literacy in young children: A whole language approach. *Passages, 3,* 44–46.

Hamayan, E., Kwait, J. & Perlman, R. (1985). *The identification and assessment of language minority students: A handbook for educators.* Arlington Heights, IL: Illinois Resource Center.

Hammond, W. D. (1982). The quality of reading miscues. In J. J. Pikulski & T. Shanahan (Eds.), *Approaches to informal evaluation of reading* (pp. 23–29). Newark, DE: International Reading Association.

Handbook for teaching Cantonese-speaking students (1984). Sacramento, CA: California State Department of Education.

Harman, S. (1991). National tests, national standards, national curriculum. *Language Arts, 68*(1), 49–50.

Harman, S. & Edelsky, C. (1989). The risks of whole language literacy: Alienation and connection. *Language Arts, 66*(4), 392–406.

Harris, S. (1982). Towards a sociology of aboriginal literacy. In D. Burns (Ed.), *Reading, writing and multiculturalism* (pp. 14–31). Adelaide, SA: Australian Reading Association.

Harste, J. C., Burke, C. L. & Woodward, V. A. (1982). Children's language and world: Initial encounters with print. In J. Langer & M. T. Smith-Burke (Eds.), *Reader meets author: Bridging the gap* (pp. 105–132). Newark, DE: International Reading Association.

Harste, J. C., Short, K. G., & Burke, C. L. (1988). *Creating classrooms for authors: The reading-writing connection.* Portsmouth, NH: Heinemann.

Harste, J. C., Woodward, V. A. & Burke, C. L. (1984). *Language stories and literacy lessons.* Portsmouth, NH: Heinemann.

Hayes, D. A. (1989). Helping students GRASP the knack of writing summaries. *Journal of Reading, 33*(2), 96–101.

Heald-Taylor, G. (1984). Scribble in first grade writing. *The Reading Teacher, 38*(1), 4–8.

Heald-Taylor, G. (1987a). How to use predictable books for K-2 language arts instruction. *The Reading Teacher, 40*(7), 656–661.

Heald-Taylor, G. (1987b). Predictable literature selections and activities for language arts instruction. *The Reading Teacher, 41*(1), 642.

Heald-Taylor, G. (1989). *Whole language strategies for ESL students.* San Diego, CA: Dormac.

Heath, S. B. (1982). What no bedtime story means: Narrative skills at home and school. *Language and Society, 33*(1), 49–76.

Heath, S. B. (1986). Critical factors in literacy development. In S. de Castell, A. Luke & K. Egan (Eds.), *Literacy society and schooling: A reading* (pp. 209–229). Cambridge, MA: Cambridge University Press.

Heimlich, J. E., & Pittelman, S. D. (1986). *Semantic mapping: Classroom applications.* Newark, DE: International Reading Association.

Herring, G. (1989). Shared writing. In N. Hall (Ed.), *Writing with reason: The emergence of authorship in young children* (pp. 100–118). London: Hodder & Stoughton.

Hilliard, A. G. III (1992). Why we must pluralize the curriculum. *Educational Leadership, 49*(4), 12–15.

Hood, W. J. (1989). "If the teacher comes over, pretend it's a telescope!" In K. S. Goodman, Y. M. Goodman, & W. J. Hood (Eds.), *Whole language evaluation book* (pp. 27–43). Portsmouth, NH: Heinemann.

Huck, C. S. (1990). The power of children's literature in the classroom. In K. G. Short & K. M. Pierce (Eds.), *Talking about books: Creating literature communities* (pp. 3–16). Portsmouth, NH: Heinemann.

Huck, C. S. & Kerstetter, K. J. (1987). Developing readers. In B. E. Cullinan (Ed.), *Children's literature in the reading program* (pp. 30–40). Newark, DE: International Reading Association.

Hudelson, S. (1981). *Learning to read in different languages.* Washington, DC: Center for Applied Linguistics.

Hudelson, S. (1984). Children become literate in English as a second language. *TESOL Quarterly, 18*(2), 221–238.

Hudelson, S. (1986). ESL children's writing: What we've learned. In P. Rigg & D. S. Enright (Eds.), *Children and ESL: Integrating perspectives (pp. 23–54).* Washington, DC: Teachers of English to Speakers of Other Languages.

Huizenga, J. (1985). *Looking at American signs: A pictorial introduction to American language and culture.* Lincolnwood, IL: Voluntad.

Irwin, P. A. & Mitchell, J. N. (1983). A procedure for assessing the richness of retellings. *Journal of Reading 26*(5), 391–396.

Irwin, P. A., & Mitchell, J. N. (1988). The reader retelling profile: Using retelling to make instructional decisions (pp. 140–41), in L. M. Morrow, Retelling stories as a diagnostic tool. In S. M. Glazer, L. W. Searfoss & L. M. Gentile (Eds.), *Reexamining reading diagnosis: New trends and procedures* (pp. 128–149). Newark, DE: International Reading Association.

James, M. O. (1987). ESL reading pedagogy: Implications of schema-theoretical research. In J. Devine, P. L. Carrell & D. E. Eskey (Eds.), *Research in reading in English as a second language* (pp. 175–188). Washington, DC: Teachers of English to Speakers of Other Languages.

Johnson, D. (1987, February 13). Written off [personal column]. *The London Times Educational Supplement.*

Johnson, D. W., Johnson, R. T. & Holubec, E. J. (1986). *Circles of learning: Cooperation in the classroom.* Englewood Cliffs, NJ: Prentice Hall.

Johnson, D. W. & Johnson, R. T. (1987). *Learning together and alone* (2nd ed.). Englewood Cliffs, NJ: Prentice Hall.

Johnson, D. W., Johnson, R. T., & Holubec, E. J. (1988). *Cooperation in the classroom* (rev. ed.). Edina, MN: Interaction.

Jordan, C. (1984). Cultural compatibility and the education of Hawaiian children: Implications for mainland educators. *Educational Research Quarterly, 8*(4), 59–71.

Kaplan, S. N. (1990). The start-up stage. *Learning, 18*(6), 42–43.

Kendall, F. E. (1983). *Diversity in the classroom: A multicultural approach to the education of young children.* New York: Teachers College Press.

Kennedy, M. (1991). Policy issues in teacher education. *Phi Delta Kappan, 72*(9), 659–665.

Kim, B. L. C. (1983). The future of Korean-American children and youth: Marginality, biculturality, and the role of the American public school. In D. T. Nakanishi & M. Hirano-Nakanishi (Eds.), *The education of Asian and Pacific Americans: Historical perspectives and prescriptions for the future* (pp. 49–64). Phoenix, AZ: Oryx.

King, M. L. (1984, Special Issue). Language: Insights from acquisition. *Theory Into Practice, 24* 358–363.

King, M. L. (1985). Language and language learning for child watchers. In A. Jaggar & M. T. Smith-Burke (Eds.), *Observing the language learner* (pp. 19–38). Newark, DE: International Reading Association.

Kintisch, L. S. (1986). Journal writing: Stages of development. *The Reading Teacher, 40*(2), 168–172.

Kirby, D., & Kuykendall, C. (1985). *Thinking through language: Book one.* Urbana, IL: National Council of Teachers of English.

Knapp, M. S., Turnbill, B. J. & Shield, P. M. (1990). New directions for educating the children of poverty. *Educational Leadership, 48*(1), 4–8.

Kolczynski, R. (1978). Reading leads to writing. In J. W. Stewig & S. L. Sebesta (Eds.), *Using literature in the elementary classroom* (pp. 51–61). Urbana, IL: National Council of Teachers of English.

Koskineri, P. A., Gambrell, L. B., Kapinus, B. A., & Heathington, B. S. (1988). Retelling: A strategy for enhancing students' reading comprehension. *The Reading Teacher, 41*(9), 892–896.

Krashen, S. D. (1982). *Principles and practices in second language acquisition.* New York: Oxford/Alemany.

Krashen, S. D., & Terrell, T. D. (1983). *The natural approach: Language acquisition in the classroom.* New York: Oxford/Alemany.

Kukla, K. (1987). David Booth: Drama as a way of knowing: *Language Arts, 64*(1), 73–78.

Langer, J. A. (1982). Facilitating text processing: The elaboration of prior knowledge. In J. A. Langer & M. T. Smith-Burke (Eds.), *Reader meets author/bridging the gap: A psycholinguistic and sociolinguistic perspective* (pp. 149–162). Newark, DE: International Reading Association.

Langer, J. A. (1990). Understanding literature. *Language Arts, 67*(8), 812–816.

Laquer, T. W. (1983). Toward a culture ecology of literacy in England, 1600–1850. In D. P. Resnick (Ed.), *Literacy in historical perspective* (pp. 43–57). Washington, DC: Library of Congress.

Larrick, N. (1987). Keep a poem in your pocket. In B. E. Cullinan (Ed.),

Children's literature in the reading program (pp. 20–27). Newark, DE: International Reading Association.

Levine, D., & Ademan, M. (1982). *Beyond language: Intercultural communication for ESL.* Englewood Cliffs, NJ: Prentice Hall.

Levstick, L. S. (1990). Research directions mediating content through literacy texts. *Language Arts, 67*(8), 848–853.

Lindauer, S. K. (1988). Wordless books: An approach to visual literacy. *Children's literature in education, 19*(3), 136–142.

Lindle, J. C. (1989). What do parents want from principals and teachers? *Educational Leadership, 47*(2), 12–14.

Lipson, M. Y. (1984). Some unexpected issues in prior knowledge and comprehension. *The Reading Teacher, 37*(8), 760–765.

Little Soldier, L. (1989). Language learning of Native American students. *Educational Leadership, 46*(5), 74–75.

Lock, D. C. (1989). Fostering the self-esteem of African-American children. *Elementary School Guidance and Counseling, 23*(4), 254–259.

Loughlin, C. E. (1977). Understanding the learning environment. *Elementary School Journal, 78*(2), 125–131.

Loughlin, C. E. (1978). Arranging the learning environment. *Insites Into Open Education, 11*(2), 2–6.

Loughlin, C. E., & Martin, M. D. (1976). A dynamic teacher role. *Journal of Teaching and Learning, 2*(2), 34–43.

Loughlin, C. E., & Martin, M. D. (1987). *Supporting literacy: Developing effective learning environments.* New York: Teachers College Press.

Loughlin, C. E., & Suina, J. H. (1982). *The learning environment: An instructional strategy.* New York: Teachers College Press.

Loughlin, C. E. & Suing, J. H. (1983, September/October). Reflecting the child's community in the classroom (pp. 19–21). *Childhood Education* (1), 19–21.

Love, M. J. (1989). The home visit: An irreplaceable tool. *Educational Leadership 47*(2), 29.

Lueder, D. C. (1989). Tennessee parents were invited to participate–and they did. *Educational Leadership, 47*(2), 15–17.

Lunge-Larsen, L. (1981). Listening comprehension: In the oral tradition. *Minnetesol Journal, 1*, 29–46.

Lynch, E. (1989). *Parental approaches to transmission of language and literacy to young children with and without handicaps: A naturalistic inquiry.* Unpublished research report, Moorhead State University, Moorhead, MN.

MacDonald, M. G. (1989). Oral dialogue journals: Spoken language in a communicative context. *TESL Reporter, 22*(2), 27–31.

Macon, J. M., Brewell, D. & Vogt, M. (1991). *Responses to literature: Grades K–8.* Newark, DE: International Reading Association.

Maeroff, G. I. (1991). Assessing alternative assessment. *Phi Delta Kappan, 73*(4), 272–281.

Manning, M., Manning, G. & Hughes, H. (1987). Journals in 1st grade: What children write. *The Reading Teacher, 41*(3), 311–315.

Marek, S., Howard, D., Disinger, J., Jacobson, D., Earle, D., Goodman, Y., Hood, W., Woodley, C., Woodley, J., Wortman, J., & Wortman, R. (1984). A kid-watching guide: Evaluation for whole language classrooms. *Occasional papers* (Report No. 9). Tucson, AZ: University of Arizona, Arizona Center for Research and Development.

Marshall, H. H. (1989). The development of self-concept. *Young Children, 44*(5), 266–271.

Marshall, J. (1987, April 26). Food for thought. *The (London) Times Educational Supplement* (p. 27).

Martinez, M., & Teale, W. (1987). The ins and outs of a kindergarten writing program. *The Reading Teacher, 40*(4), 444–451.

Mason, J., Barr, R., Kamil, M. L., & Mosenthal, P. (1984). Early reading from a developmental perspective. In P. D. Pearson (Ed.), *Handbook of reading research* (pp. 505–543). New York: Longman.

Mathews, J. K. (1990). From computer management to portfolio assessment. *The Reading Teacher, 43*(6), 420–421.

Mathison, C. (1989). Activating student interest in content area reading. *Journal of Reading, 33*(3), 170–176.

McClure, A. A., & Zitlow, C. S. (1991). Not just the facts: Aesthetic response in elementary content area studies. *Language Arts, 68*(1), 27–33.

McCracken, R., & McCracken, M. J. (1978). Modeling is the key to sustained student reading. *The Reading Teacher, 31*(4), 406–408.

McCracken, R., & McCracken, M. J. (1983). Chants, charts, and achievement. In J. B. Cowen (Ed.), *Teaching reading through the arts* (pp. 69–77). Newark, DE: International Reading Association.

McDonald, M. R. (1982). *The storytellers sourcebook: A subject, title, and motif index to folklore collection for children.* Detroit, MI: Neal-Schuman.

McGee, L. M., & Richgels, D. J. (1990). *Literacy's beginnings: Supporting young readers and writers.* Boston: Allyn and Bacon.

McKenzie, M. (1978). Learning to read through reading. In E. Hunter-Grundin & H. U. Grundin (Eds.), *Proceedings of the 14th annual course and conference of the UKRA* (pp. 45–53). London: Ward Educational.

McKenzie, M. (1985). Shared writing: Apprenticeship in writing. *Language matters, 1 & 2,* 1–5.

McKenzie, M. (1986). *Journeys into literacy: The handbook to journeys into reading, levels 1–4.* Huddersfield, GB: Schofield & Sims.

McMillan, M. M., & Gentile, L. M. (1988). Children's literature in teaching critical thinking and ethnics. *The Reading Teacher, 41*(9), 876–878.

McNeil, J. D. (1987). *Reading comprehension: New directions for classroom practice.* Glenview, IL: Scott, Foresman.

Means, B., & Knapp, M. S. (1991). Cognitive approaches to teaching advanced skills to educationally disadvantaged students. *Phi Delta Kappan, 73*(4), 282–289.

Meltzer, M. (1976). *Taking root: Jewish immigrants in America.* New York: Farrar, Straus, & Giroux.

Mercer, J. R. (1989). Alternative paradigms for assessment in a pluralistic society. In J. A. Banks & C. A. McGee Banks (Eds.), *Multicultural education: Issues and perspectives* (pp. 289–304). Boston: Allyn and Bacon.

Moffet, J., & Wagner, B. J. (1983). *Student-centered language arts and reading, K-13: A handbook for teachers.* Boston: Houghton Mifflin.

Molnar, A. (1989). Racism in America: A continuing dilemma. *Educational Leadership, 47*(2), 71–72.

Moore, D. W., Readence, J. E. & Rickleman, R. J. (1989). *Prereading activities for content area reading and learning* (2nd ed.). Newark, DE: International Reading Association.

Morris, A. & Stewart-Dore, N. (1984). *Learning to learn from text: Effective reading in the content areas.* Singapore: Addison-Wesley.

Morrissey, M. (1989). When "shut up" is a sign of growth. In K. S. Goodman, Y. M. Goodman & W. J. Hood (Eds.), *The whole language evaluation book* (pp. 95–100). Portsmouth, NH: Heinemann.

Morrow, L. M. (1985). Reading and retelling stories: Strategies for emergent readers. *The Reading Teacher, 38*(9), 870–875.

Morrow, L. M. (1987). Promoting inner city children's recreational reading. *The Reading Teacher, 41*(3), 266–274.

Morrow, L. M. (1988). Retelling stories as a diagnostic tool. In S. M. Glazer, L. W. Searfoss & L. M. Gentile (Eds.), *Reexamining reading diagnosis* (pp. 128–149). Newark, DE: International Reading Association.

Morrow, L. M., & Weinstein, C. S. (1986). Encouraging voluntary reading: The impact of a literature program on children's use of library centers. *Reading Research Quarterly, 21*(3), 330–346.

Moustafa, M. (1980). Picture books for oral language development for non-English speaking children, bibliography. *The Reading Teacher, 33*(8), 914–919.

Moustafa, M. (1987). Comprehensive input plus the language experience approach: A long term perspective. *The Reading Teacher, 41*(3), 276–286.

Moustafa, M., & Penrose, J. (1985). Comprehensible input plus the language experience approach: Reading instruction for limited English speaking students. *The Reading Teacher, 38*(7), 640–647.

Nagy, W. E. (1988). *Teaching vocabulary to improve reading comprehension.* Urbana, IL: National Council of Teachers of English.

Nathenson-Mejia, S. (1989). Writing in a second language: Negotiating meaning through invented spelling. *Language Arts, 66*(5), 516–527.

The National Assessment of Education Progress (1989, March 31). The nation's report card, *The Wall Street Journal Reports: Education (p. 15).* New York: Wall Street Journal.

National Center for Bilingual Education (1989). *Educating refugees:* Understanding the basics. *NCBE Forum,* 12(3), 1, 4.

Neilsen, A. R. (1989). *Critical thinking and reading: Empowering learners to think and act.* Bloomington, IN: Indiana University ERIC Clearinghouse on Reading and Communication Skills.

Nieto, S. (1992). *Affirming diversity: The sociopolitical context of multicultural education.* New York: Longman.

Norman, K. (1990). *Teaching talking and learning in key stage one.* York, GB: National Curriculum Council.

Norris, S. P., & Phillips, L. M. (1987). Explanation of reading comprehension: Schema theory and critical thinking theory. *Teachers College Record, 89,* 281–306.

Norton, D. E. (1991). *Through the eyes of a child: An introduction to children's literature.* New York: Merrill.

Norton, D. E. (1982). Using a webbing process to develop children's literature units. *Language Arts, 59*(4), 348–356.

Norton, D. E. (1990). Teaching multicultural literature in the reading curriculum. *The Reading Teacher, 44*(1), 28–40.

Ogbu, J. U. (1983). Literacy and schooling in subordinate cultures: The case of Black Americans. In D. P. Resnick (Ed.), *Literacy in historical perspective* (pp. 129–153). Washington, DC: Library of Congress.

Ogle, D. M. (1989). The know, want to know, learn strategy. In K. D. Muth (Ed.), *Children's comprehension of text: Research into practice* (pp. 205–223). Newark, DE: International Reading Association.

Olson, C. B. (1984). Fostering critical thinking skills through writing. *Educational Leadership, 42*(3), 28–39.

Oster, J. (1989). Seeing with different eyes: Another view of literature in the ESL class. *TESOL Quarterly, 23*(1), 89–103.

Oxenham, J. (1980). *Literacy: writing, reading, and social organization.* London: Routledge and Kegan Paul.

Paris, S. G. (1991). Assessment: Portfolio assessment for young readers. *The Reading Teacher, 44*(9), 680–682.

Parry, K. J. (1987). Reading in a second culture. In J. Devine, P. L. Carrell & D. E. Eskey (Eds.), *Research in reading in English as a second language* (pp. 59–70). Washington, DC: Teachers of English to Speakers of Other Languages.

Paulson, F. L., Paulson, P. R. & Meyer, C. A. (1991). What makes a portfolio a portfolio. *Educational Leadership, 48*(5), 60–63.

Peacock, C. (1986). *Teaching writing.* Beckenham, Kent, GB: Croon Helm.

Pearson, N. (1989). A journey into authorship. In N. Hall (Ed.), *Writing with reason: The emergence of authorship in young children* (pp. 119–130). London: Hodder & Stoughton.

Peregoy, S., & Boyle, O. (1990). *Literacy scaffolds—second language learners responding to literature.* Paper presented at the NCTE 1990 Spring Conference, Colorado Springs, CO.

Peyton, J. K. (1986). Literacy through written interaction. *Passages, 2*(1), 24–29.

Pflaum, S. W. (1979). Diagnosis of oral reading. *The Reading Teacher, 33*(3), 278–284.

Philips, S. U. (1982). *The invisible culture: Communication in classroom and community on the Warm Springs Indian Reservation.* White Plains, NY: Longman.

Piercey, D. (1976). *Reading activities in content areas: An idea book for middle and secondary schools* (abr. ed.). Boston: Allyn and Bacon.

Pinnell, G. S. (1985). Ways to look at the functions of children's language. In A. Jaggar & M. T. Smith-Burke (Eds.), *Observing the language learner* (pp. 57–72). Newark, DE: International Reading Association.

Pollard, D. S. (1989). Reducing the impact of racism on students. *Educational Leadership, 47*(2), 73–74.

Powlesland, S. (1985). Children talking about writing: Case study 4. In *Every child's language* (pp. 11–13). Clevendon, GB: Multilingual Matters.

Prior, P. (1990). Schemata, strategies and social construction: Some implications for second language pedagogy. *Minnetesol Journal, 8,* 53–72.

Pritchard, R. (1990). The effects of cultural schemata on reading processing strategies. *Reading Research Quarterly, 25*(4), 273–295.

Quintero, E., & Huerta-Macias, A. (1990). All in the family: Bilingualism and biliteracy. *The Reading Teacher, 44*(4), 306–312.

Ramsey, P. G. (1987). *Teaching and learning in a diverse world: Multicultural education for young children.* New York: Teachers College Press.

Rasinski, T. V., & Padak, N. D. (1990). Multicultural learning through children's literature. *Language Arts, 67*(6), 576–580.

Ravitch, D. (1992). A culture in common. *Educational Leadership, 49*(4), 8–11.

Rawski, E. (1983). Functional literacy in nineteenth century China. In D. P. Resnick (Ed.), *Literacy in historical perspective* (pp. 85–103). Washington, DC: Library of Congress.

Reimer, K. M. (1992). Multiethnic literature: Holding fast to dreams. *Language Arts, 69*(1), 14–21.

Reutzel, D. R., & Cooter, Jr., R. B. (1991). Organizing for effective instruction: The reading workshop. *The Reading Teacher, 44*(8), 548–554.

Reutzel, D. R., & Hollingsworth, D. M. (1988). Whole language and practitioner. *Academic Therapy, 23*(4), 405–416.

Reyhner, J. (1991). The challenge of teaching minority students: An American Indian example. *Teaching Education, 4*(1), 103–111.

Rigg, P. (1986). Reading in ESL: Learning from kids. In P. Rigg & D. S. Enright (Eds.), *Children and ESL: Integrating perspectives* (pp. 55–91). Washington, DC: Teachers of English to Speakers of Other Languages.

Rigg, P., & Hudelson, S. (1986). One child doesn't speak English. *Australian Journal of Reading, 9*(3), 116–125.

Rivers, W. (1968). *Teaching foreign language skills.* Chicago, IL: University of Chicago Press.

Robinson, A., Crawford, L. W. & Hall, N. (1990). *Some day you will no all about me: Young children's explorations in the world of letters.* London: Mary Glasgow Publications.

Roney, R. C. (1984). Background experience is the foundation of success in learning to read. *The Reading Teacher, 38*(2), 196–199.

Roney, R. C. (1989). Back to the basics with storytelling. *The Reading Teacher, 42*(7), 520–523.

Rosenblatt, L. M. (1989). Writing and reading: The transactional theory. In J. M. Mason (Ed.), *Reading and writing connections* (pp. 153–176). Boston: Allyn and Bacon.

Roser, N., & Wilson, G., (1986). Books for reading about reading: Read alouds for children learning to read. *The Reading Teacher, 40*(3), 282–287.

Rowcroft, V. (1989). Young letter writers as authors. In N. Hall (Ed.), *Writing with reason: The emergence of authorship in young children* (pp. 21–37). London: Hodder & Stoughton.

Royer, J. M., & Carlo, M. S. (1991). Transfer of comprehension skills from native to second language. *Journal of Reading, 34*(6), 450–455.

Rubin, D. L. (1985). Instruction in speaking and listening: Battles and options. *Educational Leadership, 42*(5), 31–36.

Rumelhart, D. E. (1981). Schemata: The building blocks of cognition. In J. T. Guthrie (Ed.), *Comprehension and teaching: Research reviews* (pp. 3–26). Newark, DE: International Reading Association.

Sampson, M. R., Briggs, L. D. & Sampson, M. B. (1986). Language, children and text. In M. R. Sampson (Ed.), *The pursuit of literacy: Early reading and writing* (pp. 97–101). Dubuque, IA: Kendall/Hunt.

Samuels, S. J. (1979). The method of repeated readings. *The Reading Teacher, 32*(4), 403–408.

Sanders, D. (1987). Cultural conflicts: An important factor in the academic failures of American Indian students. *Journal of Multicultural Counseling and Development, 15*(2), 81–90.

Sawyer, W. (1987). Literature and literacy: A review of research. *Language Arts, 64*(1), 33–39.

SCDC (1986). The multicultural curriculum: An "education" digest on the School Development Committee's agenda for multicultural education, *Education, 9* (May), i–iv.

Schallert, D. L. (1982). The significance of knowledge: A synthesis of research related to schema theory. In W. Otto & S. White (Eds.), *Reading expository material* (pp. 13–48). New York: Academic Press.

Scherer, M. (1992). School snapshot: Focus on African-American culture. *Educational Leadership, 49*(4), 17, 19.

Schieffelin, B. B., & Cochran-Smith, M. (1984). Learning to read culturally: Literacy before schooling. In H. Goelman, A. Oberg & F. Smith (Eds.), *Awakening to literacy* (pp. 3–23). Exeter, NH: Heinemann.

Schultz, J. (1990). Cooperative learning: Refining process. *Educational Leadership, 47*(4), 43–45.

Scott, L. E. U. (1990). The cooperative active learning model: One answer to multicultural gender-fair education in math and science. In S. Z. Keith & P. Keith (Eds.), *Proceedings of the 1989 National Conference on Women in Mathematics and Sciences.* (pp. 170–174). St. Cloud, MN: St. Cloud State University.

Scott, L. E. U. (1991). Applications for cooperative learning for inclusive education [Interview]. St. Cloud, MN: St. Cloud State University.

Shanklin, N. L., & Rhodes, L. K., (1989). Comprehension instruction as sharing and extending. *The Reading Teacher, 42*(7), 496–500.

Shaps, E., & Solomon, D. (1990). Schools and classrooms as caring communities. *Educational Leadership, 48*(3), 58–62.

Sharan, Y., & Sharan, S. (1990). Group investigation expands cooperative learning. *Education Leadership, 47*(4), 17–21.

Silvaroli, N. J. (1982). Classroom reading inventory. Dubuque, IA: William C. Brown.

Simich-Dudgeon, C. (1990). *English literacy development: Approaches and strategies that work with limited English proficient children and adults* Washington, DC: National Clearinghouse for Bilingual Education.

Skutnabb-Kangas, T. (1981). *Bilingualism or not? The education of minorities.* Clevendon, GB: Multilingual Matters.

Slavin, R. E. (1987). Cooperative learning and the cooperative school. *Educational Leadership, 45*(3), 7–13.

Slavin, R. E. (1990). Research on cooperative learning: Consensus and controversy. *Educational Leadership, 47*(4), 52–54.

Slavin, R. E. (1991). Synthesis of research on cooperative learning. *Educational Leadership, 48*(5), 71–82.

Sleeter, C. E. & Grant, C. A. (1987). An analysis of multicultural education in the United States. *Harvard Review, 57*(4), 421–444.

Sleeter, C. E. & Grant, C. A. (1988). *Making choices for multicultural education: Five approaches to race, class, and gender.* Columbus, OH: Merrill.

Smidt, S. (1985). Reading and our multi-cultural society. In C. Moon (Ed.), *Practical ways to teach reading* (pp. 35–45). London: Ward Lock.

Smith, C. B. (1989). Emergent literacy—an environmental concept (ERIC/RCS). *The Reading Teacher, 42*(7), 528.

Smith, F. (1975). *Comprehension and learning: A conceptual framework for teachers.* New York: Holt, Rinehart & Winston.

Smith, F. (1978). *Understanding reading: A psycholinguistic analysis of reading and learning to read* (3rd ed.). New York: Holt, Rinehart & Winston.

Smith, F. (1981). Myths of writing. *Language Arts, 58*(7), 792–795.

Smith, F. (1982a). What shall we teach when we teach reading? In D. Burns (Ed.), *Reading, writing and multiculturalism* (pp. 83–95). Adelaide, SA: Australian Reading Association.

Smith, F. (1982b). Writing and the writer. London, GB: Heinemann.

Smith, F. (1984). The creative achievement of literacy. In H. Goelman, A. Oberg & F. Smith (Eds.), *Awakening to literacy* (pp. 143–153). Portsmouth, NH: Heinemann.

Smith, F. (1987). *Joining the club.* Oral presentation at the Manchester Polytechnic Fourth Annual Manchester Literacy Conference, Manchester, GB.

Smith, G. R., & Otero, G. G. (1985). *Teaching about cultural awareness: Grades 4–12.* Denver, CO: University of Denver, Center for Teaching International Relations.

Smith-Burke, M. T. (1982). Extending concepts through language activities. In J. A. Langer & M. T. Smith-Burke (Eds.), *Reader meets author/bridging the gap: A psycholinguistic and sociolinguistic perspective* (pp. 163–179). Newark, DE: International Reading Association.

Smith, T. R. (1990) (Ed.), *Bilingual education handbook: Designing instruction for LEP students.* Sacramento, CA: California Department of Education.

Snow, C. E., & Goldfield, B. A. (1981). Bilingual education and first language acquisition in bilingual education. In W. E. Lambert, C. E. Snow, B. A. Goldfield, A. U. Chamot & S. R. Chair (Eds.), *Series 10: Faces and facets of bilingualism* (pp. 7–12). Washington, DC: National Clearinghouse for Bilingual Education/Center for Applied Linguistics.

Sobol, T. (1990). Understanding diversity. *Educational Leadership, 48*(3), 27–30.

Sorenson, M. (1981a). Setting the stage. In L. L. Lamme (Ed.), *Learning to love literature: Preschool through grade 3* (pp. 13–27). Urbana, IL: National Council of Teachers of English.

Sorenson, M. (1981b). Storytelling techniques. In L. L. Lamme (Ed.), *Learning to love literature: Preschool through grade 3* (pp. 28–36). Urbana, IL: National Council of Teachers of English.

Sparrow, L., & Dawson, V. (1987). *Literacy and play in a junior school.* Oral presentation at the Manchester Polytechnic Fourth Annual Manchester Literacy Conference, Manchester, GB.

Spindler, G. (1987). Why have minority groups in North America been disadvantaged by their school? In G. Spindler (Ed.), *Education and cultural process: Anthropolitical approaches* (2nd ed.) (pp. 160–172). Prospect Heights, IL: Waveland.

Squire, J. R. (1989). Research on reader response and the national literature initiative. Paper presented at the National Council of Teachers of English Annual Convention, Baltimore, MD.

Stauffer, R. G. (1969). *Directing reading maturity as a cognitive process.* New York: Harper & Row.

Steffensen, M. A. (1987). The effect of context and culture on children's L2 reading: A review. In J. Devine, P. L. Carrell & D. E. Eskey (Eds.), *Research in reading in English as a second language* (pp. 41–57). Washington, DC: Teachers of English to Speakers of Other Languages.

Steffensen, M. S., & Joag-Dev, C. (1984). Cultural knowledge and reading. In J. C. Alderson & A. H. Urquhart (Eds.), *Reading in a foreign language* (pp. 48–64). London: Longman.

Stern, J. D., & Chandler, M. O. (1987). *The condition of education: Statistical report.* 1987 Edition. Washington, DC: U.S. Department of Education, Center for Education Statistics.

Stieglitz, E. L., & Oehlkers, W. J. (1989). Improving teacher discourse in a reading lesson. *The Reading Teacher, 42*(6), 374–379.

Stiggins, R. J. (1991). Assessment literacy. *Phi Delta Kappan, 72*(7), 534–539.

Strackbein, D., & Tillman, M. (1987). The joy of journals with reservations. *Journal of Reading, 31*(1), 28–31.

Strickland, D. S., Dillon, R. M., Funkhouser, L., Glick, M. & Rogers, C. (1989). Research currents: Classroom dialogue during literature response groups. *Language Arts, 66*(2), 192–200.

Strickland, D. S. & Morrow, L. M. (1988). Emerging reading: Creating a print rich environment. *The Reading Teacher, 42*(2), 156–157.

Sulzby, E. (1982). Oral and written language mode adaptations in stories by kindergarten children. *Journal of Reading Behavior, 14*(1), 51–59.

Sulzby, E. (1985). Children's emergent reading of favorite storybooks: A development study. *The Reading Research Quarterly, 20*(4), 458–481.

Sulzby, E. (1985). Kindergartners as writers and readers. In M. Farr (Ed.), *Children's early writing development* (pp. 127–199). Norwood, NJ: Ablex Publishing Corporation.

Sulzby, E. (1988). The teacher's implementations of emergent literacy: Techniques in early childhood classrooms. Oral presentation, Twelfth World Congress, Gold Coast, Australia.

Sulzby, E. (1991). Assessment of emergent literacy: Storybook reading. *The Reading Teacher, 44*(7), 498–500.

Sutcliffe, J. (1987, February 2). Northern job famine growing at schools. *The (London) Times Educational Supplement* (pp. 16–18).

Taylor, D. (1982). *Family literacy: Young children learning to read and write.* Exeter, NH: Heinemann.

Teale, W. H. (1986). The beginnings of reading and writing: Written language development during preschool and kindergarten years. In M. R. Sampson (Ed.), *The pursuit of literacy: Early reading and writing* (pp. 1–29). Dubuque, IA: Kendall/Hunt.

Teale, W., Hebiert, E. H. & Chittenden, E. A. (1987). Assessing young children's literacy development. *The Reading Teacher, 40*(8), 772–777.

Temple, C., Nathan, R., Burris, N. & Temple, F. (1988). *The beginnings of writing* (2nd ed.). Boston: Allyn and Bacon.

Thaiss, C. (1986). *Language across the curriculum in the elementary grades.* Urbana, IL: National Council of Teachers of English.

Thonis, E. W. (1990). Teaching English as a second language: Who are the bilingual students? *Reading Today, 7*(4), 8.

Thorndike, R. L. (1973). *Reading comprehension, Education in 15 countries: An empirical study (Vol. 3).* New York: Halstead Wiley.

Tiedt, I. M., Gibbs, R., Howard, M., Timpson, M., & Williams, M. Y. (1989). *Reading/thinking/writing: A holistic language and literacy program for K-8 classroom.* Boston: Allyn and Bacon.

Tiedt, P. L., & Tiedt, I. M. (1990/1979). *Multicultural teaching: A handbook of activities, information and resources.* Boston: Allyn and Bacon.

Tierney, R. J., Carter, M. A. & DeSai, L. E. (1991). *Portfolio assessment in the reading-writing classroom.* Norwood, MA: Christopher-Gordon.

Tikunoff, W. J. (1985). *Applying significant bilingual instructional features in the classroom.* Rossburg, VA: National Clearinghouse for Bilingual Education.

Tjoumas, R. (1987). Giving new Americans a green light in life: A paradigm for serving immigrant communities. *Public Libraries, 26*(3), 103–108.

Toch, T., & Linnon, N. (1990). Giving kids a leg up. *U.S. News and World Report, 109*(16), 63–64.

Toole, G. J. (1990). Honoring differences. *Learning, 18*(6), 86.

Tooze, R. (1959). *Storytelling: How to develop skills in the art of telling stories to children.* Englewood Cliffs, NJ: Prentice-Hall.

Topping, K. (1989). Peer tutoring and paired reading: Combining two powerful techniques. *The Reading Teacher, 42*(7), 488–494.

Trabasso, T. (1981). On the making of inferences during reading and their assessment. In J. T. Guthrie (Ed.), *Comprehension and teaching: Research reviews* (pp. 56–76). Newark, DE: International Reading Association.

Troike, R. C. (1983). Bilingual si! *Principal, 62*(3), 8, 46–50.

Tunnell, M. O., & Jacobs, J. S. (1989). Using "real book": Research findings on literature based reading instruction. *The Reading Teacher, 42*(7), 470–477.

Turbill, J. (1982). *No better way to teach writing.* Rozelle, NSW: Primary English Teaching Association.

Turbill, J. (1983). *Now, we want to write.* Portsmouth, NH: Heinemann.

Tway, E. (1984). *Time for writing in the elementary school.* Urbana, IL: National Council of Teachers of English.

Urzua, C. (1980). Doing what comes naturally: Recent research in second language acquisition. In G. S. Pinnell (Ed.), *Discovering language with children* (pp. 33–38). Urbana, IL: National Council of Teachers of English.

U.S. Commission on Civil Rights. (1988). The problem: Discrimination. In P. Rothenberg (Ed.), *Racism and sexism: An integrated study* (pp. 9–19). New York: St. Martin's Press.

Van Dongen, R. (1987). Children's narrative thought at home and at school. *Language Arts, 64*(1), 79–87.

Veatch, J., Sawicki, F., Elliott, G., Flake, E. & Blakey, J. (1979). *Key words to reading: The language experience approach begins.* (2nd ed.) Columbus, OH: Merrill.

Verhoeven, L. T. (1987). Literacy in a second language context: Teaching immigrant children to read. *Educational Review, 39*(3), 245–261.

Vorhaus, R. (1984). Strategies for reading in a second language. *Journal of Reading, 28*(5), 412–416.

Waggoner, D. (1987). School holding power in the United States. In L. M. Malave (Ed.), *NABE 87: Theory, research and application* (Selected papers, 207–224). Buffalo, NY: State University at New York (at Buffalo).

Wallace, C., & Goodman, Y. M. (1989). Research currents: Language and literacy development of multilingual learners. *Language Arts, 66*(5), 542–551.

Watson, D. J. (1985). Watching and listening to children read. In A. Jaggar & M. T. Smith-Burke (Eds.), *Observing the language learner* (pp. 115–128). Newark, DE: International Reading Association.

Watson, D. J. (1990). Show me: Whole language evaluation of literature groups. In K. G. Short & K. M. Pierce (Eds.), *Talking about books: Creating literate communities* (pp. 157–174). Portsmouth, NH: Heinemann.

Watson, D. J., & Crowley, P. (1988). How can we implement a whole-language approach. In C. Weaver (Ed.), *Reading process and practice: From sociopsycholinguistics to whole language* (pp. 212–279). Portsmouth, NH: Heinemann.

Weaver, C. (1988). *Reading process and practice: From sociopsycholinguistics to whole language.* Portsmouth, NH: Heinemann.

Wells, G. (1973). *Coding manual of the description of child speech.* Bristol, GB: School of Education, University of Bristol.

Wells, G. (1981). *Learning through interaction: The study of language development.* New York: Cambridge University Press.

Wells, G. (1986). *The meaning makers: Children learning and using language to learn.* London, GB: Heinemann.

Wells, G. (1987). Apprenticeship in literacy. *Interchange, 18*(1–2), 109–123.

Whitehurst, G. J., Falco, F. L., Lonigan, C. J., Fischel, J. E., De Baryshe, B. D., Valdez-Menchaca, M. C. & Caulfield, M. (1988). Accelerating language development through picture book reading. *Developmental Psychology, 24*(4), 552–559.

Whitman, D. & Friedman, D. (1989–1990). The surprising news about the underclass: In the 90s demography may shrink the ghetto. *U.S. News and World Report* 107(25) 73, 76.

Wilson, M. (1988). How can we teach reading in the content areas? In C. Weaver (Ed.), *Reading process and practice: From sociopsycholinguistics to whole language* (pp. 280–320). Portsmouth, NH: Heinemann.

Wolf, J. S., & Stephens, T. M. (1989). Parent/teacher conferences: Finding common ground. *Educational leadership, 47*(2), 28–31.

Wong Filmore, L. (1981, Winter). Cultural perspective on second language learning. *TESL Reporter,* 23–31.

Wong Filmore, L. (1986). Research currents: Equity or excellence? *Language Arts, 63*(5), 74–77.

Wood, B. S. (1982). Oral communication: Holistic skills/functional approach. In L. Reed & S. Wood (Eds.), *Basic skills: Issues and choices approaches to basic skill instruction* (pp. 49–56). St. Louis, MO: Cemrel.

Woodbury, J. (1979). Choral reading and readers theatre: Oral interpretation of literature in the classroom. In D. L. Monson & D. K. McClenathan (Eds.), *Developing active readers: Ideas for parents, teachers, and librarians* (pp. 65–72). Newark, DE: International Reading Association.

Worthen, B. R., & Spandel, V. (1991). Putting the standardized test debate in perspective. *Educational Leadership, 48*(5), 65–69.

Name Index

Subject Index

Academic abilities, misdiagnosis of, 138, 285–286
Academic language, difficulty of, 44–45
Acculturation, 36–37
Aesthetic response, 276–277
African Americans
  disillusionment of, 18
  focus of, 9
  oral tradition of, 155, 187
  population growth of, 1
  school retention of, 18, 19
  verbal styles of, 195
  view of education, 14
Alphabet books, 170
Amish children, 16–17
Analogical skills, 15
Anecdotal records, 309–310, 311
Anglo-Saxon Protestant ethic, 6
Art expression, 223
Assessment and evaluation
  analysis, 309–330
  anecdotal records of, 309–310, 311
  checklists for, 310–312
  classroom settings for data gathering, 291–293
  decision making based on data gathered, 320–328
  developing an individual instructional plan with, 328–330
  distinguished from testing, 284
  of interactions, 304–309
  involving parents in, 292–294
  learner-referenced, 290–330
  of L2 students, 301
  model for, 290, 294–330
  noting classroom behavior, 303
  observing, 294–304 (see also Observing)
  portfolios for, 317–320
  profiles for, 312–315
  of reading, 296–299, 305–307, 308–309, 321–323
  record-keeping, 303–304, 309–320
  self-evaluation, 274–275, 316–317
  of speaking and listening, 295–296, 304–305, 321
  of writing, 296, 299, 307–308, 309, 323–328
  see also Testing
Assimilation theory, 3, 30, 57
Audience, becoming an, 187
Audiovisual resources, 88
Authors' circle, 236–237
Autobiographies, 217–218

Basal texts, 74–75, 85. See also Textbooks
Behavior management, cultural aspects of, 46
Bilingualism, 30, 232
  as a cognitive asset, 58
Bilingual parents, 172
Bilingual programs, 30
  developing, 23–24
  support for, 41
Bilingual students, 175
  determining language preference of, 301
  language tapes for, 200
Biography, 218
Black English (BE), 203, 204
Book displays, 121, 124
Book lists. See Teacher Resource Kit
Books
  alphabet, 170
  basal texts, 74–75, 85